How to Do *Everything* with Your

iPAQ™
Pocket PC

Second

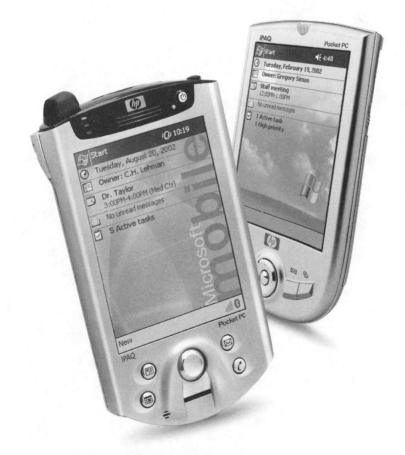

How to Do *Everything* with Your

iPAQ™
Pocket PC
Second Edition

Derek Ball
Barry Shilmover

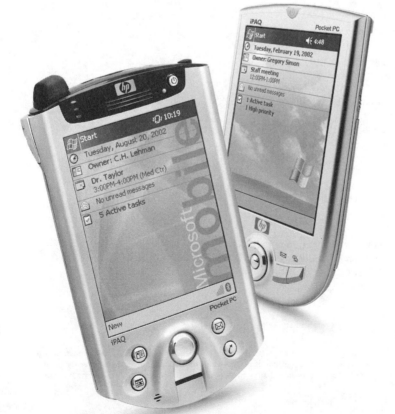

McGraw-Hill/Osborne

New York   Chicago   San Francisco   Lisbon
London   Madrid   Mexico City   Milan   New Delhi
San Juan   Seoul   Singapore   Sydney   Toronto

The McGraw-Hill Companies

McGraw-Hill/Osborne
2100 Powell Street, 10th Floor
Emeryville, California 94608
U.S.A.

To arrange bulk purchase discounts for sales promotions, premiums, or fund-raisers, please contact **McGraw-Hill**/Osborne at the above address. For information on translations or book distributors outside the U.S.A., please see the International Contact Information page immediately following the index of this book.

How to Do Everything with Your iPAQ™ Pocket PC, Second Edition

1234567890 CUS CUS 019876543

ISBN 0-07-222950-0

Publisher:	Brandon A. Nordin
Vice President	
& Associate Publisher	Scott Rogers
Acquisitions Editor:	Megg Morin
Project Editors:	Laura Stone, Elizabeth Seymour
Acquisitions Coordinator:	Tana Allen
Technical Editor:	Jason Dunn
Copy Editor:	Jan Jue
Proofreader:	Marian Selig
Indexer:	Valerie Perry
Compostition:	Tabitha M. Cagan, John Patrus
Illustrators:	Kathleen Fay Edwards, Melinda Moore Lytle, Lyssa Wald
Series Design:	Mickey Galicia
Cover Series Design:	Dodie Shoemaker

This book was composed with Corel VENTURA™ Publisher.

Dedication

For Kirsten and Dayton. For your unwavering support and friendship over the years which has added so much to the lives of my family and myself.

—Derek

I dedicate this book to my wife, Shawna, and to my two boys, Jory and Connor.

—Barry

About the Authors

Derek Ball is President and CEO of Sonic Mobility, Inc. (**www.sonicmobility.com**), a company focused on delivering solutions for handheld wireless devices such as the HP iPAQ. Derek has published nine other books on technology topics and has traveled the world speaking at conferences and seminars on emerging technology. In between trips, Derek lives in Calgary with his wife, Lesley, daughters Jamie and Carly, and golden retriever, Casey.

Barry Shilmover is the Chief Technical Officer for Sonic Mobility, Inc. Barry has published many books on system administration, network management, security, and mobile computing topics. Barry is an MCSE and has worked for many well-known technology companies including Microsoft. When not traveling throughout North America speaking and training, Barry lives in Calgary with his wife, Shawna, and their two boys, Jory and Conor.

About the Technical Reviewer

Jason Dunn is the Executive Editor of Pocket PC Thoughts, one of the most popular sources of information on the Internet for the Pocket PC community. He's also been a Mobile Devices Microsoft MVP since 1997, volunteering his time to help others with their Pocket PCs. When he's not using his Pocket PC, he runs a technology company (**www.kensai.com**) that specializes in new media communications.

Contents at a Glance

Contents

Acknowledgments

Writers are a strange lot; technical writers perhaps even more so. We have had the tremendous opportunity (curse?) to embark upon several book projects in the past. However, as is typical with "selective memory," we often forget what a monumental effort it actually takes to complete a book, not only on the part of the authors, but on the part of all the other people who are involved in the project and without whom no book would ever see the light of the sun through the book store window.

When McGraw-Hill/Osborne asked us to produce the Second Edition of the iPAQ book we realized that we had someone very important to thank. That important person is you, and all the people like you who picked up this book to help you make the most of your iPAQ. The tremendous success of the first edition, and the great feedback we received from our readers have made the second edition of the book possible. We thank you and hope that with this book we can impart information which will help enhance your mobile lifestyle.

There are a great many people we would like to thank, but thanks hardly seems to be enough. Megg Morin at McGraw-Hill/Osborne has been amazing (even through having a new baby, Cooper Burke Morin, born January 18, 2003). From the initial book proposal of the first edition, through the writing, editing, and delivering of all the elements of the book, Megg had to deal with the ins and outs and ups and downs of these two crazy authors. Then, as if she hadn't had enough punishment, she decided to do a second edition with us. Megg, you have been a fantastic source of support, for which we are deeply grateful. Congratulations on the new baby and best wishes for the future!

Special thanks also need to be extended to Tana Allan. Before, during, and after Megg's maternity leave, Tana made everything work. In case she didn't have enough work to do before, now she was doing the work of two. Tana, you have been a project manager par excellence. Thank you!

There are other key people directly involved in the editing and production of the book including Laura Stone, Elizabeth Seymour, Jan Jue, and Marian Selig. We have written many books in the past, between the two of us, and never have we had the pleasure of working with an editorial and production team of the caliber that we had on this book. Thank you all!

Our technical reviewer, Jason Dunn, has helped us to make sure our information is as accurate and up-to-date as possible. He was invaluable in validating and correcting our information. Thank you, Jason, for helping to ensure the quality of this book, and for pitching in to help with the product information.

Special thanks are due to several folks at Hewlett Packard, who went out of their way with the second edition of this book to make sure we had access to the necessary information, product samples, and people to make this book a success. Specifically, thanks go out to Mary Callahan and George Bold.

There are a number of people at Microsoft whose efforts made it possible to get this book to market. Some of these fantastic people include Chris Hill, Doug Dedo, and Jeff McKean. Thanks guys for all your help with the new Pocket PC 2003 platform!

There are many other individuals behind the scenes involved in the production of the book whose names we may not know, but whose contribution to delivering this book into your hands is no less significant. Their efforts are also appreciated.

And finally to our families, who have put up with late nights and family activities where Dad couldn't go, for encouraging and supporting us through this process. Your love and support made all of this possible. To you go our deepest gratitude and love.

Introduction

When Compaq introduced the iPAQ Pocket PC to the world, it began a revolution that saw the pendulum of the existing PDA market begin to swing from the heavily Palm-oriented world to that of the Microsoft Pocket PC. To date, more than two million iPAQ Pocket PCs have been shipped, and more are selling every day.

This remarkable device contains so much power that mobile individuals can now do things never before possible with a PDA. Beyond simple contact and calendar management, people can send and receive e-mail, write MS Word documents, build spreadsheets, make presentations, and surf the Internet—all from a device that you can slip into a pocket.

The iPAQ Pocket PC has gone through several iterations of development. The recent merger of Hewlett Packard with Compaq energized the iPAQ platform with the introduction of more powerful, flexible, and portable devices. The future of the iPAQ continues to grow more interesting as the power and battery life of these devices grow, and as they become smaller and more portable… and with the introduction of integrated wireless technology, more connected!

Who Should Read This Book

We have organized this book in sections to enable you to jump right into the area that is most relevant to you. Part I, "Meet Your iPAQ Pocket PC and Its Software," introduces you to the basic setup of your iPAQ and also explains how to use the powerful built-in software that comes with it. You will learn how to use office productivity tools such as Pocket Word, Pocket Excel, and Pocket Outlook.

Part II, "Optimize Your iPAQ Pocket PC for Maximum Productivity," switches the focus to more advanced topics such as device security, performing mobile presentations, connecting to wireless networks, and using Global Positioning Systems for personal navigation. Part III, "Select Hardware and Accessories for Your iPAQ," shows you what kind of external devices you can use to expand the functionality of your iPAQ as well as how to use the myriad third-party products designed to increase the storage of your iPAQ Pocket PC, turn your iPAQ Pocket PC into a digital camera, enable your iPAQ Pocket PC to function as a mobile medical tool, and more. The appendices of the book are there to help you troubleshoot some common problems with the iPAQ Pocket PC, as well as point you to other resources that you might want to investigate for more information on your device.

As you read through the text, you'll see we've included sidebars for points of specific interest, so watch for the sections labeled How To, Did You Know?, Caution, Note, and Tip for special information about the section you are currently reading.

We hope that you will find this book helpful as you learn to live the mobile iPAQ lifestyle! We use our iPAQs on a daily basis, and they have almost become an extension of our arms. Our most critical information is never more than a moment away, and we can consolidate many disparate information sources into one location. Your iPAQ Pocket PC can become as important a productivity tool for you as it is for us. We use them to find our way around foreign cities when we travel, give presentations while on the road, stay connected to the office wirelessly to manage our infrastructure and data, send and receive e-mail, and so much more!

If you would like to contact the authors, or have other questions about your iPAQ Pocket PC, please contact us through our website at **www.pocketpctools.com**. On this website we will address any questions that we receive from our readers as well as post updated information on new iPAQ and general Pocket PC accessories, software, tips, and news.

Part I

Meet Your iPAQ Pocket PC and Its Software

Chapter 1

Meet Your Pocket PC

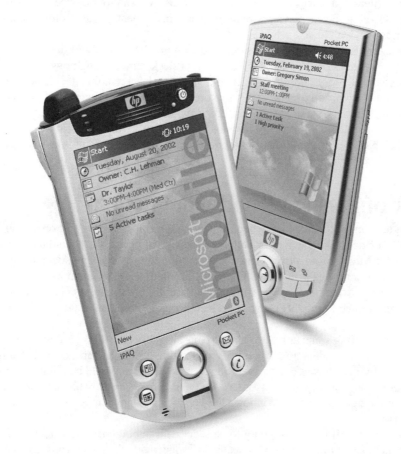

How to...

- ■ Tell one iPAQ from another
- ■ Live the mobile lifestyle

Ever since we humans learned to store information somewhere other than in our heads, we have been working on ways to not only make permanent records of our information, but also to take those records with us wherever we go. Over many millennia, this pursuit has taken us from crude paintings on cave walls, to hieroglyphics on stone tablets, to papyrus, to the printing press, to the day planner, and now to the *personal digital assistant* (PDA).

We are no longer satisfied to simply carry our information with us. We are pushing for a new era of portable information. We want our PDAs to do even more than was even hinted at by early science fiction writers and television shows like *Star Trek*. We want our devices to become an extension of ourselves, to function as a personal secretary, travel agent, guide, doctor, communicator, and entertainment device.

Hewlett-Packard has responded to this demand with the iPAQ family of devices, and the overwhelmingly popular HP iPAQ Pocket PC. With its sleek retro styling, powerful Intel XScale processor, abundant memory, and ultra-bright and clear touch screen, this device is a bestseller. In its early days it was hard to find an iPAQ on store shelves, although increased production has eliminated this problem. HP sold over 1.2 million iPAQs in 2002 alone.

It used to be that a PDA was more of a status symbol than a truly practical tool, but that is changing as they become as ubiquitous as mobile phones. With the current release of Pocket PC 2003, we are getting closer to the hand-held PDA as an extension of ourselves.

The History of Pocket PC and Windows CE

Many years ago, Microsoft realized they would need to develop a lightweight operating system (OS) for non-PC devices. Without a clear picture of the kind of device that would use the new OS, it was difficult for Microsoft to move forward. At the time, futurists prognosticated a great deal about the impact of multimedia on our culture. This resulted in one group at Microsoft wanting to push Windows CE to become heavily multimedia oriented for use in television set–top boxes. A different group wanted to strip NT down to its bare bones and use that as the new Windows CE operating system.

In an attempt to bring some unity of vision to this area, Microsoft brought all these groups together in 1994 under the direction of Senior Vice President Brad Silverberg. This team realized that what was really needed was a new operating system, one that would be compatible with the existing and future Windows operating systems, but would not necessarily be just a subset of them. This resulted in the development of Windows CE version 1.0, which appeared on the market in late 1996.

The team knew that if they were going to be successful in building a new operating system, it was critical that users not feel they were using a strange, new OS. This meant that the user interface had to mirror the already popular Windows 95 and use a similar desktop of icons as well as the start menu toolbar at the bottom of the screen.

The devices of this time were called *hand-held personal computers* (HPCs). They were extremely limited in capacity, with very little memory (usually 4MB or less), a small, grayscale screen, and a very limited processor that ran between 33 and 44 MHz.

The limited power and storage capacity led to meager adoption of the initial Windows CE device, except among the most hardy computer enthusiasts. The average business user instead tended to adopt the more portable and easy to use competitor to the Windows CE platform, the Palm OS devices, such as the well-known Palm Pilot from 3Com and the Visor from Handspring.

The next generation of the CE platform was version 2.0, which came out in 1998. The devices that ran this operating system generally had double the CPU power and RAM of the earlier devices, and on top of that, many of these featured color screens.

Microsoft hoped that this new version of CE would provide greater competition to the very successful Palm Pilot line of PDAs. Unfortunately, this wasn't to be, as sales of the Windows CE 2.0 operating system were also very slow. Microsoft had also anticipated the accelerated adoption of portable computer systems in cars. The company had hyped its Windows CE 2.0 operating system as its answer to the expected surge of "Auto PCs" (a hand-held computer installed in any car in place of an existing stereo). Through a voice interface, drivers could request directions to any address in their Pocket Outlook contact list. The adoption of the Auto PC never happened (although some still think that this is yet to come).

Microsoft followed up Windows CE 2.0 with version 2.1, which was primarily aimed at embedded developers. These developers were building applications that run on specialized devices, with the operating system embedded directly within their hardware. Examples of places where developers would use an embedded version of Windows CE would be customized gas monitors, hand-held inventory tablets, or point of sale (POS) systems.

While all this development on Windows CE was going on, Palm OS–based devices continued to gain market share. Things were not looking good for Microsoft's vision of a hand-held version of Windows.

Then in January 2000, Microsoft released Windows CE version 3.0. This product was dubbed the *Pocket PC* operating system. It overcame many of the limitations of the previous versions and also had the good fortune to come into existence when a new line of powerful processors was poised to come out of the gate. Intel's StrongARM processor would give the new devices running the Pocket PC OS several times the CPU power of the most powerful Palm device at the time. Many of these devices were also equipped with at least twice, and sometimes as much as eight times, the memory of the most well-endowed Palms.

Sales of these Pocket PC–equipped devices began to pick up. The HP Jornada took an early lead, but the release of the Compaq iPAQ handheld set a new standard. Sales of the iPAQ have soared and show no signs of slowing.

The next chapter in the Pocket PC saga occurred in October 2001. Microsoft released the next version of their Windows CE operating system, dubbed *Pocket PC 2002*. The Pocket PC 2002 operating system featured an improved user interface, better character recognition options, enhanced Pocket Outlook features, expanded Pocket Word and Pocket Excel features, Pocket Internet Explorer enhancements, Terminal Server, and more. A Pocket PC user could now expect more functionality than ever on such a compact device.

In 2002 something amazing happened. The two leaders in the Pocket PC field, HP and Compaq, merged. A great deal of confusion and concern arose among Pocket PC enthusiasts as to what this would mean. Would the HP Jornada line survive? The Compaq iPAQ? Would the two lines be "blended"? This confusion was enhanced by competitive offerings that were now hitting the market from Toshiba, NEC, Dell, and a host of other companies. The result of the HP/Compaq merger was that HP chose to keep the iPAQ line and rebranded it the *HP iPAQ*. With barely a hiccup, while the merger was occurring, HP shipped the new and improved 3900 series iPAQ. Before year's end, they shipped the current lineup of the 1900 and 5400 series, demonstrating their continued dominance in this market and their ability to deliver superior products even in the face of increased competition.

What will the future hold for the iPAQ? We will look into the crystal ball later in this chapter. The entry of Dell into this space with their Axim Pocket PC has many analysts expecting a price war between these two powerhouses. Such competition usually benefits the consumer, as the companies increase the pace of innovation (to differentiate themselves from the competitor) and at the same time drive prices down. You can expect that, at a minimum, you will continue to see increasingly powerful machines—with longer lasting batteries, better screens, and more expansion capability—for lower prices.

In May 2003 Microsoft released the latest version of their Pocket PC operating system, called *Pocket PC 2003*. It features enhanced wireless support, improved integration for hardware with integrated cellular phones, more games, and personal software. In addition, many features are designed to make the Pocket PC platform more appealing to enterprises, such as remote provisioning, e-mail configuration, sync setup, device locking, and more.

This book will focus primarily on the most recent versions of HP iPAQs that run the Pocket PC 2002 or Pocket PC 2003 operating systems.

Pocket PC vs. Palm OS

Now that you are a proud owner of a shiny HP iPAQ, you might find yourself being approached by owners of Palm OS–based devices who will try to engage you in debate about your device vs. their own. The relative merits of each OS are hotly contested among many PDA users and can be dangerous territory for any author. That said, we offer a brief comparison here of the two platforms.

The Processor

First consider the processor. The top-end processor available right now for the iPAQ is the Intel XScale processor, which runs at 400 MHz (even the older line of iPAQs runs on the Intel StrongARM processor, which runs at 206 MHz). The top-end Palm Tungsten runs with a 200-MHz Texas Instruments OMAP 1510 processor. These units are not yet very common, and most people still run the older Palm V with a 40-MHz Motorola Dragonball processor. It is important to note that the Pocket PC OS was designed for a more generic processor and hardware combination and uses substantially more of the processor for basic overhead. The extra power available for the Pocket PC also correlates to faster battery drain on the Pocket PC devices. In general, your Pocket PC processor can do much more than a Palm OS processor, but at the cost of battery life.

Memory

The Pocket PC operating system is also designed to handle much larger memory allocations than the Palm. What this means to you is that you can work with larger files and more sophisticated programs that take more memory.

Early versions of the iPAQ came with 16MB or 32MB of RAM, but all of the models shipped since 2002 (3670 and 37xx, 38xx, 39xx, 54xx, 19xx series) come with 64MB of RAM standard, and many can be upgraded (by a third party) to up to 256MB of RAM. In comparison, the most powerful Palm devices come with 16MB of RAM.

The same comment can be made in the area of memory efficiency as was made about the processor. The Palm makes very effective use of its memory as far as applications go, whereas the Pocket PC and Pocket PC applications are often larger. However, when it comes to raw data (photos, music, documents), the memory usage is essentially the same.

Multitasking

The ability for the processor to work on more than one task at a time is an important feature of the Pocket PC environment. For many day-to-day activities, this can be a mixed blessing. On your iPAQ, every time you launch a new application, the other application keeps running in the background, just as on your Windows desktop. However, because you don't see the other applications, this can get a little confusing. Suddenly, you have several applications open and running at the same time. With a little practice, this isn't hard to manage. The Palm OS, on the other hand, does not support multitasking, which means that every time you start a new application, that action effectively closes the previous application. This is a simple, tidy way to work and is very effective on a hand-held device, but can be limiting in more complex work environments.

Multitasking can become an extremely valuable feature as you learn to expand your PDA experience beyond the basic built-in applications. For example, with multitasking, you can connect to your wireless provider and download your e-mail in the background while surfing the Web and pasting information from a web site into your Pocket Word document. This complex activity isn't possible on the majority of the Palms currently in circulation. Palm's latest OS5 release is technically multitasking, but they licensed the technology from a third party and are expressly forbidden as part of the agreement from exposing the multitasking capabilities to developers. This limits the ability to do multitasking on even the newest Palm platform.

Applications

Consider two categories when looking at applications: those that come with the operating system and those that are provided by third parties. A number of applications come bundled with your iPAQ, including contact management, e-mail, notes, to-do lists, and calendaring software. Whether you prefer these built-in applications or third-party products will usually depend on what you used before you turned to your hand-held device. Users of Microsoft Outlook will likely appreciate the similarity between the Pocket Outlook features and those on their desktop.

Pocket PC also comes standard with many other applications, including Pocket Excel, Pocket Word, and Pocket Internet Explorer. Each of the applications that come with Pocket PC will be addressed in detail in subsequent chapters. At a minimum, these applications allow easy access to your existing files, or to file attachments that arrive in your e-mail Inbox.

> **NOTE** *The current version of Pocket PC does not include Pocket Money preinstalled like it was on the first versions of the Pocket PC operating system. Pocket Money can be downloaded for free at the Microsoft web site: www.microsoft.com/MOBILE/pocketpc/downloads/money.asp.*

The Palm comes with basic contact management, calendaring, e-mail, and to-do list software as well. In addition, you can purchase third-party applications separately for the Palm that will allow you to do some rudimentary work with Microsoft Word documents and Microsoft Excel spreadsheets, but these come at an additional cost and with limited functionality. Where the Palm really shines is in the variety of software designed for it; more than 10,000 third-party applications are currently available for the Palm. In contrast, fewer than half that many applications are currently available for the Pocket PC platform. The large number of Palm applications is a direct result of Palm's early ability to grab market share and Windows CE's previous inability to achieve significant market share. This ratio is coming down dramatically as consumers and businesses are buying more and more Pocket PCs. The quantity of third-party applications available for the Pocket PC platform is growing so quickly that it is getting very difficult to keep track of them all, and by some estimates, it now actually exceeds the number of Palm apps that are available. In other chapters of this book and on the **www.PocketPCTools.com** web site we will examine some of the best third-party applications that you can take advantage of to extend your iPAQ's functionality.

Another element to consider is that some companies are currently working on Palm emulators for the Pocket PC that will allow you to run any Palm application on your Pocket PC device. Although there will likely be little need to run Palm applications on a Pocket PC, and the legality of doing so is certainly questionable, should you locate a particular Palm app that you must have, with an emulator, you will be able to run it directly on your Pocket PC. A few companies have been working on emulators, but to date, no commercial emulator has ever been produced. With the increasing amount of Pocket PC-based software, we believe that a Palm emulator is becoming less and less valuable.

Expandability

The Pocket PC can be expanded through one of four standards (or any combination) depending on your hardware options. The most common expansion technique is through CompactFlash (CF) cards and Secure Digital (SD) cards. The SD card, the size of a postage stamp, is the smaller of the two. The CF card is slightly larger, but boasts a very impressive range of accessories in its format, including digital cameras, miniature hard drives, GPS units, and much more. All of the current lines of iPAQs contain built-in SD expansion slots, although the older 31*xx*, 36*xx*, and 37*xx* series units have no SD support whatsoever. The iPAQ handhelds use an expansion sleeve (a hardware add-on that allows for expansion of the iPAQ platform) to support CompactFlash (with the exception of the H1910, which doesn't support any expansion sleeves).

Another option for expanding your Pocket PC is through PCMCIA. This is the PC card standard that has been used in laptop computers for many years. This means that if you have a PCMCIA slot or expansion sleeve on your Pocket PC device, you can use almost any card that your notebook computer uses. You can share your modems, network cards, wireless accessories, VGA display adaptors, and a plethora of other tools.

The third option is available integrated within the higher-end iPAQs such as the 3870/75, 3970/75, and H5450. These units have built-in support for the new Bluetooth standard. Bluetooth is a short-range, low-power, wireless networking and connectivity protocol that allows your iPAQ to communicate with any other Bluetooth-enabled device. For example, if you have a Bluetooth-compatible phone, your iPAQ could (with add-on dialer software) automatically look up and dial numbers of contacts in your address book on your cellular phone. This feature also allows you to synchronize your iPAQ without having to plug it into a sync cable (as long as the host PC is Bluetooth enabled). The use of Bluetooth is spreading rapidly, which will result in many other ways for you to use your iPAQ without wires, such as navigating with a Bluetooth GPS, printing to any printer, surfing the Internet from a public Bluetooth node, sharing notes or Microsoft PowerPoint presentations with other Bluetooth iPAQs and devices, and much more. If you have an iPAQ that doesn't feature built-in Bluetooth support, you can add it through the CF or SD slots (except on the H1910 model, which only supports storage of data though its SD slot).

The combination of CompactFlash, PCMCIA, Secure Digital, and Bluetooth means that you will have a tremendous range of expansion and connectivity options on your iPAQ.

When comparing this with the Palm, we see that early versions of the Palm device had little expandability, but third-party licensees of the Palm technology, such as Handspring and Symbol, added to the expandability of the hardware. Handspring was one of the first to introduce hardware expansion through their proprietary Springboard module. You could plug in third-party modems, pagers, GPS units, and more. Later versions of the Palm have adopted the Secure Digital format to allow for expandability. The SD format is growing, but still has limited support for more than file storage and Bluetooth connectivity at present, in contrast to the widely supported CompactFlash format.

The Bottom Line

The Pocket PC platform is in a state of mass adoption. The devices are flying off the shelves at an unprecedented rate. The Pocket PC is continually eroding the substantial user base that Palm has garnered, and the introduction of the ultra-lightweight and inexpensive H19*xx* series is rapidly accelerating this process.

The variety and power of the hardware platforms that are available for the Pocket PC is impressive. On this hand-held device you can now perform processing that until recently was the exclusive realm of *Star Trek*, such as speech recognition and 3-D modeling. Many of the devices are well adapted to the wireless world, which will be the next major wave driving the hand-held device space. The number of applications available for the Pocket PC is growing daily and includes many of the titles that you are already accustomed to using on your desktop.

This doesn't mean that the Pocket PC platform is perfect. The hardware tends to suck battery power quickly, can be bulkier than the Palm (although the H19*xx* series again proves that a Pocket PC can be sleek and lightweight), and definitely presents a more complex environment than a Palm. The Palm was an early entry in the PDA market and secured a significant market share. It is well liked by users for its simplicity of operation, light weight, long battery life, and voluminous catalog of third-party applications. However, the Palm faces declining popularity, limited hardware expandability, limited wireless support, and limited processor power.

The Pocket PC, in formats like your iPAQ, offers the best opportunities for the future of hand-held computing.

The iPAQ Family

The term "iPAQ" has come to be used by the mass media and ourselves to refer to the sporty hand-held unit with the familiar PDA style running the Pocket PC software. That unit is the focus of this book, too. However, it is important to point out that iPAQ was originally much more. Compaq produced an entire line of consumer devices and Internet appliances all bearing the iPAQ moniker. This short section will explain what these other devices were and where they fit into the Compaq universe. With the HP merger, the only iPAQs still around today are the Pocket PC and the iPAQ Blackberry mentioned shortly. The rest of this book will be dedicated to only the hand-held Pocket PC device.

Internet Appliance

Compaq had aimed their iPAQ Internet appliance offering at the home market. These devices were essentially stripped down PCs running MSN Companion, which allowed you to access the Internet and receive e-mail. The Internet appliance came in two configurations: the IA-1, with a 10-inch display and a wireless keyboard, and the IA-2, with a 15-inch display but fewer gizmos to play with. Both came with six months of free Internet access from MSN. These devices were not well received in the marketplace and were short-lived.

Audio Players

Compaq released two audio players under the iPAQ name, one a portable unit and the other a home unit to hook into your stereo.

The portable unit was much like other MP3 players on the market. It used a 64MB MultiMediaCard (MMC) to provide up to two hours of music and supported both the MP3 and WMA music formats.

The home unit was designed to plug into your home stereo system and provide digital music playback for your MP3 and other digital format music files. It came with a CD tray and would convert your audio CDs to MP3 files and store them on its internal 20GB hard drive. Approximately 400 audio CDs could be stored on the unit. Through a network connection it could connect to Internet radio stations as well as online sources to decode the artist and song names of any audio CDs you inserted.

Blackberry

The Compaq iPAQ Blackberry is a Compaq branded version of the popular Blackberry two-way pager from Research In Motion (RIM). This device was intended as a less expensive option to the iPAQ handheld, with an expansion sleeve and CDPD card (the popular wireless option for iPAQs before GPRS and CDMA 1*x* networks became common). The Blackberry is first and foremost a two-way pager that handles e-mail through a direct e-mail link or through a Microsoft Exchange gateway. This device has some limited capability to run third-party software, but generally is only used as an e-mail device with a calendar and contact database.

This device comes in two versions; the pager-sized W1000 (aka the RIM 950), and the larger H1100 (aka the RIM 957). This device is still offered by HP today.

Compaq Residential Gateway Products

The iPAQ family of products also included networking components designed to allow home users to build shared networks in their homes that could communicate through and share a single Internet connection. This included a variety of wireless base stations, wireless cards, Ethernet cards, HomePNA (phone line–based networks) access points, and hubs. This technology competed with a host of other home networking technologies that still dominate the market, including solutions from 3Com, Linksys, and others.

Home PCs

If that isn't confusing enough, Compaq released a line of desktop PCs called the iPAQ. This line of products was aimed at the home user and was tagged as being low cost and easy to install.

Hand-Held Pocket PC

Finally we come to the line of handheld PCs for which the iPAQ label has become a one-word description. This prestigious family continues to grow as HP builds more and more into their iPAQ package.

> NOTE   *Most iPAQ models have two model numbers, one ending in zero and one ending in five. This denotes the kind of packaging the units were in and the channel they were sold through. The units themselves are identical.*

The iPAQ lineage includes

Model	Description
H3135	A grayscale screen iPAQ with 16MB of RAM and a 206-MHz StrongARM processor. Designed as a lower-cost option to the 3635 (and to keep up with demand, as the lead time to produce the screens for the 36*xx* series made them difficult to obtain in the market). This unit ran Pocket PC 2000.
H3635/3650	The color version of the H3135 with 32MB of RAM. This unit was the original "iPAQ."

Model	Description
H3670/3675	The 3650 with 64MB of RAM.
H3760/3765	The 3670, but with 32MB of ROM so it supports complete installation of Pocket PC 2002.
H3835/3850/3855	With 32MB of ROM, this unit supports Pocket PC 2002. Features the same 206-MHz processor and 64MB of RAM. Also features voice command and control software and a reflective screen that supports 65,536 colors (16-bit).
H3870/3875	The H3850 with Bluetooth support.
H3950/3955	The 39xx series models were the first to offer Intel's new 400-MHz XScale processor. They also featured the revolutionary Transflective (TFT) screen, which was brighter than any previous iPAQ. These units featured 64MB of RAM and 32MB of ROM and ran Pocket PC 2002.
H3970/3975	The 3950 with integrated Bluetooth support. These units also featured 48MB of ROM, which allowed for more room in the iPAQ File Store (as discussed in Chapter 15) and allowed the devices to be fully upgraded to Pocket PC 2003.
H5450/5455	This device was launched in November 2002 to capture the high end of the Pocket PC market. This is the "Cadillac" device with a sleek new look and all the features of the 3970. In addition, this unit capitalizes on the trend to wirelessly connect these devices. It features not only integrated Bluetooth, but also integrated 802.11b (WiFi) wireless networking. These units were also the first to offer a removable battery, so that now you could carry a spare!
H1910	This unit was introduced at the same time as the H5450 and was aimed at the Palm-using executive or price-conscious Pocket PC fan. Priced at $299, it was the least-expensive color iPAQ ever. It was also incredibly slim and lightweight, weighing in at only 4.23 oz. It featured a 200-MHz Intel PXA 250 processor and 64MB RAM (46MB user available) and 16MB Flash ROM. It features a lighter version of Pocket PC 2002 that doesn't include things like Terminal Server. It has an integrated SD slot that supports memory storage only. Additional H19xx models, expected to be released before the end of 2003, will have additional memory, integrated wireless, and Secure Digital Input/Output (SDIO)–capable expansion ports. Watch for announcements about these new models from HP and on the third-party web sites mentioned in Appendix B.
H2200	This is one of the latest in the iPAQ line aimed at the middle ground between the compact but feature-limited H1910 and the feature-rich H5450. It provides integrated Bluetooth and has both an SDIO-capable Secure Digital slot and a CompactFlash slot. This unit features the 200-MHz Intel PXA 255 processor and 64MB RAM with 32MB NAND Flash ROM.

Adopting the Mobile Lifestyle with Your Pocket PC

As PDAs have become more popular, many people seem to be carrying them around in their briefcases or pockets. However, amazingly, many people also still carry around paper-based day planners and files of business cards or keep that trusty paper phone book by the telephone (although it always seems to have been moved by someone when you need it most).

To get the most out of your hand-held device, it is important to adopt habits that will centralize all of your information in your device. You will never make effective use of your handheld if you keep some of your appointments in a paper calendar and some in your Pocket PC.

Tips for Adopting the Mobile Lifestyle

Here are some suggestions to help you integrate your hand-held device into your life.

- Pick one point in the day, usually at the very beginning or very end of the day, where you will enter any business cards that you have picked up into your Outlook Contacts folder. This will keep your Pocket PC business contacts completely up to date. Then you can discard the business cards, or, if you feel compelled to keep them, you can place them in a binder to be kept in your office.

- Whenever someone gives you personal contact information such as a phone number, resist the urge to scribble it on a piece of paper and stuff it in your pocket or briefcase. We all have drawers of unidentifiable scribbled phone numbers that are of little use. These scraps of paper also don't tend to be in your hand when you need to call that person back. Instead, take the extra 45 seconds to put that person's information into your Pocket PC. Now it is permanently preserved and will be available to you anytime you need it.

- When you book an appointment or plan an event, even in the distant future, always immediately enter the event into your hand-held calendar. If you are consistent with this behavior, you will learn to trust the calendar in your Pocket PC. If you aren't consistent, you will find yourself missing appointments or double booking as you try to organize yourself with both a paper system (or worse, your memory) and a Pocket PC.

- If you use your Pocket PC for expense management, use the same diligent technique of once a day entering all your receipts or financial information into your system.

- Whenever you think of something that you need to do, personal or professional, instead of "making a mental note," put it into your task list. You can categorize it, prioritize it, and assign a date to it.

- Every morning when you get up, look at your calendar and to-do list. If something that you know is happening that day isn't in your calendar, enter it. If there is something you need to get done that day, put it on your task list. Not only does this help to keep track of your tasks and appointments, it helps you to feel that you've accomplished something when you look back on your day. Instead of that "where did the day go, and did I actually get anything done?" feeling that sometimes comes at the end of the day, you will be able to look at your list and see at a glance all the activities and tasks that you knocked off.

- When a special event such as a birthday or anniversary occurs, record it in your calendar as a recurring event (the technique for doing this is described in detail in Chapter 5). That way your Pocket PC will become a true personal assistant by reminding you to make a dinner appointment or pick up a gift well in advance of the date!

■ Try to find things that you are already doing that you might be able to do better with the Pocket PC. For example, I work out at the gym regularly and am an avid runner. I use software to help me track my workouts and fitness goals from **www.MySportTraining .com**. If you are watching what you eat, check out **www.PocketDietTracker.com**. If you are an avid wine connoisseur, you can load databases of different wines, and so on. The amount of software now available for the iPAQ is impressive.

Keeping Your iPAQ with You

Making the best use of your iPAQ also means that you need to keep it with you as you live your mobile life. The iPAQ, although small and lightweight, isn't quite small enough to slip into your shirt pocket or the back pocket of your pants like a wallet (with the exception of the H1910, which will fit nicely into a shirt pocket), especially if you are using an expansion sleeve and a wireless card.

As future versions of the product are released, we will likely see the two form factors exhibited in the current lines continue. The integrated WiFi and Bluetooth also remove the need for bulky expansion sleeves to enable wireless communication. Hopefully, the form factor will continue to get smaller, and the overall weight lighter. Right now the best method is to carry it in a briefcase or purse when you move around. But what about those times when you don't want to carry your briefcase or purse?

Your iPAQ doesn't weigh any more than a conventional portable CD player and is as easy to carry with you. In fact, you will probably find your iPAQ works as well or better than your CD player while you run, work out, or perform any such activities. What's more, with MP3, you will never again experience that annoying skipping that even the very best "skip-free" CD players are prone to.

For casual walking around, cargo pants with the side pockets can be very useful places for storing your iPAQ. For more of a business casual appearance, Dockers has released a line of casual pants called "Mobile Pants," which contain a special pocket for holding your iPAQ. This idea is a good one; unfortunately, Dockers' execution wasn't great. The pocket (specifically identified in advertising as being good for an iPAQ) is too small. It is possible to squeeze in the iPAQ with no expansion sleeves or accessories, and the H1910 fits, but the fit is extremely tight. Unless you are standing at just the right angle, the bulge of the iPAQ is still obvious, and don't you dare sit down! Dockers has the right idea; hopefully other clothing manufacturers will actually try putting an iPAQ into the pocket and using it before they tout their clothing as "mobile" wear!

NOTE *For those people constantly on the move, finding the right cases and bags to hold all their gear is critical. RoadWired (**www.roadwired.com**) has produced the most durable and lightweight range of bags, portfolios, and cases for your iPAQ and accessories. We have been using them for several months now. The portfolio pockets aren't quite big enough for the iPAQ, but the briefcases are excellent. For a thorough review of the various bags, cases, and accessories, refer to the web site for this book: **www.pocketpctools.com**.*

One popular method for carrying the iPAQ is to get a third-party case with a belt clip. The cases that came with the older iPAQs were generally of poor quality, didn't fit the expansion pack, and did not feature a belt clip. As a result, they are mostly unusable. The current iPAQ lines don't even have cases included. If you want a case, you will need to search through third-party offerings. On the **www.pocketpctools.com** web site we review many of the cases available from third-party manufacturers and give you the pros and cons of each one.

There are other carrying methods as well, such as the secret agent–style under-the-jacket holster, or the multipocketed vest. One of the vests specifically targeted to the PDA owner is the SCOTT eVest (**www.scottevest.com**). It is a lightweight water-repellent vest that looks like a safari vest. It is loaded with pockets for all your wireless toys and has a unique feature: Velcro-enclosed conduits to hold all the wires that connect your devices together and to keep the cords tucked safely away. They call this a *personal area network* (PAN). The vest isn't something that you could wear to a business function, and for personal recreational wear, the $160 price tag is rather steep. For those of you who like leather, they have also introduced a leather jacket with the same integrated pockets and personal area network features.

Chapter 2

Get Started with Your Pocket PC

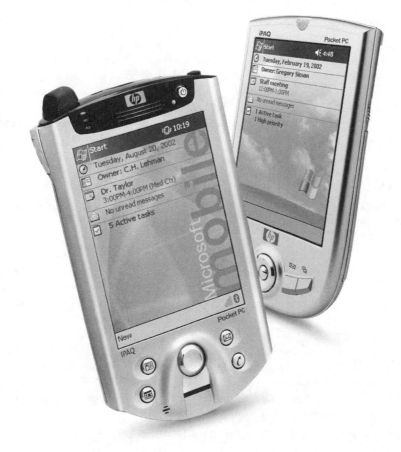

How to...

- Unpack your iPAQ
- Use your iPAQ for the first time
- Use the iPAQ controls
- Set up owner information
- Use and customize the Start and New menus
- Use the companion CD
- Enter data by hand
- Connect your iPAQ to your PC
- Set up ActiveSync
- Beam data between devices

We know how it is—you've got the box in your hands, and you can't wait to get home or to the office so you can open it up and start using your new tool. But before you can jump into scheduling appointments with Pocket Outlook or analyzing data with Pocket Excel, you'll need to get to know your iPAQ and set it up to work best for you. This chapter is to help you understand the basics of getting your iPAQ set up and ready for use, as well as what software you should add to the iPAQ from the CD that comes with it.

Unpacking Your iPAQ

Different versions of the iPAQ come packaged differently; however, what is packed inside the box varies only slightly from model to model. Your iPAQ should come with the following:

- Your iPAQ (of course!).
- A case. Depending on which model of iPAQ you have, you may or may not have received a case. The H1910 doesn't ship with a case, but a case is a must-have accessory to help protect your iPAQ from damage. The 38*xx,* 39*xx,* and 54*xx* iPAQ ship with a very practical plastic flip-top case, which is what we use on a day-to-day basis. The older models of iPAQs come with a case that is sufficient for protecting the "naked" iPAQ (without any expansion sleeves—slide-on accessories used to provide hardware expansion capability on your iPAQ), but is really inadequate for day-to-day use. Many third-party cases are worth considering for protection as well as style, but discussing all the case manufacturers is beyond the scope of this book. A full review of cases and case manufacturers can be found at **www.PocketPCTools.com**.
- A cradle (or sync cable if you purchased the H1910 or H3135 iPAQ).
- An AC adapter for charging your iPAQ.

■ iPAQ companion CD-ROM.

■ Spare stylus. (Not all models ship with a spare stylus.)

Some iPAQs, at various times, shipped with either CompactFlash (CF) expansion sleeves or PCMCIA expansion sleeves. These sleeves are addressed in detail in Chapter 14.

NOTE   *When you first pull the iPAQ out of the box, a thin film covers the screen. This is to protect the screen during shipping, and you should peel this off before using your iPAQ. Some third-party manufacturers produce similar plastic adhesive overlays that you can place on your screen to protect it during use. Many users swear by these. The ones most commonly recommended are WriteShields from* **www.PocketPCTechs.com.**

Make sure ActiveSync is fully installed before plugging your sync cable or cradle into your USB port. Setup of ActiveSync is covered later in this chapter.

Hardware Orientation

All the iPAQ models feature similar external hardware configurations with the exception of the SD slots on the newer series, the fingerprint scanner on the 54*xx* series, and small variations in button size and location.

As shown in Figure 2-1, the front of the iPAQ contains most of the items that you will use as you work with the iPAQ. From left to right, top to bottom, the features are

■ **Microphone**   The built-in microphone is useful for voice dictation and voice control software. On the 5400 series iPAQs the microphone is on the bottom left. On the H1910 it is on the very top of the unit.

■ **Light sensor**   This sensor will automatically adjust the side lighting based upon the light in the room.

■ **Power indicator/Charging/Alert light**   This light glows solid amber if your iPAQ is connected to AC power and fully charged. It is off if your iPAQ is running on battery power, flashes amber if your iPAQ is charging, and flashes green if you have an alert or reminder. On the 5400 series iPAQ it is on the left and is one of three indicator lights. The other two lights are for 802.11b wireless connection and Bluetooth connection. On the H1910 a single indicator light in the top middle is also the power button.

■ **Speaker**   Built-in speaker for any sound coming out of your iPAQ. On models prior to the 38*xx* series iPAQs, the speaker was hidden inside the Navigation Disc (see later in list).

■ **Power button**   This button turns your iPAQ on and off. It also turns the side light off and on when held down for one second.

■ **Screen**   This is a 320×240-pixel touch-sensitive screen.

■ **Button One (Calendar button)**   This programmable button is by default set to open the Calendar, but can be modified to perform a number of functions.

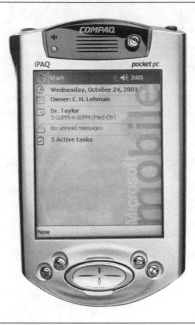

FIGURE 2-1   The front of the iPAQ is your primary interface, through the touch screen and hardware buttons.

- **Button Two (Contacts button)**   This programmable button is by default set to open Contacts.

- **Button Three (Inbox button)**   This programmable button is by default set to open the Inbox on all iPAQs since the 37xx series. On 36xx series or older iPAQs it opens the Quick Menu application.

- **Button Four (iTask button)**   This programmable button is by default set to open the iPAQ iTask program, which is used to switch between running applications or to shut down open applications. On older iPAQ models, this button opened the Compaq task switcher. On the H1910, this button will return you to the Today screen.

- **Navigation Disc**   A multiposition disc for navigating through applications and data. This disc's size and shape vary by model of iPAQ.

- **Biometric Fingerprint Reader**   This is on the 54xx series iPAQs only and compares the fingerprint of the device user against a stored fingerprint to authenticate the user. If the fingerprints do not match, the device will not allow access. Full details on using this feature can be found in Chapter 8.

Looking down on the top of the iPAQ, note three controls (from left to right):

- **Headphone jack**   Use this jack to plug in stereo headphones and listen to any of the sounds the iPAQ produces (incidentally, it makes a good MP3 player).

■ **Top microphone hole**   This is a small hole that is linked to the internal microphone like the hole on the front of the iPAQ. It lets you record a sound by pointing your iPAQ at the sound source (on the 54xx series, this hole is on the bottom).

■ **Secure Digital slot**   On the 38xx, 39xx, 19xx, and 54xx series iPAQ this slot allows you to insert Secure Digital (SD) memory cards, or SD-based devices such as a digital camera (except on the H1910, which does not support the SDIO—Secure Digital Input/Output— standard, so the slot can only be used for memory).

■ **Infrared port**   This port is used for sending and receiving information from other infrared devices. On the H1910, this port is on the left side of the iPAQ. More information on this is in the "Beaming Data for Easy Transfer" section later in this chapter.

■ **Stylus**   The stylus is conveniently stored inside the body of the iPAQ. Press the silver button to pop the stylus out of its slot if you have a 37xx series of iPAQ or earlier. If you have a 38xx series iPAQ or later, the stylus is released by pushing it down so it pops out. To slide the H1910 stylus out of its slot, slide your finger or thumb along the back-right corner in an upward motion.

On the bottom of the iPAQ you will find four items (from left to right):

■ **Adapter jack**   Use this jack to plug in an external charger. This jack doesn't exist on the 38xx, 39xx, or H1910 iPAQs, as they must be charged through the Sync port.

■ **Hard reset switch (36xx and 37xx series iPAQs only)**   Use this switch for hard resetting the device (this will wipe out the memory of the device). Hard resetting is not something you want to do by accident, so the switch to cut and restore power is covered by a sliding door.

■ **Sync port**   This port is used for plugging in an external sync cable. On most models of iPAQ this port can also be used to charge the iPAQ.

■ **Expansion port**   This port is the long port close to the back of the device. It is used to attach the iPAQ to its expansion sleeves (as discussed in Chapter 14). The H1910 does not have this port, as it does not support expansion sleeves.

■ **Soft reset switch**   Use this switch for soft resetting the system (no data is lost). This is like rebooting your computer. The switch is recessed and must be pressed with the tip of your stylus or other pointed object.

On the left side of the iPAQ you will find a single button. This button is intended for voice memos. When you press and hold it, you can record a voice memo that will be stored in the Notes area. Each press and hold will be stored as an audio file with the name "Recording X," where the X is the next sequential number that doesn't already exist in the directory. Note that on the H5450, this button can also be used to turn the volume up or down on playback of an audio file.

Finally, if you have a 54xx series iPAQ or an H1910, you have the option of removing your battery and replacing it with a spare. This is great if you are a heavy user and find you run through your battery quickly. A release button is on the back middle of the 54xx series units and on the right side (below the stylus) on the H1910.

CAUTION
Do not leave the battery out for long. Although these iPAQs contain a "backup battery" internally, it is only good for a few minutes, so switch your batteries quickly to prevent losing your valuable data and having to reinstall your programs!

Turning Your iPAQ On for the First Time

When you power up your iPAQ for the first time, the iPAQ will initialize and ask you to run through some initial calibrations. To configure the touch screen, you must tap on the screen in the various positions indicated. If you ever find that the places you tap on the screen register inaccurately, you can rerun this setup from the Settings area.

NOTE
If you have an older iPAQ (37xx series and earlier), when the device is shipped, the master power switch is turned off. To turn it on, you must open the hard reset port on the bottom of the iPAQ. Use the tip of the stylus to slide the cover to the left. Underneath the cover, you slide the switch to the left to turn on the power. Be sure to slide the switch cover back after turning on the power, to prevent it being accidentally switched off.

The initial setup will also get you to select your time zone. Once you have worked through these initial screens, your iPAQ is ready to use.

Setting Up the Owner Information

From the time your iPAQ is first turned on until you complete this task, your Today page (which is the page that will appear first) has a line reading, "Tap here to set owner information."

Tapping this line will open up the Owner Information dialog box, as shown in Figure 2-2. This is very important to set up to ensure that someone finding your iPAQ can return it to you.

FIGURE 2-2　Set up the Owner Information dialog box to make sure that if your iPAQ is lost, the person who finds it knows where to find you.

On this screen you will enter your name, company, address, telephone number, and e-mail address. You can also set an option that causes your information to be displayed every time the device is turned on. That way anyone turning it on will immediately know it's yours.

CAUTION   *The option to show your owner information on startup is very important if you decide to set a power-on password for your device (discussed in Chapter 8) because it is the only way someone finding your device will know it's yours.*

Using the Start Menu

As in the desktop versions of Windows, in Pocket PC you launch applications from the Start menu. Tapping the Start menu at any time will open the list shown in Figure 2-3. Note that when an application is launched, the Start menu is replaced by the name of the program that you are currently running, but tapping on the program name will always cause the Start menu to appear.

NOTE   *All iPAQs except for the H1910 come loaded with Pocket PC Premium. The H1910 has Pocket PC Professional, which doesn't come with some of the embedded software such as Terminal Server. Software that isn't included on the H1910 will be pointed out in the various sections.*

The top bar of the menu shown in Figure 2-3 shows the icons of up to six of the last applications that you ran. Tapping any of these icons will relaunch that program. Note that this only works for programs, not for shortcuts or documents.

Below that bar are the most commonly used programs that you can launch. This list can be customized (discussed in the "Customizing the Start and New Menus" section later), but initially provides links to the Today page, ActiveSync, Pocket Outlook applications, Pocket Internet Explorer, and the Pocket PC Media Player.

FIGURE 2-3   The Start menu is the primary launching point for applications on the Pocket PC.

The next section of the Start menu contains two shortcuts: Programs and Settings. Programs will take you to the folder where shortcuts to all programs loaded on the Pocket PC should be stored. This folder contains the full set of applications installed on your iPAQ, not just those featured in the short list above it.

The final section contains a Find tool to search for any data contained in your iPAQ. It also has the Help utility. The Help utility is context sensitive. If you are in Pocket Word and you tap the Start menu, and then tap Help, you will receive Help for the section of Word that you are in. This aspect of Help makes it particularly handy while you're getting to know the Pocket PC applications.

Using the New Menu

The New menu is in the lower left of the Today page. It is also available in other Pocket Outlook applications. When you tap the New menu in the Today page, a pop-up menu will appear, listing the types of documents that you can create, as shown here:

From this list you can create new appointments, contacts, e-mail messages, workbooks, documents, notes, and tasks. A tap on any of the commands in the list will launch the application that creates that document and open a blank entry in that format.

Customizing the Start and New Menus

Both the Start and New menus can be modified to meet your specific needs. Select Settings from the Start menu, and a window will open that displays the icons of different settings that you can modify. Tapping the Menu icon will open a dialog box where you can customize the Start and New menus.

The Start Menu tab of the Menus dialog box is focused on the Start menu. You will see a list of all known applications and subfolders on the Pocket PC that you can include on the menu. Adding a folder means that tapping it on the Start menu will open it. Modifying the menu is simply a matter of selecting the check boxes of the applications and folders you wish to appear in the Start menu, and deselecting the check boxes of those that you don't want, as shown in Figure 2-4.

The New Menu tab in the Menus dialog box controls the New menu, as shown in Figure 2-5. You cannot add new items to this list, but you can remove documents that you do not want to be able to launch directly, by deselecting those documents in the list. The more important option on this tab is Turn On New Button Menu. When this check box is selected, the New menu will show a pop-up arrow beside it. This doesn't affect how the menu works in the Today page, but in other applications with a New menu, normally New will only create a new document within

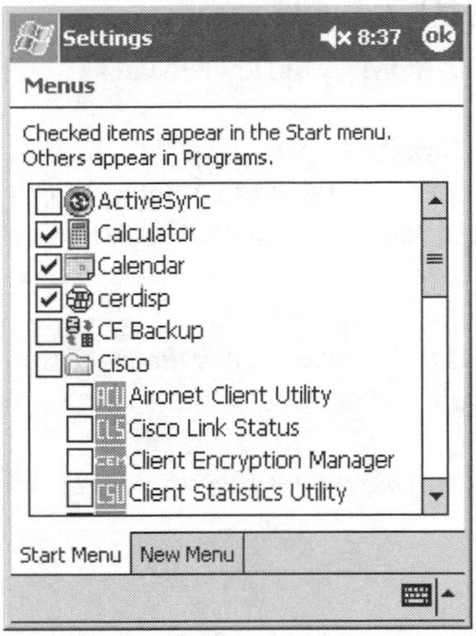

2

FIGURE 2-4   You can customize the Start menu by selecting which applications you want to appear on the menu.

that application. With the pop-up menu, you can create a new document of any type from almost anywhere at any time. For example, while editing a Word document, you could open the New menu and begin creating a new e-mail message or Excel workbook.

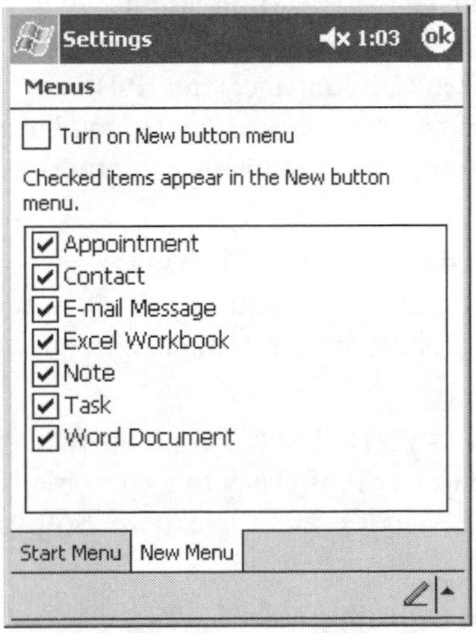

FIGURE 2-5   Documents listed in the New menu can be removed in the Menus dialog box.

What's on the Companion CD?

With every iPAQ, you receive a CD-ROM from Hewlett-Packard (HP) that contains some tools to help you make the most of your iPAQ.

To make sure that you can synchronize e-mail, the CD includes a copy of Outlook 2000, which you can install. (This isn't the most recent version of Outlook. Most people run Outlook XP.) If you are going to upgrade your Outlook installation, you should do this before you install ActiveSync.

> **NOTE** *If you are upgrading an older iPAQ to Pocket PC 2002 or 2003, you will not receive desktop Outlook as part of the bundle. Check the Microsoft Pocket PC web site at* **www.pocketpc.com** *to find the download.*

> **CAUTION** *If you need to install ActiveSync, do not plug in your sync cable or cradle until after ActiveSync is installed.*

After these basic essentials, the CD contains a set of applications (or links to downloadable applications) that can enhance the use of your iPAQ. Different versions of the iPAQ have shipped with different tools on the companion CD. We can't list every set of tools for every version of the iPAQ, so here we will look at the companion CD on the H5450. These tools are divided into five categories: Enterprise Solutions, Productivity, Mobility, Entertainment, and Tools.

Enterprise Solutions

The following enterprise solutions are either included or downloadable through links on the CD:

- **Telephone and Voice over IP (VoIP) Applications** The CD contains four applications to help turn your iPAQ into a mobile phone. These are Avaya IP Smartphone for Pocket PC, Running Voice IP, Cisco Call Manager, and IP Blue VTGO. These applications can be used to tie into your office telephone system (if you have the right brand) and perform various call functions and/or connect to another Internet-connected PC or Pocket PC and place a voice call.

- **Excellnet Afaria** Allows you to centrally manage corporate deployments of iPAQs through a client application that loads onto the iPAQ. A ten-user license is available for free at this link. This includes synchronizing content on the devices, deploying applications, and more.

- **Virtual Private Network (VPN)** The CD contains two VPN links to secure communications from a wireless iPAQ back to a corporate network. The two vendors represented are NetMotion Wireless and Checkpoint Software. This is discussed further in Chapter 9.

- **Short Range Personal Networking** This software from Colligo allows for file transferring, chatting, and instant messaging from Pocket PC to Pocket PC.

Productivity

The following applications are either included or downloadable through links on the CD:

- **Microsoft Money for the Pocket PC 2002 (often referred to informally as "Pocket Money 2002")**   Although this was once part of the standard Pocket PC install, it now must be installed after the fact. You can link to the Microsoft site and download it through this link. This application allows you to synchronize with your desktop version of Money as well as to manage your accounts, portfolio, and expenses. This application is covered in more detail in Chapter 6 along with the competing product for Intuit Quicken users.

- **Microsoft Reader**   This application is usually preinstalled on your Pocket PC 2003 equipped iPAQ. If it is not, or if you are running an iPAQ upgraded from an earlier version of Pocket PC, you can load it from this CD. This application allows you to read eBooks on your iPAQ. Many of these books are available from a variety of sources including the Microsoft site. This software is covered in more detail in Chapter 11.

- **Handango**   This isn't an application, but rather a link to the Handango.com web site, which contains a tremendously large library of applications for the Pocket PC for purchase and trial. You can find more information on Handango in Appendix B.

- **iPresentation Mobile Converter LE**   This application, included on the CD, converts Microsoft PowerPoint presentations so that they can be viewed on your iPAQ. This is a free application that the manufacturer hopes will encourage you to upgrade to their full application suite. This software and subject are covered in more detail in Chapter 10.

- **Margi Systems Presenter-To-Go**   Allows you to give presentations from your iPAQ (including PowerPoint and other formats) and with the Margi external card, present this on a monitor or projector. No more lugging around your laptop to do presentations!

- **Wordlogic Keyboard**   A predictive keyboard that aims to make your text entry on the iPAQ even easier than using the standard keyboard. Predictive keyboards use their dictionary of known words to help highlight the letters or words you may be trying to type, making it easier to enter data with your stylus.

- **QuickView Plus**   Although you can already view Word documents and Excel spreadsheets, QuickView allows you to view over 70 different file formats on your Pocket PC.

Mobility

The following mobility applications are either included or downloadable through links on the CD:

- **AvantGo**   AvantGo is already installed on your iPAQ and is accessed through Pocket Internet Explorer. AvantGo downloads information based upon a content profile that you create online and stores that information on your Pocket PC for you to browse while on the go.

■ **MS Pocket Streets**   The link to download MS Pocket Streets allows you to take content from MS Streets & Trips 2002, MS AutoRoute 2002, and MS MapPoint 2002 (these products must be purchased first) and put it onto your Pocket PC. With this ability, you can pinpoint addresses, restaurants, attractions, automatic banking machines, and more while on the move. This will be discussed more in the GPS navigation chapter.

■ **Callex**   This software allows you to record voice messages and send them to an e-mail address. The recipient can reply with text e-mail. This is the entry-level free product. If you upgrade, you can send these messages to any telephone number and enable the recipient to speak a response.

■ **Other Applications**   There are other links to software from Compaq (still using the old pre-HP-merger name) for their corporate wireless services, a conference call management application, and an electronic catalog of other Pocket PC software.

Entertainment

The following entertainment applications are either included or downloadable through links on the CD:

■ **Microsoft Pocket PC**   The Pocket PC site from Microsoft has links to many games, including favorites such as Minesweeper, Reversi, and Hearts.

■ **Microsoft Windows Media Player for Pocket PC**   Lets you listen to music and watch video on your iPAQ. This is discussed in detail in Chapter 11.

■ **Audible Player**   This application enables you to listen to a wide variety of audio content online including news, comedy, education, and much more. This web-based service offers significant free content, and, of course, premium content for an additional charge.

■ **Other Applications**   You will also find on the companion CD useful applications including multimedia (Macromedia Flash Player, the RealOne Player), games (Bust Em, PocketTT), and an application to give you a directory of places to eat, shop, and play when you travel (Vindigo).

Tools

The following utility and tool applications are either included or downloadable through links on the CD:

■ **Transcriber**   One of the most useful tools on the CD is Transcriber, which interprets your handwriting, wherever you scribble on the screen, and inserts it where the cursor is. This one is definitely worth installing (on all Pocket PC 2002 devices, Transcriber is already loaded in the ROM).

■ **Jeode Runtime**   A Java virtual machine for running Java applets or Java content from web sites on your Pocket PC.

■ **eWallet**   Trial software from Illium to keep your personal information (credit cards or other personal data) safe in an encrypted storage "wallet." List-management trial software from Illium is also included.

■ **FSecure**   If you keep important files on your Pocket PC and you are worried about losing the device (or having it stolen), you can encrypt those files with FSecure.

■ **Pocket Watch**   An interactive world clock for the avid traveler or person doing business in multiple time zones.

Entering Data By Hand

The iPAQ is designed to have data entered in a variety of formats. The most common ways of inputting data are writing characters with the stylus and typing text on a keyboard (either virtual or external).

Mastering Handwriting Recognition

The most common way of entering data into a hand-held device is to use the stylus to write characters that are interpreted into text. Pocket PC 2002 and Pocket PC 2003, which is loaded on all current models of iPAQs, come loaded with three handwriting-recognition modes for text entry: Letter Recognizer, Block Recognizer, and Transcriber.

Only one method of character recognition can be used at a time. The icon at the bottom-right corner of the screen indicates the current method of recognition that you are using. Tapping on the up arrow beside the icon will open a pop-up menu you can use to change your input method, as shown here:

Using the Letter Recognizer

The Letter Recognizer uses the area at the bottom of the screen called the *soft input panel* (SIP). This area is divided into three sections where you will draw your characters, as shown in Figure 2-6. The left third of the SIP is reserved for drawing uppercase characters. The middle section is for lowercase letters, and the right third is for numbers. The far right of the SIP contains buttons for Backspace, Cursor Left, Cursor Right, Return, Space, Help, and Special Characters.

The Letter Recognizer will interpret any characters that you write in the SIP area and put the translated characters into the currently running program wherever the cursor is, just as if you were typing on a keyboard. The dashed line through the middle of the SIP is used to ensure letters can be

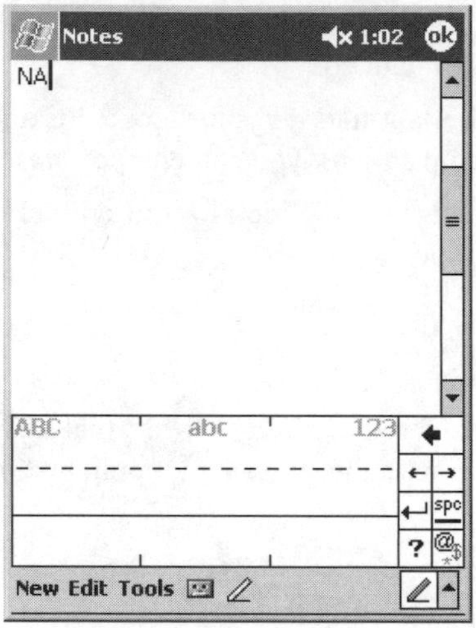

FIGURE 2-6 The Letter Recognizer divides the soft input panel into three sections.

correctly interpreted. For example, because the uppercase and lowercase forms of some letters look the same when handwritten, to write a lowercase *o* or *c,* you should write them below the dashed line, as shown here:

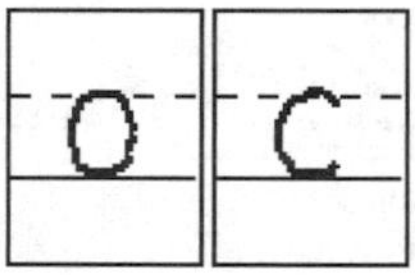

Characters with parts that descend below the normal printed line are called *descenders*. Letters such as lowercase *p* and *q* are examples. You should draw them below the dashed line, with the descending part extending below the solid line, as shown here:

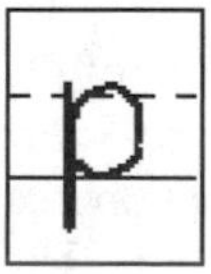

Similarly, letters with parts that extend above the dashed line, like *b* and *d,* are called *ascenders*. These should be drawn with the body below the dashed line and the ascender above the line, as shown here:

Punctuation can also be entered anywhere in the SIP Letter Recognizer, but it seems to be more effective to use the Special Characters button on the right of the SIP. This button shows three symbols as its icon: @, *, and $. When you tap this button, the SIP changes to show a number of special characters, as shown in the next illustration. You can select the character you want to insert by tapping it with the stylus. As soon as you have selected your character, the panel returns to normal Letter Recognizer mode.

The odd thing that you will need to get used to is that when you are using the Letter Recognizer, you always enter letters as lowercase, even if you want an uppercase letter. To get an uppercase *A,* you enter a lowercase *a* in the leftmost section of the SIP. This is counterintuitive and can make the Letter Recognizer a little difficult for new users. It is not our preferred method of input.

You can configure some settings to change the way Letter Recognizer behaves and tweak them for your own uses. These settings can be accessed by tapping Options in the input method pop-up menu. (To open this menu, tap the up arrow in the lower-right corner.) The first option is Quick Stroke. Turning this on allows you to write letters with a single stroke of the stylus. This is different from the Graffiti language that is used on the Palm and requires you to learn new ways of writing letters.

The second option is Right To Left Crossbar. You will turn this option on if you are in the habit of putting the horizontal line in letters like *t* and *f* from right to left instead of left to right.

The third option is Allow Accented Characters. This will allow you to enter characters that use accents such as *è* (*e* with a grave accent) in French.

Using the Block Recognizer

The Block Recognizer is similar to the Letter Recognizer in that you write letters on the SIP one character at a time. This method, however, uses the Graffiti language that is standard with Palm hand-held devices. If you are migrating to your iPAQ from a Palm, this option makes it easy to use the same input method that you are used to on the Palm. The SIP is divided into two entry sections. The left section is for letters (both upper- and lowercase). The right section is set up for numerical entry, as shown in Figure 2-7.

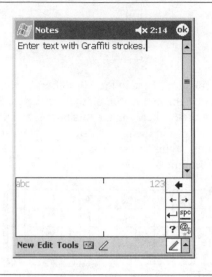

FIGURE 2-7 The Block Recognizer allows you to use Palm Graffiti to enter text into your iPAQ.

The keys on the right side of the SIP do the same as they do in the Letter Recognizer. If at any time you need help figuring out what strokes to use to make a character, tap the ? button on the right. It will enable you to launch a Demo that will show you how to draw any strokes you require.

Using Transcriber

Transcriber is our favorite way of entering text into the iPAQ, particularly when writing e-mail messages or documents. Transcriber allows you to write anywhere on the screen and then, when you pause, have your written text interpreted into words and phrases. You can print, use cursive writing, or mix it up, and Transcriber can still interpret what you are doing. Figure 2-8 shows an example of writing with Transcriber.

> **TIP** *When using Transcriber, don't write too small. The larger your text, the easier it is to interpret. On the other extreme, don't write so large that you can't fit your text on the screen. Also, remember that you can write anywhere, so use the full screen. Don't worry about writing over whatever is currently displayed; what is shown on the screen will not affect your Transcriber input. Try not to rest your palm on, or allow anything else to come into contact with, the screen.*

Another advantage to Transcriber is that it works with any Pocket PC application, but doesn't take up screen space, giving you the maximum view of your application.

Training Transcriber to Recognize Your Handwriting   The way that Transcriber recognizes your handwriting can be adapted to your unique way of forming letters. For example, if you find that Transcriber regularly misinterprets a particular letter, you can train it using the Letter Shapes Selector. You open the Letter Shapes Selector by tapping the icon in the toolbar that looks like a cursive letter *a* (fourth icon from the left). This window is shown in Figure 2-9.

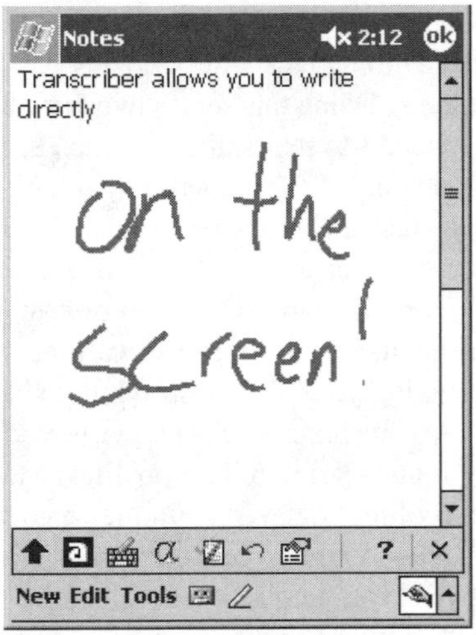

Transcriber allows you to write words anywhere on the screen and have them translated into text.

The Letter Shapes Selector window gives you all the characters of the alphabet as well as the most commonly used punctuation and special characters at the bottom of the screen. To select the character you want to train, tap it in the list (the arrows at the bottom right will move you to the next or previous character). In the top portion of the screen, you will see a series of characters displaying the different

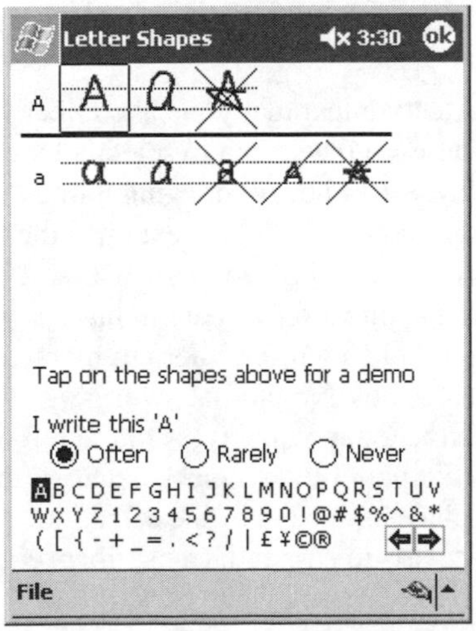

FIGURE 2-9 The Letter Shapes Selector allows you to train Transcriber to recognize the way that you write letters.

ways that Transcriber will expect to see the upper- and lowercase versions of the letter. You can select each variation and tag it as being one that is often, rarely, or never used by you. Any letter you select as rarely used will appear with one slash through the letter, and any that you mark as never used will appear with an *x* marked through the letter. Doing this serves two purposes: By eliminating letters that you never write, Transcriber has fewer letters to search through each time to find a match and can thus recognize text more quickly. The second purpose is that letters that look similar to other characters can be difficult to interpret. For example, a cursive *Q* looks very much like the number *2*. If you never use the cursive *Q* style, then you can increase the chances of the number *2* being correctly interpreted.

While in the Letter Shapes Selector, you can see a demo of how any of the shapes is drawn by tapping it. This will cause it to draw itself for your observation.

If you are concerned that by tweaking your Transcriber letter shape settings, you might make your iPAQ unusable for someone that you share the device with, you don't need to worry. The Letter Shapes Selector also allows you to set one of two profiles: Master or Guest. By default, it assumes you are editing the Master profile; however, if you lend your iPAQ to someone, you can set it to the Guest profile, so they can use standard recognition or customize the settings for their own handwriting without affecting your settings. You can select the profile in the File menu, as shown in the illustration that follows. If many people are using the same iPAQ, you can save and load profiles from this menu as well. At any point, you can revert to the default setting by selecting Use Original Settings from this menu.

Selecting Text with Transcriber   Selecting text that you have already written is a bit tricky with Transcriber. When you move the stylus on the screen to select a letter or word, Transcriber will assume that you are now entering a word and begin drawing a line. You can select text three ways. In the first method, you tap and hold the desired text until the text is selected (usually about two seconds). The text will appear highlighted to show that it is selected. The tap and hold method doesn't work very well if the application you are in has a tap and hold shortcut menu. For example, in Notes, if you tap and hold a word, a shortcut menu appears in which you are given options to insert a date, paste, or look for alternate words.

The second method to select text is to tap your stylus to the left of the text and drag it (drawing a line) across all the text that you want to select. Then, without lifting the stylus from the screen, hold the stylus in place at the end of the selection.

The third method for selecting text is to suspend Transcriber temporarily by tapping the hand icon in the bottom right of the screen. The box and white background around the hand will disappear. This means you can now use the stylus to interact with the screen without Transcriber. To return to Transcriber, simply tap the hand icon again. Suspending Transcriber enables you to drag and drop, select, and carry out other stylus activity that can be difficult with Transcriber active.

Using Drawn Gestures for Special Characters and Commands   To use Transcriber effectively, you will need to know how to use your stylus to input letter spaces, tap Enter, access commands, and perform other tasks by drawing. The sign you draw on the SIP is called a *gesture*.

Enter   (Equivalent of pressing ENTER on a keyboard.) Draw a line straight down and then turn 90 degrees to the left. Make sure the horizontal line is at least twice as long as the vertical line.

Space   (Equivalent of pressing the SPACEBAR on a keyboard.) Draw a line straight down and then turn 90 degrees to the right. Make sure the horizontal line is at least twice as long as the vertical line.

Backspace   (Equivalent of pressing BACKSPACE on a keyboard.) Draw a line straight to the left.

Quick Correct   (No keyboard equivalent for this gesture.) Draw a line straight down and then straight back up. This will open the Alternates menu (discussed later) if a word is selected, or will open the keyboard if a letter is selected.

Case change   (No keyboard equivalent for this gesture.) Draw a line straight up. This will change the capitalization of the letter, word, or text block that is currently selected. If a word is selected and it is in mixed upper- and lowercase, or lowercase only, it will be changed to all uppercase. If the selected text is all in uppercase, it will be changed to lowercase.

Undo   (No keyboard equivalent for this gesture.) Draw a line straight up and then back down again. This will undo your last action.

Copy   (Equivalent of pressing CTRL-C on the keyboard.) Draw a line to the right and then back again to the left. The currently selected text will be copied into the clipboard so you can then paste it somewhere else.

Cut   (Equivalent of pressing CTRL-X on the keyboard.) Draw a line to the left and then back again to the right. The currently selected text will be removed from its current location and copied into the clipboard so you can then paste it somewhere else.

Paste   (Equivalent of pressing CTRL-V on the keyboard.) Draw a line up and to the right at a 45-degree angle, and then back down to the right at a 45-degree angle. The text in the clipboard will be pasted into the document at the cursor's current location.

Tab   (Equivalent of pressing TAB on the keyboard.) Draw a line straight up and then turn 90 degrees to the right. Make sure the horizontal line is at least twice as long as the vertical line.

Correction   (No keyboard equivalent for this gesture.) Draw standard check mark, drawing from left to right. This will open the Transcriber correction window.

Transcriber's Correction Window   If a word has been entered poorly or was recognized incorrectly by Transcriber, you can go to the Transcriber correction window to fix the problem. First, select the word that was incorrectly recognized (the fastest way is to double-tap it). Then open the correction window by drawing the Correction gesture, as shown previously; by drawing the Quick Correct gesture and then selecting Go To Corrector from the menu; or by tapping the correction icon on the Transcriber toolbar (which appears as a red check mark over a page of writing).

The correction window will display a larger version of the word that you selected, as shown in Figure 2-10. You can correct an incorrect word by inputting directly over the letter or letters to change them. Alternatively, you can select an entire word and tap the alternates icon (appears as an uppercase *A* with a bar underneath it) in the new toolbar that is at the top of the screen.

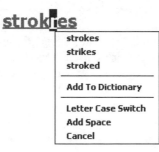

FIGURE 2-10   In the correction window, you can correct erroneous words and add words to Transcriber's dictionary.

The Alternates menu that pops up when you double-tap the word is shown in the following illustration. In this menu you can select a replacement for the wrong word from a list of dictionary words, add this word to the dictionary, change the case of the selected letter, add a space, or cancel to close the menu.

The fourth icon from the left on the top toolbar allows you to switch the correction window from full-screen mode to partial screen, as shown in Figure 2-11. In partial screen you can still see your whole document while the correction window floats in the front.

Other Transcriber Features   At any point you can tap the ? icon on the toolbar to go to the help area and learn more about the options on the toolbar. Tapping the OK button will close the correction window, returning you to the document with your modifications in place. Tapping the *X* button will close the window without making your modifications to the document.

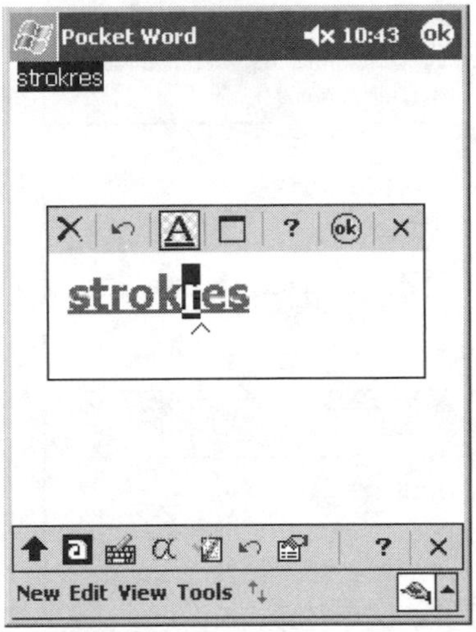

FIGURE 2-11   You can set the correction window to operate in either full-screen or floating partial-screen mode, which is shown in this figure.

Transcriber has a built-in calculator that will solve simple equations simply by writing them on the screen. For example, if you need to know the answer to 4×3, simply write **4 × 3 =** on the screen, leaving the answer blank. Transcriber will fill in the answer in the results that it transcribes into the application, as shown here:

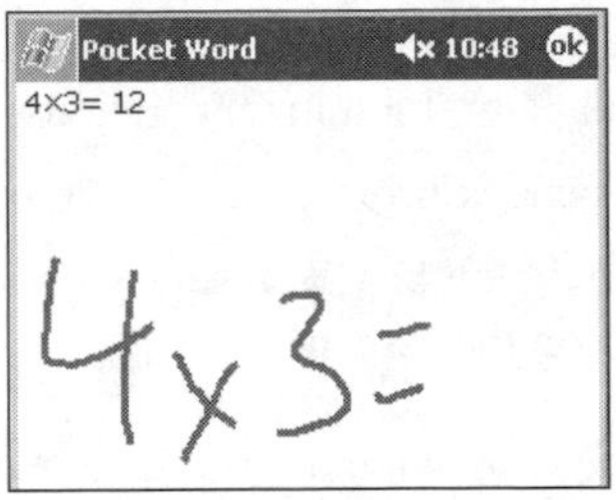

Configuring Transcriber Options   You can configure Transcriber to your particular preferences by tapping the Options button on the bottom toolbar. The Options button is located third from the right and looks like this:

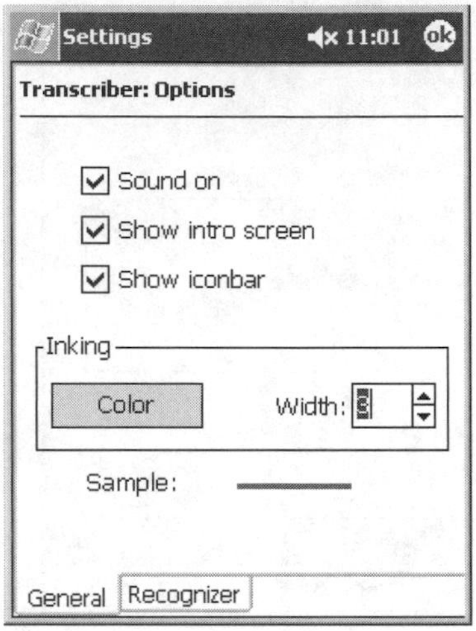

FIGURE 2-12 On the General tab of the Transcriber: Options dialog box, you can configure Transcriber.

The Transcriber: Options dialog box has two tabs: General and Recognizer. The General tab has four options you can set, as shown in Figure 2-12:

- **Sound On** Tapping this check box turns Transcriber sound effects on and off.
- **Show Intro Screen** Selecting this check box causes the Transcriber introduction screen to be shown each time Transcriber is started. This screen gives basic instructions and also shows how to draw gestures that aren't intuitively obvious, like Enter and Backspace.
- **Show Iconbar** Tapping this check box toggles the Transcriber toolbar on and off.
- **Inking** In this section of the dialog box, you select a color and width for the ink that appears when you are writing on the screen.

The Recognizer tab of the dialog box, shown in Figure 2-13, enables you to set options for how Transcriber recognizes information. The top box shows you the version number of Transcriber that you are running. Selecting the Add Space After check box will cause a space to be inserted automatically after each recognized word. Selecting Separate Letters Mode tells Transcriber that you never write with your letters connected together (that is, you print instead of use cursive). If you print all your letters, then selecting this option will speed up the character-recognition process. Use the Speed Of Recognition vs. Quality slider to choose whether you want faster recognition and less accuracy or slower recognition and increased accuracy. The final option is Recognition Start Time, which is how long Transcriber will wait before deciding that you have finished writing and it should interpret the text. The default setting is about one second (with the slider in the middle).

FIGURE 2-13	Use the Recognizer tab of the Transcriber: Options dialog box to set the speed and quality of Transcriber's character recognition.

If you find that Transcriber starts interpreting your text before you finish writing, you can drag the slider to the right to increase the time. On the other end, if you find yourself impatiently waiting for Transcriber to recognize what you have written so you can write more, drag the slider to the left to decrease the wait time.

Using a Keyboard to Enter Data

Another way to enter input into your iPAQ is through a keyboard. You can use either the built-in virtual keyboard or an external keyboard.

Using the Virtual Keyboard

The virtual keyboard is accessed by changing the input method as we did for the handwriting recognition options. Instead of choosing one of the handwriting options from the pop-up menu, you choose Keyboard. This will turn the soft input panel at the bottom of your screen into a standard QWERTY keyboard, as shown here:

You can tap any key in the keyboard, just as you would with a real keyboard, to have that character inserted where the cursor is. The 123 key at the top left of the keyboard will bring up a numerical keypad along with some special character keys, as shown in the next illustration. Tapping 123 again will return you to the regular keyboard.

Tapping the button on the lower left with the two accented characters will open a keyboard of special foreign characters, as shown next. Tapping this key again will return you to the regular keyboard.

The arrow keys on the bottom right will move the cursor in the direction indicated by the arrow.

Changing Virtual Keyboard Options

You can modify the settings for the virtual keyboard. First, select Options from the input method selection pop-up menu (opened by tapping the arrow next to the current input icon on the bottom right of the window) to open the Input dialog box with the Input Method tab active, as shown in Figure 2-14. When Keyboard is selected in the Input Method box, you can opt to use small or large keys. If you select the Large Keys option, this by necessity means that some of the less frequently used keys will disappear off the keyboard. You can also turn on an option to use gestures in the keyboard area to represent certain keys, such as BACKSPACE and ENTER.

Using an External Keyboard

If you find yourself doing a lot of typing on your iPAQ—for taking notes in meetings or for long e-mail messages, for example—you might find an external keyboard to be a very valuable accessory. As adept as you might become with the other handwriting and input mechanisms, you will never reach the speed of a touch typist on a full keyboard. The leader in the portable keyboard world is the Targus Stowaway folding keyboard. It is easy to carry with you. Folded up in its black case it is about the same size as an iPAQ and weighs only 7.9 ounces.

FIGURE 2-14   You can choose large keys or small keys for your virtual keyboard.

When attached to the keyboard, the iPAQ is propped up efficiently by a small stand at the back of the keyboard. The keyboard draws its minimal power requirements from the iPAQ.

To make the keyboard work, you must install a keyboard driver onto the iPAQ. This driver can be found on the CD that is supplied with the keyboard. More information on external keyboards is available on the **www.PocketPCTools.com** web site.

NOTE   *The iPAQ H1910 does not feature an external serial port and therefore does not currently have support for external keyboards.*

Setting Options for Word Completion and Recording

Two tabs in the Input dialog box are generally applicable to all input methods: Word Completion and Options. To open this dialog box, select Options from the Input Method pop-up menu.

The Word Completion tab, shown in Figure 2-15, enables you to turn on the automatic word completion option to have the iPAQ suggest words to you that it thinks you might be trying to enter. After you enter the specified number of characters, the iPAQ will prompt you with a list of words that contain the characters you entered. If your word appears in the suggestion list, tap it, and the word will appear in your text without further entry by you. You can select the number of letters you want to enter before word completion starts to recommend matches, as well as the number of words that should appear in the suggestion list (we prefer three words). Selecting the last check box will cause the iPAQ to insert a space automatically after the word if you make a selection from the word completion list.

Use the Options tab to set five other options:

- **Voice Recording Format**   You can set the default quality level for any voice recording done on the iPAQ. You can choose from a variety of quality levels. The amount of storage per second of recorded audio is shown next to the option so you can see how quickly you will run out of storage space.

- **Default Zoom Level For Writing**   This option defaults screen zoom to the percentage you specify (initially 200%) when you enter Writing mode for any Pocket PC applications that support Writing mode.

- **Default Zoom Level For Typing**   This option defaults screen zoom to the percentage you specify (initially 100%) when you enter Typing mode for any Pocket PC applications that support this mode.

- **Capitalize First Letter Of Sentence**   If you select this option, your iPAQ will automatically capitalize the first letter of any sentence whether or not you enter an uppercase letter.

- **Scroll Upon Reaching The Last Line**   Selecting this option will cause the screen to scroll up automatically so that the next line comes into view when you have reached the last line visible onscreen while you are entering text.

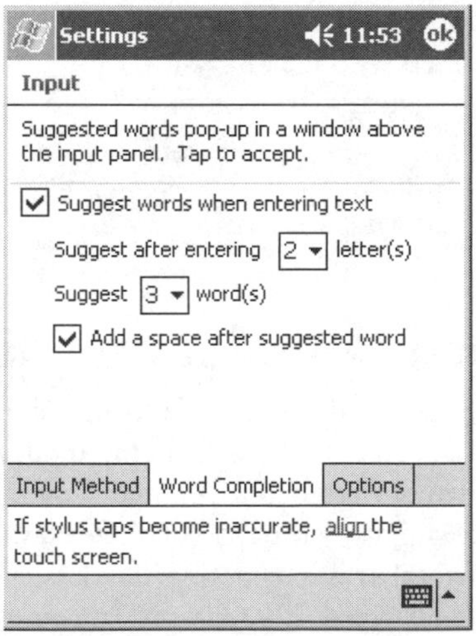

FIGURE 2-15   Word completion will suggest words you might be trying to enter as you type.

Connecting Your iPAQ to Your PC

You can connect your iPAQ to your PC in a variety of ways for synchronization and connectivity:

- Universal serial bus (USB) cable
- Serial cable
- LAN connection (wired or wireless)
- Infrared port

The most common method is to connect with a USB connection. Your iPAQ will have arrived with either a cradle with a USB or serial connector that plugs into your PC, or a sync cable that plugs into the bottom of the iPAQ and into your PC. It is important that you not connect your cables to your PC until *after* you have installed ActiveSync (described in the next section).

Also included in your iPAQ kit will be an AC adapter for charging your batteries. This adapter will plug into the back of your cradle, or can plug directly into the bottom of your iPAQ if you only want to charge and not sync. You can also buy sync cables from third parties. We highly recommend the Belkin iPAQ sync/charger cable (**www.belkin.com**). It enables you to charge your iPAQ from your USB port using a single cable. If you travel, it saves having to take your adapter with you on the road. In addition, it comes with a cigarette-lighter adapter allowing you to charge your iPAQ in your vehicle, which for road warriors is invaluable. As a final bonus, this cable costs less than one-third the price of the same cable from HP.

Most people will sync their iPAQs with a USB cable, but if you don't have a USB port on your computer (older computers may not have a USB port), then you can sync with a serial cable. The higher-end iPAQs ship with a cradle that has both a USB and a serial connector. If you have a cable with only USB and you need the serial connector, it can be obtained at significant additional expense from HP. It is probably cheaper to buy a USB card for your PC than to buy the cable. Serial syncing is also very slow, so it is not recommended.

You can also sync your iPAQ with your infrared port. Many laptop computers have infrared ports that allow you to sync with your iPAQ if the ports are aligned and the port on your laptop is active. Desktop PCs rarely have infrared ports. This is also a slow sync method and is rarely used. However, it is useful to know that it can be done if you are on the road with your laptop and have forgotten your cable at home.

The fastest way to sync your iPAQ is through a network connection. To obtain a network connection, you must use an expansion sleeve (discussed in detail in Chapter 14) to insert either a CompactFlash or PCMCIA networking card. One of the ways of networking your iPAQ that is rapidly growing in popularity is to use a wireless 802.11b wireless local area network (WLAN) card to connect your iPAQ to your network. That way, as you roam around your office, your iPAQ is always connected in real time to your network. The whole concept of how to connect your iPAQ to your network (both wired and wireless) is covered in detail in Chapter 9.

Setting Up ActiveSync

Once you have determined how you will connect your iPAQ to your PC, you must configure the software so you can synchronize information and load new software onto the iPAQ. This is accomplished using software provided by Microsoft called ActiveSync. You can install ActiveSync from the CD that came with your iPAQ. The program installs very easily and doesn't need any information from you to get it installed.

CAUTION *Do not connect your iPAQ to your PC with the sync cable until* after *you have installed ActiveSync on your computer. If you do, the install may not work properly.*

Setting Up an ActiveSync Partnership

Once ActiveSync is installed, you can physically connect your iPAQ to your PC. This will initiate a conversation between your iPAQ and the PC as they attempt to establish communication. The first time you connect a new iPAQ to your system, a wizard will open, asking whether you want to set up a *partnership* with the device, as shown in Figure 2-16. A partnership is required if you want to allow your iPAQ to synchronize calendar, contacts, notes, e-mail, and other Pocket Outlook data with your PC. If you only want to use the cable to load software or files onto your iPAQ, then you do not need to set up a partnership. Without a partnership, a device will be connected as a guest. Select Yes, With This Computer or No, and tap Next to go on to the next screen of the New Partnership Wizard. The middle option on the screen, Yes, With This Computer And A Server, is to be used *only* if your company has acquired and installed the Microsoft Mobile Information Server with ActiveSync.

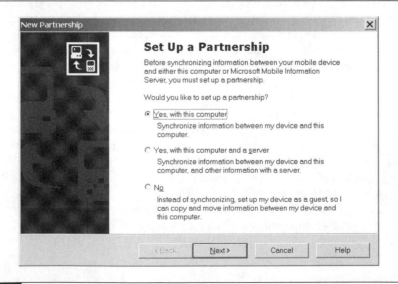

| FIGURE 2-16 | You must establish a partnership between your iPAQ and your PC to synchronize Pocket Outlook data. |

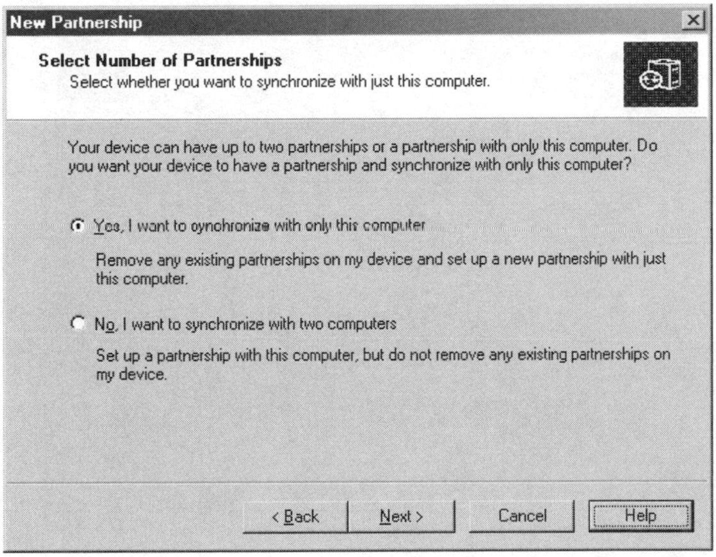

FIGURE 2-17   Select how many systems you will be synchronizing information with on this screen.

This feature is great for the mobile corporate professional and allows for syncing of your Calendar, Contacts, and Inbox of your iPAQ from remote locations over a wireless or wired connection. Setting up and working with Microsoft Mobile Information Server is covered in Appendix A.

In the second screen, you will be asked whether you want to synchronize this device with more than one computer, as shown in Figure 2-17. If you only ever synchronize with one system, then choose Yes to set up the relationship. If you choose No, then you will not be given the option to synchronize e-mail. However, if you have a computer at work and another at home and want to connect to both of them, you can configure your settings to accommodate this. Set up the computer where your primary e-mail account resides as a Yes (exclusive) relationship, but set up the other machine as a No relationship. This will synchronize your calendar and contact lists on both systems, but your e-mail will only synchronize with the machine that has the Yes relationship. Tap Next after you have made your selection.

TIP   *If you want an e-mail account to stay synchronized instead of relying on ActiveSync to keep the e-mail on your iPAQ, use a new e-mail service with IMAP4, which will always keep your Inbox in sync, no matter which computer you are syncing with.*

The next screen of the wizard will ask you which programs you want to synchronize with your iPAQ, as shown in Figure 2-18. Each of the programs has separate settings that you can configure to modify how it synchronizes. The programs to synchronize are AvantGo, Calendar, Contacts, Favorites, Files, Inbox, Notes, Pocket Access, and Tasks.

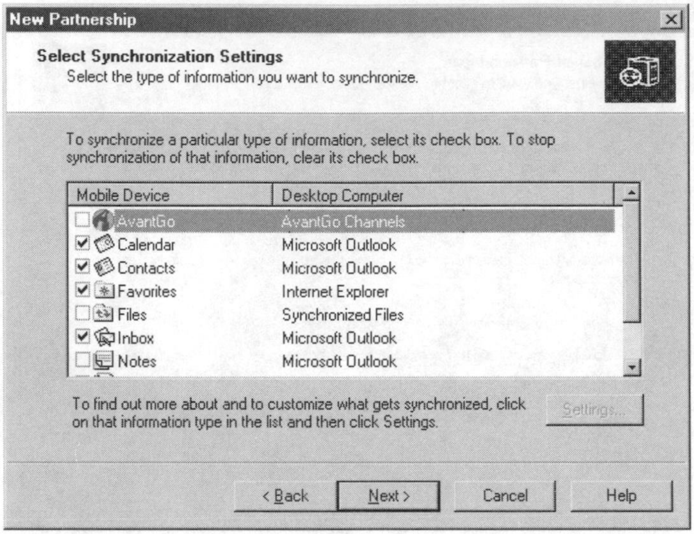

FIGURE 2-18   Choose the programs that you want to synchronize with your iPAQ.

Sync AvantGo

AvantGo is a third-party service (**www.avantgo.com**) that provides, free of charge, informational content that can be delivered to your iPAQ whenever you synchronize. You must set up a channel with AvantGo in order to use the service. (*Channels* are content that you have elected to bring down and store on your iPAQ, such as the latest news, sports scores, and so on.) You set up a channel through your iPAQ by launching Internet Explorer from the Start menu. The Pocket IE home page appears, as shown in the following illustration. Select the AvantGo link at the bottom of the page to begin setting up your channels.

The first time you use this link it will give you instructions on setting up your channels. For this to work, your desktop computer must have Internet access. If you have completed the ActiveSync New Partnership Wizard, selecting the AvantGo link will bring you to the AvantGo setup pages. The first of these pages asks you to select your preferences, including your country, ZIP/postal code, and language preference.

NOTE   *If you already have an AvantGo account, you can right-click on AvantGo, select Settings, then Properties, and change your username and password to sync against your current account. This method is a huge timesaver as compared with reconfiguring everything.*

Once you set your preferences language, you will be taken to a default page where you will see the channels that are going to be synchronized with your device. By default a set of standard channels is selected. Now you can customize those channels by using the options on the page. Because these web pages might change at any time, we won't show illustrations of the options here. But the AvantGo site operates like any other web site, so you can easily follow the links to set up your channels.

TIP   *Don't select too many channels in AvantGo. Remember that everything you select is stored on your iPAQ and will take up valuable memory space.*

Once the link is set up, you can go to AvantGo in Pocket IE at any time and read the latest news or other information from the last time that you synced your iPAQ. A new wireless version of AvantGo will allow you to get real-time updates while you are on the move between syncs. Wireless AvantGo will be discussed in more detail in Chapter 9.

Sync Calendar

If you double-click on the Calendar detail line in ActiveSync on your PC, you will be presented with the sync options for the Calendar, as shown in Figure 2-19.

The Calendar Synchronization Settings dialog box offers three options:

- **Synchronize All Appointments**   This means that all appointments both in the past and in the future will be synchronized between the device and your desktop. This is useful if you find that you often make changes to appointments that occurred in the past, and you want that information also kept on your iPAQ. This kind of syncing can take some time to complete if you have a lot of historical information on your iPAQ and desktop.

- **Synchronize Only The**   With this option you specify how far into the past and future you want ActiveSync to look when synchronizing appointments. You can select a specific number of weeks for the past (the default is two) and for the future, but given that your future data is usually the most important, we do not recommend that you change the latter from the default of All.

- **Synchronize appointments in selected categories**   You can choose specific categories of appointments that you want to synchronize. This is useful if you have certain types of appointments on your desktop (or iPAQ) that you don't want kept in sync between the two.

After you select the options you want, click the OK button to save the changes. The changes you select will only affect this device's profile.

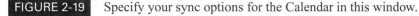

Specify your sync options for the Calendar in this window.

Sync Contacts

By double-clicking Contacts in the details of ActiveSync on your PC, you will open the Contact Synchronization Settings dialog box shown in Figure 2-20, allowing you to set the sync options for the Contacts application.

You have the following choices for syncing contacts:

■ **Synchronize All Contacts** This is the default option and will keep all of your contacts on your iPAQ and desktop PC synchronized.

■ **Synchronize selected contacts** This option enables you to select specific contacts that you want to synchronize. We don't recommend this option because any new contacts you add to a specific device will have to be set up independently in ActiveSync if you want to keep them synchronized.

■ **Synchronize contacts in selected categories** This option enables you to select specific categories of contacts that you want to be synchronized with your iPAQ. This setting is useful if you have contacts that you do not want shared between your desktop and your iPAQ.

As with the Calendar, once you have selected your options, click OK to have them applied and return to ActiveSync.

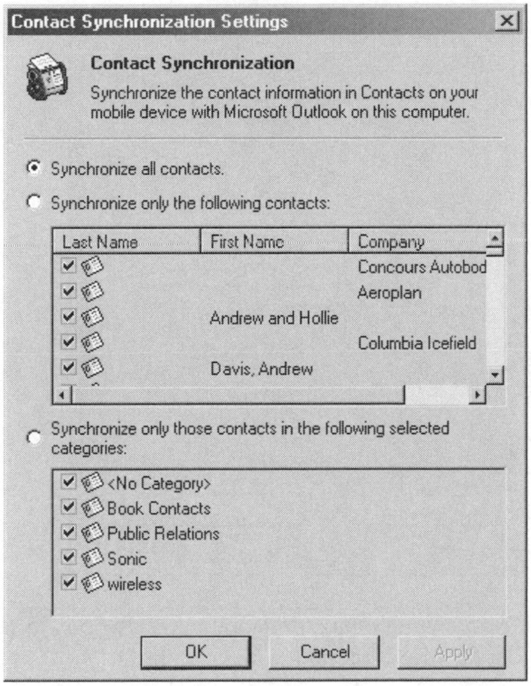

FIGURE 2-20   The Contact Synchronization Settings dialog box allows you to set the synchronization options for your Outlook contacts data.

Sync Favorites

The Favorites sync options are accessed by double-clicking Favorites in the detail area of ActiveSync. In the Favorite Synchronization Options dialog box, shown in Figure 2-21, you can set which of your Internet Explorer Mobile Favorites settings (web page addresses that you have stored in Mobile Favorites or added to Favorites on your iPAQ) you want to synchronize between your handheld and your desktop.

On the General tab you will see all the pages and folders in the Mobile Favorites folder. Each folder and page can be individually flagged to synchronize to the iPAQ. The Customize tab, shown in Figure 2-22, enables you to choose to synchronize offline content if any of your Favorites are flagged to store offline content in Internet Explorer. Because of the amount of memory that images and sound files use, you can choose to exclude those from your offline content.

Sync Files

When you choose to synchronize files between your desktop and your handheld, a special folder will be created in your My Documents folder. It will be named the same as the partnership that you set up for this device (for example, Pocket_PC My Documents). Any documents in this folder will be synchronized automatically with the My Documents folder on your iPAQ when you synchronize.

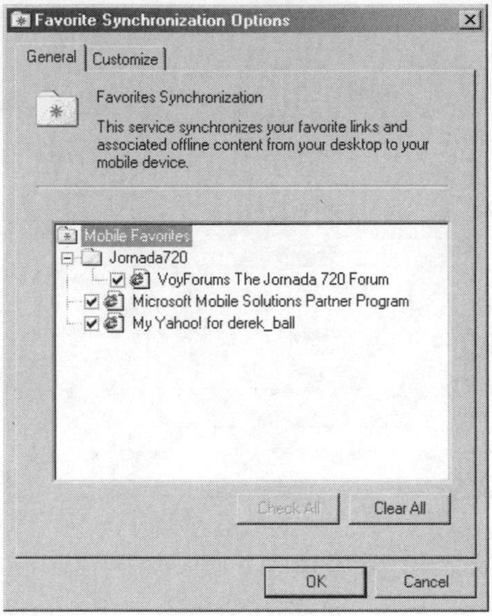

FIGURE 2-21 Use the Favorite Synchronization Options dialog box to set up how you want to sync your favorite web links with your iPAQ.

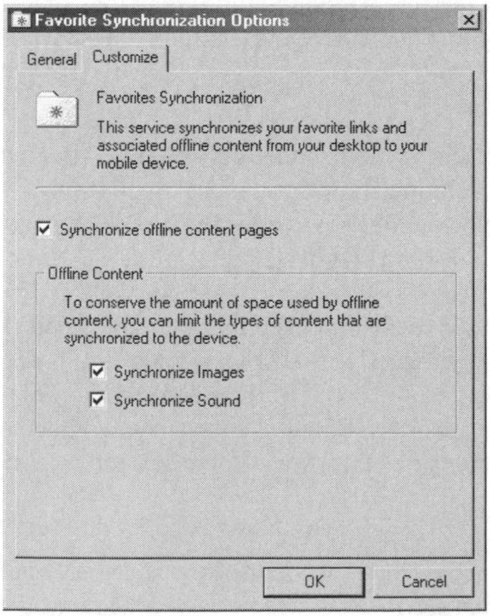

FIGURE 2-22 If you have offline content in your desktop web browser, you can sync that content with your iPAQ.

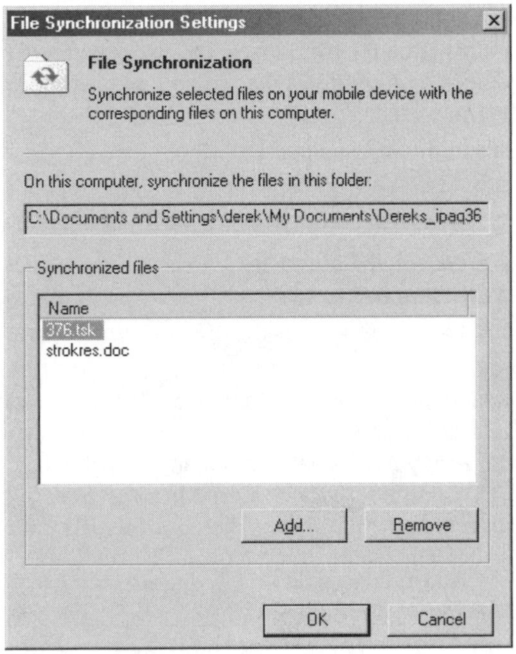

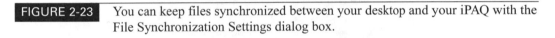

FIGURE 2-23   You can keep files synchronized between your desktop and your iPAQ with the File Synchronization Settings dialog box.

In the File Synchronization Settings dialog box, shown in Figure 2-23, you can choose to not synchronize specific files that are in these folders by removing them from the list using the Remove button. You can add files to the list by clicking the Add button and selecting the file in the File Selection dialog box.

Sync Notes

You have no options to set when you have selected to sync Notes in ActiveSync. All notes will be synchronized, and there is no way to exclude any of them.

Sync Tasks

By double-clicking the Tasks line in the details of ActiveSync on your PC, you will open the Task Synchronization Settings dialog box, shown in Figure 2-24, where you can set the sync options for the Tasks application.

Your choices for syncing the tasks are the following:

- **Synchronize All Tasks**   This option will keep all tasks fully synchronized on your desktop and your iPAQ. This isn't the default because keeping all of your historically completed tasks on your iPAQ is generally not an efficient use of memory.

- **Synchronize Only Incomplete Tasks** This is the default option. If it is selected, ActiveSync will only synchronize tasks that aren't complete yet. This way you will keep the minimum task information on your iPAQ. This works effectively as long as you don't need to refer to any notes or other items that you might have stored in relation to the task, after the task is completed.

- **Synchronize Only The** If you schedule a lot of tasks for specific dates in the future, you might not want to have all of those tasks taking up memory on your iPAQ. Instead, you can set a specific range of weeks that you want to keep current in the iPAQ with this option.

- **Synchronize Tasks In Selected Categories** This option enables you to select specific categories of tasks to synchronize.

Sync Pocket Access

A very useful feature if you want to put information from a local or corporate database onto your iPAQ is the ability to create a Pocket Access database and have it synchronize with the corporate or PC database. You can synchronize any Access database, or any database to which you have an Open Database Connectivity (ODBC) connection. This includes Microsoft SQL Server, Oracle, Informix, Sybase, and many other popular enterprise databases. There isn't actually a Pocket Access program available for the Pocket PC, so don't go looking for it on your Pocket PC. To use the Pocket Access database, you will need to use a database viewer program, SQL CE, or write your own program!

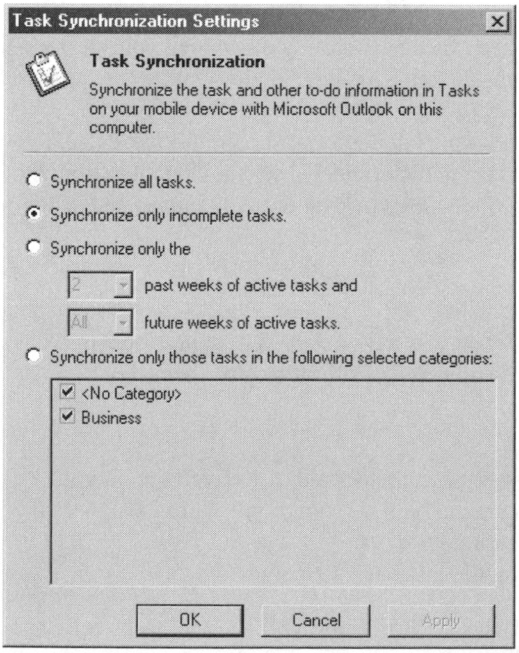

FIGURE 2-24   Set which tasks should be synced between your iPAQ and your desktop with the Task Synchronization Settings dialog box.

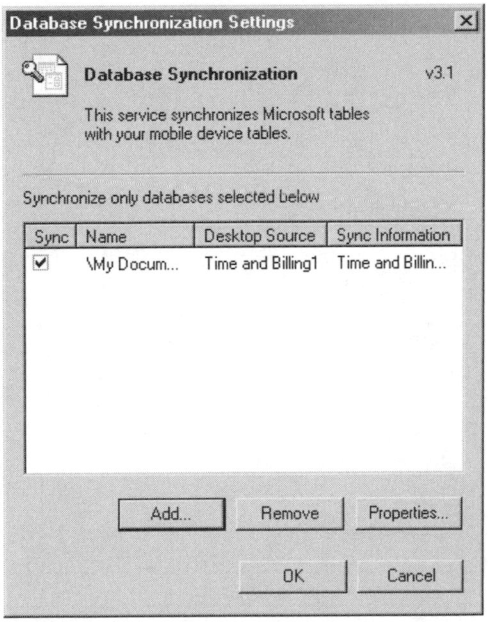

FIGURE 2-25   You can synchronize data in desktop databases using the Pocket Access sync options.

After double-clicking Pocket Access in the detail list in the main ActiveSync window, you will be prompted to add or remove a database from the list of databases, as shown in Figure 2-25.

The first time you synchronize, the system will need to create a Pocket Access (.cdb) file on your iPAQ and copy the data to it. You will select the tables and fields that you want copied using the dialog box shown in Figure 2-26.

NOTE   *Another way to synchronize a Microsoft Access file is to drag the MDB file on your desktop PC to your mobile device icon in the Mobile Devices window.*

Sync Inbox

Double-clicking Inbox in the details area of the ActiveSync program on your desktop PC will give you the opportunity to select which folders you want to synchronize with the Inbox application on the iPAQ, as shown in Figure 2-27.

The other options you can set will let you maximize your usage of memory by enabling you to:

■ Limit the number of lines downloaded to the Pocket PC Inbox

■ Restrict the number of days of messages that will be downloaded to the Pocket PC Inbox

■ Choose to include or exclude file attachments, and if including them, limit them to attachments under a certain size

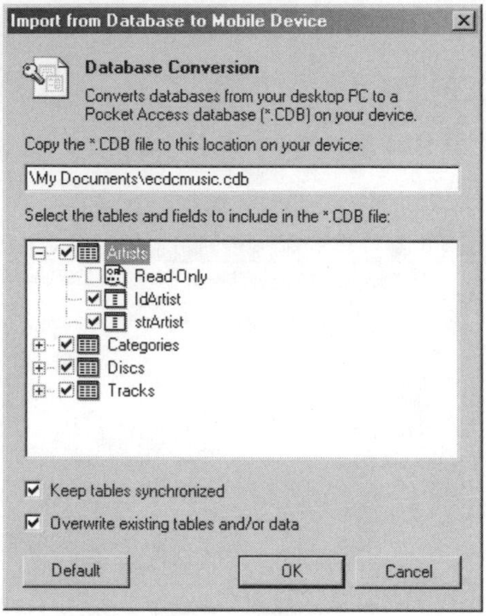

FIGURE 2-26 The Import From Database To Mobile Device dialog box lets you select which tables and fields will be copied onto your iPAQ database.

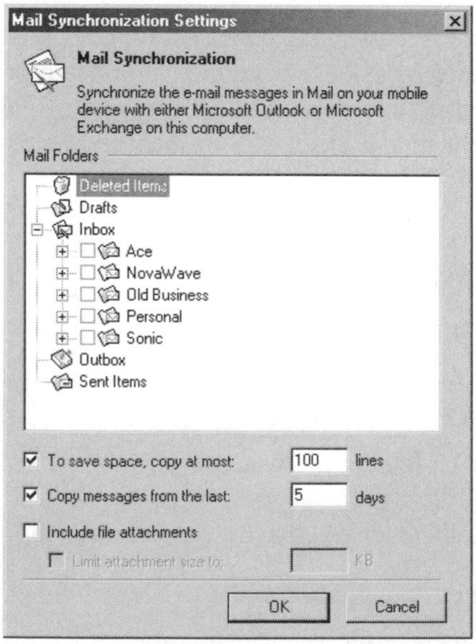

FIGURE 2-27 The Inbox sync options let you control what messages are synced to your iPAQ.

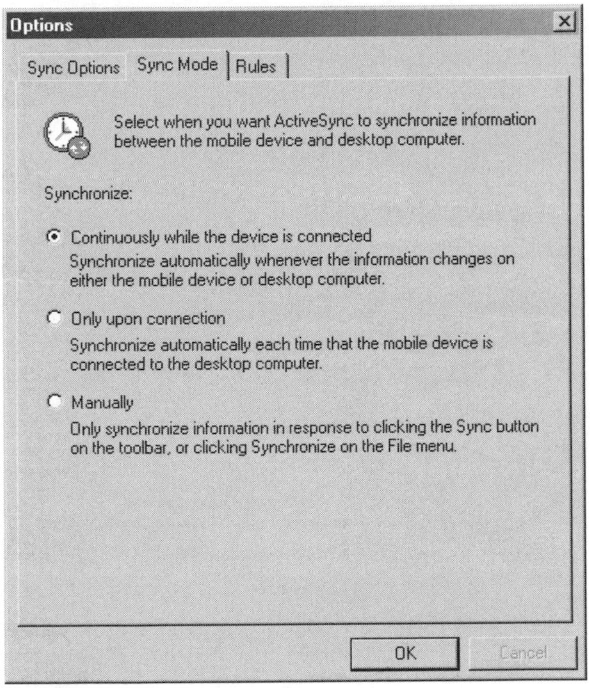

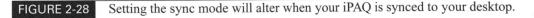

Options	×

Sync Options | **Sync Mode** | Rules |

Select when you want ActiveSync to synchronize information between the mobile device and desktop computer.

Synchronize:

◉ Continuously while the device is connected
Synchronize automatically whenever the information changes on either the mobile device or desktop computer.

○ Only upon connection
Synchronize automatically each time that the mobile device is connected to the desktop computer.

○ Manually
Only synchronize information in response to clicking the Sync button on the toolbar, or clicking Synchronize on the File menu.

[OK]   [Cancel]

FIGURE 2-28   Setting the sync mode will alter when your iPAQ is synced to your desktop.

ActiveSync Sync Mode

The Sync Mode tab of the ActiveSync Options dialog box, shown in Figure 2-28, enables you to alter how frequently the data from your iPAQ is synchronized with your desktop. By default, your iPAQ will synchronize with your desktop continuously. Every time a piece of information is changed in a desktop or Pocket PC application, the relevant record is synchronized on the other device. If this is not the behavior you desire, you can set ActiveSync to only replicate when your device is first connected to your PC, or you can set it to be manual and only synchronize when you click the Sync button in ActiveSync.

ActiveSync Rules

The Rules tab of the ActiveSync Options dialog box allows you to set three critical elements: how to resolve sync conflicts, how to do file conversions, and how to access the Internet, as shown in Figure 2-29.

For conflicts in synchronization, you can choose to have a manual resolution (in which case you are prompted about what to do with the information), or you can set it to always favor the desktop over the iPAQ, or the iPAQ over the desktop.

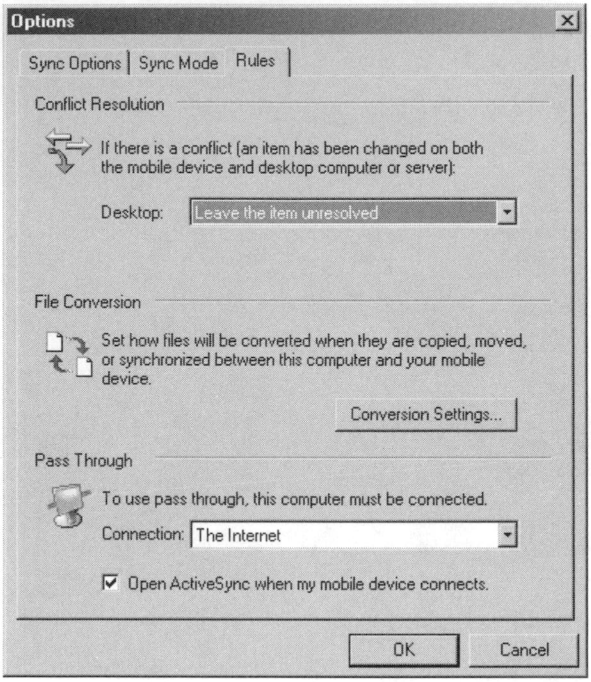

FIGURE 2-29   The Rules are important for determining how to resolve sync conflicts, perform file conversions, and access the Internet while connected to a desktop.

The Conversion Settings button will enable you to specify whether files are to be converted when moved between the Pocket PC and the desktop. You can choose to not convert files such as Word documents (or any other file type). This feature enables your Pocket PC to act as a mobile hard drive as you move among different computers, but to access the file on your Pocket PC, it will need to be converted by the relevant program.

The Pass Through setting specifies how this device will be able to connect to synchronize IMAP4 e-mail services and browse the Web. The selection you make in the Connection box is generally some type of Internet connection.

Syncing with a Server

Here's an interesting challenge. You are often out of the office, and your office manager will use your Calendar in Outlook to schedule appointments for you while you are away. At the same time, you are setting up new appointments in your iPAQ. This leads to scheduling and sync conflicts. To get around this, you have the option of setting up your iPAQ to sync with your server over your wireless connection. To do this, you need to have added Microsoft Mobile Information Server to your server. It will allow you to dial in with your wireless modem and synchronize your Inbox, Calendar, and Contacts.

If you are syncing data with a server through MS Mobile Information Server, you cannot also sync it with a desktop PC. You can only use one or the other.

To enable syncing with a server, select Options in the Tools menu in ActiveSync to open the Options dialog box. From here, select the Enable Synchronization With Server check box, and click the Configure button to go to a dialog box where you will enter the information for the server you will be synchronizing with.

For more detail on setting up Microsoft Mobile Information Server, refer to Appendix A.

Beaming Data for Easy Transfer

A very convenient way for people who have Pocket PC devices to share data is beaming information back and forth through the infrared ports that are standard on most Pocket PCs and all iPAQs.

Beaming Between Two Pocket PCs

To beam between two Pocket PCs, you simply align the two infrared ports, and then on the device that is sending information, you choose the information you want to beam. You can choose to beam contacts, appointments, notes, tasks, or files. To initiate the sending of information, you select the item that you want to send by tapping and holding the stylus on that item. For example, if you wanted to beam a particular contact on your iPAQ, you would select the contact and then tap and hold the stylus to produce the shortcut menu shown next.

The sending iPAQ will immediately begin searching for another Pocket PC to send the information to. If you have a Pocket PC 2002 or 2003 system to receive the information, it will automatically detect the beamed information and allow you to begin receiving the information. If you are running Pocket PC 2000, you will need to explicitly set your iPAQ into receive mode by running the Infrared Receive program found in the Programs folder.

How to ... Disable Incoming Infrared on Pocket PC 2003

Your Pocket PC 2003 is set up to automatically receive all incoming infrared beams. If you would like to change this default behavior, you do so under the Settings menu item (from the Start menu) on the Connections tab. You will see an icon for Beam. Tapping this will open a beaming options window, which has a single check box to enable or disable the automatic receive mode. Once it's disabled, should you want to accept the incoming infrared beam, a link at the bottom of this window will force your iPAQ to manually accept an incoming infrared transmission.

Beaming Between Your iPAQ and a Palm

Out of the box, older Pocket PCs loaded with the original Pocket PC 2000 software do not talk to Palm devices. Pocket PC 2002 and 2003 include OBEX support, which allows you to beam to a Palm device or a Nokia cell phone. If you want to use Pocket PC 2000 and beam contact and other information to and from Palm devices, you will need to use a third-party product. One of these is Peacemaker from Conduits Software. Peacemaker has both a free version and a more sophisticated full version. The free version allows you to beam contacts to and from Palm devices one contact at a time. The paid version allows you to select multiple data sets (multiple contacts, appointments, files, and so on) of information and transfer them all at the same time. You can get more information from Conduits directly at **www.conduits.com**, and you can try the evaluation version included on the companion CD.

Chapter 3

Use Pocket Word to Read and Write Documents

How to...

- Read a Word document on your iPAQ
- Create a Word document on your iPAQ
- Move documents between your iPAQ and your desktop
- Create sketches and drawings
- Capture audio in your documents
- Format a document
- Beam or e-mail a document

One of the most useful features of having a hand-held computer running the Pocket PC operating system is access to scaled-down versions of the popular Microsoft Office software. The most commonly used program in the world for documents is Microsoft Word. Your Pocket PC comes with Pocket Word, which allows you to read, compose, and edit documents on your handheld that are compatible with your desktop version of Word.

In this chapter we will examine how to use Pocket Word to not only read, but also to write and edit documents. For any of this to be of value, you will need to be able to move documents between your iPAQ and your desktop, so we will also discuss that topic. To make sure that you don't get yourself into any trouble, we will cover exactly which parts of the document you can work with in Pocket Word and which you can't, and what that means for you as a document reader or author.

What Pocket Word Can Do

Pocket Word is a scaled-down version of the full desktop Microsoft Word product. As you would expect, it has only a limited set of features, but this doesn't mean it isn't powerful enough to do almost all of what you need while away from your desk.

It is important to understand that Pocket Word doesn't actually work directly with the DOC files that are created by your desktop Word program. When you move the files over to your Pocket PC (either by copying them with Windows Explorer, syncing, or downloading an e-mail attachment), they are automatically converted from the DOC format you are familiar with to the PSW format, which Pocket Word works with. This reduced format supports the most important features of Word, but some information is stripped out. If you are moving your files back and forth between your iPAQ and your desktop, this could become a problem. To help you understand the details of what is and isn't supported, we've produced lists of the different features and characteristics.

NOTE *A downloaded e-mail attachment isn't actually converted to the Pocket Word format until it is opened. This is an important distinction because otherwise you would be unable to forward the original DOC file to someone via e-mail.*

3

The set of fully supported document characteristics includes the following:

- **Standard text formatting**   Consists of bold, italics, underlining, strikethrough, highlight, font type, and font size.
- **TrueType fonts**   Any TrueType fonts you want to use must be installed on your iPAQ (by placing them in the /windows/fonts folder). By default, Courier New and Tahoma are installed with Pocket PC, and you also get Bookdings and Frutiger Linotype with Pocket PC 2002 and 2003.
- **Bullets**   Any bulleting of text will be supported on the iPAQ.
- **Paragraph spacing and aligning**   Your paragraph spacing and aligning will be retained on the iPAQ.

A number of other characteristics are supported, but not fully, or are altered in their implementation:

- **Indentation**   This is altered to make a document more readable on the iPAQ's smaller screen.
- **Images**   The color depth of images is reduced to 256 colors.
- **Tables**   Table data is brought over and inserted as text, and any formatting information is not retained. If you move a document containing a table back to a desktop Word format, the table will appear as simple text aligned with tab stops.
- **Table of contents and index data**   This information is retained, but as with tables, any formatting is lost.
- **OLE objects**   These objects are not brought over, but are replaced by a bitmap placeholder.

When a document is transferred onto your mobile device, some document characteristics are preserved but ignored for the purposes of Pocket Word. This means that if you restore the document to a desktop environment, those settings reappear. These characteristics include

- Margins and gutter settings
- Paper size settings
- Header and footer vertical locations

It is very important to understand the characteristics that are completely ignored when you move from the desktop Word environment to the Pocket Word environment, as these settings will return to the default if you ever move the document from Pocket Word back to the desktop. These characteristics include

- Borders and shading
- Columns

- Numbered lists
- Headers and footers
- Footnotes
- Annotations and comments
- Revision marks
- Frames and style sheets
- Page setup information
- Password protection

NOTE *If you have password protection on a document, you will not be able to convert it to a Pocket Word format. You will need to remove the password protection first.*

Even with these limitations, Pocket Word is an excellent way to view attachments to e-mails that are sent to you, edit short documents while you are on the go, or reference important memos without having to carry briefcases full of paper. With applications like Transcriber (described in Chapter 2), Pocket Word becomes a great place to keep your notes while you are on the move if you want to pull them over to your desktop and edit them later. Or if you are a salesperson on the road, you can edit documents such as contracts while sitting with a client, rather than having to wait until you are back in the office to do it.

TIP *On the Pocket PC you can set a password to protect the entire unit; however, what if you only want to protect a specific file? This isn't supported natively on the Pocket PC, so a talented programmer named Francois Pessaux has written a free application called "Lucifer" that you can use to encrypt or decrypt any individual file on your iPAQ with Defense Encryption Standard (DES) encryption. If you are technically inclined to want to tinker, he even provides the source code! To download Lucifer, visit Francois' web site at http://guinness.cs.stevens-tech.edu/~fpessaux/index.html#The_other_stuff_I_did.*

Opening an Existing Document or Creating a New Document

When you tap on the icon to launch Pocket Word, you will be presented with a list of documents in the My Documents folder, as shown in Figure 3-1.

To open a specific document, simply tap on it, and it will open within Pocket Word. If you are already in Pocket Word, you can open a document by tapping OK in the upper-right corner of the title bar. This will close the document you are in and return you to the document list of Figure 3-1.

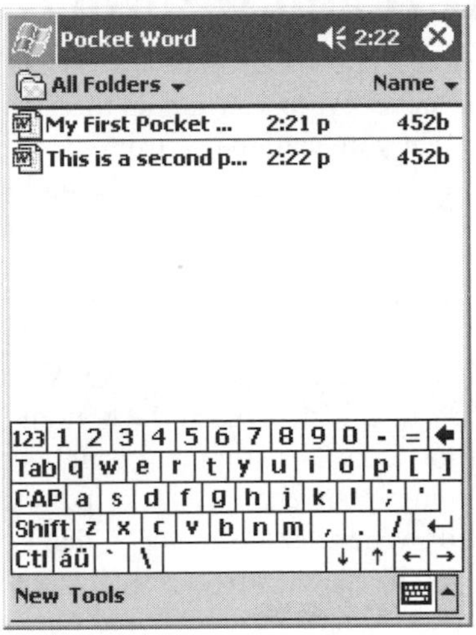

3

FIGURE 3-1 The document list window shows the Word documents stored on your iPAQ.

At the top of the document selection window, you can see a list of the folders by tapping the folders drop-down arrow in the top left, as shown here:

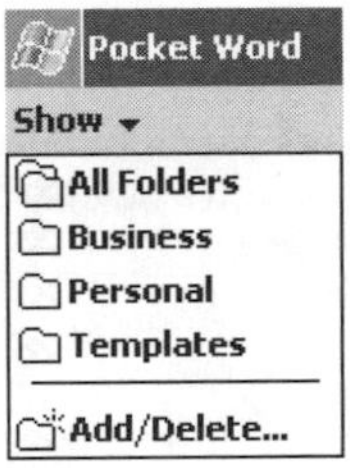

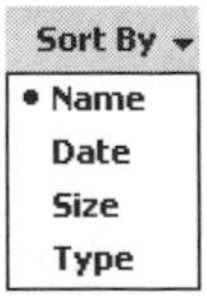

If you have many documents on your iPAQ, you can sort the document list by tapping on the Sort By drop-down arrow in the top right of the window, as shown in the illustration that follows. As with your desktop version of Windows, you can sort by filename, date, size, or type.

If you want to create a new document, you select the New option from the menu at the bottom of the document list window. If you are already in a document, you can always select New from the menu at any time to begin creating a new document.

Entering and Editing Text and Drawings

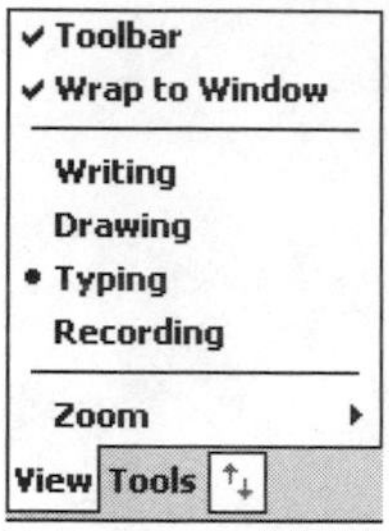

✔ Toolbar
✔ Wrap to Window
Writing
Drawing
• Typing
Recording
Zoom ▸
View Tools ↑↓

The essence of working in a document editor is to be able to enter text and information in your document. In Pocket Word you can do that in a few different ways. You can select the input mode that you want to use from the View menu. The four options are Writing mode, Drawing mode, Typing mode, and Recording mode. You select the mode that you want to use from the View menu, as shown here.

Entering Text in Typing Mode

Typing mode is the default entry mode for Pocket Word. You enter text through the soft input panel (SIP), which is the area at the bottom of the screen that appears as a keyboard or as a character recognition area. The soft input panel is covered in detail in Chapter 2.

All entries that you make in Typing mode end up as text in the document, just as they do with your standard desktop word processor. Wherever the cursor is, that is where your text will appear. You can move the cursor wherever you like in the text simply by tapping the appropriate spot with your stylus. Figure 3-2 shows text entered into a Pocket Word document in Typing mode with the soft keyboard selected.

Also visible in Figure 3-2 is the toolbar, the group of buttons above the soft keyboard. (In Typing mode, the toolbar contains buttons for formatting text.) By default, this toolbar is off, but you can turn it on by selecting Toolbar from the View menu. It can also be made visible or hidden by clicking the up/down arrow button in the menu bar at the bottom of the window, as shown in Figure 3-3. The toolbar works much the same way as its counterpart in desktop Word.

FIGURE 3-2   Typing mode with the soft keyboard visible

Toggle formatting
toolbar on and off

FIGURE 3-3   The formatting toolbar can be toggled on and off by selecting the up/down arrow in the main menu bar.

You select the text that you want, and then choose the relevant button to apply formatting to the text. The buttons on the toolbar allow you to select text formatting such as bold, italic, underline, left-justified text, right-justified text, and center-justified text, or to start a bulleted list. These formatting options are discussed later in this chapter.

Entering Text in Writing Mode

In Writing mode, the strokes you write with your stylus directly on the screen of the iPAQ are captured and saved in the document. Your handwriting is not converted to text in the document; instead, each word is saved as an image and embedded into the text.

When you switch into Writing mode, lines are displayed on the screen to help you keep your handwriting in a straight line, as shown in Figure 3-4. The text is also enlarged to make the writing easier. If you are like us, your handwriting is terrible, so you might find that you use Writing mode very rarely.

Each word that you enter is captured as a separate image, allowing you to erase one word at a time by selecting the image and deleting it.

The toolbar changes when you are in Writing mode, as shown in Figure 3-4. The first icon in the toolbar allows you to toggle the pen on and off. When the pen is on, wherever you tap with the stylus becomes a word in your handwriting. If you want to move the cursor or select text, you will need to toggle the pen off first. Next to the Pen button is the Pen Weight button, which allows you to select a different *weight* (line width) for the text that you are writing. You can even change

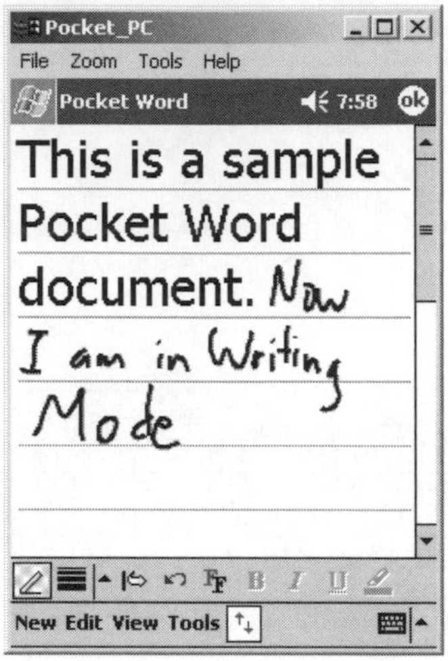

FIGURE 3-4   In Writing mode the strokes you make with the stylus are captured as images.

the weight after you have written. The following illustration shows the Pen Weight selections (Fine, Normal, Bold, and Thick) and the word "Writing" changed to a thick weight.

The third button from the left is the Insert/Remove Space button, which allows you to alter the space between words. The next button is for the undo functionality. You cannot simply backspace to correct an error when you are writing, but Undo lets you erase the last word that you wrote (or the word before that, or more, depending on how many times you tap the button). The formatting buttons are still on the toolbar, and if you select written words, the program will do its best to make bold, underline, italicize, or strikethrough the written words you have created. The button on the far right of the toolbar is the Highlight button, which works the same as it does in the desktop version of Word, allowing you to put a colored background behind the selected text.

Creating Sketches and Diagrams in Drawing Mode

Writing mode helps you to write words in straight lines across the page. If you would like to add sketches and drawings to your Pocket Word document, you will need to switch to Drawing mode. In this mode the system will not try to group your lines into words (which is what happens in Writing mode). Instead each line will be its own image, and you can select multiple lines to group. Figure 3-5 shows a Pocket Word document with a mixture of text entered in Typing mode and a drawing entered in Drawing mode.

When in Drawing mode, any text that you have entered in Typing mode is grayed out to remind you that you are in Drawing mode. You will also see a grid appear on the screen to help you align your drawing. You can adjust the zoom factor by selecting Zoom from the View menu. Figure 3-5 is shown in 300% zoom. If you adjust the zoom to 100%, you will see smaller grid boxes and be able to draw a much larger, less grainy image, as shown in Figure 3-6.

The toolbar, as shown in Figure 3-6, contains some buttons that are similar to those in Writing mode, such as the Pen toggle and Pen Weight. Next to those you have a pop-up menu for selecting the colors you want for the lines you are drawing, and one for the fill (which will fill in any closed shape that you draw). Tapping on the arrow next to the button brings up a list of colors to choose from, as shown here.

For example, let's say you would like to color the lake in the drawing in Figure 3-6 aqua. First you select the Pen Toggle button to toggle from drawing

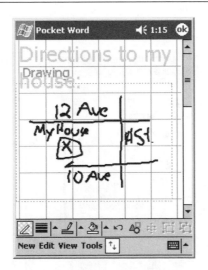

FIGURE 3-5   Drawing mode lets you add sketches to your Pocket Word document.

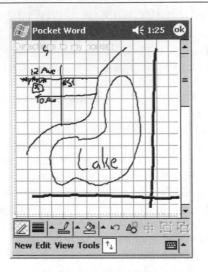

FIGURE 3-6   Changing the zoom factor can give you a larger drawing area.

to selecting. Then you select the lake by tapping on it. Next you tap on the Fill button to display the Fill pop-up menu and choose a color—for example, Aqua—from the list. Now the lake is colored, as shown in Figure 3-7.

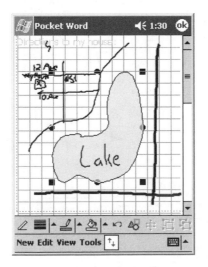

FIGURE 3-7   You can color in any closed shape by using the Fill button.

Every line that you draw in Drawing mode becomes its own discrete object. You can group these objects together by tapping and holding the stylus down and dragging a rectangle around the objects that you want to group. Once they have been selected, you can choose the Group button on the toolbar (second icon from the right showing two squares) to group them together. You can undo this action by selecting a group and choosing the Ungroup button (rightmost icon showing two squares with dark boxes in the corner of each square) on the toolbar.

An action similar to grouping can be used to align objects. Select the objects that you want to align, and then select the Align button (third icon from the right showing two small squares with arrows in each direction). This will give you a pop-up menu with the options to align all the selected objects to the left, right, top, bottom, vertical center, or horizontal center, as shown in Figure 3-8.

Tapping and dragging one of the handles (dark boxes or circles that appear on an object's or a group's perimeter) lets you resize any selected object or group of objects.

Drawing mode is good for a quick sketch, but if you want to do any serious art on your Pocket PC, you should probably acquire a third-party graphics program, as discussed in Chapter 11.

Using the Recording Mode to Capture Audio

Recording mode is used if you want to attach a live audio recording to the Pocket Word document that you are currently working on. Recording mode places a new toolbar on the bottom of the screen that allows you to use the built-in microphone on your iPAQ to record a voice or

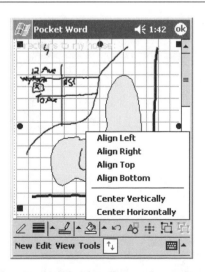

 Clicking the Align button brings up a menu of alignment options.

Quick Shape-Drawing Techniques

If you draw a shape, tap and hold on it to make the pop-up menu appear. From the pop-up menu, select Shape. This allows you to specify one of four shapes: Rectangle, Circle, Triangle, or Line. You can also resize these shapes, so if you need to do a quick organizational chart, this method works.

live audio attachment for your document. If you have an audio attachment, an icon will be shown in the top-left corner of the document. The attachment icon and the recording toolbar are shown in Figure 3-9.

The buttons on the recording toolbar are made to resemble those you would see on any tape recorder or VCR. The big red dot will start the recording when tapped. The square will stop the recording. The single right arrow will play a selected recording. The slider bar shows you where in the audio file you are and can be dragged to move to a specific position within the file. The double-arrow buttons are to skip to the beginning or end of the recording. The last button lets you adjust the playback volume.

| FIGURE 3-9 | The audio attachment icon shows when your Word document has an attached audio file, and the recording toolbar allows you to work with that attachment. |

Formatting Your Document

The amount of formatting that you can accomplish in Pocket Word is limited. Any truly fancy formatting will have to wait until you have transferred the file to a full desktop version of Word. However, you can perform some formatting on the text and paragraphs right on your iPAQ.

Text Formatting

To format text in your Pocket Word document, first you must select the text you want to work with. To select a block of text, tap and hold your stylus just before the first letter that you want to affect. Drag your stylus until just after the last letter that you want to format. This will select all the text between your initial tap and your final release. Then select the Format button on the toolbar, as shown here, or choose Format from the Edit menu. Performing either action will open the Format dialog box, shown in Figure 3-10.

In this dialog box you can use the drop-down lists to change the text font, size, weight, color, and fill color. You can also set the selected text to be bold, italicized, underlined, highlighted, or struck through. When you have finished setting the formatting options for the selected text, tapping the OK circle in the top right of the dialog box will return you to the document.

Paragraph Formatting

To change the formatting of the current paragraph of the document, you only need to place the cursor anywhere in the paragraph by tapping. If you want to affect more than one paragraph at a time, select

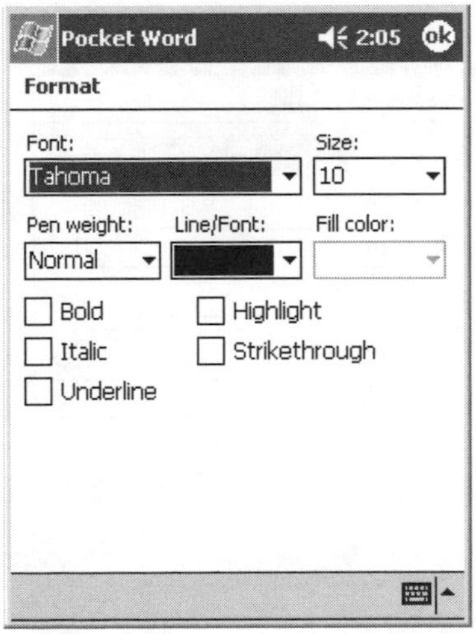

FIGURE 3-10   The Format dialog box allows you to change the characteristics of the selected block of text.

the text in the paragraphs by tapping and dragging your stylus until all the desired paragraphs have been highlighted. To select the entire document, choose Select All from the Edit menu.

Once you have selected the desired paragraphs, from the Edit menu choose Paragraph to open the Paragraph dialog box, shown in Figure 3-11.

In this dialog box you can set the alignment to be left, center, or right. You can also convert the selected paragraphs to a bulleted list by selecting the check box. Set left, right, and special indentations in this dialog box by entering the desired amounts. Special indentations include extra indentation for the first line of a paragraph and hanging indentation.

Saving Your Document

Saving your current document works slightly differently in Pocket Word than it does in the desktop version. Your Pocket Word document will be saved automatically as soon as you tap the OK button in the top-right corner to exit the document. You do not need to explicitly save the document. It will be saved into the folder that you are currently working in, with the name that you last used. If this is a new document that hasn't been saved before, Pocket Word will use the first words in the document as the filename. If you want to use a specific filename, save in a different folder, save to an external storage device (such as a CompactFlash (CF) card), or save as a different file type, you will need to choose Save Document As from the Tools menu.

Selecting Save Document As will open the Save As dialog box, as shown in Figure 3-12. Tapping OK will carry out your instructions and make a copy of the document where you have requested.

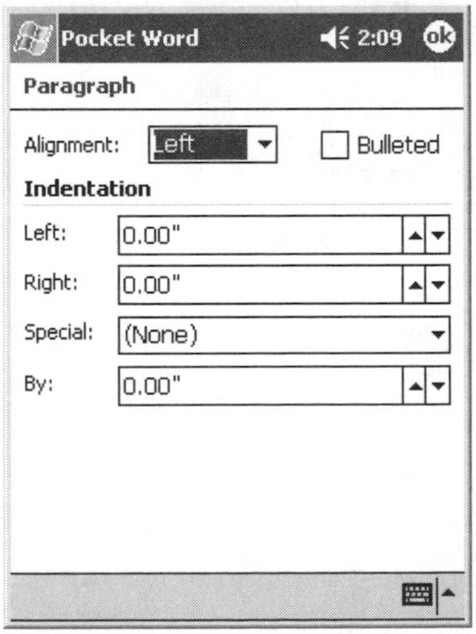

FIGURE 3-11   The Paragraph dialog box lets you change the characteristics of a paragraph.

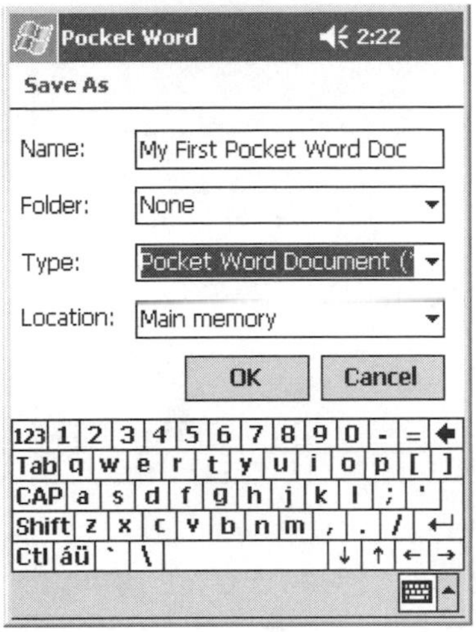

FIGURE 3-12 In the Save As dialog box you can change the filename, type, folder, and storage location of your document.

Remember that if you are editing an existing document and tap the OK button in the top-right corner, your changes will be automatically saved. When you tap this button, Pocket Word will *not* prompt you with a "Do you want to save?" message as the desktop version does; it will assume that you want to save, and the old version will be overwritten. If you have been making edits and decide you don't want to keep them, be careful *not* to exit the program with the OK button. Instead, use the Revert To Saved command on the Tools menu. You will be asked to confirm that you want to undo all the changes that you have made since opening the document. If you select Yes, the document will revert to its original state. If you select New after editing a document in Pocket Word, it will prompt you with a message asking whether you want to save, cancel, or save as prior to opening a new document.

Beaming and E-mailing Your Document

Pocket Word realizes that if you are writing documents on your iPAQ, they will likely be short, and you will probably want to be able to transmit them to someone else either by e-mail or by *beaming* (transferring information through the infrared port of your iPAQ) them to another Pocket PC owner. To make this process as easy as possible, Pocket Word has added Send Document By E-mail and Beam Document commands to the Tools menu.

Selecting Send Document By E-mail from the Tools menu will create a new e-mail message in your Outbox with your document already attached. You will need to select to whom you wish to send the message as well as add a subject line and any text to the message. Tapping the Send button will queue it up to be sent the next time you have an active wireless connection or the next time you connect with ActiveSync.

Setting up to beam a document to another Pocket PC through the infrared port

Selecting the Beam Document command will automatically set up your iPAQ to beam or transmit the document from your infrared port at the top of your unit to a receiving unit that has a physically aligned infrared port. You will see the Pocket Word beaming window, shown in Figure 3-13, which shows the status of the beam. In Figure 3-13 the device hasn't yet located an aligned infrared port that is ready to receive. If you are running Pocket PC 2000, the receiving unit must be set to receive the file by selecting the Infrared Receive program in the Program Files folder. For Pocket PC 2002 and 2003 users, the unit is always in a receive state unless you specifically turn this feature off. Once the document has been successfully transmitted, you will see the results window, as shown in Figure 3-14.

Zoom

The Zoom command on the View menu allows you to change the size of the document view. There are five preset zoom levels: 75%, 100%, 150%, 200%, and 300%. Figure 3-15 shows our sample document zoomed to 75%, the smallest setting, as well as the Zoom command fully expanded.

Undo/Redo

Undo and Redo commands are available on the Edit menu. Undo will undo the last action that you took, including formatting, zooming, typing, deleting, or other action. This command is also available on the standard toolbar. Tapping Undo multiple times will undo multiple previous actions.

3

FIGURE 3-14   The results window appears after a document is successfully beamed to another Pocket PC device.

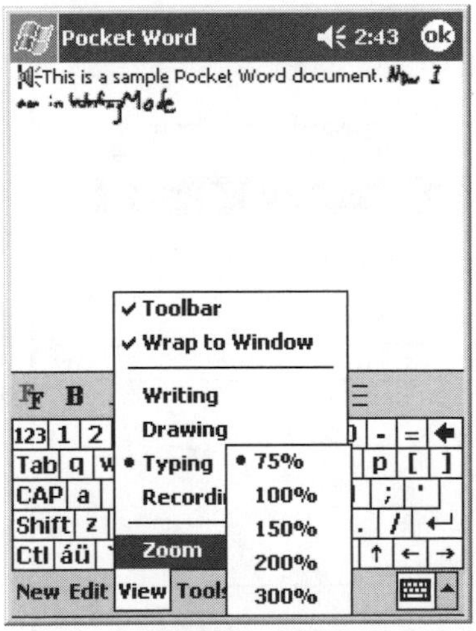

FIGURE 3-15   A document zoomed to 75% allows you to see more information on the screen at one time.

The Redo command will let you restore the change that you just undid. Redo can be useful if you tap the Undo button too many times and accidentally undo more steps than you intended to.

Spell Check

Spell check is only available with Pocket PC 2002 and 2003. If you are running an earlier version of Pocket PC or have upgraded an older iPAQ, you will not have this feature (although it can be installed separately).

You can start the spell checker by choosing it from the Tools menu.

Word Count

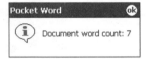

You can determine the length of your document by selecting Word Count from the Tools menu. A window will pop up that gives the count of words entered in the document, as shown here. Note that this does not include any words that you have entered in Writing mode.

Setting Your Options

You can set global options for Pocket Word by selecting Options from the Tools menu. The Options dialog box will open, as shown in Figure 3-16.

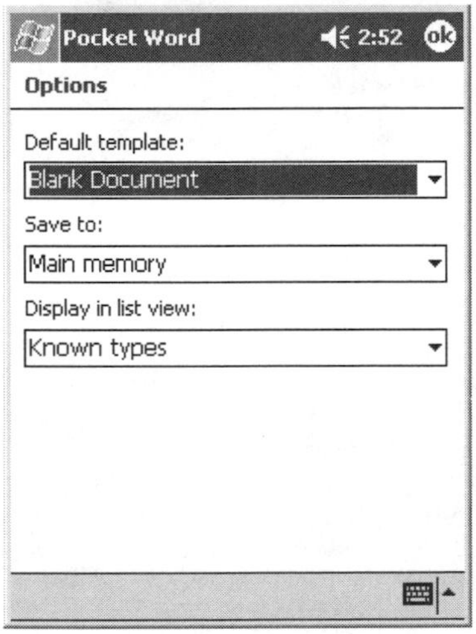

FIGURE 3-16   You can set Pocket Word options in the Options dialog box.

Default Template

The Default Template drop-down list allows you to set the standard template that will be used every time a new document is opened using the New command. It is rare that you would want to change this selection from the default Blank Document, unless you find that the vast majority of new documents you create are based on another template. The standard templates that install with Pocket Word are

- **Blank Document**   The initial default template is a completely blank document.
- **Memorandum**   This template contains a title and the standard fields To, CC, From, and Date.
- **Meeting Notes**   This template contains a title, subject, date, attendees, and action items headings.
- **Phone Memo**   This template contains a title, caller, company, phone, date and time, and message headings.
- **To Do**   This template contains a title and a list of blank bullets for entering to do items.

Alternatively, to start a document with a specific template, you can select the Templates folder from the document list window discussed in the sections "Opening an Existing Document" or "Creating a New Document" earlier in this chapter.

You can add new templates to this default set by creating a template you want and putting it in the Templates folder. For example, if you are a real-estate inspector and find that you use your iPAQ for doing inspections in the field, you could set your default Word document template to be a blank inspection report. Just remember to use the Save Document As command to avoid overwriting your initial template. (We recommend keeping an extra copy of all your templates in a different folder because at some point you will accidentally overwrite your template.)

Did you know?

You Can Edit Text or HTML Files on Your iPAQ

By default, Pocket Word likes to open only Pocket Word files. You can open other editable file types like HTML by going to the Options page and changing the Display In List View drop-down list to Known Types. You will now be able to see other editable file types such as text or HTML that you can now open in Pocket Word.

Save To

The Save To command allows you to save your documents by default to the main memory of your iPAQ or to an external storage location. External storage locations can include Secure Digital (SD) cards (if you have a newer series iPAQ with a Secure Digital slot), CompactFlash (CF) cards, external PCMCIA hard drives, or other storage devices. These storage peripherals are examined in detail in Chapter 15.

Display In List View

The Display In List View command allows you to select what types of files appear in the document list window that opens when you first launch Pocket Word. By default this list will show all known file types. You can restrict this list to show only Pocket Word documents or only Pocket Word documents and text documents.

Synchronizing with Your Desktop

Synchronizing your data with ActiveSync is covered in detail in Chapter 2, and if you need detailed instructions, you should refer to that chapter. Note that keeping a synchronized document on both your Pocket PC and desktop system can be a great convenience. Every time you make a change on your Pocket PC or desktop, the document will be synchronized with the other system. If you reference and update this document frequently, this capability could save you a great deal of time. However, keep in mind that if you modify the document on both the desktop and the handheld between synchronizations, then the next time you ActiveSync with your iPAQ you will have a conflict you will have to resolve by selecting one of the documents to overwrite the other.

An Alternative to Pocket Word

For the serious mobile writer, the limited feature set of Pocket Word might prove disappointing. If you want the ability to create and edit your Word DOC files in their native format with full functionality, you should purchase TextMaker from German software vendor SoftMaker (**www.softmaker.de**). It is an impressive program that allows you to create and edit full Word documents (no conversion of the file as with Pocket Word). It includes full support for images, tables, headers and footers, and more (for example, see Figure 3-17). TextMaker can use its own native file format, as well as support Microsoft Word, RTF, Pocket Word, and HTML files. If mobile access to and editing of documents is important to you, this software is a must-have addition to your Pocket PC.

| FIGURE 3-17 | TextMaker allows you to work with full unconverted Microsoft Word documents including many advanced features. |

Writing Resources

Many writers like to keep a dictionary and thesaurus close at hand. However, your iPAQ won't come with these installed by default. You can check out some of the following sources for Pocket PC compatible reference materials.

TomeRaider

TomeRaider (**www.tomeraider.com**) is an eBook reader that allows you to view a wide variety of reference material such as encyclopedias, dictionaries (as shown in Figure 3-18), thesauri, guides, religious works, philosophical texts, and much more. It is compact and responsive, allowing you to look up important reference information quickly and easily without consuming all of the storage space on your iPAQ. You have to purchase the software for a nominal charge, but the reference materials are free. A vast library of TomeRaider books is available at **www.memoware.com**.

FIGURE 3-18   Many portable reference books are available to load separately on your
Pocket PC.

Lextionary

Lextionary by Revolutionary Software Front is both a dictionary and thesaurus. It contains almost
140,000 words available for lookup. It is more limited than TomeRaider in that it is a single-purpose
stand-alone application instead of a generalized reference reader. You can download a free trial
copy from the Revolutionary Software web site at **www.revolution.cx/lex.htm**.

Microsoft Reader References

You can also find a variety of free Microsoft resources such as the Encarta Encyclopedia and a
Pocket Dictionary directly from the Microsoft web site at **www.microsoft.com/reader/
downloads/dictonaries.asp**.

Chapter 4

Use Pocket Excel to Work with Numbers

How to…

- Open and work with an Excel workbook on your iPAQ
- Create a Pocket Excel workbook on your iPAQ
- Move workbooks between your iPAQ and your desktop
- Create a template
- Format cells and workbooks
- Use formulas in a workbook
- Beam or e-mail a workbook

Like Pocket Word, Pocket Excel is part of the unique capabilities of the Pocket PC–based handhelds like the iPAQ. Pocket Excel allows you to view, create, and edit spreadsheets on your handheld that are compatible with your desktop version of Excel.

In this chapter we will examine how to use Pocket Excel to not only view, but also to compose and edit spreadsheets. As we did in Chapter 3, on Pocket Word, to make sure that you don't get yourself into any trouble, we will cover exactly which parts of the spreadsheet you can work with in Pocket Excel and which you can't, and what that means for you as a spreadsheet reader or author.

What Pocket Excel Can Do

Pocket Excel is a scaled-down version of the full desktop Microsoft Excel product. As you would expect, it only has a limited set of features, but this doesn't mean it isn't powerful enough to do almost all of what you need while away from your desk.

As with Pocket Word, the files that Pocket Excel works with are converted versions of the XLS files that are on your desktop. The converted Pocket Excel workbook extensions are PXL for workbooks and PXT for templates.

NOTE   *Pocket Excel files are limited to 256 columns and 16,384 rows. (This is a pretty big file, but desktop Excel can handle much larger ones.) If the Excel spreadsheet you are moving to your Pocket PC is larger than this, it will be truncated.*

When you move the files over to your Pocket PC (either by copying them with Windows Explorer, syncing, or downloading an e-mail attachment), they are automatically converted to the correct format. This reduced format supports the most important features of Excel, but some information is lost. If you are moving your files back and forth between your iPAQ and your desktop, this could become a problem. You shouldn't notice any significant problems with basic spreadsheets, but some that utilize more sophisticated functions could operate differently in Pocket Excel. To help you understand the details of what is and isn't supported, we've produced lists of the different features and characteristics.

This is the set of fully supported spreadsheet characteristics:

- ■ **Standard text formatting**   Bold, italics, underlining, highlight, font type, font color, and font size formatting are fully supported.
- ■ **TrueType fonts**   Note that any TrueType fonts you want to use must be installed on your iPAQ. By default, Courier New, Tahoma, Bookdings, and Frutiger Linotype are preinstalled.
- ■ **Cell formatting**   Standard and custom formats are supported for cells including General, Number, Currency, Accounting, Date, Time, Percentage, Fraction, Scientific, and Text.
- ■ **Alignment**   Horizontal and vertical alignment options are supported along with word wrap within a cell.
- ■ **Row heights and column widths**   Adjustment of row heights and column widths are supported.

A number of other characteristics are supported, but not fully, or are altered in their implementation:

- ■ **Formulas with arrays**   You cannot use arrays in your formulas. When you copy a spreadsheet that contains arrays from your desktop, the arrays in the formulas will be converted to values in Pocket Excel.
- ■ **Formulas with unsupported functions**   Many of the functions in Excel are supported in Pocket Excel, but not all. We won't list all the functions here, but to give an example, the Round() function is not available in Pocket Excel. You can see a full list of supported functions from the Insert Function command on the Tools menu. When you copy a spreadsheet that includes unsupported functions from your desktop, those functions will be converted to values.
- ■ **Pivot tables**   Pivot tables are not supported in Pocket Excel, and, like the unsupported formulas, will be changed to values if brought over from desktop Excel.
- ■ **Borders**   Borders are supported, but not if you try to be fancy. You can only create borders with single lines. Any different borders that are brought over from desktop Excel will be converted to single-line borders.
- ■ **Vertical text**   Vertical text is not supported and will be changed to horizontal text if brought over from a desktop file.
- ■ **Hidden names**   Any hidden names that are brought over from a desktop file will be displayed.
- ■ **Passwords**   You can set a general password for your spreadsheet in Pocket Excel, but you can't choose options like adding a password in order to modify the spreadsheet, or flagging it as read-only.

4

When a spreadsheet is brought onto your mobile device, one characteristic is converted, but is ignored for the purposes of Pocket Excel: cell shading. This means that if you restore the spreadsheet to a desktop environment, the cell shading originally assigned to a cell reappears.

It is very important to note which characteristics are completely unsupported when you move from the desktop Excel environment to the Pocket Excel environment, as these settings will return to the default if you ever move the spreadsheet from Pocket Excel back to the desktop. These characteristics are

- Graphics of any kind (images, object charts, picture controls, drawing objects, and so on)
- AutoFilter
- Add-ins
- Data validation
- Cell notes
- Cell patterns
- Cell and sheet protection
- Scenarios
- Text boxes
- Hyperlinks
- VBA scripting

Pocket Excel is a very handy way to whip together quick calculations, write up expense sheets while on the go, gather sports statistics at the park, calculate a tip at the restaurant, and more. The wonderful Transcriber application we've already mentioned also works well with Pocket Excel.

NOTE *If you need some of the functions that are not provided in Pocket Excel, third-party applications may be the answer. For example, the ClearVue viewers from Westtek (**www.westtek.com**) allow you to view full Excel documents including charts and graphics, but do not allow for editing.*

Opening an Existing Spreadsheet or Creating a New Spreadsheet

When you tap the icon to launch Pocket Excel, you will be presented with a list of workbooks in the default folder, as shown in Figure 4-1.

To open a specific workbook, simply tap it, and it will open within Pocket Excel.

If you are already in Pocket Excel, you can open a workbook by tapping OK in the upper-right corner of the title bar. This will close the workbook you are in and return you to the list shown in Figure 4-1.

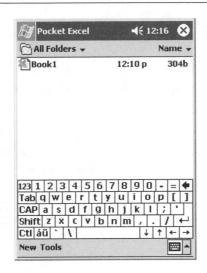

FIGURE 4-1   The workbook list window shows the Pocket Excel workbooks stored on your iPAQ.

At the top of the workbook selection window you can browse through the folders by tapping the show folders drop-down arrow in the top left, as shown here:

One of the folders in the list is the Templates folder. Templates are preformatted read-only documents. A Vehicle Mileage Log template comes preloaded as part of Pocket Excel. Templates retain their same base formatting forever, which is great for standard forms that you need to fill out often, such as expense sheets.

If you have many workbooks on your iPAQ, you can sort the list by changing the Sort By setting. To change the sorting method, tap the drop-down arrow in the top right of the window, shown next, and make a selection from the list. As with your desktop version of Excel, you can sort by filename, date, size, or type.

If you want to create a new workbook, select New from the menu at the bottom of the workbook list window. If you are already in a workbook, you can always select New from the menu at any time to create a new workbook.

Entering Data and Formulas into Cells

The benefit of spreadsheet software like Pocket Excel is that you can analyze groups of numbers or information by entering the data into the spreadsheet and then building formulas to calculate and manipulate the values automatically. Typical examples of this include tracking expenses, tallying up sales for a group of stores, keeping sports statistics, or any other numerical activity. For nonnumeric activities, the software might contain items like your grocery list or Christmas gift list.

How to ... Graph with Pocket Excel

Pocket Excel doesn't support graphs, but if you need to display graphs on your Pocket PC, you can do so with third-party applications such as AutoGraph from Developer One (**www.developerone.com**). It is easy to use. You copy the range of cells you want to graph into the clipboard by selecting the range and choosing Edit | Copy from the Pocket Excel menu. Next, you start Pocket AutoGraph and paste the cells. You can now choose your graph format and display a visual picture of your information. Next time you are on a plane with the sales manager and you want to show her or him the sales trend for the East Coast region, you know how to do it!

Selecting Cells

Before you can enter data into a cell, you must select the cell or group of cells that you want to work with. To select a single cell, tap the cell you desire with your stylus, as shown in Figure 4-2.

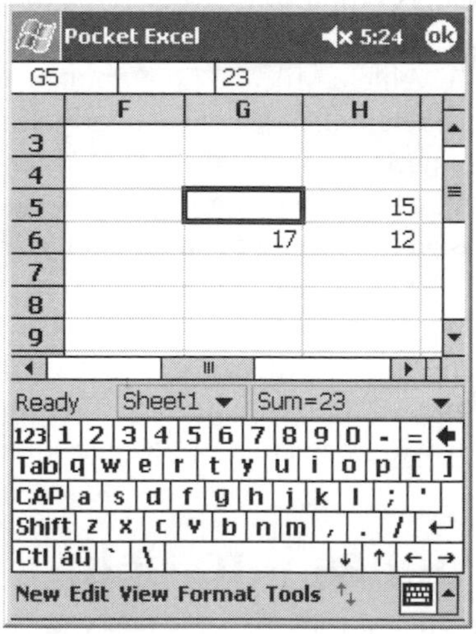

FIGURE 4-2   Before you can enter data into a workbook, you must select the cell or cells you want to work with.

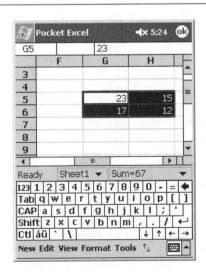

If the cell you want is not visible, you can scroll using the scroll bars on the right and bottom, or you may use the Go To command in the Tools menu. Selecting Go To will open the dialog box shown here, allowing you to specify a particular cell (which you can name by its cell address, H9, for example—or if you have named ranges in your workbook, you can use the name).

The Go To Current Region command will select a rectangular cell range around the currently selected cell bordered by blank rows or columns, as shown in Figure 4-3.

You can select a range of cells by tapping with the stylus and dragging the rectangle so that all the cells you desire are contained within the shaded area.

Entering Data into a Cell

Once you have selected a cell or range of cells, you can enter data, labels, or formulas into the current cell. You can enter data in the standard ways, through the character recognizer, keyboard, or Transcriber.

When you start typing in characters, they will appear in the entry bar where the current cell value is displayed, as shown in Figure 4-4. To the left of this bar you will find the address of the current cell, a button to cancel your entry, and a button to complete your entry (which is the same as pressing ENTER on the keyboard). There is also a button for creating formulas, which is addressed later in this chapter.

  FIGURE 4-3 The Go To Current Region command will select the set of all cells around the current cell that contain data.

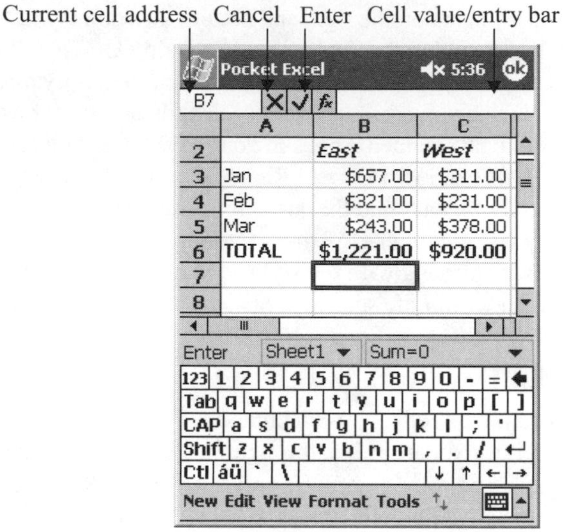

Current cell address Cancel Enter Cell value/entry bar

FIGURE 4-4 Data that you enter appears in the cell value box with buttons to cancel or accept your entry.

The difference between using the Enter button on the entry bar and ENTER on your keyboard is that tapping the Enter button will leave you in the current cell, whereas pressing ENTER on the keyboard will accept your entry and will make the cell below the current cell the new current cell. The latter action is convenient for entering a long list of data.

Entering a Formula

Being able to enter formulas to perform calculations on numbers is where the real power of a spreadsheet program like Excel becomes evident. Usually you are after more than just a list of numbers. You need to be able to add up those numbers, find an average, or perhaps perform a net present value calculation. All of this is possible with Pocket Excel formulas.

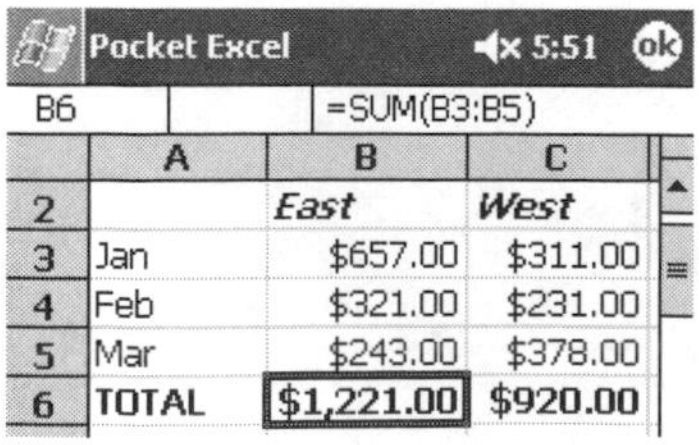

To enter a formula, first select the cell in which you want the result of your formula to be displayed. To tell Pocket Excel that you are creating a formula, enter an equal sign (=) in the cell value box. Next, type in the formula that you desire along with any information that it needs to make its calculation, as shown here. (Note that the three buttons between the cell address and the cell value only appear when you are editing a specific cell.)

This illustration shows an example of one of the most commonly used formulas, the Sum formula. It is very likely, if you are a frequent user of Excel, that you will know the most common formulas such as Sum, Average, and Count, but you may not know all the other functions that are available. To access these, you can go to the Insert Function command under the Tools menu or tap the *fx* button to the immediate left of the cell value area. Any of these actions opens the Insert Function dialog box, shown in Figure 4-5.

To select which subset of functions you want to look at, make a selection from the Category drop-down list. The default setting is to show all functions, but you can choose to view subsets of Financial, Date and Time, Math and Trigonometry, Statistical, Lookup, Database, Text, Logical, and Informational.

The Function list shows all the available functions that match the category you selected. The arguments that the function expects are presented in parentheses. When you select a function in the list, a brief description of it will appear beneath the list. To list every function in detail is beyond the scope of this book, but if you have access to the desktop version of Excel, you can look up the details of each function; they work the same way in Pocket Excel as they do in the desktop version.

Once you have selected the function you desire, tap OK to return to the cell value box where the selected function will be pasted into place. Next, simply replace the argument placeholders with the values that you desire. In addition to typing in the cell addresses by hand, you can tap specific cells to enter them into your formulas. Or, to enter a range, tap and hold a cell and then drag the stylus over the range of cells you would like to select.

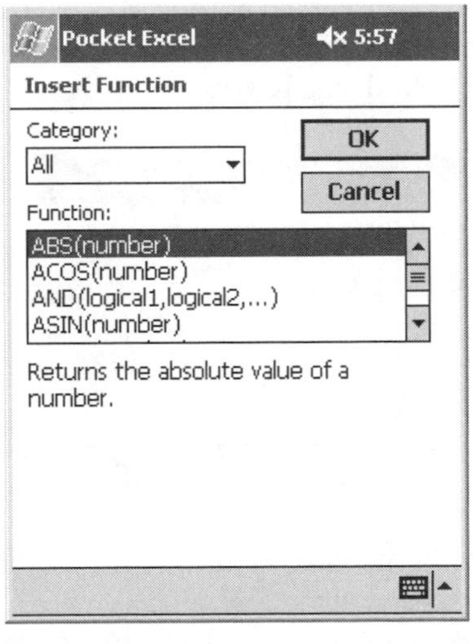

FIGURE 4-5   You can select from a list of all available functions in the Insert Function dialog box.

Tapping and Holding a Cell

If you tap your stylus and hold it on a cell without moving the stylus, you will be presented with a pop-up menu to make it easier to perform common functions on a specific cell, as shown in the following illustration.

> **NOTE** *Tap-and-hold functionality is only available in Pocket PC 2002 and 2003. If you are running an earlier version of Pocket PC, tapping and holding will do nothing.*

From this pop-up menu you can easily cut or copy the selected cell (or cells) into the clipboard, from which they can be pasted elsewhere in the spreadsheet. You also have commands to open the Insert Cells, shown next, or Delete Cells dialog boxes.

The Delete Cells dialog box works the same as the Insert Cells dialog box except that rows are shifted either left or up, or entire rows or columns are deleted.

Use the Format Cells command on the pop-up menu to edit the formatting of the selected cells.

Formatting Cells

The amount of formatting that you can accomplish in Pocket Excel is limited when compared with that available in the desktop version. Any truly fancy formatting will have to wait until you have transferred the file to a full desktop version of Excel. Nevertheless, you can still format a number of items in Pocket Excel.

When you select Format Cells from the tap-and-hold pop-up menu, or from the Cells command under the Format menu, the Format Cells dialog box will open. Along the bottom of this dialog box are five tabs to choose from: Size, Number, Align, Font, and Borders.

Size

You can format the row height and column width of the currently selected cell on the Size tab in the Format Cells dialog box, as shown in Figure 4-6. Only these two properties may be edited.

Row height is measured in points, and column width is measured in characters based upon the standard font. Row height can be set anywhere from 0 to 409. A value of 0 will make the row a hidden row. Column width can be set anywhere from 0 to 255 characters (decimal points are allowed) based upon the standard character font. Setting the column width to 0 will hide the column.

Number

You can change the data type of the number in a cell on the Number tab of the Format Cells dialog box. The Category list box contains a list of all the valid formats for Pocket Excel. You can scroll through this list and select the format that is appropriate for what you are doing. When you select a format, appropriate formatting options for that data type will appear below. For example, in

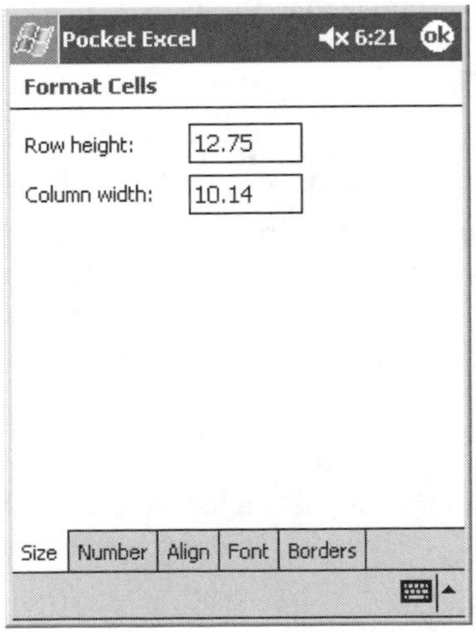

FIGURE 4-6   The physical size of the selected cell(s) can be adjusted by setting the Row Height and Column Width values on the Size tab of the Format Cells dialog box.

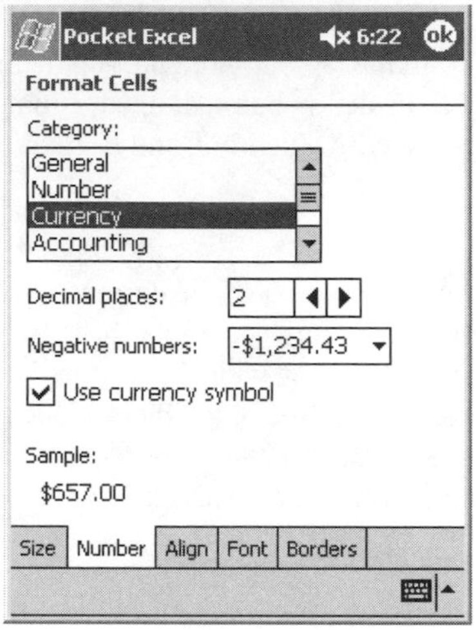

FIGURE 4-7 You can select the data type for a cell with the Number tab of the Format Cells dialog box.

Figure 4-7 the Currency data type has been selected; the options for this data type are the number of decimal places, how to display negative numbers, and whether you want the currency symbol to be shown. A sample of a number formatted as this data type is displayed below the options.

The format types available are General, Number, Currency, Accounting, Date, Time, Percentage, Fraction, Scientific, Text, and Custom.

Align

The Align tab is used to set the alignment properties of the currently selected cell. From here you have the option to set the horizontal alignment to General, Left, Center, Right, or Center Across Selection. You can set the vertical alignment to Top, Center, or Bottom. Also, a check box will allow to you wrap text onto multiple lines within a cell, as shown in Figure 4-8.

Font

On the Font tab you can select from the drop-down lists to change the selected cell's font, color, and size. You can also set the cell to be bold, italic, or underlined, as shown in Figure 4-9.

Borders

On the Borders tab you can select the options for a border around the currently selected cell or cells. You can only create one style of border—a single line—unlike desktop Excel, which has many line weights and types. You can set a line color and fill color for the cell from the drop-down lists.

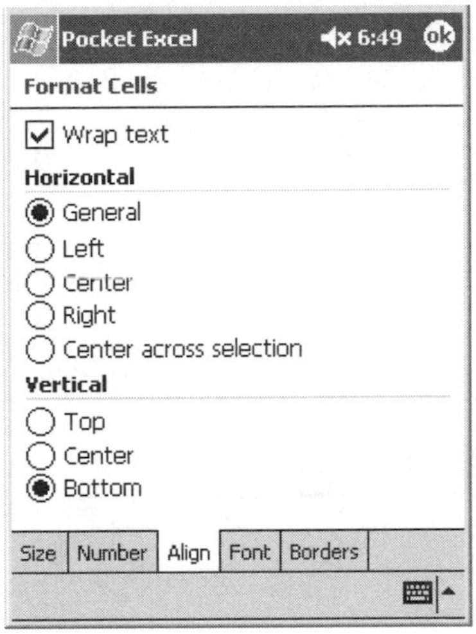

FIGURE 4-8 Use the Align tab to set options for horizontal and vertical alignment as well as word wrapping within a cell.

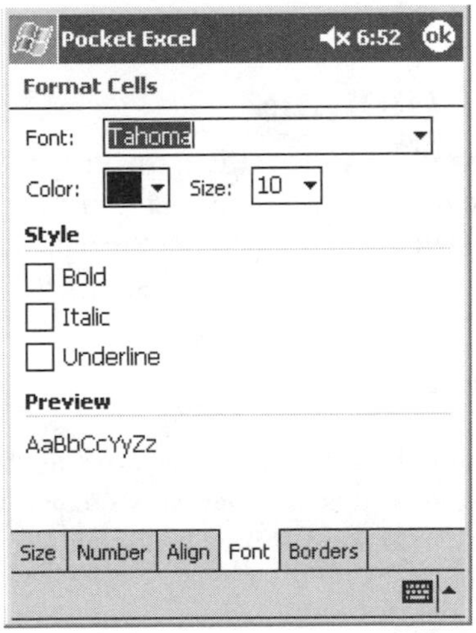

FIGURE 4-9 You can format the font settings for the selected cell on the Font tab.

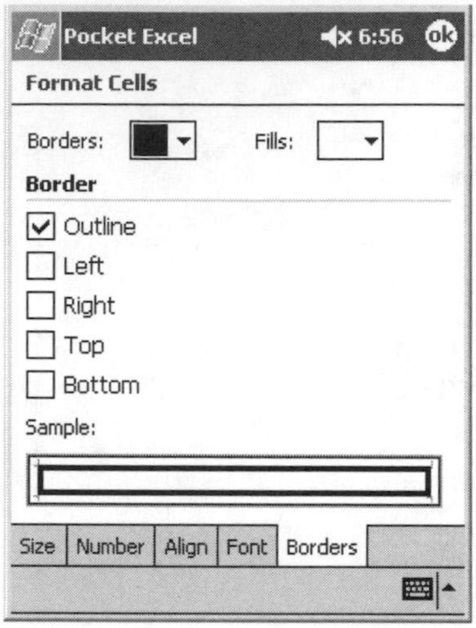

FIGURE 4-10   You can format the borders for your cells with the Borders tab.

Given that almost all Pocket PCs available today have full-color screens, the use of colors in a spreadsheet can be very effective. You can also set which side of the cells you want to see a border on by checking the appropriate boxes for Outline, Left, Right, Top, and Bottom, as shown in Figure 4-10.

Formatting Rows and Columns

Under the Format menu are commands to set specific formatting for rows and columns. These do not deal with colors or fonts of the rows and columns, but rather allow you to either hide or show the selected rows/columns or set them to AutoFit. AutoFit means that the row height or column width is adjusted to automatically accommodate the widest or tallest data in the row/column.

Working with Sheets

Workbooks in Pocket Excel accommodate multiple sheets, just as the desktop version of Excel does. When you create a new workbook, it is automatically created with three sheets. You can see what sheet you are currently in by looking at the Sheet area of the status bar (immediately above the menu), as shown in Figure 4-11.

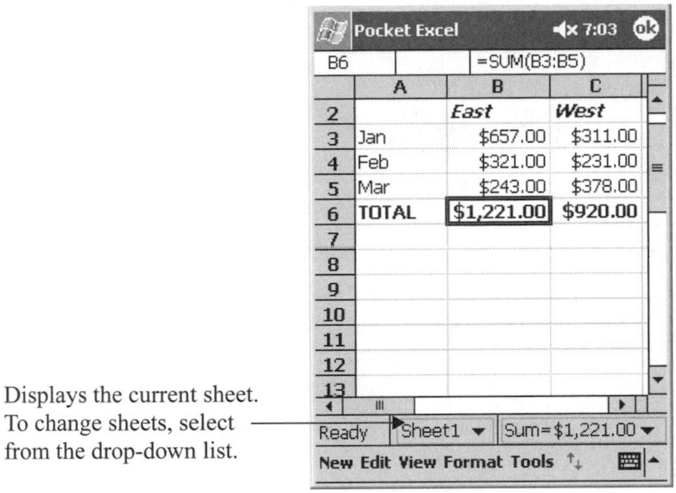

Displays the current sheet. To change sheets, select from the drop-down list.

FIGURE 4-11 See or change the current worksheet with the Sheet box in the status bar.

You can add, remove, reorder, or rename sheets in your workbook by selecting Modify Sheets from the Format menu, which opens the dialog box shown here.

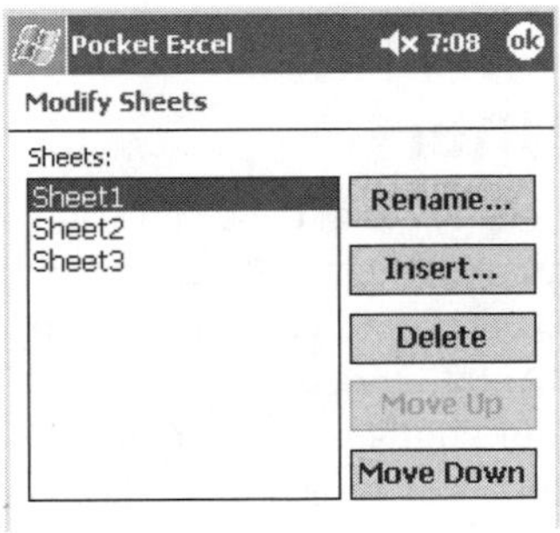

Using the AutoCalculate Feature

The status bar in Pocket Excel also contains a box for automatically showing calculated values on the currently selected range of cells. For example, if in the spreadsheet shown in Figure 4-12 we wanted to see the total of sales across both the East and West regions for January, we would select the relevant range of cells, and the AutoCalculate box in the status bar would show that the total sales are $968.00, as the figure shows.

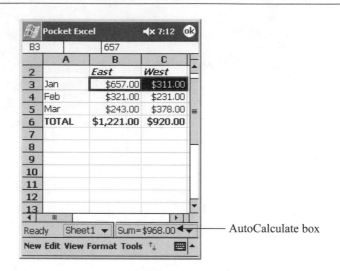

AutoCalculate box

FIGURE 4-12 The AutoCalculate feature will perform automatic calculations on a selected range of cells.

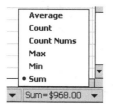

To change the kind of calculation being performed, tap the drop-down arrow in the box, and make a selection from the list of calculations. The choices are Average, Count, Count Nums, Max, Min, and Sum, as shown here.

Using AutoFilter

Sometimes you have a large set of data, and you want to be able to easily jump between subsets of that data. For example, if you had a list of all your employees across the country, you might want to be able to quickly filter the list to only show those employees in a given city. You can do this using the AutoFilter command on the Tools menu. To use AutoFilter, select a cell in the title or header row of your spreadsheet, and then select AutoFilter. Drop-down arrows will then appear in all the columns of your row, as shown in the following illustration:

Click the drop-down arrows in any column, and select from the list to filter for a specific column value, get all the data, see the top ten items, or set a custom filter, as you can see next:

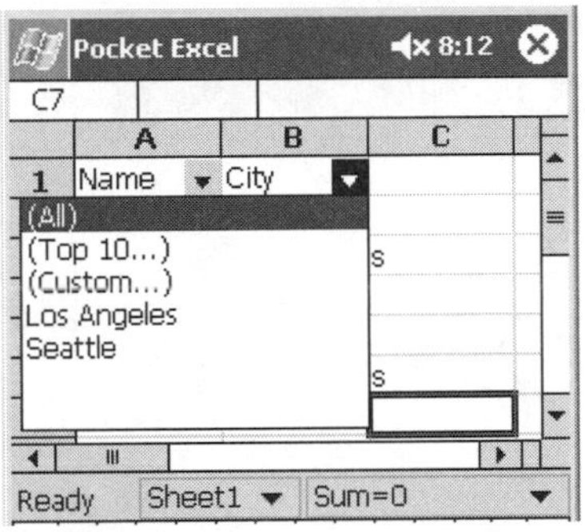

The following illustration shows the result of filtering an employee list for a specific city, in this case, Seattle.

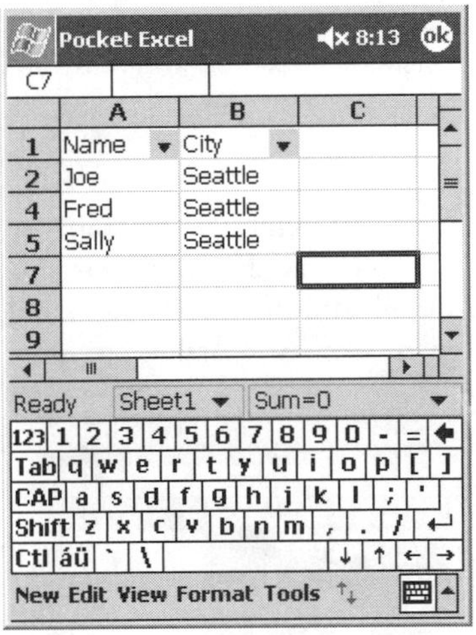

Selecting Custom opens the Custom AutoFilter dialog box, as shown in Figure 4-13. This dialog box allows you to set custom filter criteria. You can select one or two conditions where the selected column is equal to, not equal to, greater than, less than, greater than or equal to, less than or equal to, or begins with a value that you enter in the second field. You can then set an AND or OR condition with a second criteria that you can choose.

| FIGURE 4-13 | With the Custom AutoFilter command you can build complex filter criteria with up to two elements that can be joined by an AND or OR condition. |

Sorting

When you are working with lists of data and numbers, the ability to sort the information in a meaningful way is critical. To sort data in Pocket Excel, first select the range of cells that you want to sort, as shown in the following illustration. (You can include or exclude the header row; you have the option of excluding it later in the Sort dialog box.)

Once you have selected the cells you want, choose Sort from the Tools menu. The Sort dialog box will open, as shown in Figure 4-14. You have the option to sort by up to three columns. If the first column you select has two values that are the same, then the second column will be evaluated when choosing which row of data to place first, and so on, with the third. The check box to the right of each column allows you to specify whether you want to sort in ascending or descending order.

The check box at the bottom of the dialog box allows you to exclude the header, or title, row if you included it in your selection. If this box is selected, the column title will appear in the drop-down lists that currently show Column A, Column B, and so forth.

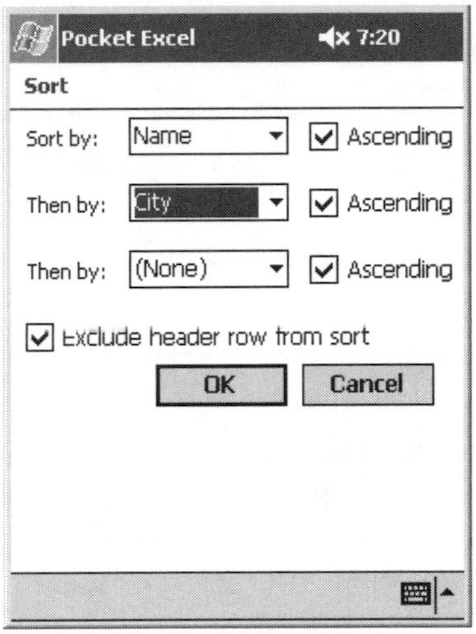

4

FIGURE 4-14   The Sort dialog box allows you to select which columns to sort by.

Inserting Symbols

If you find that you need to insert special characters in your text, you can do that with the Insert Symbols command on the Tools menu. Typical examples of special characters include currency characters such as pound (£) or yen (¥) and letters with special accents and certain characters from the Latin alphabet as well as characters from the Hebrew, Arabic, Cyrillic, Greek, and other alphabets. When you choose Insert Symbols, the Insert Symbol dialog box opens, as shown in Figure 4-15.

From here you select the font that you want to work with from the drop-down list, as shown next.

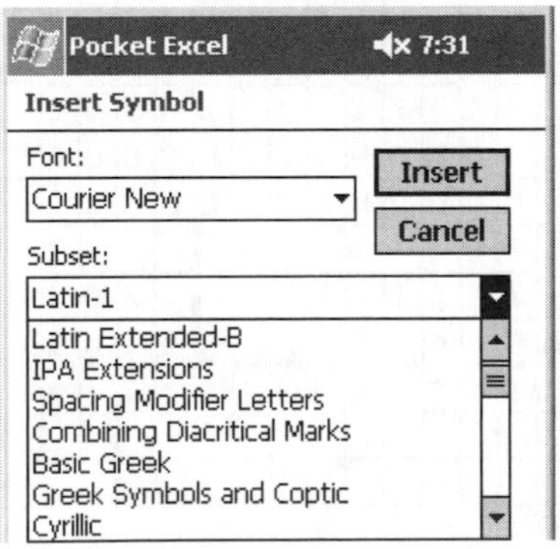

Then you can select the subset of the font. For example, the subsets available for Courier New include a few Latin choices, some special formatting and spacing characters, Greek,

FIGURE 4-15   Use the Insert Symbol dialog box to insert special characters into your
worksheet.

Cyrillic, Hebrew, Arabic, Armenian, Devanagari, Gurmukhi, Gujarat, Oriya, Tamil, Telungu,
Kannada, Malayalam, Thai, Lao, Basic and Extended Georgian, Hangul Jamo, and many more
special sets of characters, drawing symbols, pictograms, and others.

The graph that displays all the characters is extremely small and difficult to read. It would
be nice if future releases would provide a general zoom option on this window. In the meantime,
you can see the character better by selecting it. This will show an enlarged version of the selected
character, as shown here:

Now tap the Insert button, and that character will be inserted into your workbook at the point
where your cursor is.

Defining Names

A seldom-used feature of Excel is the ability to assign a name to a cell or range of cells. This allows you to reference the cell by name when using it in formulas instead of having to remember the cell's address every time you want to use it. This technique can be very useful for large spreadsheets that contain a number of formulas. For example, if we take our list of sales by region, we can add names to the regions and then use those names in our formulas. To define the name for a region, we first select the region. In the following illustration, we have selected all the sales for the East region.

	Pocket Excel	◀× 7:44	ok
EastSale		657	
	A	**B**	**C**
2		*East*	*West*
3	Jan	$657.00	$311.00
4	Feb	$321.00	$231.00
5	Mar	$243.00	$378.00
6	TOTAL	$1,221.00	$920.00
7			

To give this range of cells a name, we select Define Name on the Tools menu to open the Define Name dialog box, shown in Figure 4-16. In this dialog box you can enter a name for the selected region. In our example, we call this region EastSales. Tapping Add adds the name that you enter to the list of defined names. The Refers To field below the list allows you to see which cell or range is included in the selected name.

FIGURE 4-16 In the Define Name dialog box you can give a name to your selected cell or range of cells.

Once a name is defined, you can substitute it for any cell reference (if it names a specific cell) or any cell range in any formula. In our example, we named a range of cells EastSales. In the formula in cell B6, as shown in the following illustration, we are summing the range of cells from B3 to B5. This is the same range we named EastSales, so we can substitute the range in the formula with EastSales, and Excel will perform the correct calculation.

A final feature to mention in this section is the Paste List button shown in Figure 4-16. If you make extensive use of defined names, you may want to have a list somewhere in your workbook of all your defined ranges for reference. You can create such a list by placing your cursor where you want the list to be inserted and then opening the Define Name dialog box and selecting Paste List. A list of defined names that looks something like the one shown here will be pasted into your workbook.

Using the Fill Feature

The Fill feature of Excel allows you to fill a range of cells with data quickly and easily. Fill can be used for static copying of data from an existing set of cells or can include filling the range with a series or data that is different in each cell, such as an increasing number or date. To perform a copy type of fill, you must select the cells that you want to copy and then at the same time, select all the cells that you want to fill in with the copied data. The original data must be on one edge of the selection range. This can be any of the top, bottom, left, or right edges. Once the data and range are selected, you choose the Fill command from the Edit menu to open the Fill dialog box, as shown in Figure 4-17.

4

FIGURE 4-17   The Fill dialog box allows you to fill a selected range of cells with data.

To perform your copy, you simply indicate which row the original data is in by choosing your fill direction from the list of Down, Up, Left, or Right. The Fill Type in this case will be Copy. Once you've made your selections, tap OK to copy the original data into the range.

It's likely you will also use the Fill command to fill a range of cells with series data, such as a range of numbers or dates. When building a series, it helps to think in advance about what cells you need to select. For example, if you wanted to produce a list of days of the week on the left of your worksheet, you could enter the first day **Mon** on the first line. Then you would select the Mon cell along with the six cells beneath it, as shown here:

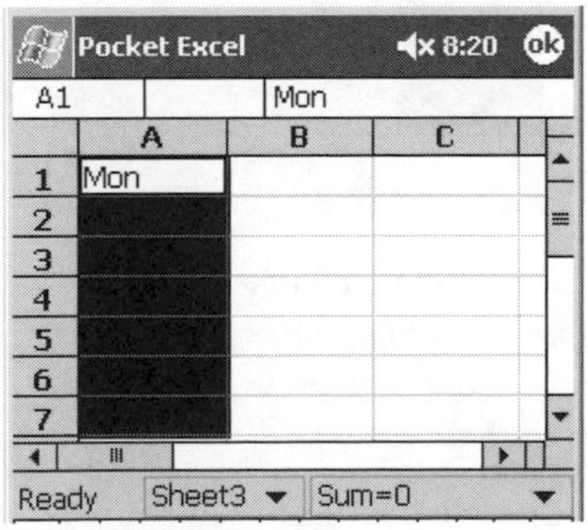

Select Edit | Fill, and in the Fill dialog box select a direction of Down, a Fill Type of Series, and a Series Type of Autofill, as shown in Figure 4-18.

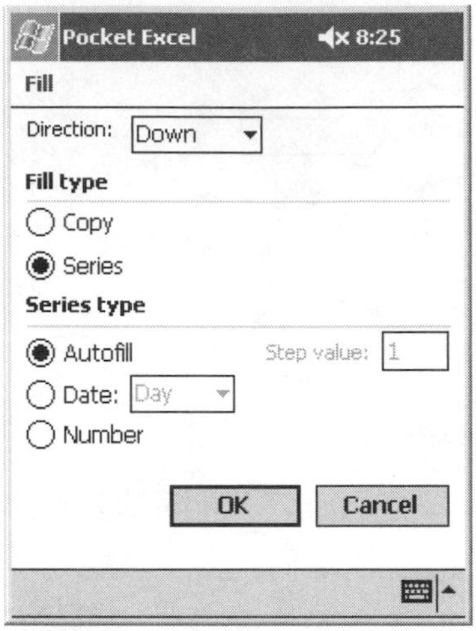

FIGURE 4-18   You can set the options in the Fill dialog box to produce an Autofill of days of the week.

Autofill instructs Excel to examine the data in the selected range and to extend the range. In our example, entering **Mon** on line 1 tells Autofill to fill the lines in the range with the subsequent days of the week. Tapping OK will produce the results shown next.

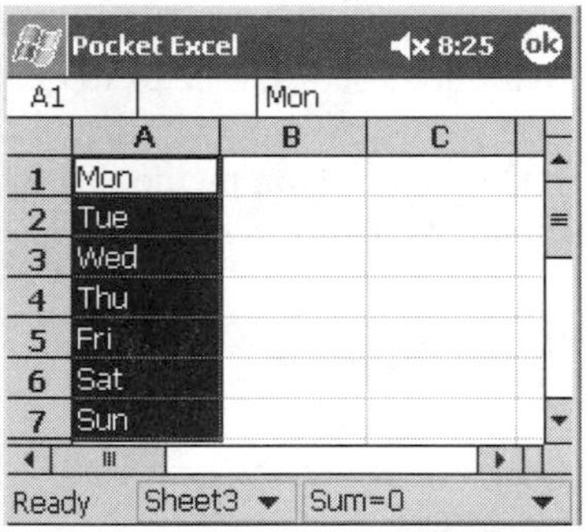

CAUTION   *We found a bug in Pocket PC 2002 that still exists in PPC 2003. If you attempt to use Autofill with numerical data, it will not enter a series, but will instead copy your data from the first cell into all the remaining cells. You can work around this bug by using the Series Type of Number instead of Autofill.*

The other Series types that you can select are Date and Number. Selecting one of these means that the primer data that you have entered in the fill range only includes the starting point for the series (that is, the first day or number that you want). For the rest of the information you will indicate what you want to fill in (days or numbers). If you choose days, you must choose the type of date information that you want to fill in, Day, Month, or Year. Then with either option you must

4

choose the increment or *step value*. This is the number that the Fill function will increase each subsequent line or column in the fill. For example, to fill a range with the first day of each week, you would put your first date such as **Jan 1** on the first line in your range. Then in the Fill dialog box you would select a Fill Type of Series, a Series Type of Date, and a Step Value of 7. Tapping OK would produce a worksheet like the one shown here:

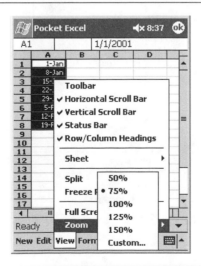

Zoom and Full Screen View

The Zoom command on the View menu allows you to change the view of your worksheet to make the workspace larger or smaller. This useful feature allows you to see more of your worksheet at one time or focus on a small area of it, although you might sacrifice resolution and readability, depending on the scale you select. There are five preset zoom levels you can select from—50%, 75%, 100%, 125%, and 150%—or you can choose Custom to set your own zoom percentage. Figure 4-19 shows our sample worksheet zoomed to 75%, and also the Zoom command fully expanded.

 FIGURE 4-19   A worksheet zoomed to 75% allows you to see more information on the screen at once.

Panes/Splitting

If you want to view two different parts of the same worksheet at the same time, you can split your screen into panes. This can be done so you can look at two different sets of data or to keep certain information fixed at the top and left of your worksheet while you scroll around in the main part of the worksheet. Figure 4-20 presents an example of a divided screen where we have split our regional sales spreadsheet to allow us to scroll through the data section while keeping the column and row headers in place.

To break a spreadsheet into panes, select the cell where you want the split to occur. Then select Split from the View menu. To remove the split from any worksheet you are in, select Remove Split from the View menu.

The Freeze Panes command under the View menu works in a very similar way. The difference is that in a split, you have the ability to scroll anywhere on the spreadsheet within any of the panes. With a freeze, only the main "unfrozen" area freely scrolls in all directions. When you hit the boundary of a frozen pane, the cursor will automatically jump into the correct pane for editing purposes. Another difference is that frozen panes are displayed with a single, static line rather than the double, movable line used with a split screen. Choosing Unfreeze Panes from the View menu turns off the Freeze Panes command. An example of frozen panes is shown in Figure 4-21.

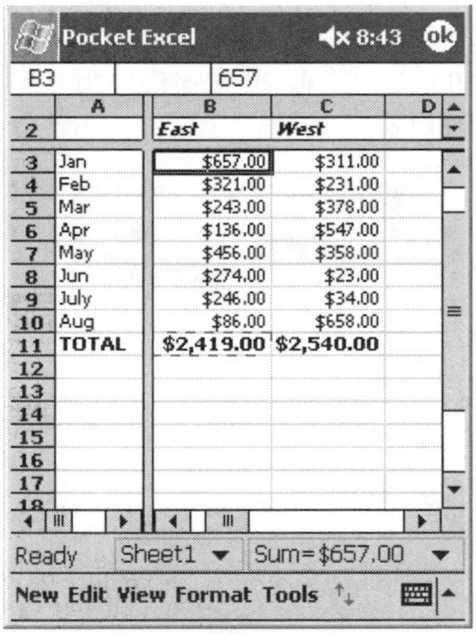

FIGURE 4-20   Windows can be split into panes to allow you to work with different sections of a worksheet at the same time.

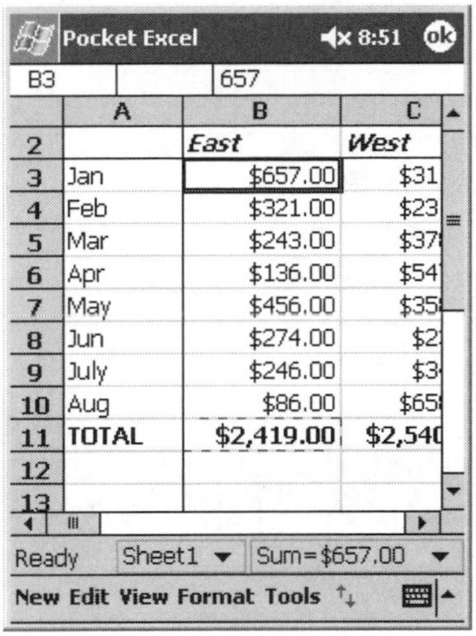

4

	A	B	C
2		*East*	*West*
3	Jan	$657.00	$31
4	Feb	$321.00	$23
5	Mar	$243.00	$37
6	Apr	$136.00	$54
7	May	$456.00	$35
8	Jun	$274.00	$2
9	July	$246.00	$3
10	Aug	$86.00	$65
11	TOTAL	$2,419.00	$2,540
12			
13			

Ready   Sheet1 ▼   Sum=$657.00 ▼

New Edit View Format Tools ↑↓

FIGURE 4-21   Frozen panes are displayed with a solid, static line.

The Toolbar

By default, the toolbar for Excel is hidden, but you can make it appear by tapping the up/down arrow icon in the menu bar. This button toggles the toolbar on and off. From the toolbar, shown here, you have quick access to cell formatting, alignment, common functions, number formatting, and a button to toggle through all the zoom settings.

Undo/Redo

Undo and Redo commands are available on the Edit menu. Undo will undo the last action that you took, including formatting, zooming, typing, deleting, or other action. Tapping Undo multiple times will undo multiple previous actions. The Redo command will let you restore the change that you just undid. This feature can be useful if you tap the Undo button too many times and accidentally undo too many steps.

Find and Replace

To locate any specific text in your workbook, you can use the Find/Replace command on the Edit menu. Selecting this command opens the Find dialog box, shown in Figure 4-22.

You enter any text string that you are looking for in the Find What box. Then you can set options to require it to match case or to only match if the entire cell content matches your text. You must

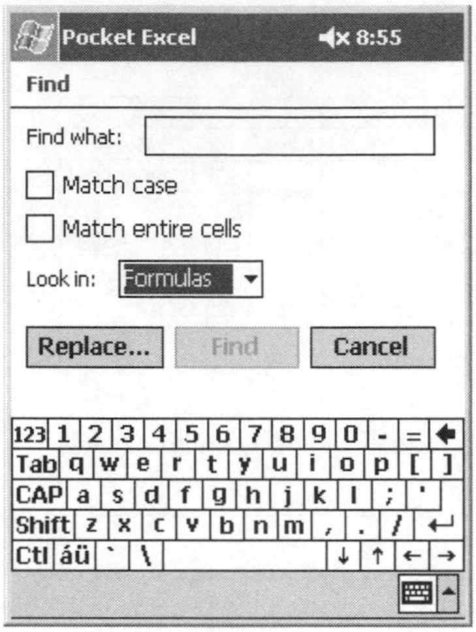

FIGURE 4-22   The Find dialog box allows you to search for and replace text strings in your workbook.

then select whether you would like to search in cells that contain formulas or cells that contain values. If you like, you can specify a value to replace the search text with by tapping the Replace button. In the new dialog box that opens, you specify your replacement string.

If you tap the Find button, Excel will find and make current the first cell after your current cell that contains the string. A new toolbar will also be displayed, as shown in Figure 4-23.

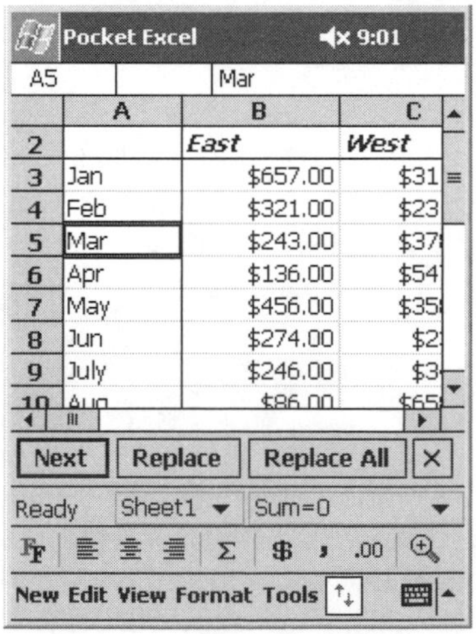

FIGURE 4-23   In the middle of a Find/Replace action, you will have an additional toolbar on your worksheet that includes Find and Replace commands.

This toolbar allows you to move on to find the next instance of your text string, replace the text (using the replacement text that you specified), or replace all instances (it will stop asking you to confirm each one). Or you may cancel your Find/Replace action by tapping the *X* button.

Saving Your Workbook

Saving your current workbook is slightly different in Pocket Excel than in the desktop version. Your Pocket Excel workbook will be saved automatically as soon as you tap the OK button in the top-right corner to exit the workbook. You do not need to explicitly save the workbook. It will be saved into the current folder you are in, with the name that you last used. If this is a new workbook that hasn't been saved before, the filename of the workbook will be Book1, Book2, and so on, depending on how many workbooks you have in the directory that have already been named that way. If you want to use a specific filename, save in a different folder, save to an external storage device (such as a CompactFlash card), or save as a different file type, you will need to choose Save Workbook As from the Tools menu.

Selecting Save Workbook As opens the Save As dialog box, shown in Figure 4-24. Tap OK to carry out your instructions and make a copy of the workbook where you have requested.

Remember that if you are editing an existing workbook and you tap the OK button in the top-right corner, your changes will be saved automatically. When you tap this button, Pocket Excel will *not* prompt you with a "Do you want to save?" message as with the desktop version. It will assume that you want to save, and the old version will be overwritten. If you have been making edits and decide you don't want to keep them, be careful *not* to simply exit the program with the OK button. Instead, use the Revert To Saved command on the Tools menu. You will be

FIGURE 4-24   In the Save As dialog box you can change the filename, type, folder, and storage location of your workbook.

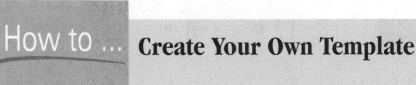

Create Your Own Template

If you want to create your own templates for any documents you use often (such as expense sheets, telephone contact logs, purchase orders, and so on), you can do this during the Save As process. At the stage where you are specifying the filename and location, you have the option to save the document as a Pocket Excel template. You can save it anywhere, but it would be convenient to save it in the Templates subfolder.

asked to confirm that you want to undo all the changes that you have made since opening the workbook. If you select Yes, the workbook will revert to its original state.

If you select New after editing a workbook in Pocket Excel, it will prompt you with a message asking whether you want to save, cancel, or save as, prior to starting a new workbook.

Beaming and E-mailing Your Workbook

Pocket Excel realizes that if you are writing workbooks on your iPAQ, they will likely be short, and you will probably want to be able to transmit them to someone else either by e-mail or by *beaming* (transferring information through the infrared port of your iPAQ—discussed in more detail in Chapter 5) them to another Pocket PC owner. To make this process as easy as possible, Pocket Excel has added Send Workbook By E-mail and Beam Workbook commands to the Tools menu.

Selecting Send Workbook By E-mail creates a new e-mail message in your Outbox with your workbook already attached. You will need to select to whom you wish to send the message as well as add a subject line and any text. Tapping the Send button will queue it up to be sent next time you have an active wireless connection or next time you connect with ActiveSync.

Selecting Beam Workbook will automatically set up your iPAQ to beam the workbook from your infrared port at the top of your unit to a receiving unit that has a physically aligned infrared port. The Pocket Excel Beaming window, shown in Figure 4-25, will appear, showing the status of the beam. In Figure 4-25 the device hasn't yet located an aligned infrared port that is ready to receive. The receiving unit must be set to receive the file by selecting the Infrared Receive program in the Program Files if you are running Pocket PC 2000. If you are running Pocket PC 2002 or 2003, it is set to receive automatically.

Once the workbook has been successfully transmitted, you will see the results message box, as shown in Figure 4-26.

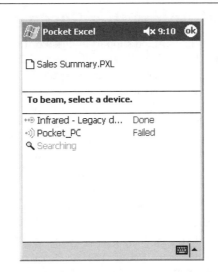

FIGURE 4-25   Setting up to beam a workbook to another Pocket PC through the infrared port

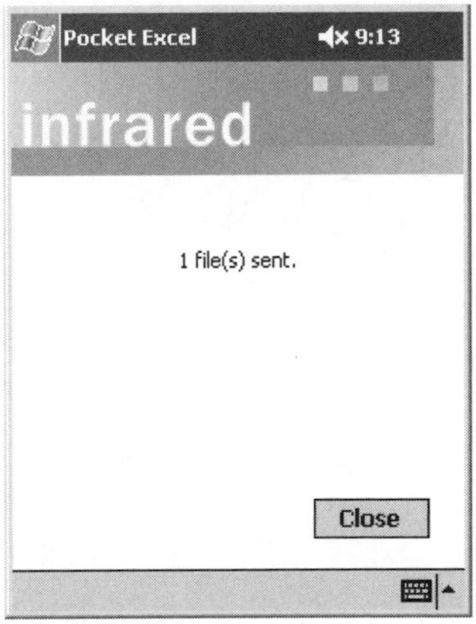

FIGURE 4-26   The results message box appears after a workbook is successfully beamed to another Pocket PC device.

Protecting Your Workbook with a Password

Unlike Pocket Word, Pocket Excel has limited support to password protect your workbook. This is a single-level password, meaning that it either allows full access or denies access to the workbook.

Pocket Excel does not have commands for access to read-only or modify as does the desktop version of Excel.

You can add or change a password on the Pocket Excel workbook by choosing the Password command from the Edit menu. In the Password dialog box that opens, shown here, you can add a password to your document or change the existing password.

Pocket Excel ◀× 9:17 **ok**

Password

Set or change password for 'Sale...':

Password: [   ]

Verify password: [   ]

Synchronizing with Your Desktop

Synchronizing your data with ActiveSync is covered in detail in Chapter 2, and if you need detailed instructions, you should refer to that chapter. Note that keeping a synchronized workbook on both your Pocket PC and desktop system can be a great convenience. Every time you make a change on your Pocket PC or desktop, the workbook will be synchronized with the other system. If you reference and update this document frequently, this capability could save you a great deal of time.

Chapter 5

Use Pocket Outlook to Take Control of Your Mobile Life

How to...

- Use and customize the Today page
- Manage appointments with the Calendar
- Create new appointments
- Set reminders and categories and invite meeting attendees
- Navigate and manage contacts
- Create new contacts
- Customize the Contact manager
- Read and compose e-mail
- Set up inboxes and connect to a mail server
- View attachments
- Attach files to an e-mail
- Read, edit, and compose tasks
- Read, edit, and compose notes
- Beam information
- Set up ActiveSync for all Outlook functions

The single most useful thing the average person does with an iPAQ is to keep track of personal information such as contacts/address book, appointment book, personal notes, to-do lists, and, of course, e-mail. These activities fall into a general category called *personal information management* (PIM). Microsoft Outlook has become the most widely used e-mail and PIM tool around today. A Pocket version of this popular tool is preinstalled on your iPAQ.

What Is Pocket Outlook?

Pocket Outlook isn't a single application. It is actually five applications that each perform a different part of the PIM job, but all interact together and synchronize with your desktop version of Outlook. Pocket Outlook doesn't have all the bells and whistles of the desktop version, but it has everything you need when you are on the move and is extremely effective. Speaking from personal experience, until we started using Pocket Outlook, we used to carry our Palm Pilot PDAs and paper-based day planners. After using Pocket Outlook, for the first time, we went fully digital and stopped using our paper day-planners.

The five applications that make up Pocket Outlook are

- **Calendar**   Lets you schedule appointments and events to make sure you don't double-book and are in the right place at the right time.
- **Contacts**   Keeps a database of all of your contacts and their relevant information. At your fingertips is complete contact information for anyone you know: phone numbers, e-mail address, notes, pictures, audio narratives, and more.

- ■ **Notes**   Allows you to take notes on your handheld instead of scratching them on little pieces of paper that you easily lose track of. We use it to keep track of an incredibly diverse range of miscellaneous information.

- ■ **Tasks**   Provides a convenient to-do list that lets you prioritize your tasks. It also includes boxes so you can check off tasks on your list when they are completed.

- ■ **Inbox**   Allows you to receive your e-mail on your handheld and to read and respond to your messages on the go. You can create new messages, attach files, and everything you would do from a full-sized PC. If you are wirelessly enabled, you can receive your e-mail from anywhere at any time (for details, see Chapter 9).

See What's Up with the Today Page

The Today page is the jumping off point to any of your personal information that is handled by Pocket Outlook. It allows you to see, at a glance, what appointments you have upcoming today, how many unread messages are in your Inbox, and how many unfinished tasks are on your to-do list, as shown in Figure 5-1.

Tapping any line item will take you to the appropriate application to view the item selected. You can modify the Today page in a number of ways.

Tapping the time line will bring you to the Settings window for the clock, where you can set the current time for your home time zone, or for the time zone you happen to be in if you are away from home, as shown in Figure 5-2.

You can customize the appearance and functionality of the Today page by going to the Settings command under the Start menu and choosing the Today icon. This opens the Settings window shown in Figure 5-3. From here you can select different themes for your Pocket PC. The theme changes the picture behind the Today page and the Start menu.

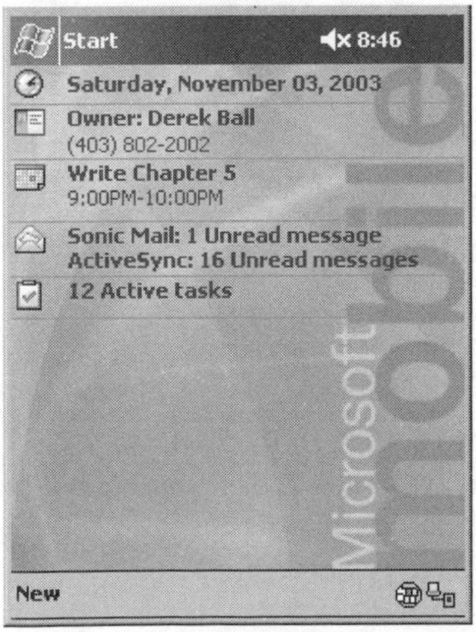

FIGURE 5-1   The Today page lets you see all of your important information.

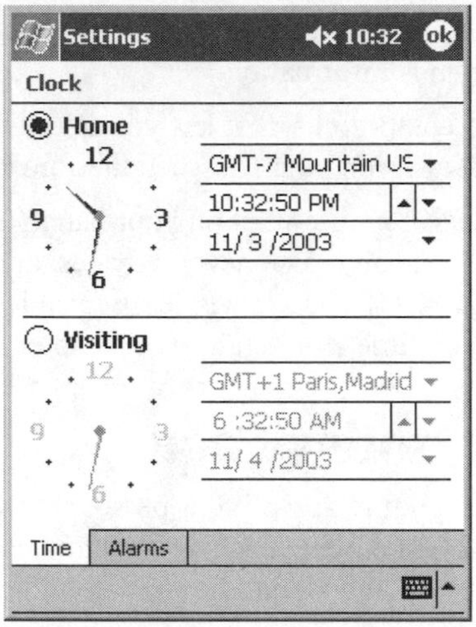

FIGURE 5-2   The Settings window for the clock lets you both set your current time and select a second time zone for when you are traveling.

FIGURE 5-3   The Settings window for the Today page allows you to select different themes for your Pocket PC.

You can select any theme you like from the list of available themes. By default, only the default theme is loaded on your Pocket PC. You can download new themes from a variety of web sites. One site, which you can access at no charge, is solely devoted to Pocket PC themes: **www.pocketpcthemes.com**. To download a theme, you simply copy the theme file to your My Documents directory on your iPAQ. It will automatically appear in the list of available themes. In addition, this site has theme-related links, such as links to software for building your own themes and much more.

> TIP   *Do you want to really personalize your iPAQ and maybe create your own theme? You can do this with software from BVRP called Pocket Theme Manager, which helps manage your theme collection, create your own themes, and more! You can try it for free at **www.bvrp.com**.*

5

If you want to share a theme with a friend, you can select the theme and tap the Beam button to send it to another Pocket PC user via the infrared port. You can also select any picture to be your theme by selecting the Use This Picture As The Background check box and then browsing to your picture file.

Keeping Your Appointments with the Calendar

The Calendar application is an invaluable tool that can immediately make the purchase of your iPAQ worthwhile. I was always struggling with appointments, often double-booking myself or losing track of where I was supposed to be for a specific appointment. I found my paper day-planner cumbersome, and I wasn't always diligent about updating it (not to mention it was large and heavy to carry around). Now, I always have my iPAQ in my pocket, and if someone asks me whether I am free for a meeting next week, I can pull it out, see my schedule, pick a mutually convenient time, and enter the meeting into my timetable. When I am back in the office, my new appointment is automatically synced with my desktop Outlook calendar application, which is hooked into Microsoft Exchange. Everyone in my office shares calendars, so anyone who wants an appointment with me can see when I am available. Over the past year, the number of appointments I have missed or double-booked has dropped to virtually zero, making me much more effective at work and in my personal life.

> TIP   *Although the built-in Calendar application is everything most people will need, if you want to take it up a level, check out Agenda Fusion from Developer One (**www.developerone.com**). It features improvements in appointment viewing and scheduling, including drag and drop functionality and color coding. It also has enhancements to other PIM applications like Contacts, enabling you to actually dial a contact phone number (with the appropriate phone integration).*

How to ... Customize Your Today Page

At the bottom of the Settings window, you will find another tab, the Items tab. From here you can select what items appear on the Today page, as shown here.

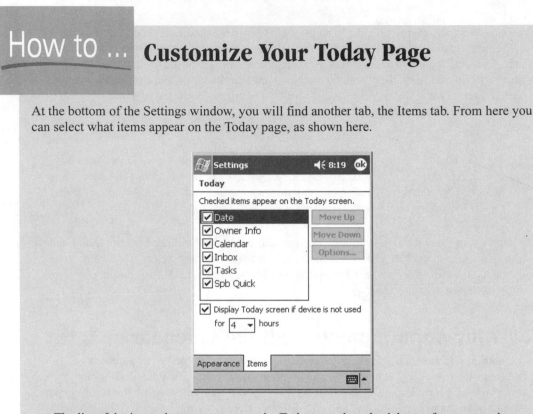

The list of the items that can appear on the Today page has check boxes for you to select which items you want to appear on the Today menu. You will notice the option for Spb Quick, which is Pocket PC personal finance software that syncs with Quicken. If this is checked, it will show you your account balances on the today screen. You can also adjust the settings to cause the Today page to appear if your iPAQ is not used for a specific number of hours.

Some of the items in the list also have options you can configure, such as the Calendar. If you tap the Options button after selecting Calendar, you will see the options shown in this illustration.

For the Calendar you can choose to see the next appointment only or all upcoming appointments. You can also choose to show or not show all-day events.

Starting the Calendar Application

You can launch the Calendar application on your iPAQ in a number of ways. First, when looking at the Today page, you can tap the calendar icon to be taken directly to today's appointments. You can also get to the Calendar application by selecting Calendar from the Start menu. The iPAQ provides four small hardware buttons to launch specific applications. These buttons are configurable, but in their default out-of-the-box configuration, the leftmost button will launch the Calendar application, giving you a quick and easy way to access one of the most-used applications on your iPAQ.

Viewing the Calendar

After you open the Calendar application, what you will see will depend on the view that you last used. If this is your first time accessing the application, you will see the Agenda view. The Calendar has five different methods by which you can look at your data. It is always the same data, but shown in different levels of granularity. The five views are

- Agenda view
- Day view
- Week view
- Month view
- Year view

The Agenda view, shown in Figure 5-4, contains a listing of all of today's appointments and their times. All of the views share most of the standard navigation icons and options shown in Figure 5-4.

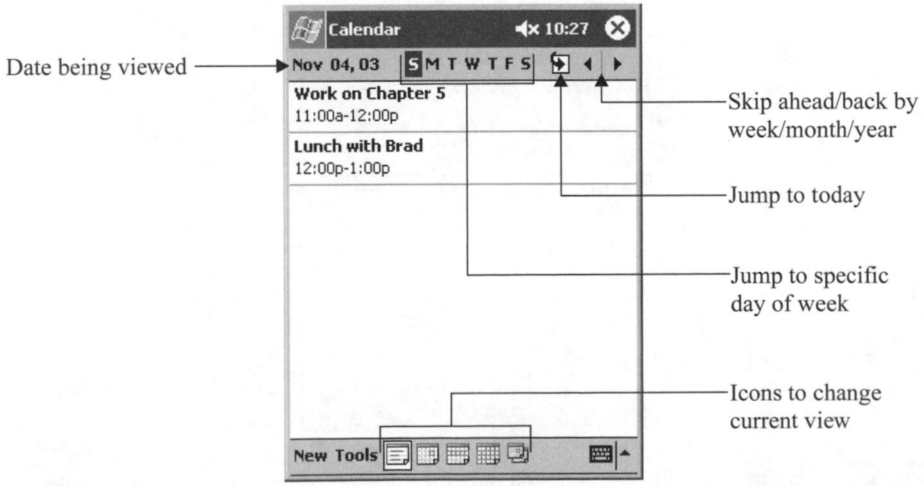

FIGURE 5-4   The Agenda view, featuring a list of today's appointments, contains many standard navigation items found in all views.

The top-left corner always shows the current day, date, month, or year being viewed. Immediately to the right of that are the days of the week (represented by the first letter of the day), which can be tapped to jump to that specific day of the week. If you have Pocket PC 2003, the Saturday and Sunday letters show up in colors different from the regular weekdays to make them easier to differentiate. If a day other than the current date is being viewed, the current date will appear with a white square around the day letter. Tap the icon to the right of the day of the week letters (the one with a white square and a curved arrow) to jump immediately to today's date. The left/right arrows on the far right will scroll you ahead or back within the calendar. In the Agenda, Day, and Week views, it will scroll by one week. In the Month view it will scroll by a month, and in the Year view, it will scroll by a year.

The five view icons at the bottom of the window will allow you to jump to any of the views directly. You can also change the view you are currently looking at by pressing the hardware Calendar button. Each press changes the view down one level of granularity. The navigation dial on the hardware of the iPAQ is also useful with the calendar. It allows you to move from the current date being viewed to the next date by pressing the disc to the right or down. Pressing the disc to the left or up will move you to the previous day.

Tapping any item in the list in the Agenda view will open the details of that appointment, as shown in Figure 5-5. If you want to edit the appointment or add notes, tap the Edit menu. This will open the appointment in an editable window where you can change all the information such as subject, date, time, location, or notes.

The Day view looks more like a traditional day-planner and like the desktop version of Outlook. It shows a single day divided into one-hour blocks with all of your appointments recorded in their relevant time slots, as shown in Figure 5-6.

FIGURE 5-5   Tapping the Edit menu opens the current appointment in an editable window so you can change all the details such as date, time, and more.

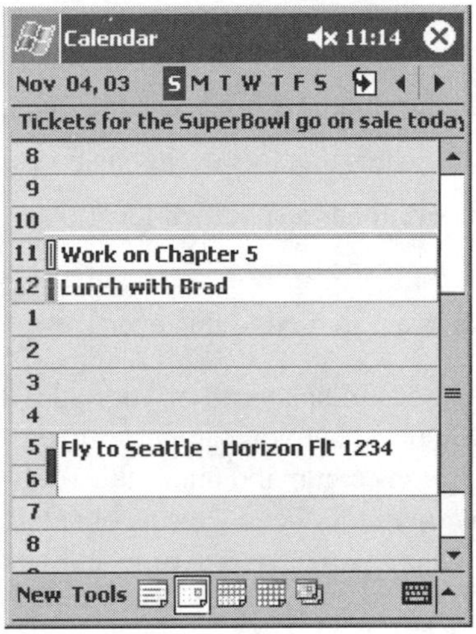

FIGURE 5-6   The Day view divides the entire day into one-hour slots where all of your appointments are shown.

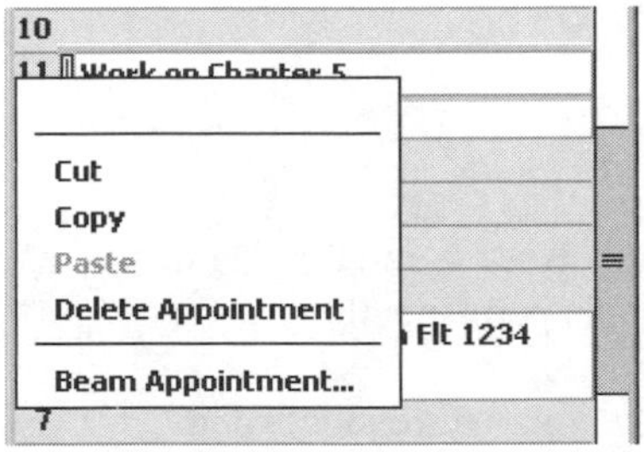

All of the controls work the same as they do in the Agenda view, but here you will use the scroll bar on the right to scroll through the entire day. In all views, when looking at a specific appointment, you can tap and hold your stylus on the appointment to open a shortcut menu, as shown here. This enables you to move or copy an appointment to another point in your calendar.

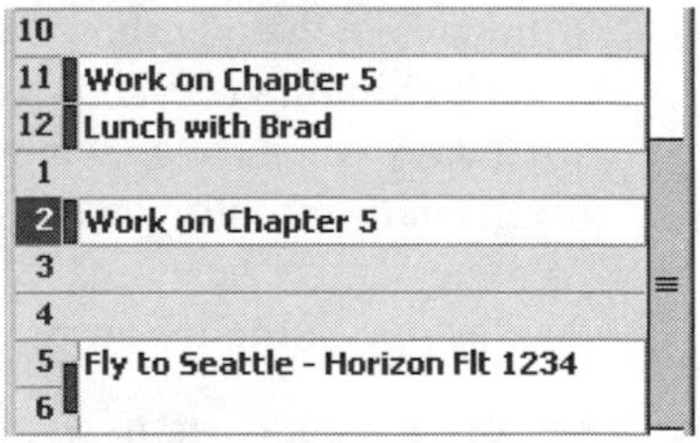

Looking at Figure 5-6, if I wanted to make another appointment to work on Chapter 5 after my lunch with Brad, I would tap and hold to open the shortcut menu, and select Copy to copy the appointment to the clipboard. Then I would select another time slot, tap and hold to open the shortcut menu, and paste the appointment into the new time. The new schedule would look something like the one shown here.

In the Day view, you will also see any relevant icons beside the appointment if this option has been turned on in the Options dialog box, as shown here.

You might see the following icons:

- **Bell**   Indicates that a reminder alarm has been set for this appointment
- **Circle with arrows**   Indicates that this is a recurring event
- **Note page with pencil**   Indicates that this event has notes
- **House**   Indicates that this event has a specified location
- **Key**   Indicates that this is a private event
- **Heads**   Indicates that others are invited to this event

The Week view, shown in Figure 5-7, displays all of your appointments for a week. By default, the week is defined as seven days, but you can customize this setting to show a five-day or six-day week by selecting the Options command under the Tools menu.

All of your appointments show up in the Week view as blue blocks in their appropriate date and time slots. You can easily see where you have free time and where you do not. To view the details of a specific appointment, tap on the blue block. This will open a small box at the top of the screen, which will display the details of the appointment, as shown here.

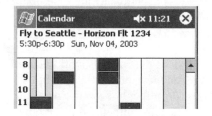

After ten seconds, the box will disappear, returning you to the default Week view. Tapping in the appointment box before it disappears will open the appointment details permanently in a window like the one shown back in Figure 5-5.

The Month view, shown in Figure 5-8, enables you to see at a glance your entire month and what days you have appointments on. Each square in the view represents a day. If the current date is in the month you are viewing, that day will be outlined in red.

The Month view uses icons to give you a quick feel for how busy that day is. Each day will display one of the following icons to indicate the density of appointments:

- **No icon**   Indicates there are no appointments for the day
- **Triangle (pointing to top left)**   Indicates at least one appointment in the morning
- **Triangle (pointing to bottom right)**   Indicates at least one appointment in the afternoon
- **Dark square**   Indicates appointments in both the morning and afternoon
- **White square**   Indicates an all-day event

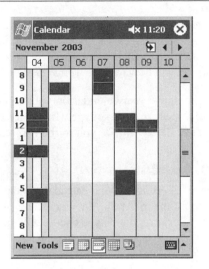

FIGURE 5-7   The Week view enables you to see your schedule for the entire week at a glance.

FIGURE 5-8   The Month view shows you an entire month's appointments in one window.

5

NOTE *If you are unable to get the white square to appear for an all-day event, it is because it only shows up if the appointment option Show Time As is set to "Busy" or "Out Of Office," which is not the default setting for an all-day event. If you change this setting to the default and resync, the white square will show up. This trick also works for multiple-day events. Tapping on any specific date in the Month view will take you to the Day view for the day you selected.*

The Year view will display the entire year calendar on your screen at once, as shown in Figure 5-9. The current date will appear in inverse type. (In Figure 5-9, the current date is November 4.) Tapping on a specific date will take you to the Day view for the selected day.

Entering a New Appointment

To begin entering a new appointment or event into your calendar, tap the New menu. Alternatively, you can tap and hold the stylus on a time in the Day or Week view, and when the shortcut menu appears, select New Appointment. Whichever option you choose will open the New Event dialog box.

Entering Details

You will enter the details of your new appointment or event in the New Event dialog box, shown in Figure 5-10.

You can fill in as many or as few details as you choose. The minimum information required to create a new event is a subject and a time. The subject line includes a drop-down arrow, enabling you to select from commonly used words for appointments such as "Meet with," "Lunch," "Dinner," "Visit," "Call," "Birthday," and "Complete." You use the onscreen keyboard or other input mechanism to enter the text for the rest of the subject.

FIGURE 5-9 The Year view shows you an entire calendar year at a glance.

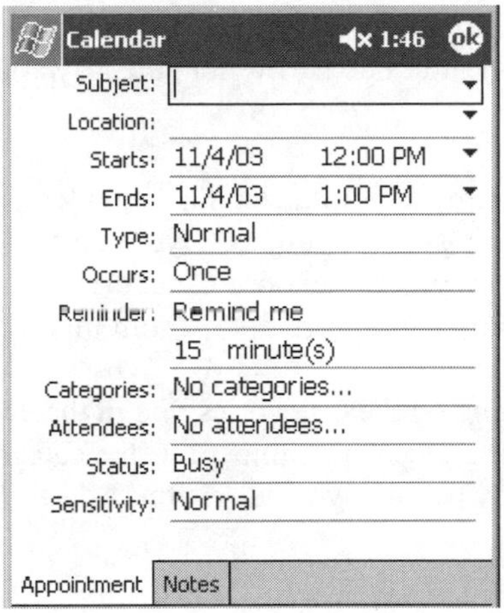

FIGURE 5-10   The New Event dialog box is where you can enter the details for the new appointment.

You can also enter a location, and a start and an end time for the appointment. On the Type line you can choose to make the appointment an all-day appointment. The Status line will change how this appointment appears to anyone who looks at your public calendar through Microsoft Exchange. You can set the time to appear as Free, Busy, Tentative, or Out Of Office. The Sensitivity line enables you to mark the appointment as private, which means that someone looking at your public calendar will not see the subject line of the event. Instead, they will simply see "Private" as the subject. Thus, you can keep your medical appointments and other personal information private from outside observers.

Setting Reminders

The Reminder line in a new event allows you to specify whether you would like an alarm and pop-up note to remind you about an event. You can set a reminder to occur anywhere from minutes in advance of an appointment to months. For example, I set my reminders for events such as birthdays a week in advance so I have time to buy a gift and card. I set reminders for events such as internal meetings at only five minutes.

On the Reminder line, you can select from two options in the drop-down list: None and Remind Me. If you select Remind Me, you will have to select the time before the event to remind you by first selecting whether you want to be reminded minutes, hours, days, or weeks in advance, as shown here.

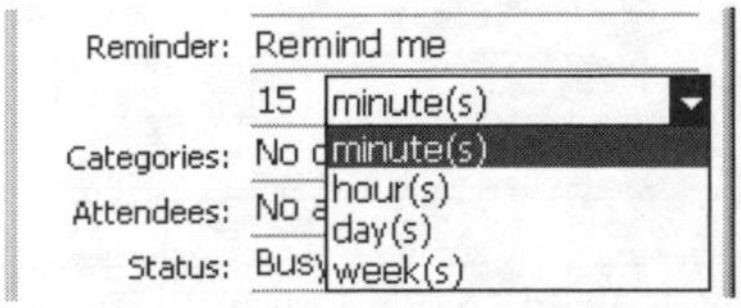

Once you have selected the units, you select the quantity by tapping the number to the left of the units. You can select from the drop-down list, or type in your own quantity. Setting a reminder will cause an alarm bell icon to appear beside the event in the Day and Agenda views.

Setting Categories

You can also select a category for the appointment. This enables you to view at one time just those appointments related to a specific subject. By default, the Calendar will display the appointments for all categories, but you can choose Categories from the Tools menu to open a dialog box similar to the one shown in Figure 5-11. From this dialog box you can check the categories that you would like to show.

You select a category by tapping on the Categories line in the event detail dialog box. You can choose multiple categories for a given appointment. If the category you want hasn't been created yet, you can add a category (or remove one) via the Add/Delete tab at the bottom of the category selection dialog box.

Inviting Attendees

As in the desktop version of Outlook, you can invite individuals to meetings or other events by using the Calendar. In Pocket Outlook you do this on the Attendees line in the event detail dialog box. Tap the Attendees line to open a dialog box showing your list of contacts with check boxes beside their names, shown here.

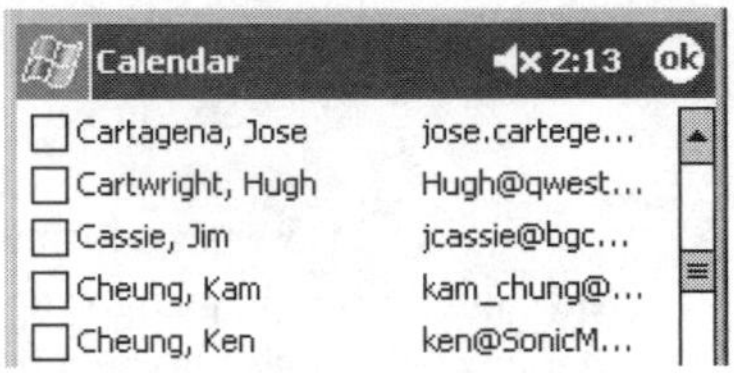

You can select as many attendees as you like by selecting their check boxes and tapping OK. A Microsoft Exchange event invitation will be mailed automatically to each of the selected individuals. To invite an individual to an event, he or she must have an entry in your Contacts list with a valid e-mail address.

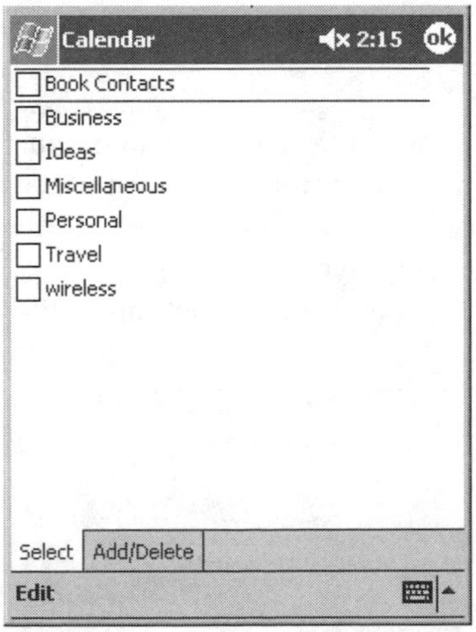

FIGURE 5-11   You can select the categories that you want to be visible in the Calendar to see subsets of your tasks.

How to ...   **Set Up a Recurring Appointment**

Many appointments that you schedule will occur on a regular basis, such as weekly status meetings and birthdays. You can set these appointments to recur automatically. Tapping on the Occurs line in the event detail dialog box opens a drop-down list of the most common recurrence options, shown here.

From this list, you can select the option to make this event repeat every week, on the same day every month, or annually. If your recurrence pattern for your event is not listed, choose Edit Pattern. Doing so will open the first of three windows that make up the Recurrence Wizard, shown here.

Here you set the duration of the appointment and have the option to remove the recurrence of the event. Once you have set the duration, tap the Next button to open the second window of the wizard, shown here.

In the second window you can choose the following options:

- **Daily**   You can set the recurrence as every X number of days or every weekday.

- **Weekly**   You can set the recurrence as every X week(s) and also specify any combination of days of the week you want the event to occur on.

- **Monthly**   You can select which day of the month to have the event recur on and then set it to recur every X month(s). Alternatively, you could have it occur on a specific day of the week in a month every X month(s), such as the third Tuesday of every month.

- **Yearly**   You can select which day of the year you want the event to recur on. Alternatively, you can have it occur on a specific day of the week in a specific month. For example, Mother's Day occurs on the second Sunday of every May.

The third window in the wizard is where you will set the start and end date for the pattern, as shown next. You can choose to have the pattern not end, end on a specific date, or end after a certain number of occurrences of the event.

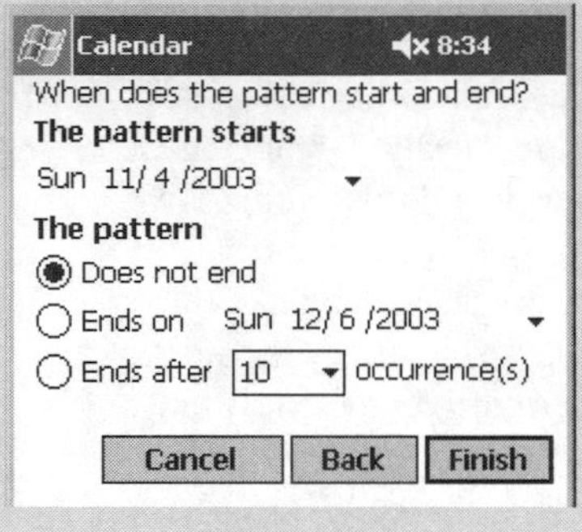

Adding Notes

You can add notes to any appointment by selecting the Notes tab at the bottom of the event detail dialog box. From here you can add any notes you want by typing in the input area, using Transcriber, or using a keyboard. You can also tap the pencil icon to add sketches and drawings, as shown in Figure 5-12.

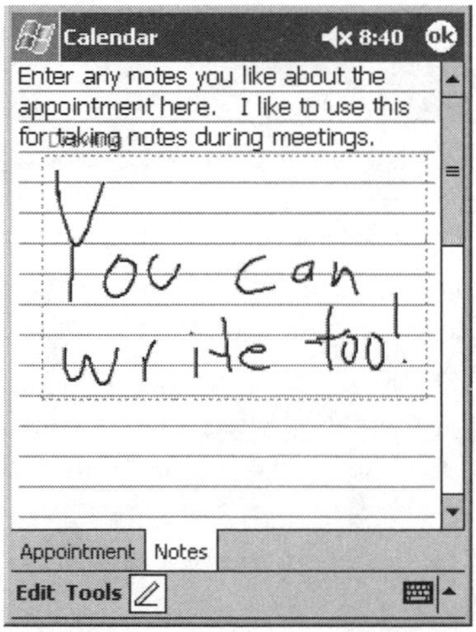

FIGURE 5-12   You can enter text as well as drawings in the Notes area.

Beaming an Appointment

Imagine you are sitting with someone, trying to plan a meeting together. You can enter the details of the meeting into your Calendar. Then, by tapping and holding a specific appointment, you can choose Beam Appointment from the shortcut menu. This will start the process of searching for and transmitting the appointment to a Pocket PC with an aligned infrared port. The receiving Pocket PC device will be given the option of accepting the beamed appointment. Beaming to non-Pocket PC devices is possible with all the new iPAQs, or if you have an older iPAQ, with third-party add-in software. For details about beaming outside the Pocket PC universe, see Chapter 2.

ActiveSync Settings for the Calendar

You can set three options in ActiveSync on your desktop PC to change what information is shared in the Calendar application:

- ■ **Sync All Appointments**   This setting can lead to very memory-intensive and time-consuming syncing, but will ensure that any modifications made to past appointments in either your iPAQ or your desktop are all up to date.
- ■ **Sync Only The**   This default setting will enable you to set the number of past weeks to synchronize (defaults to two weeks) and the number of future weeks (defaults to all).
- ■ **Sync Only Selected Categories**   This setting enables you to select only specific categories of appointments to synchronize. This can be useful if you synchronize with multiple desktop systems or if multiple people share the same iPAQ.

Managing Your Contacts

The other personal information management tool that is right at the top of the list with the Calendar is keeping track of all your contacts. The Contacts application in Pocket PC is extremely useful and flexible. In addition, it seamlessly synchronizes with the contacts in your desktop version of Outlook, enabling you to access this crucial information both at your desk and when you are on the move.

Navigating Your Contacts

You can launch into the Contacts application by pressing the hardware button for opening Contacts (second from the left in the default configuration) or by selecting Contacts from the Start menu. Either action will open a window similar to the one shown in Figure 5-13.

By default, you will see a list of all of your contacts sorted in alphabetical order. If you are like me, you probably have hundreds of contacts. There are many ways to make it easier to sort through your reams of associates. On the top left you will see a drop-down arrow. Tap this arrow to display a list from which you can select a subset of your contacts to view. In the categories list, you can choose to see All Contacts (the default), Recent (the most recent contacts you have looked at), or choose to view a subset based on the preassigned category you have given each one. To do this, you will need to have assigned one or more of the static categories in Outlook to each of the contacts.

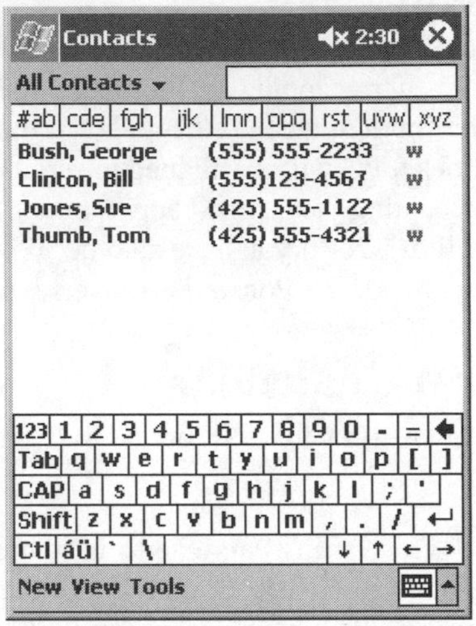

FIGURE 5-13   The Contacts window is your personal address book for your iPAQ.

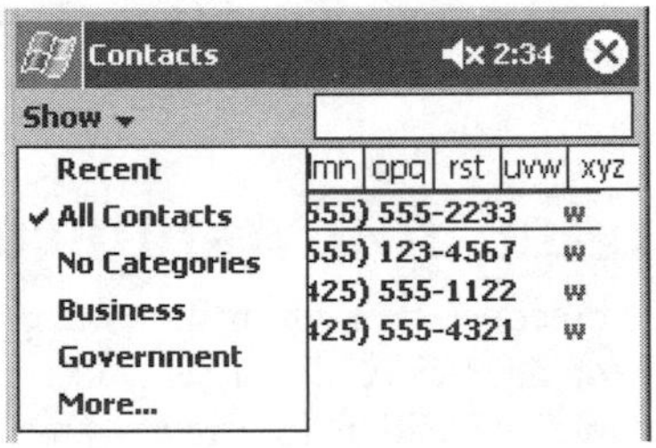

In our sample data, I have four contacts, which have been divided into two groups: Government and Business, as shown in this illustration. The drop-down list shows me all my categories and one No Categories option for any contact who does not have categories assigned. The More option in the drop-down list will take you to the full list of categories where you can select a specific category you would like to view. You select the category by tapping on a check box, or you can select multiple categories by tapping on multiple check boxes.

In the box to the right of the categories drop-down list, you can type specific text that you want to search for in your list. Any text that you enter will be matched against the first or last name of the contact. For example, with our set of data, entering **b** in the text search box will cause it to filter the list to show *Bush, George* (a last-name match), as well as *Clinton, Bill* (a first-name match), as shown here.

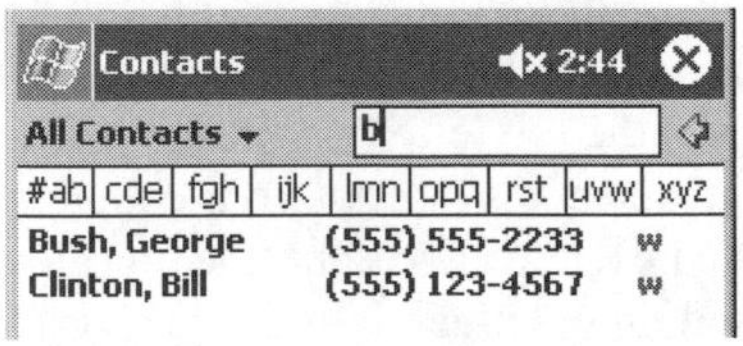

Immediately below the categories drop-down list and the search text box you will see a series of boxes, each containing three letters of the alphabet. Tapping any one of these boxes once will cause the view to scroll to the appropriate subsection of the contacts list. If you are currently viewing your contacts sorted by last name, then tapping the *ijk* box would cause the list to scroll to show those contacts with last names starting with *I*. If you are viewing your list sorted by company name, then it would scroll to show company names beginning with *I*. If you tap the box again, it will scroll to the second letter in the box, *J*. A third tap will scroll to *K*; the same method applies to the rest of the letter boxes.

You can use the three preceding techniques alone or together to narrow your list of contacts. For example, you could select Government from the drop-down list of categories, type a **b** into the text search box, and tap the *cde* box to get a list of all the contacts categorized as Government with first names starting with *B* and last names starting with *C*.

You can also navigate through your list of contacts with the scroll bar on the right side of the window if your list of contacts is more than will fit in one window (which it almost always is). You can also use the hardware navigation disc and press up to scroll up your list or down to scroll down your list. If you hold the button down, a large box will appear and cycle through all the letters of the alphabet, enabling you to scroll to the specified letter, as shown in Figure 5-14.

By default, when you enter the Contacts application, you are looking at a view of your contacts sorted by name. You can change this to see a list of companies instead, if this is your preferred method of navigation. Change your sort rule by selecting View | By Company. The resulting window will look something like this.

The number in parentheses after the company name is the number of contacts that you have in your list who work for that company.

How to ... Eliminate Duplicate Outlook Contacts

When I used to sync my Palm, I frequently ended up with duplicate contacts. Each duplicate had to be deleted by hand, and it seemed like as soon as I did, they would reappear on the next sync. ActiveSync is fairly good at eliminating duplicates, but they can still occur. If it happens to you, you can try a couple of freeware programs:

- Outlook Contacts Scrubber at **www.teamscope.com/contacts_scrubber.htm**
- Outlook Duplicates Remover at **www.hlyspirit.org.uk/outlook.php**

The first link will scrub contacts only, whereas the second one will search for duplicates in all parts of Outlook. To be safe, make sure you back up your Outlook PST file first!

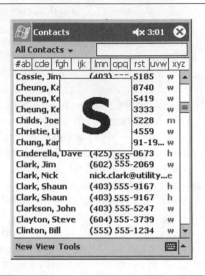

FIGURE 5-14   Holding down the hardware navigation disc will enable you to scroll through all the letters of the alphabet.

In your list of contacts you will see a blue letter to the right of each entry's contact information. This letter tells you what type of contact information is being shown. For example, a small blue *e* indicates an e-mail address, a *w* is a work phone number, an *f* is a work fax number, an *h* is a home number, and so on. If you tap this letter, you will see a drop-down display of that individual's contact information. A black dot indicates which contact information is currently set to appear in the list view, as can be seen in this illustration. If you want to change this default, tap on the line that you would prefer to show as the default.

Tapping any contact name or phone number in the list will open the contact's detail information, as shown in Figure 5-15.

The Summary tab shows all the contact information you have for the contact. The Notes tab contains any notes that you have for the contact. Notes can include text, drawings, images, and sound recordings. Tapping the Edit menu will enable you to enter and change any of the information displayed here. Tap Tools in the menu bar to change your view (on the Notes tab only), delete the contact, send an e-mail to the contact, or beam the contact to another Pocket PC.

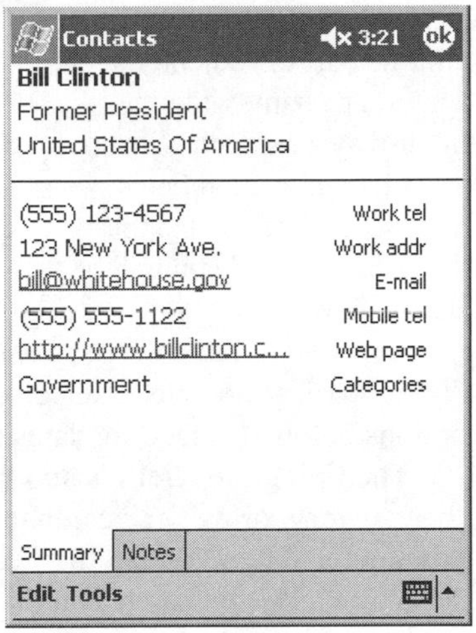

FIGURE 5-15   Tapping a contact name or number will open that individual's contact information window.

Tapping and holding any name in your list of contacts will open up a shortcut menu via which you can copy or delete the contact, send an e-mail to the contact, or beam the contact to another Pocket PC.

Entering a New Contact

To add a contact to your list, tap the New menu at the bottom of the Contacts dialog box to open the new contact form, shown here.

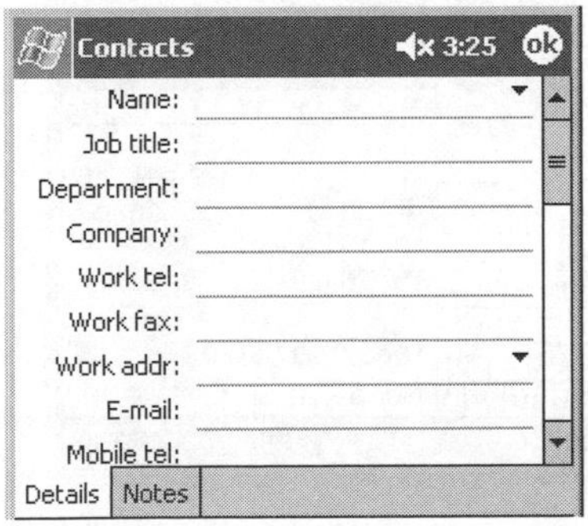

From this window you can enter an entire range of information. These fields mirror the fields found in the desktop version of Outlook, allowing seamless synchronization of information.

A number of the fields are contractions of information held in multiple fields. For example, the Name field is a combination of the Title, First, Middle, Last, and Suffix fields. As you enter a name, Contacts will try to place the appropriate names into the appropriate fields. If it is unsure, it will display a red icon with an exclamation mark at the end of the line. All combination fields include a drop-down arrow at the end of the field. If you tap the arrow, all the subfields involved will be displayed, and you will be able to enter the data into each subfield, as shown here.

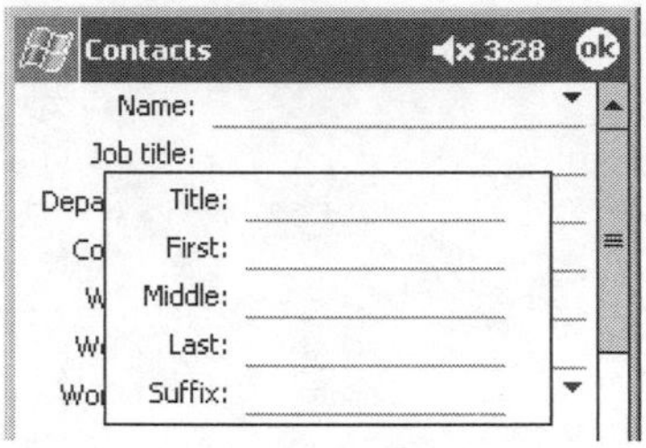

Date fields, such as Birthday and Anniversary, enable you to select a date from a drop-down calendar, as shown in Figure 5-16. If no date is selected, the field will show None. The drop-down calendar also has options below the specific dates to select Today or None.

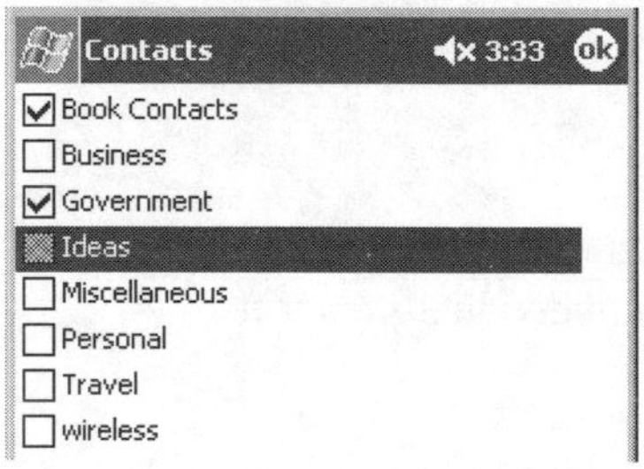

The Categories field is another unique field. It displays the category, or categories, that you have assigned this contact to. When you tap the field, it will open a separate form in which you can select al the categories you want to apply to this contact from a list of categories. You can select multiple categories by selecting multiple check boxes, as shown here.

FIGURE 5-16   Date fields include drop-down calendars to make selecting a date easier.

If the category that you want isn't in the list, you can add a category (or delete one you no longer want) using the Add/Delete tab at the bottom of the categories dialog box shown next.

This tab features a list of all the categories. You can select a specific category and tap the Delete button to remove a category. To add a category, place the cursor into the text box at the top of the form, enter the category name, and then tap the Add button.

TIP *Categories in Pocket Outlook are synced over from your desktop Outlook installation. Setting up and managing your categories is easier on the desktop, so you should do the bulk of your planning there instead of on your iPAQ.*

Customizing the Contact Manager

Even on the Pocket PC, you can customize a few options in your software. This list is limited in the Contacts application, but you can change a few items in the view as well as some default information for when you are entering details.

Selecting Tools | Options will open the Options dialog box, shown here, where you can make changes to your Contacts application.

The three check boxes allow you to show or hide the ABC tabs, show contact names only (that is, not show phone number or e-mail address), or switch to a larger font if you find the standard size hard to read.

You can also change the default area code, which is automatically included with every new contact you enter, and default country.

You can set three options in ActiveSync on the desktop PC for your Contacts:

- ■ **Sync All Contacts** This default setting will ensure that all modifications made to contacts in either your iPAQ or your desktop are up to date.

- ■ **Sync Only The Following Contacts** This option enables you to choose only specific contacts to synchronize. This is very limiting because any new contacts added to your iPAQ will not be automatically sent over to your PC.

- ■ **Sync Only Selected Categories** This setting enables you to select only specific categories of contacts to synchronize. This can be useful if you synchronize with multiple desktop systems or if multiple people are sharing the same iPAQ.

Keeping in Touch with E-mail

For the Internet, e-mail is the killer application. It was e-mail that drove people to get Internet connections to every corporate desktop and in every home. Many PDA experts expected that being able to get e-mail anywhere, anytime, would be the driving force that would cause millions to adopt PDAs. This ended up being a bit of a pipe dream, as most PDAs until now were not wirelessly connected, so e-mail could only be sent or received while your PDA was attached to your computer with a sync cable.

Out of the box, your iPAQ is not wirelessly enabled (unless you have a newer model with WiFi or Bluetooth network connectivity), but it can sync your Outlook Inbox with its own Inbox application, allowing you to take your e-mail with you. With some simple wireless add-in products, you can easily extend your iPAQ to allow you to send and receive your e-mail anywhere, at any time. For details about wireless iPAQ, see Chapter 9. This section will focus on the specifics of using the Inbox application, whether you are wirelessly connected or not.

Setting Up Your Inbox and Services

You can work with e-mail on your Pocket PC in two ways: through your ActiveSync connection or by connecting to an external mail server.

E-mail with ActiveSync

ActiveSync will keep a copy on your Pocket PC of the messages in your current desktop Outlook folders. All of the setup for this is done in your ActiveSync application on your PC. With each synchronization, the appropriate messages are transferred to your iPAQ so that you can read them when you are disconnected. You can also compose replies to the e-mail you read, and these will be sent by your desktop version of Outlook the next time you synchronize your iPAQ.

NOTE   *Remember that your Inbox will only synchronize with one desktop Outlook partnership, so if you are syncing with multiple desktops, as discussed in Chapter 2, make sure you set up your partnerships correctly and sync with your Inbox partner first. For more information, see "Setting Up ActiveSync" in Chapter 2.*

To set up ActiveSync synchronization of your desktop, open ActiveSync on your PC, and select the check box beside Inbox, as shown in Figure 5-17.

After selecting the check box, you will want to adjust the settings for your mail synchronization. Click the Settings button to open the Mail Synchronization Settings dialog box, shown in Figure 5-18.

From here you can specify which subfolders you want to be synchronized with your iPAQ. Select the check box before the name of any subfolder whose messages you want copied to the Inbox program on your iPAQ. Then you can specify whether you want only a limited number of lines of a message to be copied to your iPAQ. This reduces the amount of data stored on the device, so you don't run out of room. However, I recommend not selecting this option because if, just once, you receive an important long message, and it is truncated, you might get so annoyed you will toss your iPAQ into the nearest trash can. Instead, I recommend keeping only a limited number of days of messages. By default, the system will only synchronize five days of messages,

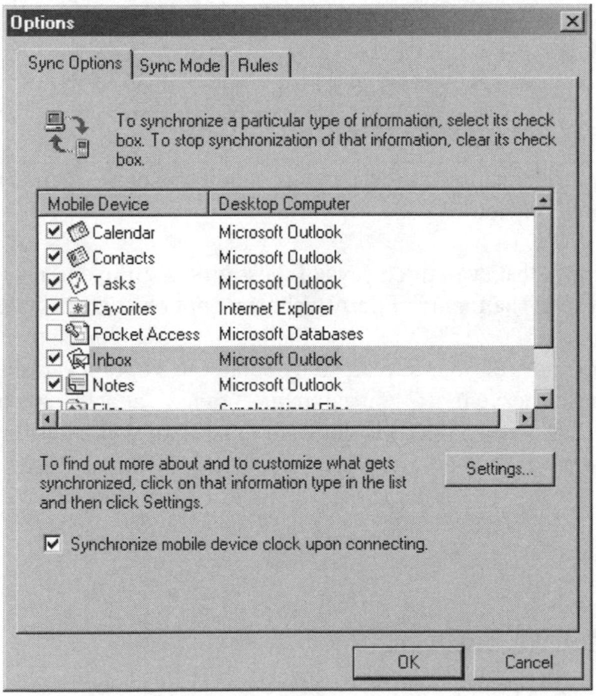

FIGURE 5-17   To synchronize your Pocket Inbox with your desktop Outlook, select the Inbox check box in the ActiveSync setup.

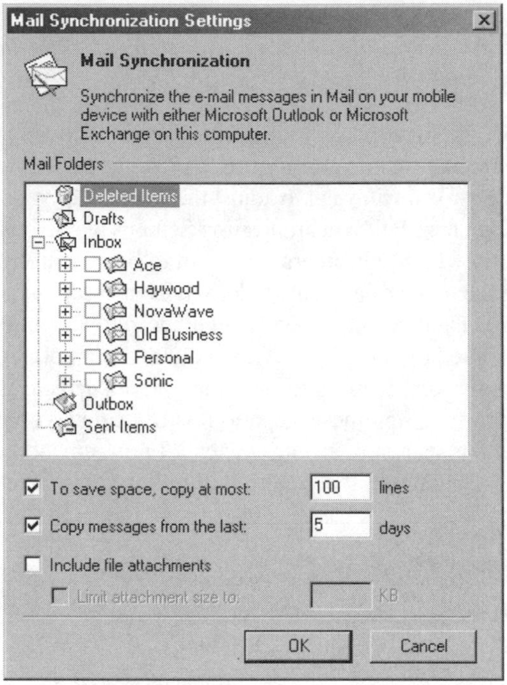

FIGURE 5-18   The Mail Synchronization Settings dialog box enables you to determine what is stored on your iPAQ.

or one working week. I find that even three days of messages is sufficient, unless I am on the road for an extended period. The Include File Attachments option enables you to automatically copy file attachments to your Pocket PC, or leave them unless you request them. Attachments can quickly fill up the memory of your device, so by default this option is turned off, and I would usually recommend that you leave it off. You can request to have attachments downloaded from your iPAQ as needed. Alternatively, if you really want to keep all your attachments, you can use the Options section to set attachments to be stored to an external storage card.

NOTE   *Sent Items and Drafts folders cannot be synced with your desktop Outlook program.*

Connecting to a Mail Server

Your iPAQ can also be configured to connect to other types of mail servers and bypass your desktop Outlook program altogether. For this configuration to work, your iPAQ must be able to connect to the Internet. You can connect your iPAQ to the Internet in one of three ways:

- ■ **Wireless connection**   Through a third-party wireless modem, Bluetooth connection, or WiFi network card, you can connect to the Internet from almost anywhere.
- ■ **Wired connection**   Through a third-party network card, you can get onto a corporate or home network with an Internet gateway.
- ■ **ActiveSync connection**   If the desktop PC that you ActiveSync with has an Internet connection, you can use the pass-through option (discussed in Chapter 2) to connect to an outside mail server.

You must set up the properties of the outside mail server by configuring a new service on your iPAQ. From the Services menu, select New Service. This will open the E-mail Setup Wizard, which will help you configure your service. The first window asks you for your e-mail address, as shown here.

Enter your e-mail address in the box provided, and then tap the Next button to bring up the second window of the wizard, as shown next.

Here the wizard will attempt to automatically configure your e-mail service by reading from a configuration file kept on the Microsoft servers. A number of the major ISPs are referenced there. If you are not using a major ISP, or cannot be configured automatically, you can tap Skip to configure the service yourself. Tap Next to open the third window of the wizard, shown in this illustration.

In this window you will enter your user information, including your full name, username, and password. You have the option to save the password and not be prompted each time it tries to synchronize your e-mail. When you have entered all your information, tap Next to open the fourth window of the wizard, as shown here.

In this window you will configure your server type and name for this service. You can connect to two types of servers: POP3 and IMAP4. The name you choose for the service can be anything you like, but should be descriptive enough to let you differentiate it from your other mail services (if you are connecting to more than one).

Almost every mail server that you might connect to supports POP3. It is an older protocol, but widely supported. With POP3, your e-mail is copied down to your device. The protocol has little intelligence for handling folders or synchronization with the server.

It is very likely that the mailbox being accessed by your handheld is also accessed from one or more desktops. In this case, it is probably better to use the newer, more efficient, IMAP4 protocol. In my situation, I have an office e-mail service that is run from a Microsoft Exchange server. At work, my desktop accesses the exchange server through Outlook. I have a computer at home with a cable modem that keeps synchronized with my mail server using IMAP4. This way, no matter which desktop system I am using, when I read, compose, delete, or file messages, it is in one common message store that all my systems share. When I chose to connect my iPAQ to this message store, IMAP4 was the obvious choice, as it would participate in this tidy little family of e-mail handlers by synchronizing with the central Microsoft Exchange message store.

When you have entered the relevant account information, tap Next to open the wizard's final window, as shown here.

The fifth and final window of the wizard (unless you choose to set options!) is where you will specify the Internet address of your mail server. You must specify the address of your POP3 or IMAP4 server in the Incoming Mail box. Mail is always sent using *Simple Mail Transfer Protocol* (SMTP). To send mail, you must have an address for an SMTP server, which is the one that you will enter in the Outgoing Mail box. Usually this server will be the same as your incoming mail server, but not always. Check with your ISP or system administrator if you do not know what to enter in these boxes. If your mail server uses a network connection that requires a specific domain to connect to, you will enter that value in the Domain box.

From this window you can access an additional three option windows to configure such items as changing the time intervals for downloading new messages, downloading attachments, and limiting what portion of a message is downloaded. Tap the Options button to open the first window, as shown here.

The first Advanced Options window enables you to set the frequency to check for new messages. By default it will check every 15 minutes. You can clear the check box to have the Inbox check for new messages only when you specifically request it. If your outgoing e-mail server requires authentication, you can select that check box. Requiring authentication is becoming more common as the junk e-mail problem grows. You can also specify a specific connection by which to send outgoing messages in the Connection drop-down list. When you have set the options you want, tap Next to move on to the second Advanced Options window, as shown here.

The second Advanced Options window lets you set how much of the message you want to bring back. The drop-down list enables you to choose whether you want to download the message headers only or a full copy of the message. If you are downloading only the headers, you can choose to include a specific amount of the message. By default you will download the first 2KB, but you can download more (or less) by changing the number in the box. The second check box lets you choose to receive the attachments to a message (by default they are not brought into the Pocket Inbox) and alternatively to pick a maximum size for any attachments you are going to download. When you have finished setting these options, tap Next to open the last window.

The third and final window is very simple. It enables you to set a maximum number of days of messages to hold in your Inbox. I recommend holding only three days' worth of messages, which is the default.

Your new e-mail service is now fully configured and ready to be used.

Navigating Your Inbox

When you open the Inbox, it will open the inbox of the last e-mail service you used. You will see the list of e-mail messages, as shown in Figure 5-19.

How to ... Receive Notification When New E-mail Arrives

If you have set up an Internet connection with your Pocket PC, you can have it periodically check for new e-mail as in the preceding setup. However, your iPAQ may not be set up to give you an alert when the e-mail arrives. To do this, go to Service | Properties and tap Next. Under the Check For New Mail Every setting you can select either Play A Sound or Display A Message to inform you when a new e-mail has arrived.

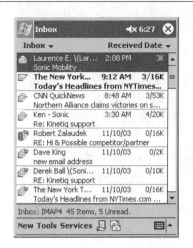

FIGURE 5-19   Opening the Inbox application will show you the messages from the last e-mail service you used.

If an e-mail message has been read, it appears in normal text; an unread message appears in bold. You can see whom the message is from, the time/date received, the size, and the subject. The envelope icon to the left of any message provides a great deal of information about the message as well:

- If the bottom-right corner of the envelope is missing, this means that the message has not been downloaded from the server. If it is there, then the message has been downloaded.

- A closed envelope indicates an unread message. An open envelope indicates the message has been read.

- A paper clip attached to the envelope means that the message includes attachments.

At the top left you can tap the drop-down arrow to choose which e-mail service and inbox you want to look at, as shown here.

Tap the drop-down arrow on the top right to change how the messages in the current folder are sorted. By default they are sorted by received date, but you can also choose to sort by the sender or subject, as shown here.

The bottom of the window contains a status bar that will indicate what operation is currently being performed. If no operation is being performed, it will indicate which mail service you are viewing, the total number of messages, and the number of unread messages.

Below the status bar is the menu bar. The icons to the right of the menu options will, left to right, connect this mail service to its server (assuming you are connected to the Internet) and check for new mail.

Reading a Message

To read a message, tap on it with the stylus. This will open the message details, as shown in Figure 5-20.

The top section of the window contains the header of the message. In its default, short view, you can see who sent the message, the subject, and when it was sent. To see the longer header information, tap the two down arrows in the bottom-right corner of the top section; this will display the To, Cc, and size information.

You can read the message by using the scroll bar on the right side of the window to move up and down within the message. Alternatively, you can use the hardware control disc to scroll the message up or down.

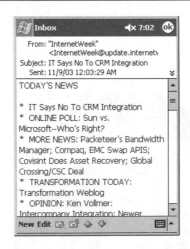

FIGURE 5-20   An open e-mail message

From the menu bar you can use the blue up and down arrows to scroll to the next or previous message. Tapping the envelope with a red *x* on it will delete the current message and load the next message. Tapping the envelope with an arrow on it will enable you to reply to the message.

The Edit menu contains several commands:

- **Mark As Unread** This command returns the message to bold in the message list, as though it had never been read.

- **Mark For Download** This command will cause the entire contents of the message to be downloaded from the mail server the next time you are connected.

- **Move To** Use this command to move the message to a folder.

- **Language** This command enables you to select the language font for the message. This is useful if you receive messages in other languages.

- **Select All** With this command you can select all the text in a message if you are in Edit mode.

- **Copy** This command copies any selected text to the clipboard for pasting somewhere else.

- **Edit My Text Messages** Use this command to change the predefined My Text Messages list (for details, see "Using My Text Messages," later in this chapter).

Handling Attachments

E-mail attachments are used all the time to send Word documents, spreadsheets, and more. Being able to receive, read, and work with these attachments on your Pocket PC makes it a very powerful tool. Attachments to e-mail messages appear in a separate area below the main body of the message, as shown in Figure 5-21.

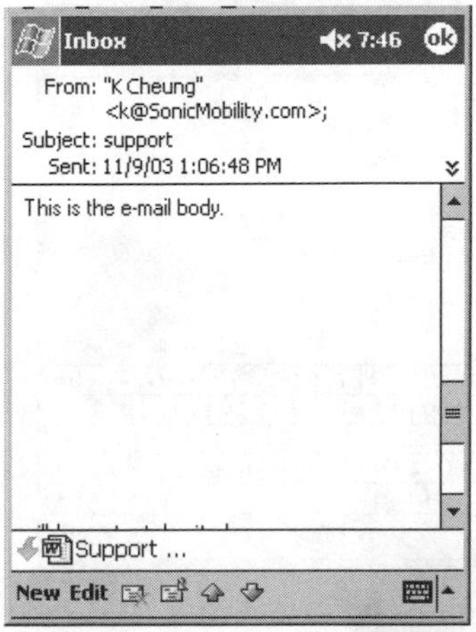

FIGURE 5-21 E-mail attachments appear in a separate area below the main body of the message.

To the left of the icon for the attachment is an arrow. The arrow is gray if the attachment is not downloaded. It is green if the attachment has been flagged for download. Tapping the attachment icon will cause it to be flagged to be downloaded, and if it has been downloaded, it will open the attachment. You can tap and hold the stylus on the attachment to perform a Save As operation if the attachment has been downloaded.

NOTE   *Once an item is flagged for download, it is not actually downloaded until your next send/receive cycle. You can manually initiate this cycle by tapping the "connect to server" or "check for new mail" icons in the menu bar at the bottom of the window.*

Composing a Message

To create a new message, simply tap New at any time. This will open the New Message window, as shown in Figure 5-22. The top box contains a header row with only To and Subject fields. You can enter the e-mail address of the person to whom you want to send the message, or you can select a contact from your Contacts application by tapping the To field, as shown here.

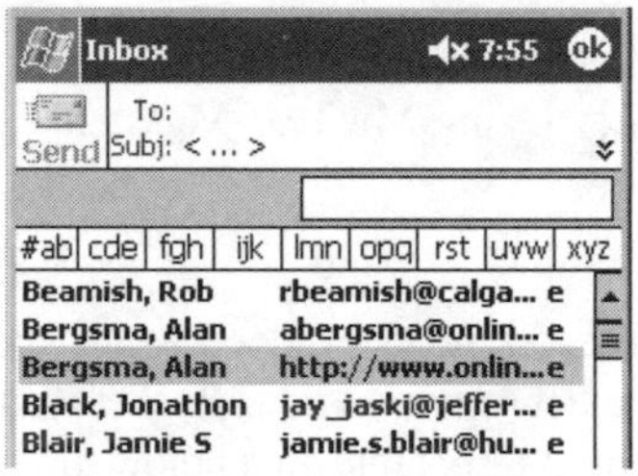

FIGURE 5-22   Tapping New will open a window for creating new messages.

How to ... Enter Extended Header Information

To enter extended header information, you can tap the double down arrow on the bottom right of the header area. This will cause the header area to expand to show Cc and Bcc rows as well as enable you to select which e-mail service you want to send your message from (if you have more than one registered). The expanded header area will look something like this.

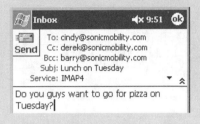

Alternatively, you can access the contacts list by tapping the contact icon (the one that looks like an ID card) in the menu bar. To select more than one recipient, just keep tapping until you are done. When you are finished, tap in the Subject field to make the list of contacts go away.

At any time you can tap in the message body and enter the text of your message. A slick trick that I like is to record a quick voice memo and e-mail it to someone as a WAV file. You can do this by tapping the record icon (the cassette tape) on the menu bar. This will open the full record toolbar, as shown in Figure 5-23. From here you can use the built-in iPAQ microphone to dictate a quick message, which will be attached as a WAV file to your e-mail message. What a great way to whip out a quick note to someone when you don't have time to write it down. We can all talk much faster than we can type, especially on a miniaturized virtual keyboard!

How to ... Create an E-mail Signature

If you are running the latest Pocket PC 2003, you can create an e-mail signature to attach to all of your outgoing e-mail. This is done under the Options menu item. Tapping this opens the Options box where on Pocket PC 2003 there is a Signatures button at the bottom. Tapping on this button will open the Signatures window, where you can specify a different signature for each e-mail profile you are using on your device. You can enable or disable the signature for each profile independently, and then enter the text for your signature.

5

FIGURE 5-23   Voice attachments are a great way to send a quick note to someone when you are on the move and don't have time to type.

When you have finished composing your message, tap the Send button in the top-left corner to send your message to your Outbox for transmission next time you are connected to your service.

Using My Text Messages

Many e-mail messages can be replied to with a brief message. Pocket Outlook has a handy function called My Text Messages, which helps you respond very quickly to your e-mail. My Text Messages provides a list of common replies, which you can select with one tap and drop into your message. To access My Text Messages, tap My Text to open a pop-up list of standard messages, as shown in Figure 5-24. The list includes convenient one-word responses such as Yes and No, as well as status updates such as "I can't talk right now," "I'll be right there," and "I'm running late."

You cannot change the total number of items in this list, but you can change ones that you don't use often into something that may be more useful to you. To do so, select Edit | Edit My Text Messages. This will open the My Text Messages dialog box, shown here, where you can select any item and change it.

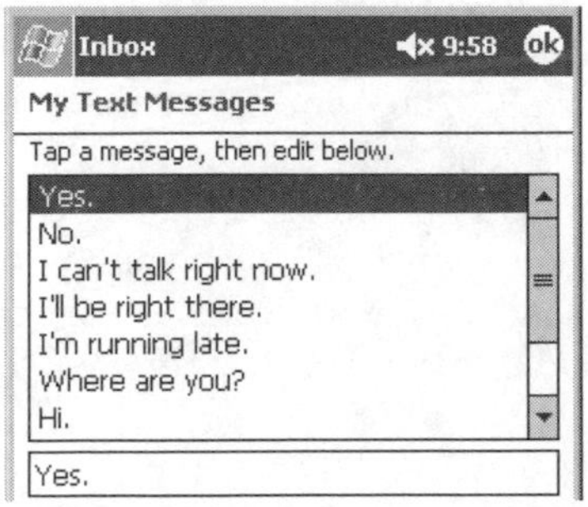

FIGURE 5-24   A set of standard responses can be inserted into your message with the My Text command.

NOTE   *Your My Text messages are shared between the MSN Messenger client and the Inbox application.*

Customizing Your Inbox

You can edit or modify a number of areas in the Inbox application. One thing to keep in mind is that if you need to change the basic properties of your e-mail service, you cannot do this while you are connected to it. If you need to change the name of a mail server or something fundamental, you must be disconnected from your service; then you can go to the Tools menu and select Options. This will open the dialog box shown in Figure 5-25. From here you can select any service in the list to modify. You will notice that ActiveSync is not in the list. This is because that is the one mail service that is set up from the PC, not from your iPAQ.

Notice the four tabs at the bottom of the Inbox Options dialog box. These tabs let you open other dialog boxes with other settings. On the Message tab, shown in Figure 5-26, you configure options for what part of the message body to include when replying and how to format it. You can choose to keep a copy of sent messages in the Sent folder, what action to take after deleting a message, and how to dispose of deleted items.

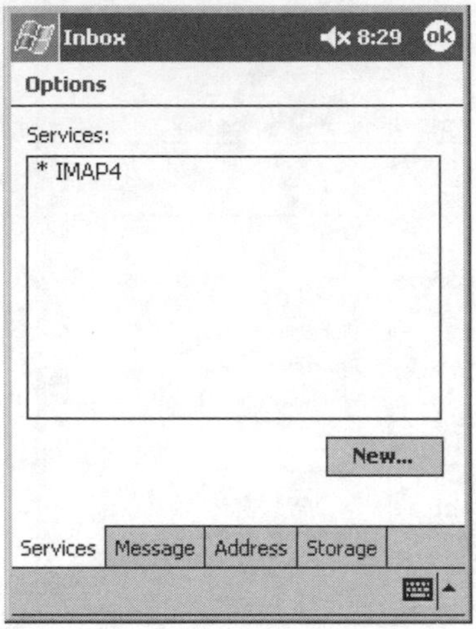

FIGURE 5-25   To edit the base properties of a service, select it from the list in the Inbox
Options dialog box.

The Address tab, shown in Figure 5-27, enables you to customize how Pocket Inbox looks up addresses. It can select addresses from all e-mail fields in your Contacts folder, or only a specific field. You can also set it to look up e-mail addresses against a Contacts folder on a mail server (if the mail server supports this action).

FIGURE 5-26   The Message tab under Options lets you set behavior when working with messages like what to do after a delete, how to reply, and when to empty deleted items.

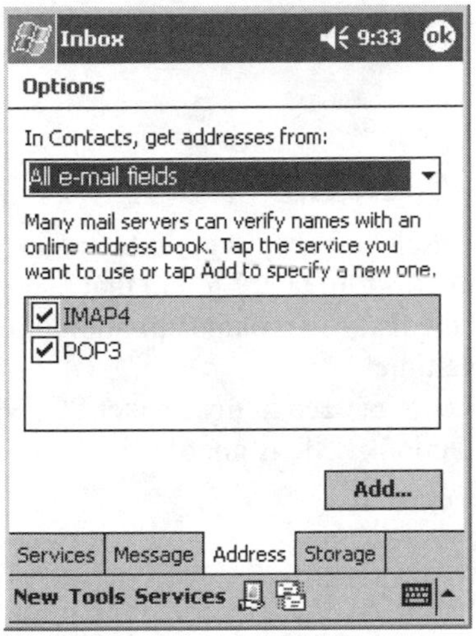

FIGURE 5-27   Customize how addresses are looked up with the Address tab under Options.

How to ... Do Name Lookups Against an External Mail Server

If you want to perform name lookups on a mail server that isn't one of your base e-mail services, you can do this by tapping the Add button on the Address tab of the Inbox Options dialog box. This will open the dialog box shown in this illustration. You must specify the directory and server to search for the names. The server likely may require you to log on and authenticate. If so, select the authenticate check box and fill in your username and password.

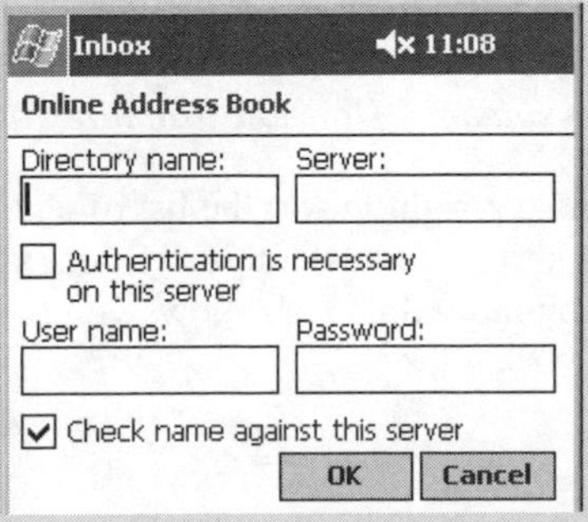

The final tab of the Inbox Options dialog box, Storage, simply allows you to select a check box to store attachments to e-mail messages on an external storage card if you have a CompactFlash or other external storage card.

Keeping on Top of Your Tasks

If you are like me, you have many tasks that always seem to run in parallel; keeping track of those tasks can require a Herculean effort. In fact, I found that every time I had something to add to my task list, I couldn't find the list, so I would start another one. Next thing I knew, I had several to-do lists going at the same time!

Now I keep all of my to-do tasks organized in my Pocket PC, which seamlessly integrates them with my desktop version of Outlook. Life is good!

Navigating Your Tasks

You open the Tasks application by tapping Tasks in the Start menu, or by navigating to it from the Today page by tapping the Tasks item in the list. Either action will open the main Tasks window, shown in Figure 5-28.

Tap the drop-down arrow on the top left of the window to view a subset of tasks. Your choices include the following:

- **All Tasks**   A list of all tasks.
- **Recent**   A list of tasks you have looked at most recently.
- **Category**   A list of all the categories that you have assigned to tasks. You can view any single category you select.
- **No Category**   A list of any tasks that do not have specific categories assigned.
- **Active**   A combination with one of the other lists to show only the subset of tasks that are active.
- **Completed Only**   Like the Active option, works with the other list items to further subcategorize by completed items only.

NOTE   *By default, only active items are kept on your iPAQ, so that when you next sync your device, any completed items will be removed from the iPAQ, although a full record is still kept in your desktop Outlook. Details on customizing this ActiveSync configuration option can be found in the sidebar "How to Customize Tasks," later in this chapter.*

Tap the drop-down arrow on the top right to sort the list of tasks. By default they are sorted by priority. You can also choose to sort by Status, Subject, Start Date, or Due Date.

The check box to the left of each individual task allows you to mark a task as completed, thus changing its status.

5

FIGURE 5-28   Keep track of all of your to-do items in the Tasks application.

Tapping on a specific task will allow you to view the details for that task, as shown here.

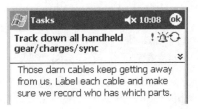

Note the line about one-third of the way down the page. Above this line are the details of the task properties. Below the line are any notes that you have entered for the task. You can tap Edit to change any of the task properties, or to enter notes for the task. The Tools menu contains commands to delete the task or beam it to another device.

Creating a New Task

You can add a new task to the list by tapping New in the menu bar or by using the entry bar.
The New command will open the new task dialog box, shown in Figure 5-29.

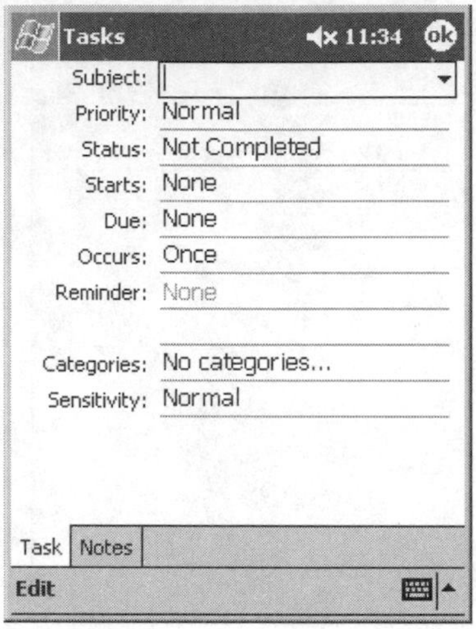

FIGURE 5-29   Use the new task dialog box to add a task to your to-do list.

You can enter information in the following fields in the new task dialog box:

- **Subject**   The name of the task that you need to perform.

- **Priority**   Normal (default), High, or Low. Selecting High will cause a red exclamation mark to be displayed next to the task in the list. Selecting Low will cause a blue down arrow to be displayed next to the task.

- **Status**   Either Completed (active) or Not Completed.

- **Starts**   Defaults to None, but can be set to any date when the task should become active. This allows you to put future tasks on your list that you don't want to appear until a specific date. Note that if you assign a start date to your task, it will also automatically receive a due date.

- **Due**   Defaults to None, but can be set to any date that the task needs to be finished by. If the current date is past the due date, the task will appear in red in your task list.

- **Occurs**   Allows you to set recurrence for a task, just as you do for an appointment. For example, I give my dog medication on the first of every month, so I could set a recurring task that starts on the first of November and recurs on Day 1 of every month, which will make that task appear on my task list on the first of every month.

- **Reminder**   Enables you to set a reminder alarm so that your iPAQ will announce a task and remind you to finish it. This can only be set if your task has a due date. After choosing the reminder option, you can tap the date to select a date from the calendar.

- **Categories**   Enables you to place this task in a category. The categories will be the same as those that you have set up for appointments and contacts. All Pocket Outlook programs share the same categories list. You can assign multiple categories to a task. This is particularly useful if you have a very large number of tasks in your list and need to be able to see the various subsets. You could enter all the groceries you need to pick up as separate tasks and then categorize them under a group called Shopping List.

- **Sensitivity**   Normal (default) or Private. Setting this as Private means that if you are sharing your calendar with people on a Microsoft Exchange server, they will not be able to see the details of this task. They will merely see that a task exists and that it is private.

- **Notes tab**   This is a separate tab where you can add any notes you like to a task. Like the notes in other Pocket Outlook applications, your Inbox notes can include text, drawings, and audio recordings.

When you are finished setting up your new task, tap OK in the upper-right corner to have the task added to your list.

An alternative way to add tasks is to change the standard interface to show the *entry bar*. To view the entry bar, select Tools | Entry Bar. Making this selection again will hide the entry bar. When the entry bar is visible, a new line will appear below the bar that contains the category and sort drop-down lists, as shown here.

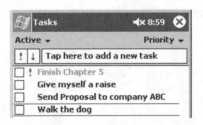

When you use the entry bar, you simply enter a new task by entering the task name into the edit box. You can select the priority by tapping the exclamation mark or down arrow icons to the left of the entry box. Tapping in the list area will cause your new task to be created. I like this feature because I often add new tasks to my list as they come to mind. When you create tasks this way, all the other properties of the task are defaulted (normal priority, no recurrence, no due date, normal sensitivity, and so on).

Keeping Track of Your Notes

The Notes program is another useful tool for helping to eliminate the scraps of paper in your life. If you need to jot something down, or find yourself in a meeting for which you must take notes, or need to make a quick dictation, you can do all of this with Notes.

How to ... Customize Tasks

You have only a few options to choose from when customizing the iPAQ interface for the Tasks application. To modify the interface, choose Options from the Tools menu to open the Tasks Options dialog box, shown here.

The first check box enables you to configure the system to automatically set reminders for any new tasks you create. Selecting the second check box will make start and due dates visible, as shown in this illustration. This feature is useful, but means that you can only view half as many tasks in your list at any given time.

The final check box enables you to use a slightly larger font if you find the default font a little too small to read.

Other options to be aware of are those that you can set on the ActiveSync module on your PC. The options in ActiveSync can be reached by opening the ActiveSync application and then clicking the Tasks line in the detail area. This will open the Task Synchronization Settings dialog box, as shown here.

There are four options you can set in ActiveSync:

- **Synchronize All Tasks**   This setting will synchronize all tasks on both the iPAQ and the desktop.

- **Synchronize Only Incomplete Tasks**   This default setting will synchronize only tasks that are not yet completed. Once completed, it will only leave information on the PC, not on your iPAQ.

- **Synchronize Only The**   This setting enables you to set the number of past weeks to synchronize (defaults to two weeks) and the number of future weeks (defaults to All).

- **Synchronize Only Those Tasks In The Following Selected Categories**   This setting enables you to select only specific categories of tasks to synchronize. This can be useful if you synchronize with multiple desktop systems or if multiple people are sharing the same iPAQ.

Navigating Your Notes

The Notes application can be accessed from the Start menu. Launching Notes will open a list showing all the Notes files in your My Documents folder, as shown in Figure 5-30.

Notes are shown with their first line as their title (which can be modified after saving the note the first time), the date or time they were created, and their size. The icon on the left will show you if it is a regular note or an audio file. If the note is an audio file, its size will show as the number of seconds of the recording. To open and view a particular note, simply tap it with your stylus. If you tap and hold a note, the shortcut menu gives you the option to create a copy of the note, delete the note, select all the notes, e-mail the note, beam the note, or rename/move the note.

An open note can be edited at will. The commands on the Edit menu enable you to perform operations such as Cut, Copy, Paste, Undo, Redo, Clear, and Select All. You can tap the cassette tape icon to embed an audio recording within a text note. The pencil icon that appears at the bottom of the window when editing will drop you into Writing or Drawing mode, where you can handwrite text or draw an image. If you handwrite text, you can select the text and choose Recognize from the Tools menu to have the handwriting interpreted into text. If the Recognizer gets a word wrong, you can tap and select the word and then choose Alternates from the Tools menu to see a list of alternate words to select from.

The Tools menu also includes commands to e-mail or beam the note, to change the current zoom factor from 75% to 300%, and to rename, move, or delete the note.

Creating a New Note

To create a new note, you can tap New on the menu bar at any time. Or, from any application, at any time, you can press the Record hardware button on the iPAQ to begin creating a new voice note immediately.

Your new note will open in the default entry mode that you have chosen. Out of the box, your iPAQ is configured to be in Writing mode, where you can draw and write characters on the

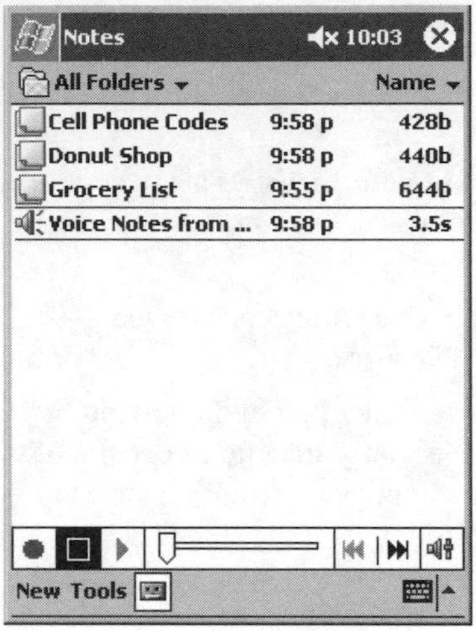

FIGURE 5-30   Each note is stored as its own file in the My Documents folder on your iPAQ.

screen. The default mode can be changed in the Notes Options dialog box (for details, see the sidebar "How to Customize Notes"). The Notes entry mode looks and works like the entry mode discussed in the Chapter 3. Once you have created the note you desire, you can tap the OK button to save the note. By default it will be saved in the My Documents folder using the first line of text that you entered as the filename.

Syncing with Outlook Express, Lotus Notes, or Other PIMs

If you want to sync your data on your Pocket PC with something other than Outlook, you can do this with third-party add-in software. A wide variety of applications is available (at a wide variety of prices and available support). Depending on what information is important to you, and which platform, you can check out some of these links:

- SyncData will sync Outlook Express only for $16. You can download it at **www.syncdata.it** (a free trial is also available).

- Companion Link (**www.companionlink.com**) has sync software available for Outlook Express, Lotus Notes, ACT!, and Goldmine in the $50–$75 price range.

- Handango (**www.handango.com**) also has a category for sync software that has some other alternatives.

How to ...   **Customize Notes**

You can customize the Notes application by selecting the Options command from the Tools menu. The Notes Options dialog box will open, as shown here.

```
Notes                    ◀x 10:22  ok

Options

Default mode:
Writing                              ▼

Default template:
Blank Note                           ▼

Save to:
Main memory                          ▼

Record button action:
Switch to Notes                      ▼



Global Input Options
```

You can set the following four options:

- **Default Mode**   This is the mode that the system will drop into whenever a new note is opened. You can select Writing mode, which enables you to write characters (and draw), or you can select Typing mode, which only selects typed characters or recognized characters from the soft input area.

- **Default Template**   You can select a standard template to use for each new note that is created. By default, a blank template is used, but you can select a template for meeting notes, memo, phone memo, or to-do. This type of note will be the one that is created every time, so unless you generate a lot of one type of note, you probably should not change this option.

- **Save To**   This option enables you to choose to save your notes to the main memory of your iPAQ or to an external storage card if you have one plugged in.

- **Record Button Action**   By default, when you press the hardware record button, the application switches to the Notes application, and a new voice recording is created. The other option available here is to remain in the current program.

Getting Hotmail E-mail on Your iPAQ

If you use a Hotmail e-mail box, it is not automatically available to you on your iPAQ. You can get your Hotmail e-mail in two ways:

■ If you have your iPAQ connected to the Internet (as explained in Chapter 9), you can access your Hotmail account through a special Pocket PC–compatible mobile section on MSN. Open Pocket Internet Explorer and go to **mobile.msn.com/pocketpc**. You will find a conveniently formatted Pocket PC interface waiting for you!

■ If you want to sync your Hotmail so it is available on your Pocket PC while you are disconnected, you will need to purchase a third-party utility to do it for you. Handango (**www.handango.com**) has a list of the most popular. Currently leading the pack is Pocket Hotmail, which costs only $5 and has a free trial available.

Chapter 6

Manage Your Finances with Pocket Money or Quicken

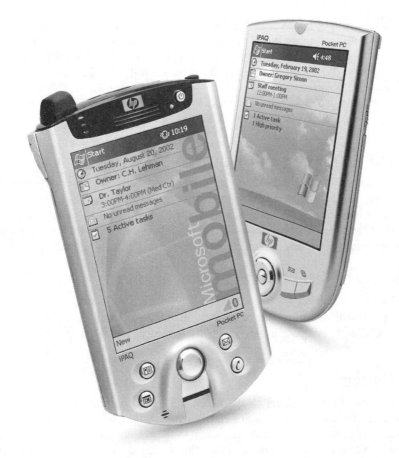

How to…

- Download and install mobile Money or mobile Quicken software
- Manage your accounts
- Work with the account register
- Manage your investments
- Categorize your financial information
- Manage your payees
- Protect your information with passwords
- Set ActiveSync options to sync with desktop Money and Quicken

This chapter will focus specifically on what you can do on your iPAQ with Pocket Money or mobile Quicken software. It is not our intention to teach you how to use Money and Quicken, but rather to show you how your Pocket PC can factor into your personal financial management.

Chances are you will use either Money or Quicken, but not both. To make it easier, we've divided this chapter into two parts. The first part focuses on Microsoft Pocket Money (a free download for your iPAQ), and the second part looks at third-party mobile Quicken alternatives for users of the popular Quicken software from Intuit.

What Can You Do with Pocket Money?

Pocket Money does not come preinstalled on your Pocket PC. You must download it from Microsoft to install it on your iPAQ (discussed in the next section).

Once you have installed Pocket Money, you can see a summary list of all your accounts and balances, see the details of a specific account, monitor all of your investments, set and manage categories for tracking your expenses, and manage your list of those you make payments to.

Downloading and Installing Pocket Money

You can download Pocket Money for free from the Microsoft web site at **http://www.microsoft.com/ mobile/pocketpc/downloads/money.asp**. Before you download the file, you must have already installed Microsoft Money on your desktop PC, otherwise the two programs will not synchronize properly.

Account Manager

The primary window of Pocket Money is the Account Manager, as shown in Figure 6-1. In the Account Manager window is a list all of your accounts with their current balances. The net balance of these accounts is displayed at the bottom of the window, which, if you have every account entered, will be your approximate net worth. Tapping on a checking, savings, or credit card account will take you to the Account Register for that account. Alternatively, you can

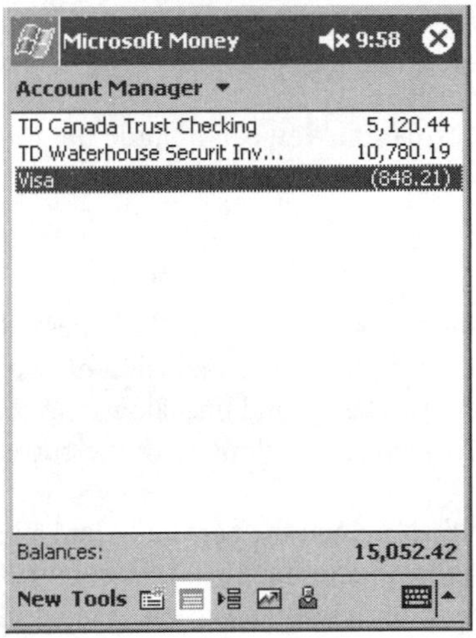

FIGURE 6-1   The Account Manager window lists all your accounts and the current balance.

navigate through the Pocket Money options by using the drop-down menu in the top left of the window as shown here.

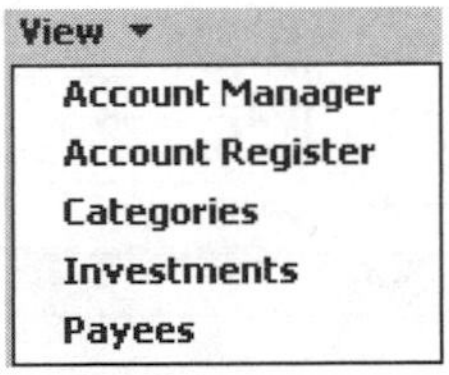

At the very bottom of the window is the menu and icon bar that you can also use to navigate through the different Pocket Money windows. Tapping the New command in the Account Manager will enable you to set up a new account in Money. The dialog box that opens will give you the opportunity to fill in all the required information for the account:

- **Name**   The name that will let you tell this account apart from the others in your list.
- **Account Type**   Bank, cash, credit card, or line of credit.
- **Opening Balance**   The balance in the account at the time you create it.
- **Credit Limit**   The limit on the account if it is a credit card or line of credit.
- **Interest Rate**   The rate that you are charged or credited on any account balances.

■ **Display Account On Today Screen**   This check box allows you to have the account show up in the Today screen with the current balance. This is very useful for tracking your most commonly used accounts.

In addition to the required information, you can include the following optional information: account number, institution name, contact name, and phone number.

Account Register

The Account Register window, shown in Figure 6-2, can be accessed by tapping any account in the Account Manager window. Each entry in the register consists of two lines. The top line shows the date and the amount of the transaction. The second line shows the party involved in the transaction (who the money was paid to or received from) along with the current balance in the account after the transaction.

The bottom of the window will show you the current balance in the account. You can switch between accounts using the drop-down list in the top-right corner of the window. You can see the details of any transaction by tapping it with the stylus. This will open the transaction detail dialog box shown here.

The Type field will define the transaction as being a withdrawal, deposit, or transfer. The Account field lets you put the transaction into any of your existing accounts. The Payee field remembers all of your current payees (managed as a separate list, as described shortly). It will automatically try to match what you type in this field with the available list of payees. The Date field lets you enter a date for the transaction. The Amount field stores the amount.

On the Optional tab you can enter or modify additional information about the transaction including the following:

■ **Check Num**   The number of the check (if paying by check).

■ **Category**   The expense or income category for tracking and reporting purposes.

■ **Subcategory**   A subcategory for the category selected earlier.

■ **Status**   A status of blank, R (for reconciled), C (for cleared), or V (for void).

■ **Memo**   Your personal notes on the transaction.

FIGURE 6-2 Manage individual transactions in the Account Register window.

The Split command at the bottom of the Optional tab in the transaction detail dialog box allows you to define different categories and subcategories for different elements in the transaction, as shown in Figure 6-3.

In this example, we have taken our total bill of $79.56 at Safeway and categorized $34.56 of it as Food, and $45 as Gifts. The Unassigned line will show you the total amount of the transaction that you haven't assigned to a category yet. You can add new subelements by tapping New. If you enter the split amounts and realize that you have entered the total amount of the transaction incorrectly, you can tap Adjust Total and have Pocket Money adjust the total of the transaction to match the sum of your split items. Tapping OK will return you to the transaction dialog box.

Tapping New on the menu bar in the Account Register window will open up a blank transaction where you can enter all the new information on the fly. This is convenient for recording transactions while you are at the checkout instead of trying to remember them all later.

Categories

The Categories window allows you to maintain the set of categories and subcategories used by Money. The full list of categories and subcategories is displayed when you enter the window, as shown in Figure 6-4.

Categories cannot be edited in Pocket Money. This activity is reserved for the full desktop version of Money. You are restricted to creating new categories and deleting existing categories.

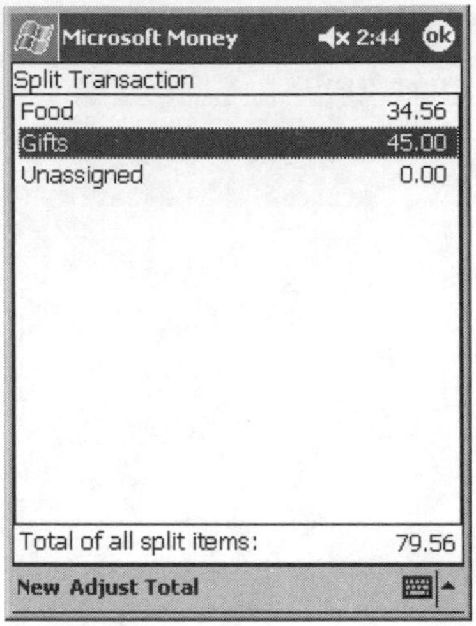

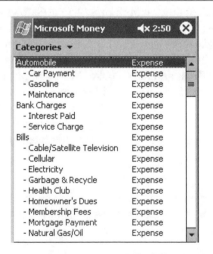

FIGURE 6-3   The Split Transaction window allows you to define different categories and subcategories within a transaction.

FIGURE 6-4   Display all the categories and subcategories available to you in the Categories window.

Tapping and holding the stylus on any category or subcategory will open a shortcut menu enabling you to delete that item from the list. If any transactions exist on your device that use this category, then you will not be able to delete it. Tapping a particular item in the list will open up a dialog box for you to view the properties of the category, as shown here.

6

NOTE *To create a new category, tap New in the menu bar at the bottom of the Categories list. This will open up a blank version of the window shown in the preceding illustration allowing you to specify a category name, type (expense or income), and whether it is a subcategory of another category. You can also add a memo to give a longer description of the category.*

Investments

One of the most useful features of Pocket Money if you invest or trade regularly in the stock market is the ability to manage your portfolio from your iPAQ. The Investments window will show your current portfolio of investments that you have chosen to sync over to your iPAQ. You can keep up to date on the current prices of your stocks while on the move if you have a wireless connection (for details, see Chapter 9). This is very powerful and if up-to-date mobile access to your portfolio valuations is important to you, you should be aware that currently Pocket Money is the only mobile personal finance software that we are aware of that allows this. The various Quicken-related products discussed later in this chapter do not currently offer this functionality.

TIP *You will not see each individual investment account in Pocket Money. Instead, it will sync specific securities that you want to monitor from your iPAQ. You set this up in the ActiveSync options, as described in "Money ActiveSync Options," at the end of this chapter.*

Selecting Investments from the drop-down list in the top left of your window, or tapping the Investments icon in the icon bar at the bottom of the window, will open the Investments window, as shown in Figure 6-5.

Each investment that you are tracking is shown on its own line. The stock symbol is shown along with the number of shares that you are holding and the last known price. Below that you will see the current market value of your holdings. At the bottom of the window you will see the total market value of your tracked portfolio as well as when the last price quote update was

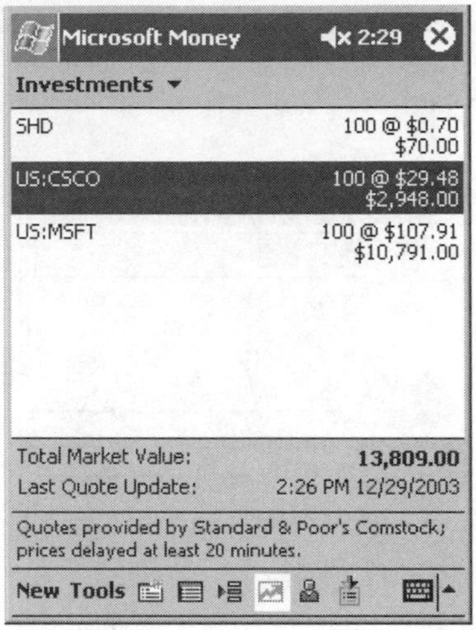

FIGURE 6-5   The Investments window allows you to track your individual stocks and see how they are performing.

completed. If you are connected to a computer with a sync cable or have another connection to the Internet (Ethernet card or wireless access), you can get a price update at any time by tapping on the Update icon in the icon bar (the last icon on the right, with a green down arrow).

Tapping any specific investment will open a detail dialog box for that investment, as shown here.

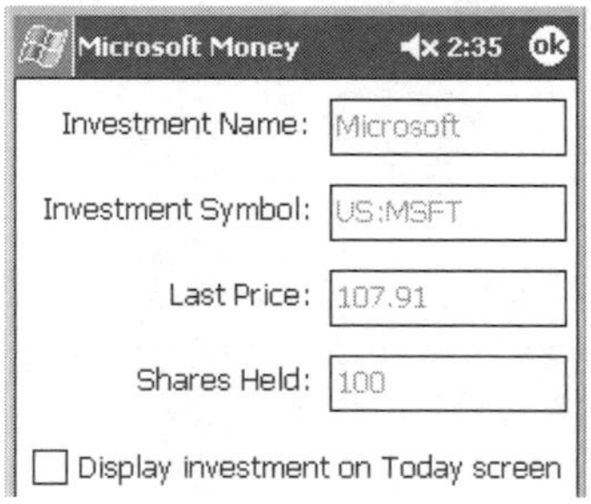

You can see the full name of the investment, the last known price, and the number of shares held. You can also flag a stock so that it shows up on your Today screen (for particularly volatile stocks!). Tapping New in the menu bar at the bottom of the Investments window will also bring you to this dialog box so that you can enter a new investment to track. Tapping and holding on a specific investment will give you a pop-up menu allowing you to delete it from your list of investments.

TIP *If you delete an investment from your list, it will only be gone temporarily. Next time you synchronize, it will be back. To stop an investment from syncing over to your iPAQ, you must set it to not sync in the ActiveSync options (discussed in "Money ActiveSync Options," later in this chapter). To remove an investment from your portfolio permanently, you must do it from the desktop version of Money.*

Payees

Pocket Money will keep your full list of payees synchronized on your iPAQ. You can see this list by selecting the Payees command from the drop-down list on the top left of the window or by tapping the Payees icon in the icon bar (the image of a person). This will open the Payees window, as shown in Figure 6-6.

In this list you can see the names of your payees and also their phone number (if you have one on file). Tapping on any given payee will allow you to see and edit the details of that payee as shown for Company ABC here:

FIGURE 6-6   Open the Payees window to view the complete list of payees synchronized on your iPAQ.

Tapping New in the menu bar will open a blank version of this window, in which you can enter the information for the new payee.

TIP   *Whenever you enter new payees in the Account Register window, they will automatically be added as payees in the Payees list. You do not need to manually add every payee to the Payees list prior to using them in the Account Register.*

As with categories, tapping and holding a specific payee will delete that payee; however, if you have used that payee in any transaction (even if the transaction is not synced over to the Pocket PC), the payee will not be permanently deleted and will reappear the next time you sync your information.

Money Options

Selecting Options from the Tools menu will take you to the Pocket Money options dialog box, shown in Figure 6-7.

Here you have two tabs to work with: Editing and Proxy Server. The Editing tab lets you set three options:

- **Use AutoComplete+**   Selecting this option will cause Pocket Money to try to match any entries that you are entering as they are being typed. This saves you from having to type in the whole payee name or category name if it has been used before.

- **Use AutoFill**   Selecting this option will cause Pocket Money to remember the most recently used amount and category for each payee; the next time you enter that payee in a new transaction, Pocket Money will automatically fill in the amount and category. This is very useful for regularly occurring transactions such as rent, phone bills, and so forth.

- **Use Large Font**   Selecting this option will cause a larger font to be used in all windows. This makes each window easier to read, but reduces the amount of data that can be shown at one time.

On the Proxy Server tab you can specify whether you want Pocket Money to access the Internet via a proxy server when updating information (such as investment prices). Your system administrator will tell you if this is necessary. In general, it is only an issue if you are working in a protected corporate network. You will need to select the check box to tell Pocket Money to use a proxy server and then fill in the HTTP (HyperText Transfer Protocol) address (such as **http://sonicproxy.sonicmobility.com**) and the port number to use.

At the bottom of the options dialog box is a link that when tapped will allow you to link one of the hardware buttons on your iPAQ to Pocket Money. For example, if you do not use the voice recorder button on the side of the iPAQ, you could set it to launch Money (or any other application that you use frequently) instead. The link takes you to the appropriate Settings option to change your hardware button settings.

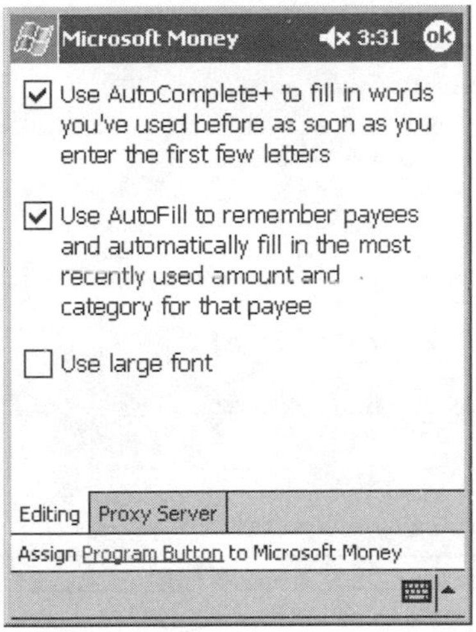

Microsoft Money ◀× 3:31 **ok**

☑ Use AutoComplete+ to fill in words you've used before as soon as you enter the first few letters

☑ Use AutoFill to remember payees and automatically fill in the most recently used amount and · category for that payee

☐ Use large font

Editing | Proxy Server

Assign Program Button to Microsoft Money

FIGURE 6-7   The Pocket Money options dialog box lets you customize how Pocket Money works.

Setting a Money Password

Your financial information is private and sensitive information. If you have not already secured your iPAQ from unauthorized use by employing a device password or one of the other techniques described in Chapter 8, you can add a password specifically to the Money application to prevent unauthorized access (or if you are particularly paranoid, you can use all of the above for extra levels of security).

To set a password for Pocket Money, open Pocket Money and select Password from the Tools menu. A dialog box will appear in which you can set and confirm the password you want to use. From this point on, you will be asked to enter the password whenever you start Pocket Money.

Money ActiveSync Options

To optimize the use of Pocket Money, you must set up the correct information in the ActiveSync program. Double-click the Microsoft Money line in the Details area of ActiveSync to open the Microsoft Money Synchronization Settings dialog box, shown in Figure 6-8.

The most important piece of information in this dialog box is the pointer to the Microsoft Money file that you wish to synchronize with. This path can be changed by clicking the Browse button and navigating to the appropriate file.

In the bottom half of the dialog box are three tabs: Transactions, Investments, and Tools. On the Transactions tab you can select the accounts you want to synchronize over to your iPAQ as

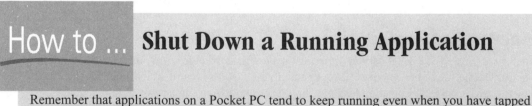

Microsoft Money Synchronization Settings

Microsoft Money for the Pocket PC
Synchronize Microsoft Money on this computer with Microsoft Money on your mobile device.

Select a Microsoft Money file to synchronize:

C:\Documents and Settings\derek\My Document   Browse...

Transactions | Investments | Tools |

○ Synchronize all transactions for the accounts selected below.

◉ Synchronize only the last [4 weeks   ▼]
of transactions for the accounts selected below:

Name	Type
☑ TD Canada Trust Checking	Checking
☑ TD Waterhouse Securit Invest...	Investment
☑ Visa	Credit Card

All accounts and their balances can be synchronized with your mobile device. By default, only those account types that can also synchronize their account registers have been selected.

[OK]   [Cancel]

FIGURE 6-8   Use the Microsoft Money Synchronization Settings dialog box to set the ActiveSync options.

How to ... Shut Down a Running Application

Remember that applications on a Pocket PC tend to keep running even when you have tapped OK to close the application. They just become idle. So closing Pocket Money and powering off your iPAQ does not necessarily mean that your password will stop someone from coming to your iPAQ, turning it on, and looking at your accounts. You must specifically close the task to log out. This can be done from the iTask application that comes with your iPAQ. On older versions of the iPAQ prior to the 38xx series, you do this by pressing the rightmost hardware button, which will open a list of all open applications. From this list, if you tap and hold on a specific application, you will see a pop-up menu allowing you to close that particular application/task, close all applications/tasks, or close all background applications/ tasks. On the 38xx series and later iPAQs, you can run the iTask software from the Programs folder and accomplish the same result. (See Chapter 7 for more details on using iTask to shut down applications.)

Also remember that setting a password will not stop the account balances and information that you have requested from being displayed on the Today page when the iPAQ starts up.

well as set an option to synchronize all transactions (synchronizing all transactions is time-consuming and memory intensive on your iPAQ, so it isn't recommended unless you have very small financial files), or synchronize only a set number of previous weeks of transactions (from none to 52 weeks of previous transactions; the default is 4 weeks).

On the Investments tab you can choose to synchronize over to your iPAQ all of your investments or only specific investments selected from the list.

The Tools tab gives you two tools to help you with managing your Pocket Money install. The first tool will perform a full synchronization between your iPAQ and your desktop version of Money. If things get out of sync, or if you have changed the file you are using on your desktop, click this to resync all of your data. The second tool allows you to remove all Pocket Money data from your iPAQ. It is important to remove this data before you give your iPAQ to someone else or send it in for servicing. This tab also has a check box to tell ActiveSync to remember your Money password and use it next time you sync data.

What About a Pocket Version of Quicken?

A question that we have received ever since the iPAQ began shipping is "I use Quicken at home. Is there a version of that for my Pocket PC?" Until recently the answer was "No," but now two companies have answered the call for a mobile version of Quicken. However, as this software doesn't come from Microsoft and isn't included with your purchase of your Pocket PC, you must buy one of these products separately. The two vendors are as follows:

- Landware makes Pocket Quicken for the Palm platform. The Pocket PC version of their product will be available by the time this book hits the shelves. The prerelease copy of the product we evaluated for this book was of extremely high quality, and we have no concerns in recommending it. You can check for current information on this product on their web site at **www.landware.com**.

- Spb Software (**www.spbsoftwarehouse.com**) had the first mobile Quicken software on the market, Spb Quick. This product can be downloaded directly from the vendor at the web link. It is very reasonably priced, and useful if you do your home finances on the computer.

With both of these products you can see your accounts on your iPAQ, allowing you to find out the balances in all your accounts wherever you are. Now when you write checks, you can enter the information into your Pocket PC and automatically sync it back into your Quicken file. You can also view graphs of your accounts to see how you are managing your money over time!

Unfortunately, one significant limitation of the Spb Quick product is that it will not track your investment accounts, and thus doesn't allow you to see your portfolios or get real-time stock price quotes like Pocket Money does. Spb Soft has suggested this may change for version 2.0 of the software due out soon.

Landware's Pocket Quicken will allow you to track your investment accounts, but the current release also will not provide real-time stock price updates for your portfolio. If you like to monitor the current trading information for the stocks in your portfolio while mobile, neither of these products will be satisfactory to you.

Both products function in a similar fashion. We will use the SPB Quick product to explain these functions.

Account Manager and Register Tab

Spb Quick opens to the Account Manager tab as shown in Figure 6-9.

Selecting a specific account and then tapping the Register tab on the bottom of the screen will take you to the account register detail for the selected account, as shown in Figure 6-10.

The detail lines of the Register tab show you the same data you are accustomed to seeing in Quicken: date, payee, transaction type, category, reconcile status, and amount. In Spb Quick, you

FIGURE 6-9   The Spb Quick Account Manager tab shows you the list of all of your accounts and the current balance.

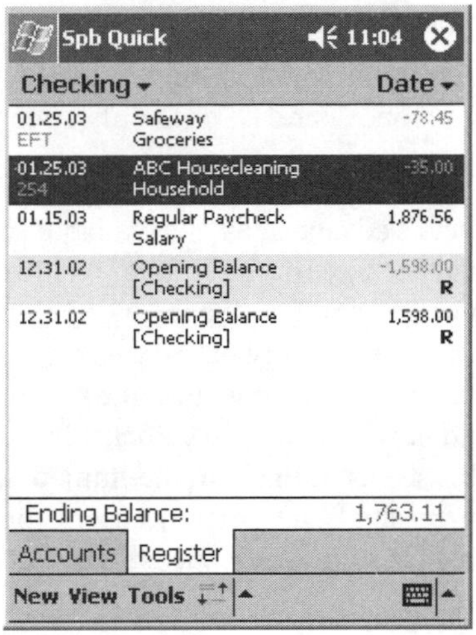

FIGURE 6-10   The Register tab allows you to see all the detailed transactions for a selected account.

cannot edit any existing transaction. Only new transactions or transactions that have not yet been synced with the desktop Quicken can be edited.

When you choose New from the bottom menu, you have the option to create a new payment, deposit, or transfer. This is convenient when you are writing a check at the supermarket or making a transfer at an ATM.

The View menu gives you the opportunity to view all the categories for classifying your transactions. However, in the current version, you cannot add new categories. You also have options for viewing memorized transactions (but again, not editing) and for viewing account balances or income/expense transactions as a graph.

Under the Tools menu you have access to setting options for regional settings and autocomplete. Also, you can set Spb Quick to show the balances of specific accounts on your Today screen so that you always know how much money you have in your account before you write that check! In addition, you can use a password setting under the Tools menu so you can restrict access to this data on your iPAQ.

On your desktop PC where your Quicken file that you will sync with your iPAQ resides, you can set some options in the Spb Quick sync properties (accessed through the ActiveSync window just as with other sync-capable data). From here you can

■ Choose which Quicken file to sync with your Pocket PC, and if it is a password-protected file, input the password

■ Filter so that only transactions after a specific date will be synced to your iPAQ, and also choose only a subset of accounts to sync

■ Set the sync schedule to run continuously (which actually doesn't work in the first version), sync once per hour, once per day, or to only sync when you manually request it

The bottom line for managing your finances on your Pocket PC if you are a Quicken user is that the available software is not yet as advanced as the available software for Microsoft Money, and the disadvantage is you will have to pay for the software. However, given the rapid growth of the Pocket PC platform, and Quicken's rank as the most popular home finance software, we anticipate you will see this software improve very quickly.

In closing this section on mobile Quicken we would like to add that it would be nice if Intuit, the manufacturer of Quicken, would provide someone's Pocket PC Quicken software to all Quicken users for no additional cost, but this seems unlikely in the immediate future. As mobile access to important information becomes increasingly important to users, the need to buy your mobile Quicken software from a third party (at additional expense) may drive some Quicken users to switch to Microsoft Money instead.

Part II

Optimize Your Pocket PC for Maximum Productivity

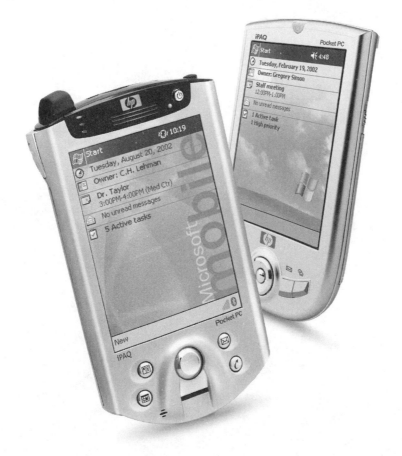

Chapter 7

Optimize Your Pocket PC—Better, Faster, and Longer

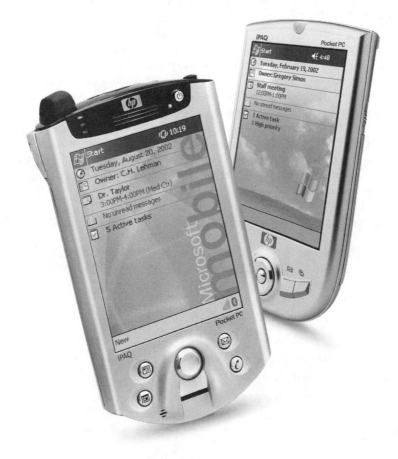

How to...

- Control running applications
- Manage the iPAQ's built-in memory
- Increase your iPAQ's storage
- Maximize your iPAQ's battery life

An old saying in the computer industry is "What Intel giveth, Microsoft taketh away." That is not to say that if your iPAQ slows down, it's Microsoft's fault. Far from it. It's just another way of saying that no matter how fast the processors become and how much memory our devices have, a better and faster model will always be on the horizon. So until the future iPAQs with 512MB of RAM and 1-GHz Intel XScale processors arrive, we have to live with our "slow" 206-MHz and 400-MHz iPAQ devices. Table 7-1 lists the iPAQ devices and the processor (and speed) they use.

One of the strengths of the iPAQ is its ability to multitask, that is, its ability to run multiple programs at the same time. This can be both a blessing and a curse. Being able to run Word, then switch to Excel without saving and exiting Word, and then switch back is something that we have gotten used to in the desktop world. Our iPAQs work the same. But as we run more programs, the processor has to perform more tasks, and the iPAQ appears to slow down.

In a desktop environment, we have hard drives. This allows the operating system to "free" memory by saving portions of it to the disk (called *paging*). In the Pocket PC world, we do not have that luxury because all of the iPAQ's software is stored in either ROM or RAM. Therefore, all our programs need to be stored in that memory (although the storage cards available for the iPAQ today make this easier to live with).

One of the problems with the iPAQ (and all other Pocket PC devices) is that as applications are executed, they take up more storage and therefore slow down the device. This chapter will

iPAQ Series	Processor and Speed
31xx	Intel StrongArm, 206 MHz
36xx	Intel StrongArm, 206 MHz
37xx	Intel StrongArm, 206 MHz
38xx	Intel StrongArm, 206 MHz
39xx	Intel XScale, 400 MHz
54xx	Intel XScale, 400 MHz
H1910	Intel XScale, 200 MHz
22xx	Intel XScale, 200 MHz or 400 MHz

TABLE 7-1   iPAQ Models and Their Processors

deal with some of the tasks that you can perform to ensure that your iPAQ will run better, faster, and longer.

Although we could try to divide this chapter into Better, Faster, and Longer sections, it makes more sense to group the Better and Faster sections together and leave the Longer section apart. As you will see, better and faster go hand in hand.

Optimizing your iPAQ is one area in which the older iPAQs (running Pocket PC 2000) and the newer ones (running Pocket PC 2002) differ significantly. We will therefore cover both iPAQ/ operating system combinations, and we will illustrate the differences between them.

Controlling Running Applications

Both versions of the Pocket PC operating system lack a way for you to easily and quickly control which applications are running. Though they both have the Memory control panel, it falls short in what it can do and how easily accessible it is. For this reason, Compaq decided to include special applications for controlling the running applications quickly and easily.

QMenu

The original iPAQ shipped with a piece of software installed in ROM called QMenu or Compaq Menu. QMenu performed two tasks. First, it allowed you to control the applications currently running on your iPAQ. You could choose to stop a single application or all the applications running on your device, as well as choose the application that you would like to switch to. QMenu's second role was simply as a shortcut to some of the control panels you might need regularly. What's interesting is that most of these control panels fall into the Better, Faster, or Longer category.

There are a couple of ways to launch QMenu. You can either navigate to it in the Program menu (Start | Programs | QMenu), as illustrated here, or press the "Q" button on the front of the iPAQ (just to the right of the Navigation pad).

When you run the QMenu application, you will see a menu similar to the one shown in Figure 7-1. At this point, you can perform one of the following actions:

- Close the active task
- Close all tasks
- Switch to a running application
- Run File Explorer
- Run the Power control panel
- Run the Volume control panel
- Run the QUtilities program
- Run the Backlight control panel

In this section, we will look at the first three actions in the preceding list. The other options will be covered later in this chapter.

If you choose the Close Active Task command, then the application (or task) that is running below QMenu—Pocket Excel in this example—will close. QMenu will then close. Note that you will not be asked to confirm this process. It will simply close the application, and you will lose any modifications or data that the application has stored but that you haven't saved.

The Close All Tasks command simply closes all the currently running applications. Again, QMenu will close and all applications will be terminated without any confirmation on your part. This command provides a very quick way to clear the deck—get the iPAQ into a state where no applications are running.

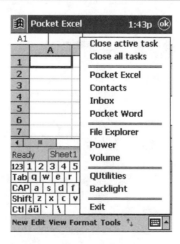

FIGURE 7-1   The QMenu menu allows you to control many features of your iPAQ.

Although there is no option to switch applications, this can be easily done. If you want to switch to another application, simply tap the desired application from the QMenu menu.

iTask

New to the native Pocket PC 2002 iPAQs (37xx, 38xx, 39xx, and 54xx series) is an application that replaces QMenu called iTask. iTask is similar to QMenu in its ability to control running applications on the iPAQ. Where it differs is that it enables you to customize its menus. Before we look at customization, let's look at some of the built-in features of iTask.

The H1910 iPAQ device does not ship with iTask, so if you own the H1910, you can skip this section.

iTask can be launched from the Programs menu, as shown here, by navigating to Start | Programs and tapping the iTask icon. It can also be launched by pressing the iTask button on the iPAQ (located on the far right of the Navigation pad). This button will be labeled with the same icon as the iTask application.

7

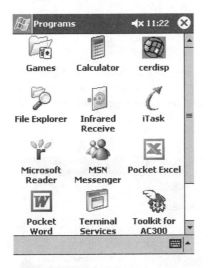

You will notice that iTask is divided into two sections, as shown in Figure 7-2. In the upper part of the menu, the running applications are listed, whereas the lower section displays three buttons.

Much as with the QMenu application, iTask enables you to close a selected task or application as well as close all tasks. A new feature also allows you to close the background tasks. To close a selected task, simply tap and hold the name of the application that you want to close. A new menu will appear, as shown in Figure 7-3. Choose Close This Task from the menu, and the application will close. As with QMenu, no confirmation is required to terminate the application.

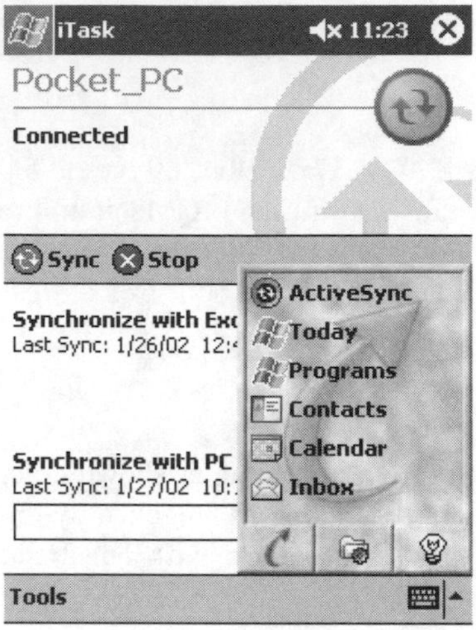

FIGURE 7-2   iTask enables you to control running applications.

To close all tasks, simply tap and hold any application listed in the iTask menu, and choose Close All Tasks from the menu. All running applications and tasks will terminate. Again, no confirmation is required. Be aware that some items on the iTask menu can never be closed. These

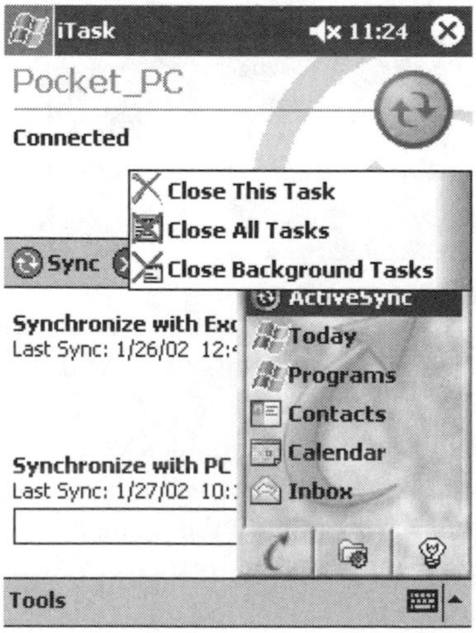

FIGURE 7-3   The iTask menu opens when you tap and hold a task or application name.

include Today, Programs, and ActiveSync. Some of these tasks can be closed manually by tapping on the close or OK button in the top-right corner of the screen.

You may find that an application you launch is running extremely slowly because of the number of other applications running at the same time. With the previous Pocket PC operating system (Pocket PC 2000), your only real option was to either close all the applications using the QMenu program (and then relaunch your desired application) or to close each of the other applications manually through the Memory control panel (covered later in this chapter). With iTask, you can simply tap and hold the application that you would like to keep running and choose Close Background Tasks from the menu. This will terminate all running applications except for the one you selected.

Configuring iTask

One of the coolest features of the new iTask application is your ability to configure it. As we mentioned previously, three buttons are on the bottom of the iTask window. By default, these are known as (from left to right) the iTask, Settings, and Brightness buttons. You can modify these buttons, the commands that appear on the buttons, and their icons.

But first, let's list the options that are set by default on the 37*xx*, 38*xx*, 39*xx*, and 54*xx* series devices. The menus accessed by tapping the Settings and the Brightness buttons are the same for all these series.

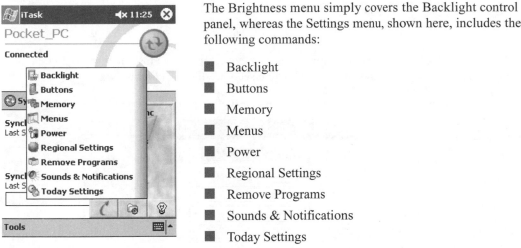

The Brightness menu simply covers the Backlight control panel, whereas the Settings menu, shown here, includes the following commands:

- Backlight
- Buttons
- Memory
- Menus
- Power
- Regional Settings
- Remove Programs
- Sounds & Notifications
- Today Settings

The iTask option enables you to control many tasks on your iPAQ. The 37*xx* series iTask menu contains the following options:

- CF Backup
- Save Contacts
- Expansion Pack
- iTask Settings

■ iTask Help

■ Microphone AGC

■ Asset Viewer

■ Auto Run

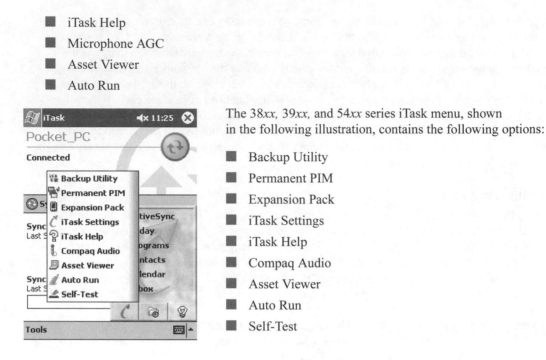

The 38*xx,* 39*xx,* and 54*xx* series iTask menu, shown in the following illustration, contains the following options:

■ Backup Utility

■ Permanent PIM

■ Expansion Pack

■ iTask Settings

■ iTask Help

■ Compaq Audio

■ Asset Viewer

■ Auto Run

■ Self-Test

As we mentioned, you can configure the options that exist on the iTask menus. To do this, open the iTask Settings control panel in the System section, shown in Figure 7-4.

FIGURE 7-4   Use the iTask Settings control panel to modify your iTask menus.

To add an application to iTask, choose the menu where it is to be displayed from the Label drop-down list, choose its location on the menu (from the Menu Item drop-down list), and choose the application from the Replace With drop-down list. You can also choose the icon to be displayed on one of the three buttons in iTask from the Icon drop-down list. Be aware that each of the three menus is limited to ten items.

Optimizing Memory

It is important to understand how the iPAQ uses its memory for operation. When the 32MB version of the iPAQ came out, it was heralded as having more than sufficient capacity to do everything imaginable with the Pocket PC. It then became clear that because the applications are stored in the iPAQ's RAM, as you added more applications, you quickly ran out of memory. The 64MB models solved that by doubling the iPAQ's storage. Remember that the iPAQ's RAM is used to store both programs and data (programs are applications that are running on the device, whereas data is the files that are stored in RAM).

7

NOTE   *Although we cover some information on storage in this chapter, Chapter 14 covers storage in much greater detail.*

The Memory control panel (launched from the System section of your iPAQ's Settings) has three tabs: Main, Storage Card, and Running Programs. We will now look at each of these tabs in detail.

The Main Tab

The Main tab in the Memory control panel enables you to control the percentage of the total memory that is used for storage and for programs. As you will notice in Figure 7-5, by simply moving the slider to the left, you will increase the amount of memory used for storage, whereas moving it to the right will increase the amount used for programs. The blue bar underneath the slider shows the total amount of free memory.

It is important to note that although the iPAQ has RAM (32MB, 64MB, or more), it assigns this RAM differently. If the memory is used for storage, then only data files can be stored on it, and applications cannot be executed from that memory section. Applications are executed from the programs section of memory. If an application is stored in the storage section and you execute it, it will be copied to the program section first. You will notice this when you launch a large application from a storage card on your iPAQ. You will notice that there will be a delay on the iPAQ before the application starts.

The Storage Card Tab

It will become clear to you as you use your iPAQ that 64MB of memory is just not enough. You will most likely find yourself requiring more storage memory. Chapter 14 covers some of the external storage solutions that exist for the iPAQ today, but for now we will look at the Storage Card tab of the Memory control panel, shown in Figure 7-6. On this tab you can view any storage cards and devices that are installed on your iPAQ and find out the amount of free or used space that exists on them. You will also notice a category for RAM called Extra. This is an upgrade that was performed on this iPAQ to increase its physical memory. More on this upgrade in Chapter 14.

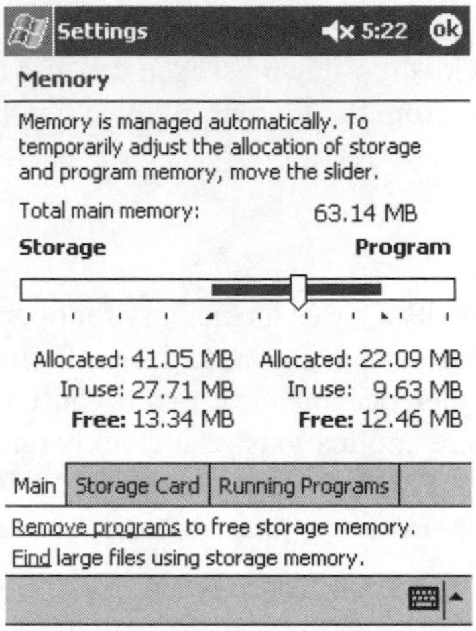

FIGURE 7-5   The Main tab of the Memory control panel allows you to control the way your iPAQ stores data and applications.

You will notice that the iPAQ "sees" all storage external to the built-in memory as a Storage Card. This is true if it is a MultiMedia Card (MMC), Secure Digital (SD) card, CompactFlash (CF) card, a hard drive, or upgraded memory.

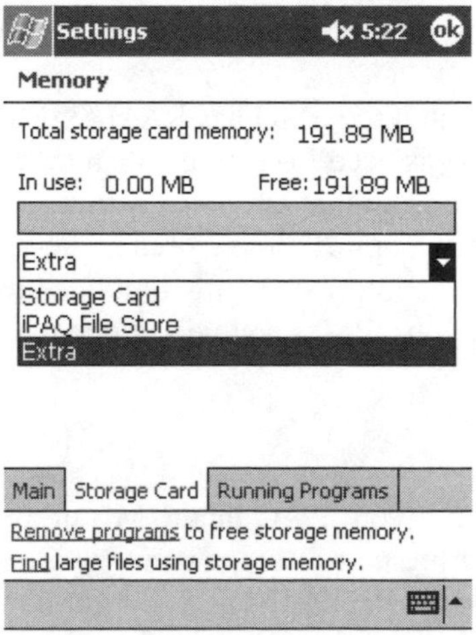

FIGURE 7-6   The Storage Card tab of the Memory control panel allows you to view the configuration of your storage cards.

If you have one of the newer iPAQs (37*xx*, 38*xx*, 39*xx*, and 54*xx* series), you will notice that a mystery "storage card" appears on the device. This storage card is called the iPAQ File Store and is approximately 6.59MB.

The solution as to where this storage comes from is an easy one. Most of the original iPAQs shipped with 16MB of ROM. It is in ROM that the operating system was stored. A few lucky iPAQ owners got one of the original iPAQs with 32MB of ROM. The reason for the different ROM sizes is that when the iPAQs were built, 16MB ROM chips were not available and 32MB ones replaced them. Because the operating system required less than 16MB of storage, this was never an issue.

With the release of Pocket PC 2002, however, the operating system grew to be greater than 24MB (because it included MSN Messenger, Terminal Server, and Microsoft Reader). This meant that most of the iPAQ devices now ship with 32MB of ROM. Two of the new iPAQs, the H1910 and the 545*x*, do not. Instead, they ship with 0MB and 48MB of ROM, respectively. The H1910 actually uses some of its 64MB of RAM to store the operating system. Because the iPAQ has the ability to store information in ROM (for upgrades of the operating system you can *flash*—overwrite the iPAQ's memory—the ROM), Compaq decided to make the extra ROM available to the user. This extra ROM appears as the "iPAQ File Store."

One aspect, however, differentiates the File Store from RAM. Because it is ROM and can be flashed, it is semipermanent. What this means to you is that any program that you store in the iPAQ File Store will be retained even if you lose battery power completely and all the data/applications in the iPAQ. It is therefore recommended that you place in the File Store data or applications that you always require on your iPAQ, such as network card drivers. You can also make your contacts and appointments permanent by storing them in this flash ROM, but more on that later in this chapter. Although you can use the File Store to store applications, you may only want to use it for data. If you install applications to it, then lose power on your device and it hard resets, you won't be able to use the applications in the File Store because the registry entries will be gone, DLLs in the /windows directory will be gone, the icon will be gone, and so forth.

Going back to the storage cards, you can simply view the size of the storage cards in this control panel without making changes. The process involved in storing information to a storage card or the iPAQ File Store is covered later in this chapter.

The Running Programs Tab

While the iTask application is available for you to control running applications (as well as to launch them), the Pocket PC operating system has a feature for controlling running applications built in. This is the Running Programs tab of the Memory control panel, shown in Figure 7-7.

Like the Task Manager in Windows NT or Windows 2000, this tab enables you to view all the programs that are currently running in memory, as well as to control them.

As you can see in Figure 7-7, a list of all running programs is presented to you. You then have one of three options: Activate, Stop, or Stop All. If you select an application from the list and tap the Activate button, the Memory control panel will close, and the selected application will be brought to the foreground. By selecting an application and tapping on the Stop button, you will terminate it. And by tapping the Stop All button, you will force the iPAQ to terminate all nonoperating system programs.

The Memory control panel contains two other options: Remove Programs To Free Storage Memory and Find Large Files Using Storage Memory.

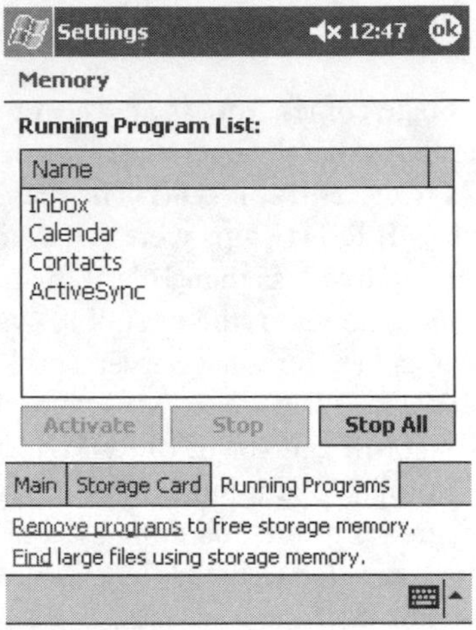

Settings   ◀× 12:47 **ok**

Memory

Running Program List:

Name
Inbox
Calendar
Contacts
ActiveSync

| Activate | Stop | **Stop All** |

| Main | Storage Card | Running Programs | |

Remove programs to free storage memory.
Find large files using storage memory.

FIGURE 7-7   The Running Programs tab of the Memory control panel allows you to control the running programs.

You can use the Remove Programs option (simply by tapping the link at the bottom of the Memory control panel) to remove (or uninstall) applications from your iPAQ. You will then be presented with a list of the installed applications, as shown here. When you tap an application, a confirmation dialog box will appear, at which point you can choose to remove the application from your iPAQ. Be aware, however, that this only removes the application from the iPAQ. Because most applications are installed from a desktop system, you will need to uninstall the application on the desktop, too.

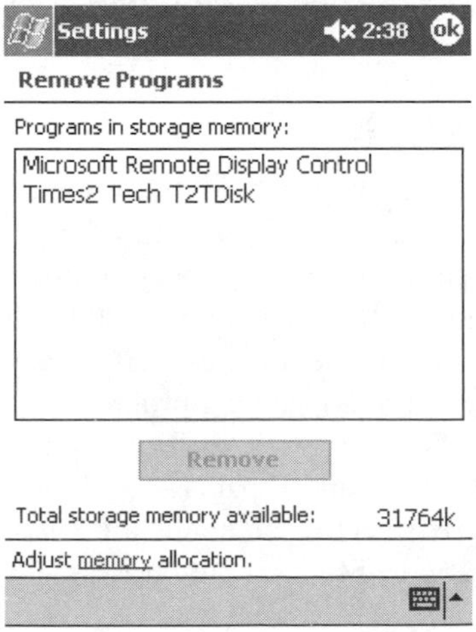

Settings   ◀× 2:38 **ok**

Remove Programs

Programs in storage memory:

Microsoft Remote Display Control
Times2 Tech T2TDisk

| Remove |

Total storage memory available: 31764k

Adjust memory allocation.

Most Pocket PC applications install themselves on the desktop first, at which point, ActiveSync transfers the application to the iPAQ and installs it. These applications are usually installed in directories directly below the ActiveSync directory (C:\Program Files\Microsoft ActiveSync, for example). If you want to uninstall an application, simply follow these steps:

1. Connect your iPAQ to your desktop.

2. Make sure that ActiveSync recognizes the iPAQ and connects to it.

3. Choose Add/Remove Programs from the Tools menu in ActiveSync.

4. Select the application to be removed in the Add/Remove Programs dialog box, shown in Figure 7-8.

5. Click on the Remove button.

6. Click the OK button to confirm the application's removal. The application will now be removed from both the desktop and the iPAQ.

7

Because the iPAQ has a finite amount of memory, Microsoft included a little utility to allow you to quickly find files on your iPAQ based on some criteria. This utility is launched by tapping the Find link at the bottom of the Memory control panel, which opens a window like this:

You can type in a search item in the Find field, or simply search for all files that fall into the criteria set in the Type field. You can choose from the following file types:

- All data
- Calendar
- Contacts
- Help (only in Pocket PC 2002)

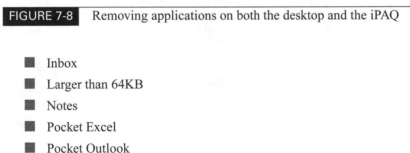

FIGURE 7-8   Removing applications on both the desktop and the iPAQ

- Inbox
- Larger than 64KB
- Notes
- Pocket Excel
- Pocket Outlook
- Pocket Word
- Tasks

You will notice that Microsoft has included most of the files that will require a large amount of storage space on your iPAQ, such as Pocket Excel and Pocket Word files.

Permanent PIM

Because the newer iPAQ models have extra storage available in the nonvolatile ROM, an application exists to enable you to store some of your most important information in it. Compaq decided that the information most people will want to ensure they do not lose is their appointments and their contacts. For this reason, they included the Permanent PIM control panel.

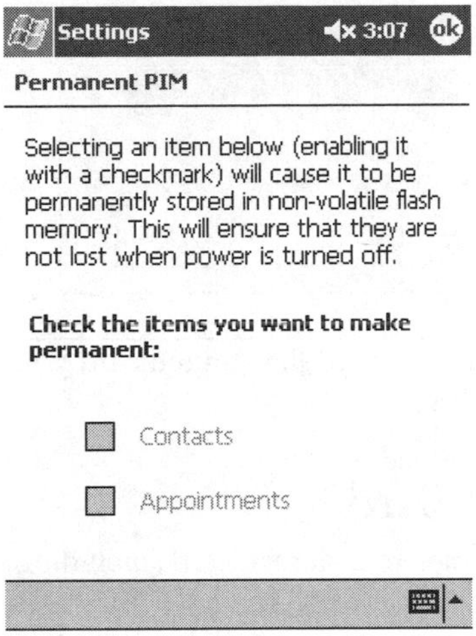

FIGURE 7-9   Storing your contacts and appointments in nonvolatile ROM

The Permanent PIM control panel, shown in Figure 7-9, enables you to control whether your contacts and/or appointments are to be stored in nonvolatile ROM. By selecting the desired check boxes, you can ensure that this information is retained even if the iPAQ's battery runs out completely.

Installing Applications on the iPAQ

Most Pocket PC applications will automatically launch the Add/Remove Programs utility covered earlier in the chapter. Some, however, do not, or you might not have your iPAQ synced with the desktop when the application attempts to install. For this reason, in this section we will cover the process of installing an application to both the iPAQ's main memory and a storage card.

Installing to Main Memory

The process of installing to main memory is a simple one. All you need to do is launch the Add/Remove Programs utility of ActiveSync and answer Yes when asked whether you would like the application installed to the default directory, as shown here:

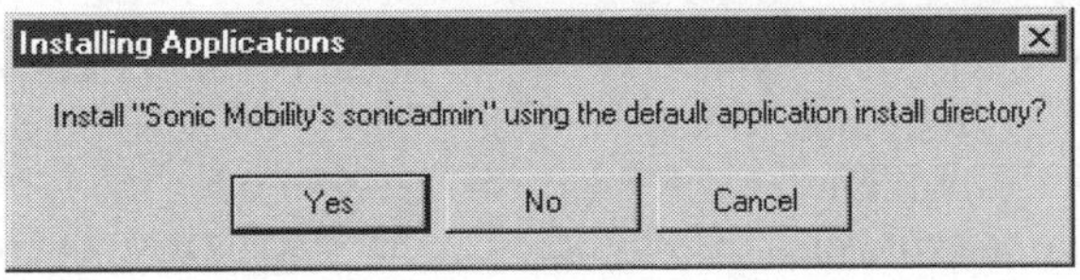

The application will now be installed into main memory and into the directory specified by the application vendor.

FIGURE 7-10   Select or enter the name of the storage card you want to install the application to in this dialog box.

Installing to a Storage Card

The process of installing an application to a storage card (including the iPAQ File Store) is almost as easy as that of installation to main memory. The only difference is that when presented with the prompt shown earlier, simply answer No. The dialog box shown in Figure 7-10 will open, where you can choose which storage card (assuming that multiple ones are available) the application is to be installed to.

Maximizing Your iPAQ's Battery Power

One of the biggest misconceptions about the iPAQ and other Pocket PC devices is that they have zero battery life. Although it is true that the iPAQ uses more battery power than, say, a Palm device, it is important to remember that several things set the iPAQ apart from such devices. First and foremost is the iPAQ screen, which is arguably one of the best hand-held screens on the market.

The iPAQ screen is lit from the side and requires quite a bit of power to maintain. For this reason, several features have been built into the iPAQ to enable you to control the brightness of the screen, as well as how the iPAQ will react to different power situations, such as when on battery power and connected to AC power.

Conserving Battery Power

Two different control panels are used for controlling power usage in the iPAQ: the Power and the Backlight control panels. Each of these is covered in detail in the next sections.

The Power Control Panel

The Power control panel simply allows you to view the current battery status and control what the device should do when on battery power or when connected to external power. As can be seen in the following illustrations (from left to right: the earlier iPAQ model, the H1910, and the 54xx series), the top half of the control panel displays the battery status (with the Main battery and an External battery if one exists). The bottom half allows you to set whether the iPAQ is to be turned off after inactivity if on battery or external power, and the amount of time before the iPAQ is to be turned off.

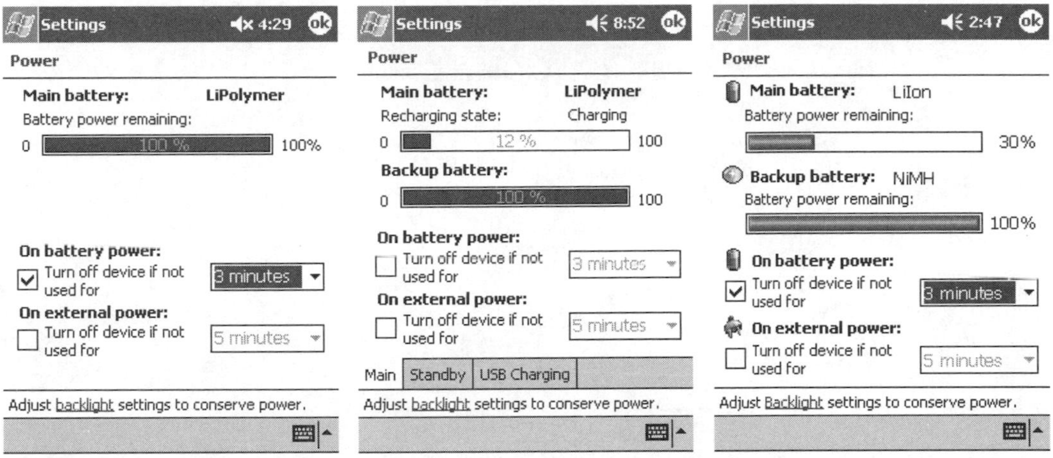

The Backlight Control Panel

The Backlight control panel contains three tabs: Battery Power, External Power, and Brightness. The first two tabs, Battery Power and External Power, are identical in all iPAQ models, whereas the Brightness tab is different on the 38xx series.

The Battery Power tab, shown in Figure 7-11, enables you to configure the threshold at which the backlight is to be turned off when the device is not in use and whether to turn the backlight on if the screen is tapped or a button is pressed.

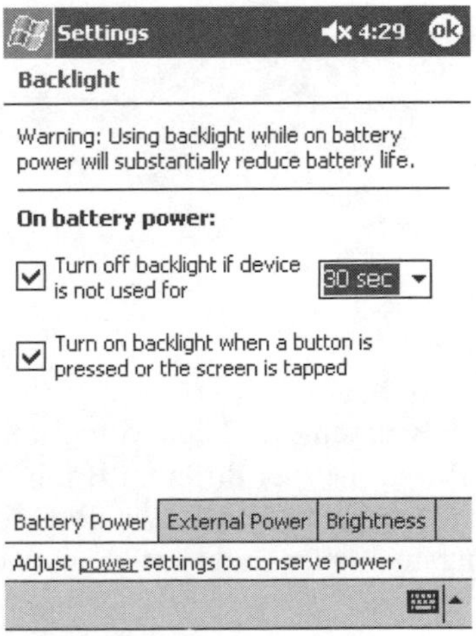

FIGURE 7-11   The Battery Power tab for monitoring your iPAQ's configuration when running on battery

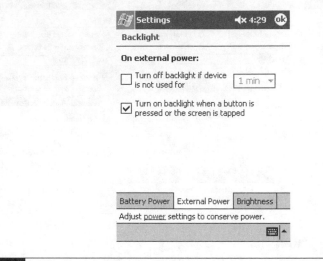

FIGURE 7-12   The External Power tab for monitoring your iPAQ's configuration when
running on external power

The External Power tab, shown in Figure 7-12, is used to configure the same settings as the
Battery Power tab, except when the iPAQ is running on external power.

The last tab, the Brightness tab, differs depending on which model of iPAQ you have. If you
have a 36*xx* or 37*xx* series iPAQ, the tab will appear as shown in Figure 7-13. There are six options
for brightness levels, and a Power Usage graphic is displayed on the right. The following options are
available:

- Automatic
- Super Bright
- High Bright
- Med Bright
- Low Bright
- Power Save

The Power Save option will simply turn the backlight completely off. This setting will conserve
the most battery life out of your iPAQ. The four different Bright settings are simply different
levels of brightness. The top option, Automatic, allows the iPAQ to choose the brightness level
automatically. This is done by using an ambient light sensor, which is located to the left of the
Compaq logo. The iPAQ will brighten the display in dark environments and turn it off in bright
environments.

As we mentioned, the Brightness tab differs significantly on the 38*xx*, 39*xx*, 54*xx*, and H1910
series iPAQs. Figure 7-14 illustrates the Brightness tab on the 38*xx* and 39*xx* series iPAQs; you

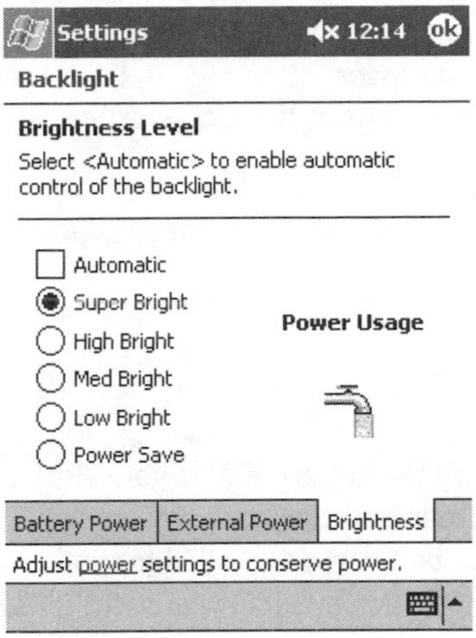

FIGURE 7-13   The Brightness tab on the 36*xx* and 37*xx* series iPAQ for controlling the brightness of your iPAQ's screen

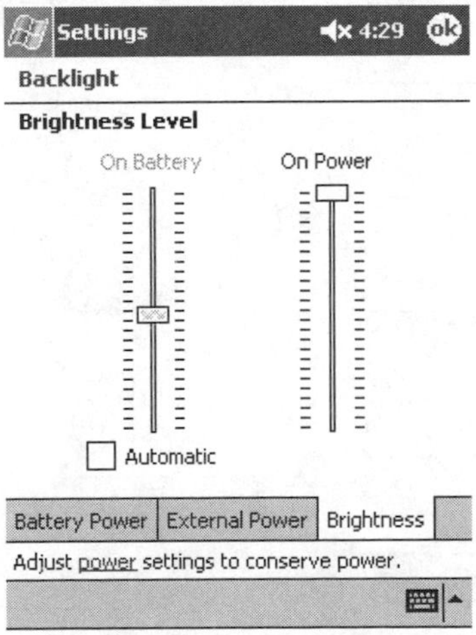

FIGURE 7-14   The Brightness tab on the 38*xx* and 39*xx* series iPAQ is very different from the previous versions.

can choose the brightness levels differently for battery or external power. It also offers many more levels of brightness. As with the 36xx and 37xx series iPAQs, an automatic option is available, and it too uses an ambient sensor.

On the H1910 and the 54xx series iPAQs, these tabs differ greatly again, as shown in Figure 7-15.

TIP *You can quickly turn the backlight on or off by pressing and holding the Power button.*

Emergency Power

Several solutions exist for extending the battery life of your iPAQ. We examine three different solutions in this section, although many others exist.

The first product that you should be aware of is called Instant Power (**www.instant-power.com**). This solution is unique in that it uses a zinc-air cell to charge the iPAQ. The zinc-air cell is stored in a sealed bag. When you need to charge your iPAQ, simply remove the cell from the bag and plug it into the iPAQ. The cell will then start to react with the air and produce enough power to charge the iPAQ three times. When you are done with the cell, simply store it in a special bag until the next time you need to use it. It remains usable in the bag for two to three months.

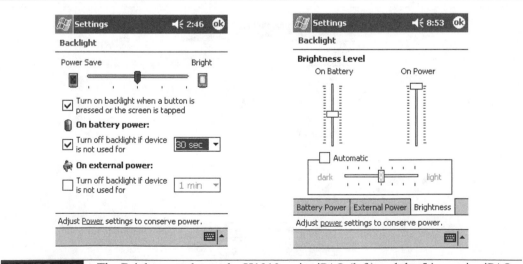

FIGURE 7-15   The Brightness tabs on the H1910 series iPAQ (left) and the 54xx series iPAQ (right) are once again different from the previous versions.

The second product is not specifically a battery product, but a dual CompactFlash expansion sleeve. We mention it here because it has removable batteries. This capability has always been lacking with the iPAQ and is finally available with the Nexian Dual CF and Power Pak for the iPAQ (**www.nexian.com**).

The final product covered here is a new battery for the iPAQ that replaces the existing one. To install this battery, you have to open your iPAQ (possibly voiding your warranty, but then again, if it was under warranty and your battery failed, you would probably send it back to Compaq). This battery also has a vibrate option, which means you can be silently notified by your iPAQ when events such as appointments take place. This do-it-yourself battery is available from **www.kingrex.net**. More on these extra add-ons in Chapter 15.

Modifying the Processor Speed

The new XScale processors can scale their speed to conserve battery power or to allow you to choose the best battery-to-speed ratio for your needs. Shortly after the release of the H1910, which was published as using the 200-MHz XScale processor, it became known that the processor within the device could actually be clocked to 300 MHz. This is known as *overclocking*. Before long, some applications started to appear that allowed you to modify the speed of the H1910 to take advantage of this extra power. A version is also available to overclock your 39*xx* and 54*xx* series iPAQs to 500 MHz.

CAUTION   *Using some of these tools may void your device's warranty or damage the device. The authors of this book are not responsible for any damages that may occur with the use of these programs.*

Although this might seem like a good idea at first, read the caution just before this paragraph. If you are okay with that caution, read it again! If you are really okay with it, you may proceed.

At the writing of this book, four different products existed that allowed you to overclock your XScale iPAQs:

- XCPUScalar (**http://immiersoft.pocketmatrix.com/**)
- Pocket Hack Master (**http://www.pockethackmaster.com/**)
- Clear Speed (**http://www.revolution.cx/**)
- XScaleCtrl (**http://wince.wibble-wobble.com/xscalectrl/**)

Search some of the Pocket PC Software sites (such as Handango and PocketGear) with the "Overclock" keyword for downloads and more information on these products.

Chapter 8

Secure Your iPAQ Pocket PC

How to…

- Secure your iPAQ with a password
- Upgrade the built-in iPAQ security
- Use hardware security products with your iPAQ
- Sign into your iPAQ with your signature

By now, you'll have gotten a sense of the power of the iPAQ. It is more than a hand-held PDA; it is a hand-held computer. It offers laptop/desktop–like capabilities in many arenas for a fraction of the cost. There is, however, one problem with it. It is portable.

"Why is that a bad thing?" you might ask. Because the iPAQ is so portable and powerful, you will probably use it all the time, which increases the chance that you will lose it or it will be stolen. Particularly if you are storing sensitive data, such as bank account numbers, personal documents, lists of passwords or PINs (personal identification numbers), and correspondence on your iPAQ, you will want to ensure that no one can access that information. How can you make your iPAQ more secure? It's easy, if you take some simple precautions.

This chapter will discuss some of the tools (both built-in and third-party) that can be used to secure your iPAQ. Losing your iPAQ will always be an inconvenience, but you can make sure it isn't a disaster.

Using the Built-In Security Tools

All iPAQs have a built-in password utility, which you can access on the Personal tab of the Settings window, shown in Figure 8-1. To open the Settings window, select Start | Settings.

The Password application will look different and have different capabilities depending on which version of the Pocket PC operating system you have (which is not necessarily determined by which iPAQ you have). The version that shipped with the original Pocket PC operating system (now called Pocket PC 2000) was very basic in its function. You were simply able to enter a four-digit PIN-type password to secure your iPAQ (as shown in Figure 8-2). As you can imagine, if someone was going to go to all the trouble of stealing your iPAQ, then a few hours in front of the television guessing which of the 10,000 combinations you chose is not a huge deal. To avoid this scenario, Microsoft implemented a system where after five tries, the timing between entries would double. Every failed entry would cause it to double again. This means that after 15 failed tries, you would have to wait 2 minutes before you could try again, and that to try 50 combinations would take a full day.

To set a password, simply launch the Password utility, enter a four-digit number, and reset the device. The next time you power-on the iPAQ, you will notice a similar keypad displayed on the screen, at which point, you will need to enter the password to gain access to the iPAQ. If you own a Pocket PC 2000 iPAQ and would like a more secure password utility, consider the strong password protection offered by Microsoft's Password PowerToy, available at **http://www.microsoft.com/mobile/pocketpc/downloads/powertoys.asp.**

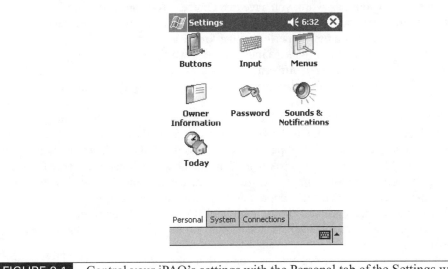

8

FIGURE 8-1 Control your iPAQ's settings with the Personal tab of the Settings window.

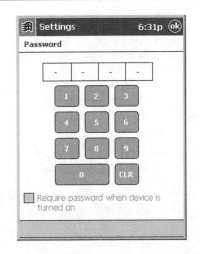

FIGURE 8-2 Set your password for a Pocket PC 2000 iPAQ through the Password dialog box.

Should you ever forget your password, you have two choices. You can sit in front of the television and try to guess your password, or you can perform a hard reset of the device. (Check your iPAQ users manual on how to perform a hard reset.)

With Pocket PC 2002, Microsoft provides a much more powerful Password utility. As Figure 8-3 illustrates, you are given three different options in this new dialog box. You can choose to not have a password, use a four-digit password, or use a strong alphanumeric password.

The first option of the dialog box is straightforward. No password is set, and therefore anyone can access the device. The second option is the same as the one offered by the Pocket PC 2000 operating system. You must enter a four-digit password to access the iPAQ, as shown in Figure 8-4.

The final option enables you to choose a password that uses an alphanumeric sequence (similar to what you would use on the Internet or at work). As you can see in Figure 8-5, you use the keyboard (or another mode of data entry) to choose and confirm your password.

No matter what type of password you choose with Pocket PC 2002, if you forget it or lose it, you will need to perform a hard reset of the iPAQ to access your data, just as you would with earlier versions of the operating system.

Once you enable any of the password options, you will be presented with a password prompt (shown in Figure 8-6) when you attempt to synchronize with your desktop via ActiveSync. As you can imagine, all this security would be for naught if all you had to do was sync the data over to a desktop.

FIGURE 8-3   On a Pocket PC 2002 iPAQ, the Password dialog box is slightly different.

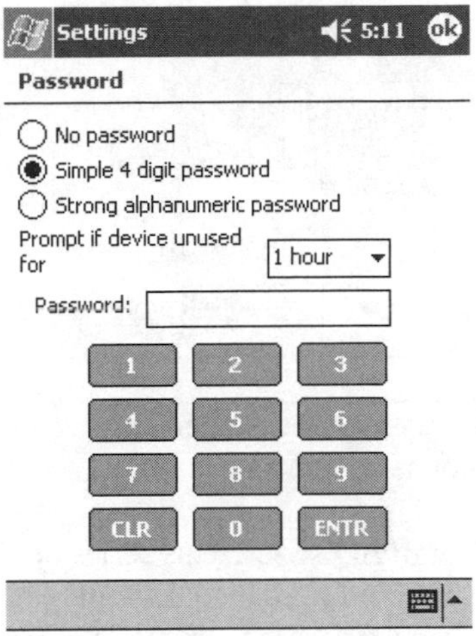

FIGURE 8-4   Use the numeric keypad in the Password dialog box to choose a four-digit password.

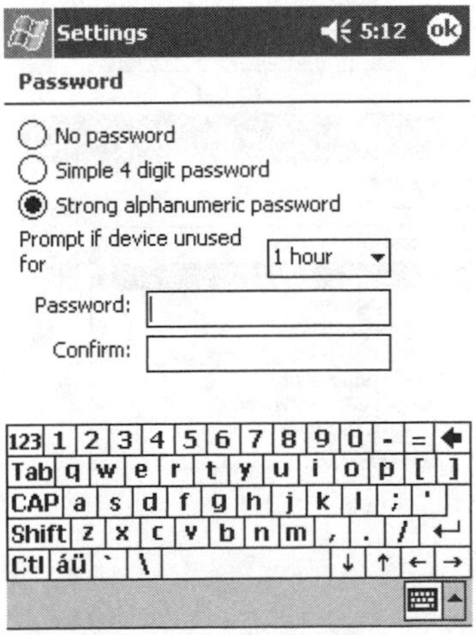

FIGURE 8-5   If you select the Strong Alphanumeric Password option, a keyboard will appear that you can use to enter your password.

Password Protected

This mobile device is password protected. In order to connect to the device, you must enter its password.

Password: [   ]

☐ Save password

[OK]

FIGURE 8-6   If your iPAQ has a password assigned to it, you will have to enter it before ActiveSync can connect to it.

All of this changed with the 54xx iPAQ series. This series of iPAQ devices has a built-in fingerprint scanner. You can therefore configure it so that only your fingerprint can unlock the device, giving you a much stronger way to secure your data. Since this requires extra configuration steps, we discuss it in its own section, next.

Securing the 54xx iPAQ Series

The password control panel on the 54xx iPAQ series, as shown in Figure 8-7, gives you much more control over how you can secure your iPAQ. Before you can use some of the more advanced security features, such as Fingerprint Recognition, the device must be trained.

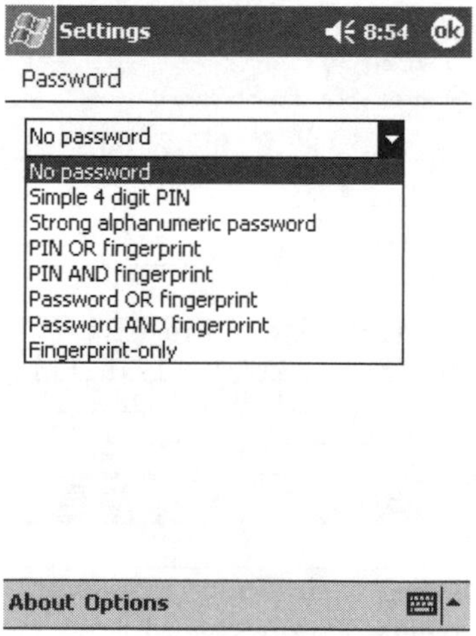

Settings   ◀€ 8:54   **ok**

Password

No password ▼

No password
Simple 4 digit PIN
Strong alphanumeric password
PIN OR fingerprint
PIN AND fingerprint
Password OR fingerprint
Password AND fingerprint
Fingerprint-only

About Options

FIGURE 8-7   Configuring the Password control panel with the 54xx Series iPAQ

The following options are available when configuring the 54*xx* iPAQ series:

- No password
- Simple 4 digit PIN
- Strong alphanumeric password
- PIN OR fingerprint
- PIN AND fingerprint
- Password OR fingerprint
- Password AND fingerprint
- Fingerprint-only

If you choose to configure the Fingerprint Recognition, you will need to first train it by having it scan your finger successfully at least six out of eight times. A successful scan is shown in Figure 8-8, while an unsuccessful one is shown in Figure 8-9.

Once you successfully scan your fingerprint, you will need to have the device test the scans. You must get seven successful scans before the finger can be stored. You can configure up to ten fingers (choose the finger to use by tapping the correct finger on the hand image on the right). Figure 8-10 illustrates a successful reading of your finger.

> NOTE   *We have found that the best way to scan a finger is to place the finger being scanned on the D-Link pad and to slowly pull the finger down past the scanner to the bottom of the iPAQ.*

8

FIGURE 8-8   A successful fingerprint scan

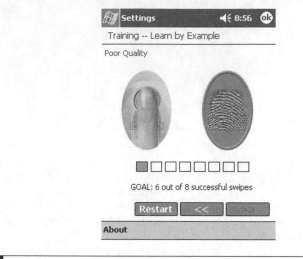

FIGURE 8-9 An unsuccessful fingerprint scan

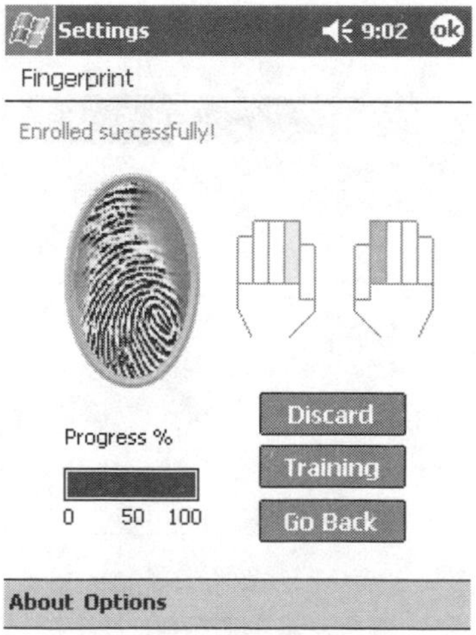

FIGURE 8-10 A successful reading of a fingerprint

Extending the Built-In Security

For many people, iPAQ's built-in password security is just not good enough. If you are one of those people, several software and hardware products are available to serve your needs. Two extremely similar software products, Sign-On by CIC and PDALok by Penflow, enable you to not only use the PIN-type password, but also your signature to secure your iPAQ. The hardware products offered by Biocentric Solutions enable you to use your fingerprint for iPAQ security.

Sign-On

Sign-On by CIC (**www.cic.com**) is a security utility that enables you to use your signature as well as a password to lock your iPAQ. After you install Sign-On, the Sign-On icon replaces the Password icon on the Personal tab of the Settings window, as shown in Figure 8-11. (Don't worry, the Password icon reappears if or when you uninstall the program.)

Before you can use Sign-On's signature feature, you need to "enroll" your signature, that is, train the application to recognize it, by writing your signature on the screen three times, as you can see in Figure 8-12. You can then test the signature, as well as set a four-digit PIN-type password for ActiveSync (and, if desired, startup).

PDALok

PDALok from Penflow (**www.pdalok.com**) is very similar to the Sign-On product. The only real difference is that PDALok requires that you write the signature six times before the application

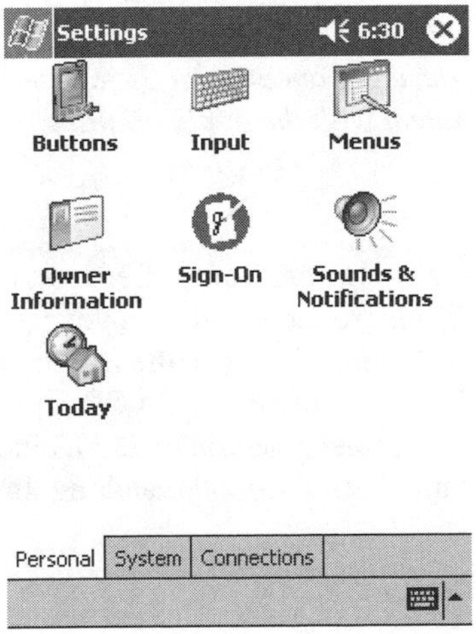

FIGURE 8-11   Once Sign-On is installed on your iPAQ, an icon will appear on the Settings window.

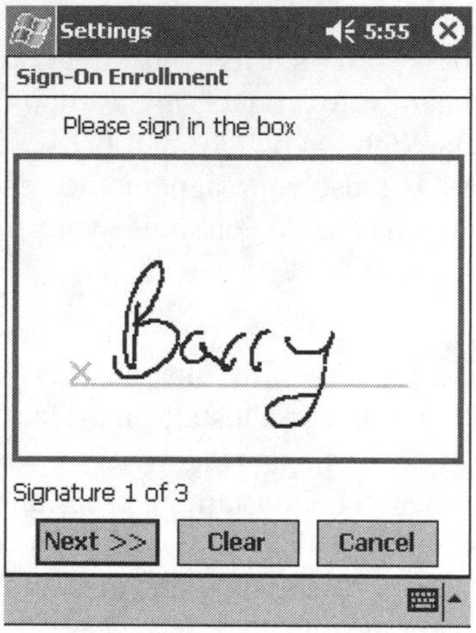

FIGURE 8-12   Enrolling your signature with Sign-On

will enroll it (see Figure 8-13). As with Sign-On, the PDALok icon replaces the Password icon in the Settings window.

> **TIP**   *Before you even think about using one of these tools, make sure that you have completely backed up your iPAQ. After configuring PDALok to recognize my signature, I tried unsuccessfully to unlock my iPAQ—although the signature was validated, the program would not let me into the device. I am unclear as to whether this was a conflict with the operating system or a problem with the application.*

BioSentry and BioHub

Biocentric Solutions (**www.biocentricsolutions.com**) offers two different hardware options for the iPAQ: BioSentry and BioHub. Both products will scan your fingerprint and grant you access based on the fingerprint. The only difference between the BioSentry and BioHub solutions is that the former is an iPAQ expansion sleeve and the latter is a CF card–based solution. The BioSentry sleeve has a built-in CompactFlash slot to enable you to add memory storage to your iPAQ. Both offer 56-bit, triple DES encryption and half-a-second matching time.

Browsing the Internet Securely

Many of us now rely on the Internet for help with our day-to-day tasks. Just as e-mail has become a must for many professionals today, Internet banking has become a "can't live without it."

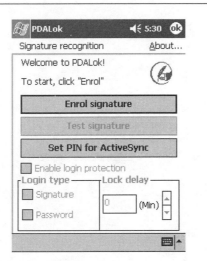

FIGURE 8-13   Enrolling your signature with PDALok

The problem with Internet banking from the iPAQ is that out of the box, Pocket Internet Explorer (PIE) is not running at 128-bit encryption. Without this level of encryption, most banks (at least the reputable ones) will not allow you to access sensitive information such as your account information. The same is true for just about any purchases that you may complete online.

If your iPAQ has the Pocket PC 2002 operating system (or has been upgraded to it), you will not need to install the High Encryption Pack because PIE will already support it.

NOTE   *Microsoft was aware of this shortcoming of PIE and released the Microsoft High Encryption Pack for Pocket PC v1.0. The High Encryption Pack (which is available as a free download from **www.microsoft.com/mobile/pocketpc/downloads/ssl128.asp**) extends the functionality of PIE to allow it to encrypt/decrypt data using 128-bit encryption. You will only need this download if your iPAQ runs the Pocket PC 2000 operating system.*

Now when you navigate to a secure site, you will be allowed to perform the desired transactions. If you need to find out whether the connection used is a secure one, simply check the properties of the page (choose View | Properties) from PIE. You will notice that in the Security field, the page will be listed as Secure, as shown in Figure 8-14.

Another indication that you are on a secure web page is the Security prompt message that appears when you try to leave a secure page to go to an insecure page. This message box, shown in Figure 8-15, warns you that you are leaving a secure connection and gives you the opportunity to change your mind.

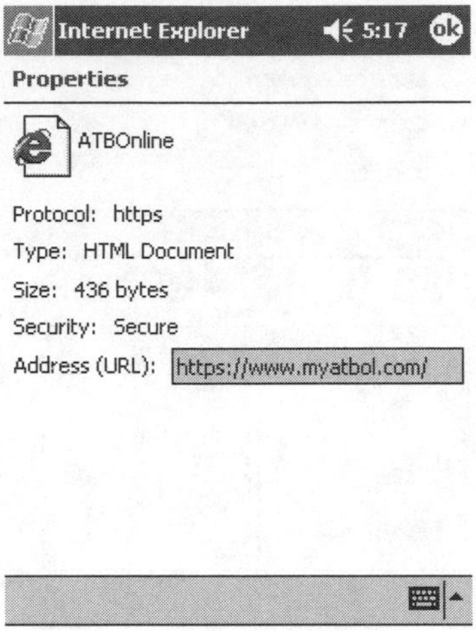

FIGURE 8-14 You can check the web page's Properties sheet to determine whether it is secure.

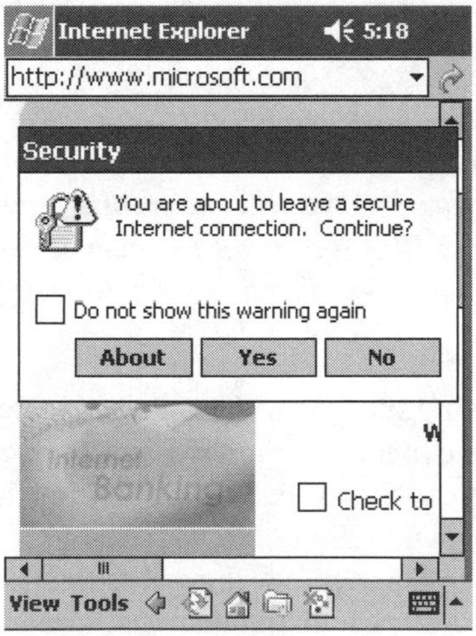

FIGURE 8-15 The Security prompt includes options to continue leaving a secure page or to return to it.

Securing Your Personal Data

When it comes to storing personal information on your iPAQ securely, three products perform the task perfectly: eWallet from Ilium Software (**www.iliumsoft.com**), CodeWallet Professional from Developer One (**www.developerone.com**), and FlexWallet from Two Peaks Software (**www.twopeaks.com**).

These products, known as *electronic wallets,* offer similar functions; they all enable you to store information about your bank, credit card, and frequent flyer accounts; information about insurance, health, and prescriptions; emergency numbers; and other personal data. Each account is treated as a card kept in your electronic wallet. You can easily secure all the cards, some cards, or the different categories of your wallet. Figure 8-16 shows eWallet and CodeWallet Professional in a side-by-side comparison.

You will immediately notice the similarities between the two products. One difference that stands out is that with CodeWallet Professional any locked category or card appears in red. This enables you to see at a glance which are password protected and which are not.

eWallet includes the following card types:

Bank account	General purpose	Picture card
Calling card	Health numbers	Prescription
Car info	ID card	Serial number
Clothes sizes	Insurance policy	Social Security number
Combination lock	Lens prescription	Software serial number
Contact	Library card	Voice mail info
Credit card	Membership info	Voter card
Driver's license	Note card	Web site
Emergency numbers	Passport info	
Free form	Password	

CodeWallet Professional includes these card types:

Bank account	Library card	Travel: flight detail
Calling card contact	Local government	Travel: flight summary
Contact favorites	Lock combination	Travel: ground transportation
Credit card	Notes	Travel: hotel
Dining: restaurant	Online shopping account	Travel: long-term parking
Dining: take-out	Passport	Travel: places
Emergency numbers	Password	Vehicle: dealer
Event	Personal insurance	Vehicle: driver's license
Exercise	Prescription	Vehicle: maintenance

Gift ideas	Security System	Vehicle: profile
Home services	Social Security card	Voice mail codes
ID/Account number	Software license/key	Warranty
Insurance policy	Stock/Investment	Web favorites
Internet service provider	Travel: car rental	Web site

Both products have a desktop component to them. eWallet's desktop companion (shown in Figure 8-17) is included with the eWallet suite. The desktop version offers all the functionality of the iPAQ version, plus the ability to export records, back up the database, compact the database, and synchronize it with the iPAQ version.

The desktop version of CodeWallet Professional (shown in Figure 8-18) has all the features of its iPAQ counterpart, except that it can back up the database, export it to a text file, and create custom cards. When creating a custom card, you have the ability to choose all the fields and properties for the new card.

You can purchase the Pocket PC and the desktop versions of these applications separately or together in a Mobile Sync Pack.

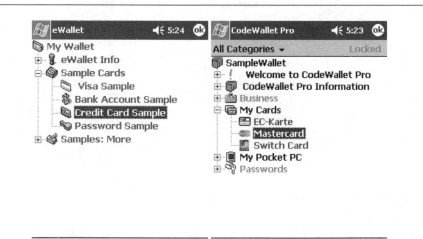

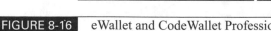

FIGURE 8-16   eWallet and CodeWallet Professional let you store your important card information securely on your iPAQ.

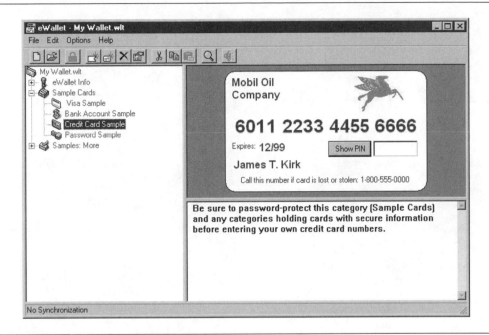

FIGURE 8-17   Instead of adding cards on your iPAQ, you can use eWallet on the desktop.

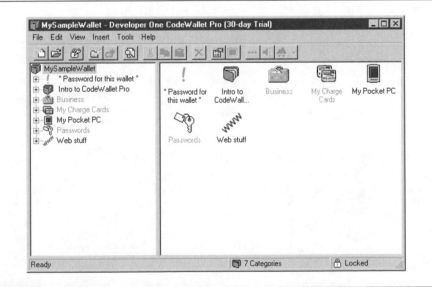

FIGURE 8-18   Simplify your card entry process by using CodeWallet Professional desktop edition.

Chapter 9

Connect Wirelessly with Your iPAQ Pocket PC

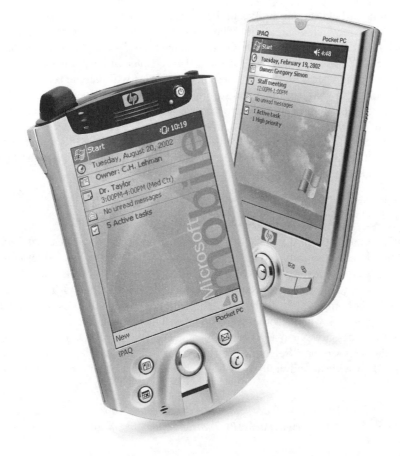

How to...

- Set up your iPAQ to connect to a wireless network
- Select from the various wireless networks available
- Choose the sleeves and cards that are right for you
- Install and configure the drivers for Sierra Wireless and Novatel wireless modems
- Configure and use the built-in networking capabilities of your iPAQ
- Send and receive e-mail, chat, and surf the Internet through a wireless connection
- Use a local wired or wireless connection
- Configure Bluetooth with your iPAQ

The future of all hand-held computing lies in the arena of wireless connectivity. Eventually, every iPAQ will have built-in wireless capability. The most recent addition to the iPAQ line, the 5450, contains both built-in WiFi and Bluetooth wireless connectivity, while the two previous versions (the 3870 and the 3970) had only built-in Bluetooth. This chapter will explain and evaluate different methods for connecting your iPAQ to a wireless network. This will include real-time sending and receiving of e-mail from your handheld and surfing the Internet with Pocket Internet Explorer. In addition, we will discuss third-party software that can provide even more value on a wirelessly enabled iPAQ, such as wireless network systems administration. This chapter will also include an assessment of the different combinations of hardware that can be used to achieve a wireless connection from PCMCIA cards (CDPD, CDMA, CDMA 1xRTT, GSM, GPRS, and so on), and CompactFlash modems.

Connecting to Wireless Networks

Before the 3870, none of the iPAQs had built-in capability to access a wireless network. The 3870 and 3970 only have the ability to access a Bluetooth wireless network. Bluetooth is short range and has yet to really take hold in North American. What this means is that to connect your iPAQ to a wireless network, you will need to add some external ingredients. The newest iPAQ, the 5450, includes not only Bluetooth, but also 802.11b wireless capabilities. If you want to use a private wireless network with the other iPAQs, you will need to acquire an 802.11b wireless LAN card and the necessary expansion sleeve to connect it to your iPAQ. Your options for this are covered in the next section, "Selecting the Hardware for Your Wireless Connection." The 802.11b cards will provide a bandwidth of 11 Mbps, but you must be within range of your wireless access points.

NOTE   *Currently, the iPAQ H1910 does not have any wireless capabilities. That, however, might change. Check **www.PocketPCTools.com** for any updates to the H1910's wireless capabilities.*

If you want to use one of the larger wireless networks that circle the globe, you will need to identify which wireless provider you will be using. Selecting your wireless provider will depend on where you reside, where you plan on using your wireless card, and how much bandwidth you need. Each wireless network carrier uses different protocols that have different transmission speeds. Without going into too much detail, Table 9-1 contains a comparison of the protocols that you can consider. For a full list of which carriers provide which protocols, their coverage, hardware requirements, and more, check **www.pocketpctools.com**.

Protocol	Bandwidth	Details
CDPD	19.2 Kbps	This protocol enjoys the widest coverage in North America at present. It is slow but fairly reliable. Good for getting your mail and running applications, but not particularly practical for Internet surfing or e-mail with large attachments. It is, however, being phased out by GPRS and 1xRTT.
CDMA	14.4 Kbps	The CDMA protocol works like a standard dial-up modem on a PC, where you enter the number to dial, and you must have an existing account with that ISP to get Internet access. This protocol is also largely limited to North America.
GSM	9.6 Kbps–14.4 Kbps	GSM is the dominant protocol used almost everywhere else in the world. It has extensive coverage throughout Europe and Asia. It will work much the same as CDMA, with the need to dial up an existing ISP account to get Internet access.
GPRS	56 Kbps–118 Kbps	GPRS is the digital and data upgrade from GSM. Most GSM providers have now moved to GPRS. The coverage is now very good in Europe, Asia, and in North America. GPRS is configured in *channels*. Each channel supports 14.4 Kbps of data traffic. The carrier can configure the number of channels, up to eight, with each connection. Most carriers are currently configuring four channels. Each channel supports data in one direction, so current GPRS offerings usually download data at 33.6 Kbps (three channels) and upload data at 14.4 Kbps (one channel). Alternatively, some carriers configure the service with 28.8 Kbps (two channels) in each direction. Both of these are called 56-Kbps service by the carriers. When the carriers choose to upgrade to eight-channel service, it will become a 118-Kbps service.
CDMA 1xRTT	56 Kbps–384 Kbps	CDMA 1x, or CDMA ONE service is an upgrade from current CDMA and CDPD networks. It is similar to GPRS and can be configured up to 384 Kbps, but initial offerings will likely be 56 Kbps.

TABLE 9-1 Wireless Network Protocols

Selecting the Hardware for Your Wireless Connection

After choosing the provider that you will use for your wireless connection, you will need to choose the hardware that you will connect with. You might use two different protocols. For example, you might use an 802.11b card while you are in the office because it has much faster bandwidth and no airtime charges. But when you leave the office, you may plug in a CDPD card connected to AT&T, which has much lower bandwidth, but much greater coverage.

In this section we will look at the different hardware that you might select. In the next section will we show you how to set up the Novatel Wireless G100.

Most of the wireless modems and LAN cards that you can choose from come in the form of a PCMCIA, or PC card. These cards are interchangeable with your laptop standard, which is convenient when you want to share one wireless access account between your laptop and your iPAQ. Also, a number of CompactFlash cards are emerging that support the 802.11b standard for wireless LAN and the Bluetooth standard for PANs (personal area networks). Table 9-2 presents the options by protocol. Note that we only cover a few of the newest products from each vendor for each protocol, rather than all the products. Each vendor, however, may have more than one

Vendor and Model	Description
CDPD	
Sierra Wireless AirCard 300 for Handhelds	Sierra offers a version of this card for handhelds only, and one for handhelds and laptops. The primary difference is the power consumption of the cards. More information can be found at **www.sierrawireless.com ProductsOrdering/300.html**.
Novatel Wireless Merlin Platinum Special Edition	This card is specifically designed for use in both handhelds and laptops and will drain less battery power from your iPAQ than the standard Merlin card. Maximum connection speed is 19.2 Kbps. More information can be found at **www.novatelwireless.com/pcproducts/ merlinplatinumSE.htm**.
Enfora Pocket Spider	This is a CompactFlash CDPD modem that will work with your iPAQ CompactFlash expansion sleeve. More information can be found at **www.enfora.com**.
CDMA	
Sierra Wireless AirCard 510	This card is meant for both handhelds and laptops. It uses the CDMA protocol, which allows you to dial up an ISP with whom you already have a dial-up account. Check with your provider, but some of the CDMA providers, such as Bell Mobility in Canada, provide their own ISP dial-up service to their AirCard 510 customers. More information can be found at **www.sierrawireless.com/ProductsOrdering/510nb.html**.
Others	Note that the dual-band CDMA 1xRTT wireless modems described next can support the standard CDMA protocol and will likely be a better buy given that all CDMA networks are expected to upgrade to CDMA 2000 in the near future.

TABLE 9-2   Wireless Modems and LAN Cards, by Protocol

Vendor and Model	Description
CDMA 1xRTT	
Sierra Wireless AirCard 550	This card operates on the CDMA 2000 networks, which have now launched in North America. This version of the card offers single-band access to the North American PCS network. The theoretical top-end data speed of this card is 153 Kbps. More information can be found at **http://www.sierrawireless.com/ProductsOrdering/AC5501xRTT.html**.
Sierra Wireless AirCard 555	This is the dual-band version of the AirCard 550, which will operate on international CDMA 1xRTT networks as well as the North American networks. This modem can also connect to the circuit-switched CDMA networks at 14.4 Kbps. More information can be found at **http://www.sierrawireless.com/ProductsOrdering/AC5551xRTT.html**.
Novatel Wireless Merlin C201	This is a dual-band CDMA 1xRTT card with essentially the same functionality as the Sierra Wireless AirCard 555. One of the nice features of this card is that it incorporates an integrated antenna, which means no long antenna to break, lose, or get in your way. More information can be found at **www.novatelwireless.com/pcproducts/merlinC201.html**.
GSM/GPRS	
Sierra Wireless AirCard 710	This is a single-band GSM/GPRS card that is suitable for North American usage only. One of the nicest features of this card is that the antenna is retractable and is stored internally, making it less likely to get lost or damaged. More information can be found at **www.sierrawireless.com/ProductsOrdering/AC710-750GSM.html**.
Sierra Wireless AirCard 750	This is the tri-band version of the AirCard 710 and can function on any of the GSM/GPRS networks in the world. Rather than a retractable antenna, it features an external hinged antenna. More information can be found at **www.sierrawireless.com/ProductsOrdering/AC710-750GSM.html**.
Novatel Wireless Merlin G100	This is a single-band GSM/GPRS card that is suitable for North American usage only. It features up to 53.6 Kbps throughput in areas featuring GPRS coverage, and 14.4 Kbps in areas offering only GSM coverage. More information can be found at **www.novatelwireless.com/pcproducts/g100.html**.
Novatel Wireless Merlin G201	This card is similar to the G100 described earlier, only with dual-band capability. The dual-band GPRS PC card for the 900-MHz and 1800-MHz bands can be used for GSM/GPRS networks in Europe, Asia, Africa, and the Middle East. More information can be found at **www.novatelwireless.com/pcproducts/merlin201.html**.
Novatel Wireless Merlin G301	This is the tri-band version. The tri-band PC card is used for worldwide access to e-mail, the Internet, and corporate databases on the GSM/GPRS 900-MHz, 1800-MHz, and 1900-MHz bands. More information can be found at **www.novatelwireless.com/pcproducts/index.html**.

TABLE 9-2   Wireless Modems and LAN Cards, by Protocol *(continued)*

9

Vendor and Model	Description
Option Wireless Globetrotter	This is a universal tri-band GSM/GPRS card that is suitable for worldwide use. It also has a headset plug-in, which enables you to use your iPAQ as your cell phone and make voice calls. The antenna is fully internally retractable. More information can be found at **www.option.com**.

TABLE 9-2   Wireless Modems and LAN Cards, by Protocol *(continued)*

solution for a given protocol. Also, the two main players in this field, Sierra Wireless and Novatel Wireless, will probably have a solution for the wireless network that meets your needs.

Other Hardware

Of course, to make any of the previously mentioned modems work, you will require an expansion sleeve. All the expansion sleeves are discussed in detail in Chapter 13. You can get an expansion sleeve from Compaq that includes a built-in GSM/GPRS modem.

Setting Up Your Wireless Modem

In this section we will show you how to install and configure one of your wireless cards. We will explain one GPRS card from Novatel Wireless. The other cards and vendors will be similar.

Setting Up a Novatel Wireless Merlin G100: GSM/GPRS

The Novatel Wireless Merlin G100 is a Type II PCMCIA card. This means that you will need an expansion sleeve for your iPAQ that supports PCMCIA cards. Either the single or the dual sleeve will work. If you have all the equipment, then follow these steps:

1. Slide your iPAQ into the sleeve until it is firmly seated. You should see a window with the message "Initializing Expansion Pack" on the screen for a moment while your iPAQ and your sleeve set up their communication. *Do not* insert the wireless modem until after you have installed the drivers.

2. Connect your iPAQ to your PC with your ActiveSync cable, and make sure there is an active connection. Once this is established, you are ready to install the drivers onto your iPAQ.

3. Install the necessary drivers for your Merlin. These likely came on a CD-ROM with your card, but if not, you can download the latest drivers from the Novatel Wireless web site (**www.novatelwireless.com**). Once you have the install program, run it, and the install should initiate through your ActiveSync connection to your iPAQ.

4. Insert your SIM (Subscriber Identity Module) chip into your Merlin G100. The SIM chip is a piece of plastic smaller than a postage stamp that identifies you to the network. It will have been provided to you by your carrier. This automates communication method setup.

Once you are all set up, you just need to connect to your network. The GPRS Modem Manager, shown in Figure 9-1, should launch by default, but if it doesn't, you can launch it from the Programs folder. The status window will enable you to see whose network you are going to connect to, or are already on, what the service type is, what carrier is managing your signal, and the strength of the signal in your location.

At the bottom of the dialog box is a menu. You can use this menu to initiate a connection or disconnection, or to see the properties of the modem, as shown in Figure 9-2.

The Roaming tab will give you the option to set the modem to automatically roam onto any GPRS network when you are away from your home network. Or you can require manual network selection where it will find all the available networks, and then let you select from the list of networks to connect to one.

Use the Tools menu to get a detailed history of activity on the modem and find out useful statistical information such as the percentage of errors encountered. You can set modem options and also configure the connection manager in case you have multiple GPRS accounts. For example, I might be using the AT&T network in North America, but have a separate account with MMo2 when I am in the United Kingdom. I can configure the connection manager with the relevant information on both networks. By having the two, I will likely reduce my overall costs by paying fewer roaming charges.

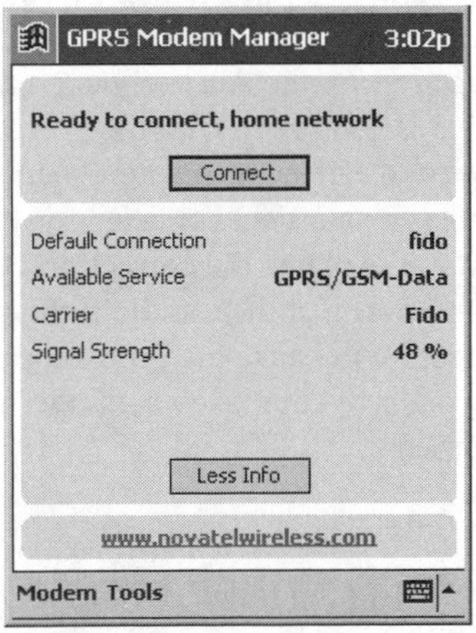

FIGURE 9-1   Use the GPRS Modem Manager dialog box to establish a connection with your GPRS network.

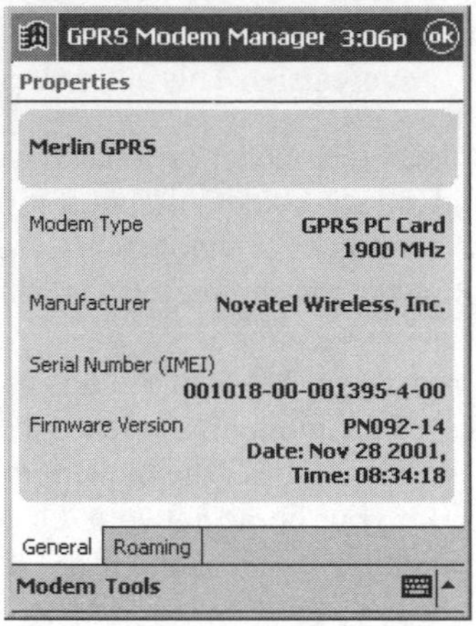

FIGURE 9-2 The modem properties will tell you all the specific attributes of the modem you are using.

Sending and Receiving E-mail Wirelessly

By far the most useful thing that average users can do today with a wireless connection is send and receive e-mail from their iPAQ in real time. This does not happen from the ActiveSync folder on your handheld where we worked with e-mail in Chapter 5. You will need to set up a standard Internet e-mail service (or set up an enterprise Internet replication strategy with IIS) to send and receive real-time e-mail. I have stopped using the ActiveSync e-mail sync and instead use only an Internet connection. When my iPAQ is connected with the sync cable, it updates my mail using the Internet pass-through feature discussed earlier in Chapter 2 and works as well as the ActiveSync feature, but also updates through a wireless connection. For details on how to specifically set up a new e-mail service, refer to Chapter 5, which explains the correct process in detail.

Tapping the send-and-receive e-mail icon at the middle right of the toolbar at the bottom of the window, or the check new mail icon, will cause the Inbox application to update your mailbox through the wireless connection. If you have composed messages that are sitting in your Outbox, they will be sent through the same process.

TIP

We recommend using the IMAP4 protocol wherever possible because it is a much more efficient protocol than POP3, meaning it will perform better across your low-bandwidth wireless connection. IMAP4 also enables you to replicate and synchronize the folder structure of your e-mail.

Surfing Wirelessly with Pocket Internet Explorer

Your iPAQ will come preloaded with Pocket Internet Explorer. This is to allow you to browse web pages and surf the Internet while connected (either wirelessly or wired) to an Internet source. You may find surfing on your Pocket PC to be a less than satisfactory experience. This is largely due to three factors:

- **Low bandwidth**   The wireless modems that we use to surf the Internet are very low bandwidth. Even the latest GPRS and CDMA 1xRTT modems only provide a 53.6-Kbps connection, which is about the same as the best dial-up modem you can buy for your PC. Most web sites you will want to visit are optimized for the high-bandwidth connections that many of us now have at home and at the office. Maximizing the user experience on the desktop has resulted in a very poor user experience on the handheld.

- **Small screen**   iPAQs have very small screens, only a fraction of the size of the usual desktops, resulting in the need for a lot of scrolling to see the web page. Even with scrolling, many pages still come up formatted in an irregular fashion.

- **Early in the adoption cycle**   We are still very early in the adoption cycle of Pocket PCs. As more people get these devices, organizations with web sites will begin building multiple front-ends to their web site. In such a setup, the web site can automatically detect when you connect from your desktop, and provide a broadband-rich media user experience. And when you connect from a handheld, the web site can send you a stripped-down page with fewer graphics, formatted to fit your screen. Although this technology exists today, very few web sites have taken advantage of it. Expect to see this capability become much more common as time goes by, and for your hand-held surfing experience to improve.

When you first start up Pocket IE (by selecting it from the Start menu), it will take you to the default home page. This is a local page, not actually pulled from the Internet, with links to PocketPC.com, Compaq, MSN Mobile, and AvantGo. The interface of Pocket IE has a number of similar features to the full version of IE, as shown in Figure 9-3.

You can type any address you like in the Address bar and then tap the Go button to be taken to that site. The Back button will back you up to the last site you visited. By default, if you have been to a site before, Pocket IE will try to reuse the page from memory to save the download time. This can cause you to not get the most up-to-date information from sites that change frequently. Tapping the Refresh button will download the latest version of a page that you are viewing. The Home button will take you to your home page (you can designate your home page in the Options dialog box, discussed later in this section). The Hide Pictures button is very useful for sites that use a lot of graphics. Tapping this button will toggle between hiding or showing the graphics on a page. If they are hidden, they will not be downloaded, causing the page to be loaded much more quickly. If you are operating this way, but find that you want to see a particular graphic, you can tap and hold on the graphic and then choose Download from the shortcut menu to bring that one graphic down to your device. This gives you the power of choice to only view those graphics that are important to you.

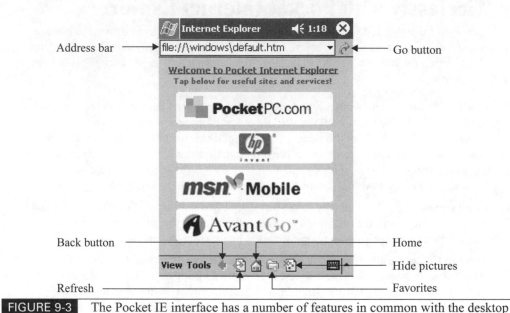

FIGURE 9-3   The Pocket IE interface has a number of features in common with the desktop version of IE.

The Favorites button will open the Favorites folder allowing you to jump to any sites you have bookmarked (you can synchronize these with your desktop IE through the ActiveSync settings, as discussed in Chapter 2). The Favorites folder is shown in Figure 9-4.

Tapping the Add/Delete tab at the bottom of the window will take you to a similar window where you can organize your favorites into folders, add new favorites, or delete ones that you no longer wish to keep in your list.

The View menu in the main Pocket IE window includes commands that enable you to change how the window appears:

- You can choose to hide or show the Address bar.

- You can also turn the Fit To Screen option on or off. By default this option is on, and IE will wrap text onto the next line to make it fit into the screen. If this option is off, IE will not try to make lines fit the screen, and you will have to use the horizontal scroll bar to move back and forth across the window.

- There are five commands under the View menu that enable you to select five different text sizes. This will allow you to display more or less text in the window. The more text you show, the less scrolling you will have to do, but the harder it will be to read.

- The History command opens a list of the previous pages you've visited in case you want to return to one of them.

FIGURE 9-4   Tapping the Favorites button will open your folder of favorite sites to visit. Tapping any of these sites will take you directly to that site.

9

■ The Properties command opens a window that displays the properties of the web page you are currently viewing, as shown next.

The Tools menu contains the following commands:

- **Send Link Via E-mail**   Sends the current URL link by composing a new message in the Inbox application.
- **Cut**   Cuts any selected text and places it on the clipboard.
- **Copy**   Copies any selected text to the clipboard.
- **Paste**   Pastes text from the clipboard into the document where the insertion point is currently positioned.
- **Select All Text**   Selects all the text on the page for you to copy onto the clipboard.
- **Options**   Enables you to configure options for Pocket IE, as described next.

Selecting the Options command opens the options dialog box, where you can set how you want Pocket IE to behave. This dialog box contains two tabs; one for general options and one for advanced options.

The General tab, shown in Figure 9-5, includes options for the following:

- **Home Page**   You can set which page you want to come up by default when you open Pocket Internet Explorer. To do this, you must surf to the page you want as your home page, then open the options dialog box and select Use Current.
- **History**   You can set how many days of past links you want saved to the History list and also can clear the history list with a click of a button.
- **Temporary Internet Files**   You can delete any stored temporary Internet files from memory.

The Advanced tab, shown in Figure 9-6, enables you to set options for the following:

- **Cookies**   You can choose whether to allow or deny cookies, and to clear cookies currently stored on your iPAQ.
- **Security Settings**   You can set the option to warn you when you are shifting from a secure page to one that is not secure.
- **Language**   You can set the default character set used by Pocket IE.

Instant Messaging and Chatting with Your iPAQ

If you are part of the massive online chatting craze, you will be happy to know that most online chat utilities have versions that will run on your wireless iPAQ, enabling you to chat while waiting in line at the grocery store, sitting in a dull meeting, or anywhere your wireless connection works! Here are some of the commonly used chat programs that you can use on your Pocket PC:

- **MSN Messenger**   This is built right into the full Pocket PC 2002 install, so you needn't install anything. We will show you how to access and set this up next.

FIGURE 9-5 Use the General tab of the options dialog box to set home page, history, and temporary file options.

9

FIGURE 9-6 The Advanced tab of the options dialog box enables you to set your preferences for cookies, security warnings, and default language.

- **AOL Instant Messenger (AIM)** This application was designed for Pocket PC 2000, not 2002, but appears to work fine in PPC 2002. For more information and to download the application, go to **http://www.aim.com/get_aim/win_ce/latest_wince.adp**.

- **ICQ** A client for the ICQ instant messenger can be downloaded from ICQ at **http://www.icq.com/download/ftp-pocketpc.html**.

- **Yahoo Instant Messenger** A full Pocket PC client can be downloaded at **http://messenger.yahoo.com/messenger/ce/downloads_ce_msgr.html**.

With MSN Messenger, start the program by tapping on the MSN Messenger link in the Programs folder. This will open a prompt where you will enter your sign-in name and password, as shown here:

You can choose to retain the password by selecting the Save Password check box, so you won't have to sign in each time you launch Messenger. Tapping Sign In will take you to the main MSN Messenger window, as shown in Figure 9-7.

You can initiate a chat with another person by tapping on his or her name. You can respond to a request to chat as they pop up on your screen. If you enter a chat, you will be taken to the chat window, as shown in Figure 9-8.

The chat window includes three menus at the bottom of the screen: Tools, Chats, and My Text.

The Tools menu includes the following commands:

- **Sign In / Sign Out** Signs you in or out of Messenger.

- **My Status** Allows you to change your status to Online, Busy, Be Right Back, Away, On The Phone, Out To Lunch, or Appear Offline.

- **Add A Contact** Takes you to a window to enter the information for a new contact to add to your list.

- **Edit My Text Messages** Allows you to create your own custom messages, which will then be available in the My Text menu.

- **Invite** Invites an additional person into your chat.

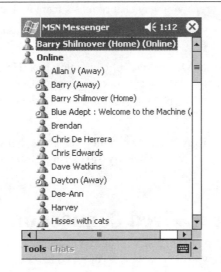

FIGURE 9-7   The MSN Messenger window lets you see who is online to chat with.

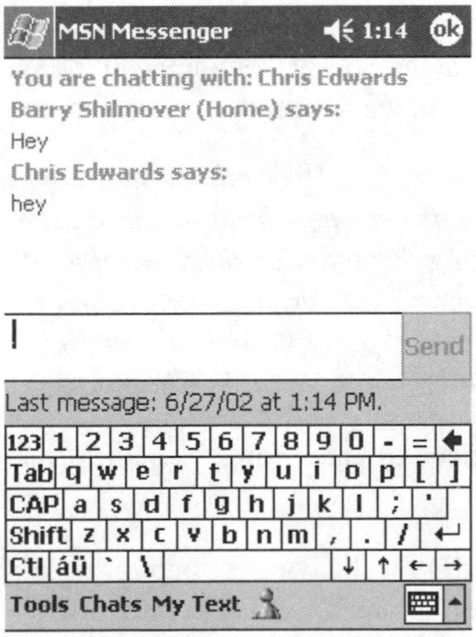

FIGURE 9-8   The chat window lets you talk with one or more of your friends who are online.

- **Block**   Stops you from receiving any chat requests from a blocked user.
- **Chat Members**   Gives you a list of all the contacts currently involved in your chat session.
- **Options**   Opens the MSN Messenger Options dialog box. Here you can designate your screen name (the name that appears to others online), set the program to open automatically upon connection to a network, manage your Allow or Block lists, and configure Passport and Exchange accounts.

The Chats menu enables you to switch between multiple chats that you have under way. The My Text menu enables you to insert one of your My Text strings into the chat (My Text strings are discussed in Chapter 5).

Choosing 802.11b or a Wired Connection

When working in your office or anywhere else with access to a local area network, you can choose to connect your iPAQ to the LAN with either a wireless or wired LAN card. The standard for wireless LAN at present is 802.11b. You can find a variety of manufacturers who make a card that will fit your iPAQ. To make any of the cards work, you will need to set up a wireless access point. A number of other facilities are also setting up wireless 802.11b networks that you will be able to access while moving around. Starbucks Coffee, for example, is installing 802.11b wireless access points into their stores so you will be able to check your e-mail and surf the Web while sipping your morning espresso!

In this section, we will not go through the setup of each wireless card because each vendor is slightly different. We will look at two different setups. The first will look at the built-in WiFi in the 5450, while the second will look at the Socket Communications WiFi Card. We will also provide a listing of the various wireless cards that we have tested and where to get more information on them.

> **TIP**   *Although wireless access with 802.11b or other wireless protocols is extremely convenient, you need to be cautious on the security front because there are many well-known ways to crack through the native encryption on these wireless devices. Make sure that any software you implement for business purposes has adequate built-in security in the software layer, or take advantage of third-party Virtual Private Network (VPN) technology. Security and your iPAQ is discussed in more detail in Chapter 8.*

Before we continue, you will need to know some basic information about your network to continue, including the following:

- **SSID**   This is the unique ID for the wireless network that the card will connect to, similar to the name of a domain on a local area network.
- **Client Name**   This is the name for this client device.
- **Do you use DHCP?**   Dynamic Host Configuration Protocol (DHCP) is where an IP address is assigned to each card as it accesses the network. The alternative is static IP addressing, in which case you will need to know which IP address you should use.

- **Do you have Wireless Equivalent Protocol (WEP) encryption turned on?**   You can choose to use WEP or not to use WEP; however, keep in mind that WEP has been shown to be very insecure, so you shouldn't count on WEP to protect your sensitive information.

- **Authentication Mode**   Here you indicate whether you are using Open or Shared key authentication.

Setting Up the 5450 Built-In Wireless LAN

The iPAQ 5450 is the first device from HP that offers built-in WiFi functionality. Having your wireless network as part of the device without the need for an expansion pack and wireless card is wonderful in that the expansion pack can be used to connect other devices to the iPAQ.

On the flip side, however, some people prefer not to have the wireless functionality built-in. Wireless cards have different chipsets and features. The Cisco Aironet cards, for example, support an encryption method known as Lightweight Extensible Authentication Protocol (LEAP). If your organization uses LEAP, then Cisco Aironet cards are your only option.

This section will step you through the steps required for you to configure your built-in wireless functionality. Follow these steps:

1. On your 5450, tap Start, choose iPAQ Wireless, and choose iPAQ WLAN. If the wireless is currently turned off, you will be presented with a message stating that "The WLAN power is off. Tap Yes to Power On or tap No to exit." Tap Yes to power on the WLAN.

2. You will be presented with the main iPAQ WLAN screen, as shown in Figure 9-9. Tap New to create a new profile.

3. The Profile Wizard will start (see Figure 9-10). On this screen you will need to enter, as a minimum, a name for the Profile and your SSID. You can also choose whether to use Power Management, what your Network type is (Infrastructure or Ad-Hoc), your Region, the Channel to use, and the Transmit Rate. Tap on Next when you are done.

9

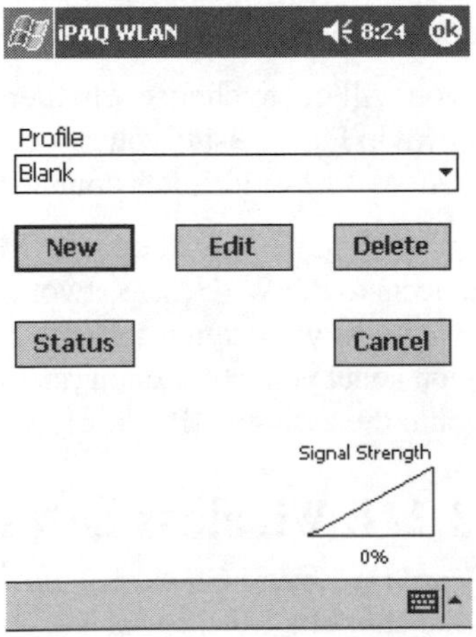

FIGURE 9-9   The iPAQ WLAN initial configuration screen

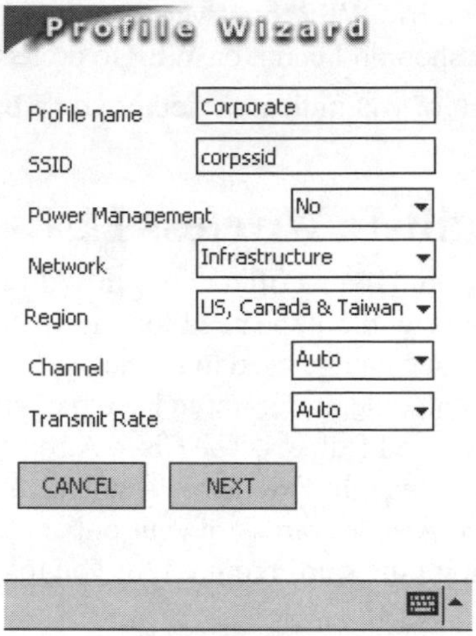

Profile Wizard

Profile name	Corporate
SSID	corpssid
Power Management	No
Network	Infrastructure
Region	US, Canada & Taiwan
Channel	Auto
Transmit Rate	Auto

CANCEL   NEXT

FIGURE 9-10   Enter your wireless profile information using the Profile Wizard.

NOTE   *The main difference between Infrastructure mode and Ad-Hoc mode is that Infrastructure mode is normally used when you have a wireless access point in place, while Ad-Hoc is used to connect multiple WLAN devices together without an access point.*

4. On the next wizard screen you will have to choose how your device will receive its TCP/IP information. Most networks dynamically assign TCP/IP addresses to your device. If this is the case, leave it on the default setting, Use Server-Assigned IP Address. Otherwise, choose the Use Specific IP Address option, and enter your address information (this is common for Ad-Hoc networks). Tap Next when you are done.

5. On the final wizard screen, you will get to choose whether your wireless network uses WEP (recommended). As shown in Figure 9-11, you can choose one of three WEP options on the screen: Disabled, 64-bit, and 128-bit. Enter your WEP key(s) and tap Finish.

6. The new settings will be applied. You will now be returned to the main iPAQ WLAN screen. Once your iPAQ connects to the Wireless Network, the signal-strength icon in the bottom-right corner should show your signal strength. You can also tap on the Status button to view more information about your connection (including the software and hardware versions, the MAC address, and the assigned IP address).

Setting Up a Socket 802.11b Wireless LAN Card

The Socket 802.11b Wireless LAN card is a Type I CF card. This means that you will need an expansion sleeve for your iPAQ that supports CF cards or PC cards (with a PC card–to–CF

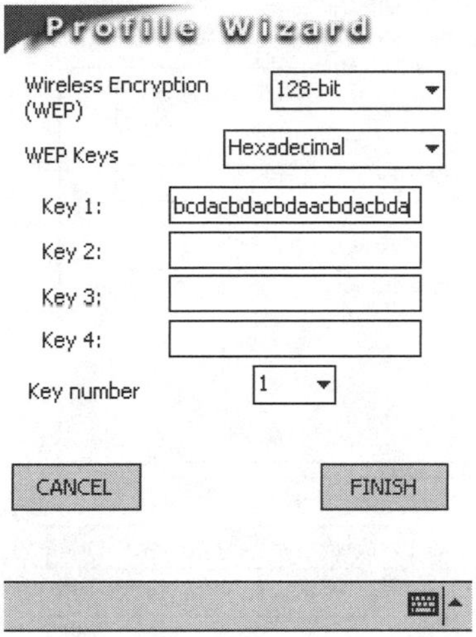

Profile Wizard

Wireless Encryption (WEP)   [128-bit ▼]

WEP Keys   [Hexadecimal ▼]

Key 1:   [bcdacbdacbdaacbdacbda]

Key 2:   [ ]

Key 3:   [ ]

Key 4:   [ ]

Key number   [1 ▼]

[CANCEL]   [FINISH]

FIGURE 9-11   The WEP information is mandatory on a WEP-enabled network.

9

converter). Either the single or the dual sleeve will work. If you have all the equipment, then follow these steps:

1. Slide your iPAQ into the sleeve until it is firmly seated. You should see a window with the message "Initializing Expansion Pack" on the screen for a moment while your iPAQ and your sleeve set up their communication. *Do not* insert the Socket card until after you have installed the drivers.

2. Connect your iPAQ to your PC with your iPAQ cradle, and make sure an active connection exists. Once this is established, you are ready to install the drivers onto your iPAQ.

3. Install the necessary drivers for your card. These likely came on a CD-ROM with your card, but if not, you can download the latest drivers from Socket Communications' web site (**www.socketcom.com**). Once you have installed the program, run it, and the install should initiate through your ActiveSync connection to your iPAQ.

4. Review the onscreen instructions and follow them as indicated. You may be asked to soft reboot your iPAQ.

5. Now you may insert your Socket Wireless LAN card into the slot in the expansion sleeve.

The drivers are installed, but the card is still not quite ready to go.

NOTE   *You might need other settings, depending on which brand of card you are using. If you encounter settings you are not familiar with, contact your network administrator.*

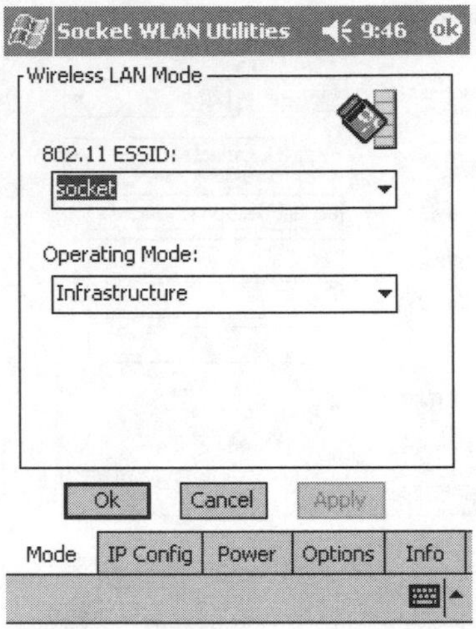

FIGURE 9-12   The Socket WLAN utility allows you to set all the necessary options for the Socket card.

With this information in hand, you are ready to configure your card. With the Socket card, Socket WLAN utility will launch the first time the card is inserted. After that, you can launch them by tapping on the icon on the bottom bar on the Today screen. The dialog box shown in Figure 9-12 appears.

You can now configure the card with your settings by entering the information in the correct sections (tap on the tabs at the bottom of the screen). One of the most powerful features of the Socket WLAN card (aside from its low power consumption) is the advanced options for the card. To access the Advanced features, tap on the socket icon in the menu bar on the today page (bottom right) and choose the Advanced option. The advanced options screen is shown in Figure 9-13. From this utility you can check your signal strength, ping hosts on your network, view the detected access points, and control your Encryption.

Setting up 802.11b cards is not as straightforward as setting up a CDPD or GPRS card and often requires a little trial-and-error before you get it right.

Wireless LAN Cards We Have Used Successfully

Table 9-3 contains a list of cards that we have successfully configured on our iPAQs.

Using a Wired Ethernet Connection

In addition to using a wireless 802.11b card, you can certainly use a wired Ethernet connection, although this will remove the single biggest advantage of your Pocket PC—its portability.

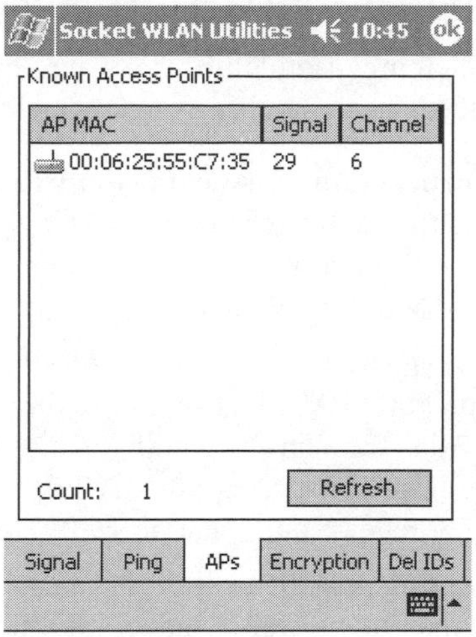

FIGURE 9-13   The Socket WLAN Advanced utility allows you to perform and set advanced options for the Socket card.

You can insert any standard PCMCIA or CF card (using the appropriate sleeve) as long as the appropriate Pocket PC drivers exist for the card. Using the same instructions for the Cisco Aironet card given earlier, install your drivers, insert your card, plug it into a LAN cable, and you should be in business!

Vendor and Model	Type	Information Site
Compaq WL100 & WL110	PCMCIA Type II	http://www.compaq.com/products/wireless/wlan
Linksys Wireless PC Card	PCMCIA Type II	http://www.linksys.com/products/product.asp?grid=22&prid=156
Linksys Wireless CF Card	CF Type II	http://www.linksys.com/products/product.asp?grid=33&scid=36&prid=434
Symbol CF Card	CF Type I	http://www.symbol.com/products/wireless/flash_card.html
Symbol PC Card	PCMCIA Type II	http://www.symbol.com/products/wireless/pc_card.html
Socket CF Card	CF Type I	http://www.socketcom.com
Intel PC Card	PCMCIA Type II	http://www.intel.com/network/connectivity/products/wlan_family.htm

TABLE 9-3   Wireless LAN Cards We Have Used Successfully

Performing Advanced Network Diagnostics

In addition to e-mail, surfing, and chatting, useful third-party applications can add value to having your iPAQ wirelessly enabled. Check out these vendors and products as examples:

- **Cambridge Computer Corporation (www.cam.com/vxutil.html)** Produces a product called vxUtil that is invaluable for troubleshooting your wireless network and contains very useful tools for a network and system administrator. The tool set includes DNS Lookup, Finger, Get HTML, Info, Ping, Port Scanner, Trace Route, Whois, and more.

- **Steve Makofsky (www.furrygoat.com)** Produces a tool that allows you to control your TCP/IP information on your iPAQ. It is similar to the IPConfig utility that ships with Windows NT/2000/XP and the WinIPCfg utility that ships with Windows 95/98/ME. The product, ceIPConfig, allows you to view your TCP/IP information on each of your network cards, and release or renew your dynamic TCP/IP configuration.

- **Sonic Mobility Inc. (www.sonicmobility.com)** Produces a tool that allows network and systems support personnel to securely connect into their back-end network and servers and diagnose and repair mission-critical problems from their wireless iPAQ from anywhere at any time. Start and stop services and processes; change user passwords and properties; reboot frozen servers; get command-line access to NT, Win 2000, UNIX, Linux, and VMS servers; and more.

As time goes by, you will begin to see even more tools emerging for wirelessly enabled iPAQs. This is truly the wave of the future for these devices.

Bluetooth

Several of the iPAQ models (3870, 3970, and 5450) offer Bluetooth technology as a built-in function. Bluetooth is a wireless standard and protocol that is designed for short-distance personal area networks (PANs). The most common uses for Bluetooth is for connecting your Pocket PC to a Bluetooth-enabled phone and then to the Internet, and for using wireless Bluetooth headsets for talking on your Bluetooth phone.

For your non-Bluetooth iPAQs, other solutions are available, including Socket Communications' (**www.socketcom.com**), Pretec's (**www.pretec.com**), and Anycom's (**www.anycom.com**) Bluetooth cards. For more information on configuring these cards, check out either their sites or the Pocket PC Tools site (**www.pocketpctools.com**).

We cannot cover the configuration for every Bluetooth card out there. We have therefore posted links to instructions for connecting your 3870/3970 to the Sony-Ericsson T39/T68i and the Nokia 6310i phones at **www.pocketpctools.com/modules.php?name=News&file= article&sid=59**. We will, however, cover some of the basics of using the Bluetooth Manager on the 5450.

With the iPAQ 5450, HP replaced Bluetooth Manager from the 3870/3970 with a new wizard-driven Bluetooth Manager. To access the Bluetooth Manager, follow these steps:

1. On your 5450, tap Start, choose iPAQ Wireless, and choose Bluetooth Manager.

2. You will be presented with the main Bluetooth Manager screen, as shown in Figure 9-14. Tap New and Connect to launch the Bluetooth Wizard.

3. From the Bluetooth Connection Wizard (Figure 9-15) you can choose one of several options, including:

- Explore A Bluetooth Device
- Connect To The Internet
- Join A Personal Network
- Partner With A Cell Phone
- ActiveSync Via Bluetooth
- Browse Files On A Remote Device

4. Select the task you would like to perform, and tap Next to continue the wizard and configure Bluetooth.

Microsoft has made Pocket PC 2003 more "wireless friendly." One of the ways they accomplished this is by embedding some of the software and drivers that you would need to perform wireless tasks. For example, drivers for both Bluetooth and WiFi cards are already installed within the operating system. This means that with many devices, you can simply insert the wireless card and know that the operating system will automatically detect it and allow you to use it. The Socket Bluetooth Card, for example, is automatically recognized by the operating system and can be used immediately.

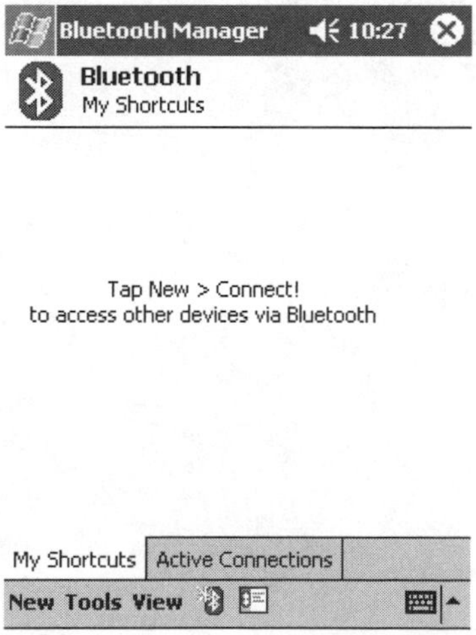

9

FIGURE 9-14   The Bluetooth Manager allows you to detect and configure Bluetooth devices.

FIGURE 9-15   The Bluetooth Wizard utility is used to connect to and configure different Bluetooth devices with your iPAQ.

There are some negative sides to this implementation. First, the drivers installed for the wireless devices may not be the most up to date, nor might they be the best drivers around. Secondly, both the WiFi and Bluetooth stacks are fairly basic, without many of the features found in the drivers that ship with the devices. With the Socket Bluetooth card, for example, the built-in Pocket PC 2003 Bluetooth stack will initialize the card and allow you to do some basic searching and connections with your Bluetooth devices. The drivers that come with the Socket Bluetooth card, however, are feature rich and have some great wizards to allow you to not only search for devices, but also to connect to them and configure them.

Chapter 10

Take Your Presentations on the Road

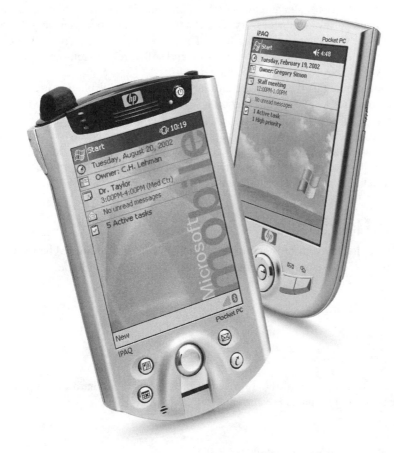

How to...

■ Convert and transfer your PowerPoint or other presentations to the iPAQ

■ Display the iPAQ screen on an external monitor or projector

■ Manage and edit your presentations on the iPAQ

■ Convert PowerPoint presentations to Pocket PC formats

This chapter introduces you to the power of the iPAQ as a presentation tool. Many businesspeople today use applications such as Microsoft's PowerPoint to get their ideas across to their customers and clients. Until recently, the only way to deliver such a presentation was with a laptop. With the speed and power of the iPAQ, these presentations not only can be stored on and presented from an iPAQ, but also can be edited on it.

To enable the iPAQ to manage and display these presentations on a monitor or through a projector, specialized hardware is necessary. The chapter will begin by describing these hardware add-ons and continue with the software products. The presentation tools can be divided into two categories: PowerPoint presentation tools (hardware and software) and remote desktop tools. Both categories will be covered within the chapter.

It is important to note that the hardware currently available for displaying presentations via iPAQ has some limitations. If your presentation has video or audio in it, the software or hardware will not support it. The Voyager CF card, for example, will only do about 4 frames per second (fps), which is too slow for video, not to mention it has no audio support. Another product, iPresentation Mobile Client LE, is a little bit of a mystery in this area—we don't think it will convert a PowerPoint presentation with an embedded MPEG clip. To convert the video to their presentation format, you must use their special software.

Presentation Hardware

To use the iPAQ to display your presentations, you will need some additional hardware. The presentation hardware add-ons available today use the following technologies:

■ PC card

■ CompactFlash (CF) card

■ Expansion sleeve

■ InfraRed

Some manufacturers offer multiple formats for their presentation hardware, others are exclusive. The following products are currently available:

■ Margi Presenter-to-Go

■ Presenter-to-Go Infrared Remote Control

- ColorGraphic Voyager VGA Adapter
- FlyJacket i3800
- Irma, Mobile Presenter

The next sections discuss these products and the technology they use.

Presenter-to-Go

Margi Systems' Presenter-to-Go (**www.presenter-to-go.com**) is an all-in-one solution. It includes both the necessary hardware (in either a PC card or a CF card format) and the necessary software. Because Presenter-to-Go falls into both the software and hardware categories, this section will only discuss the hardware side of the solution.

The Presenter-to-Go system ships with different hardware depending on which of the two versions is used. The PC card version includes the following:

- Presenter-to-Go PC card
- 12-inch VGA adapter cable with power port
- 14-button infrared remote control
- AC adapter power supply
- Gender adapter for direct connection to projectors

The CF card version includes the following hardware:

- Presenter-to-Go CF card (Type I or II)
- VGA adapter cable
- 14-button infrared remote control
- Male-to-male VGA cable for direct connection to projectors

Both versions of the card ship with not only the software necessary to convert and display your PowerPoint presentations, but also the software drivers needed for the iPAQ to recognize and run the card itself. Two software packages ship on the CD-ROM as well, Margi's Mirror application and Presenter-to-Go. Both products are covered in the software section of this chapter.

10

NOTE   *Although the PC card version ships with an external AC power adapter, the CF card version does not and can only run off either the internal iPAQ battery or through the iPAQ AC adapter.*

As mentioned, an application called Margi Mirror is also installed during the installation procedure. This application simply echoes or mirrors what is displayed on the iPAQ screen directly to the Presenter-to-Go card. This allows the PowerPoint viewer application (discussed in more detail in the software section of this chapter) to display the presentations on the screen even though they do not support the video cards themselves.

Presenter-to-Go Infrared Remote Control

Both the Presenter-to-Go cards have the same infrared remote control. The remote control has a complete numeric pad (numbers 1 through 0) and a Return button. This enables you to quickly jump to any slide in your presentation by choosing the slide number and pressing the Return button.

Three other buttons are located on the top to move forward and backward in the presentation and to set the presentation to auto (which will automatically advance slides).

As Figure 10-1 illustrates, the Margi Mirror application allows you to manually enable the VGA card. By doing this, everything that is displayed on the iPAQ will be mirrored through the display card to the projector or monitor. You can also double the size of the screen and rotate it. As you will see with the PowerPoint viewer applications, this will enable you to use them to display your presentations on a monitor or projector.

NOTE

Margi does have a Secure Digital (SD) card model of their Presenter-to-Go. As of the writing of this book, the iPAQ models do not support SDIO and therefore do not support this card. As drivers become available for the iPAQs to make them SDIO compatible (they are SDIO-Ready now meaning that they can support SDIO cards with the proper drivers), this card should be supported.

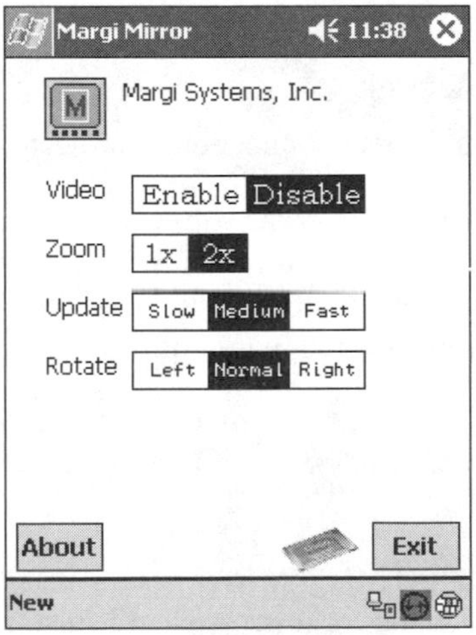

FIGURE 10-1   The Margi Mirror application is used to mirror your iPAQ screen to the VGA card.

Voyager VGA Adapter

ColorGraphic's Voyager VGA adapter (**www.ColorGraphic.net**) is another product used to display the iPAQ screen on an external monitor or projector. Although the Voyager VGA adapter used to be sold in a PC card verrsion, only the CompactFlash version is now available. It does, however, ship with a PC card adapter, which allows for the CF version to be used in the PC card expansion sleeve.

The Voyager VGA CF adapter will handle analog VGA and composite/S-video TV outputs, and ships with a three-foot cable for connecting to these outputs. It also ships with Voyager Shadow, the driver and control application. As shown in Figure 10-2, with Voyager Shadow you can

- ■ Set the screen update to either real time or timed (with the timed interval configurable)
- ■ Choose the desired output (VGA, composite, or S-video)
- ■ Specify the presentation orientation (portrait or landscape) with options to center the output and stretch the image to fit the screen resolution
- ■ Choose whether a background is to be displayed (and its color)
- ■ Select the video mode (resolution and refresh rate) at which to display the presentation

FlyJacket i3800

FlyJacket i3800 by Lifeview Animation Technologies (**www.lifeview.com**) is different from the other presentation hardware products discussed so far. Instead of using a video display card, Lifeview Animation Technologies decided to create an expansion sleeve to house all the

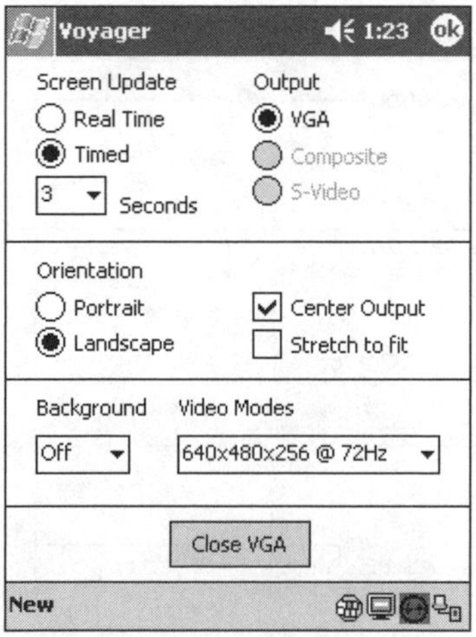

10

FIGURE 10-2   Voyager Shadow controls the output of the Voyager VGA adapter.

hardware for their system. Therefore, instead of needing to purchase a separate expansion sleeve (either the CF or the PC card expansion sleeve), all you need is this one solution. FlyJacket is smaller than Compaq's dual–PC card expansion sleeve and is about the same size as the PC card expansion sleeve. Another thing that sets it apart is that it has an internal battery (for supplying power to FlyJacket itself and to a CF slot). Other features include the following:

- Video input and output
- AV cable (composite video)
- S cable (S-video)
- NTSC/PAL auto scan
- Infrared remote control
- Laser pointer

Along with the hardware, FlyJacket ships with several software packages. These include the drivers (LifeView Shadow), presentation software (LifeView PowerShow), and a third-party presentation suite, which is partially covered in "IA Presenter," later in this chapter.

LifeView Shadow contains both the drivers for the expansion sleeve and the configuration software. As Figures 10-3 and 10-4 illustrate, LifeView Shadow enables you to configure the following:

- The position of the display
- The size ratio of the screen

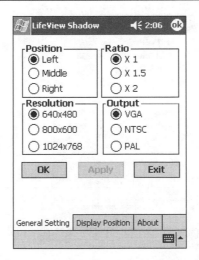

FIGURE 10-3   Controlling the FlyJacket using the LifeView Shadow application

- The resolution to be used
- The type of output used (VGA, NTSC, or PAL)
- The display position of the screen

The FlyJacket also has a camera attachment, known as the FlyCAM, which allows you to record and view videos. These videos can then be stored in the memory of the iPAQ or on a storage card in the FlyJacket.

Irma, Mobile Presenter

Irma, the Mobile Presenter, from Corporate Keys (**www.corporatekeys.com**), is another product that differs from the other Presentation hardware covered in this chapter. The Irma device connects directly to the monitor or presentation. The iPAQ then sends the presentation information to the device via InfraRed.

The Irma ships with the software drivers to push the PowerPoint presentations through the InfraRed port.

Presentation Software

Now that we have seen the presentation hardware available for the iPAQ, it is time to look at the software. Unfortunately, little standardization exists among the different players in this category. We will therefore cover each of the applications separately and discuss what you need to do to get your PowerPoint or other presentations to be displayed by them. It is important to note that

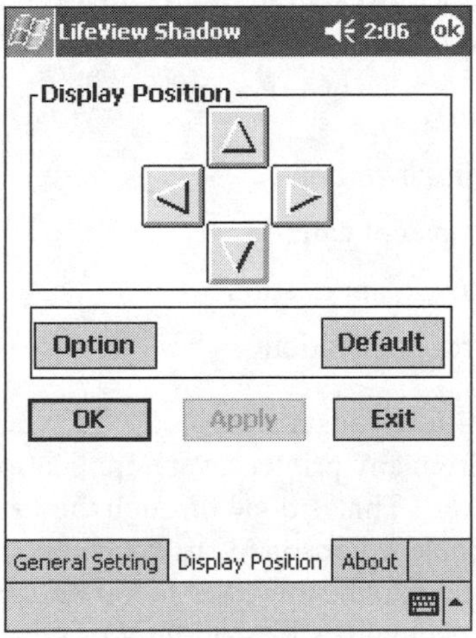

10

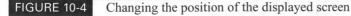

FIGURE 10-4   Changing the position of the displayed screen

some of these applications support VGA themselves, whereas others require applications such as Margi Mirror or Voyager Shadow to drive the VGA cards. The applications that require a secondary application to drive the display card are really just PowerPoint viewer applications, rather than PowerPoint presentation applications. Note that we are using the term "PowerPoint" as a generic word to mean a projected visual presentation.

Therefore, we will break these software packages into two distinct categories: VGA-enabled and PowerPoint viewers. This section discusses the following VGA-enabled software packages:

- Presenter-to-Go
- IA Presenter
- Pocket Slides
- Pocket SlideShow
- iPresentation Mobile Client LE

The PowerPoint viewer applications covered in this section are the following:

- AlbatrosSlides
- ClearVue Presentation

A third type of application is used more to control the presentation than to actually display it; both Periscope and Slide Show Commander fall into this category. We will cover this type of application last.

Presenter-to-Go

Margi System's Presenter-to-Go (**www.presenter-to-go.com**) kit ships with either the CF or the PC card video adapter. Installation includes the following:

- The Presenter-to-Go Printer
- The Presenter-to-Go icon in PowerPoint
- The Presenter-to-Go desktop application
- The Pocket PC Presenter-to-Go application
- The Pocket PC Margi Mirror application

The Presenter-to-Go suite of applications makes it easy for you to convert and transfer PowerPoint files and information from any printer-aware application (that is, any application that can send information to a printer). This is done through the Presenter-to-Go Printer. For example, if you wanted to take a simple Microsoft Word document and present it as a PowerPoint presentation, all you have to do is print it to the Presenter-to-Go Printer (as illustrated in Figure 10-5), which generates a presentation that contains slides of the Word document.

Once you click the OK button, Microsoft Word will "print" the document to the printer, which will begin converting the document into a PDB file (the format used by Presenter-to-Go).

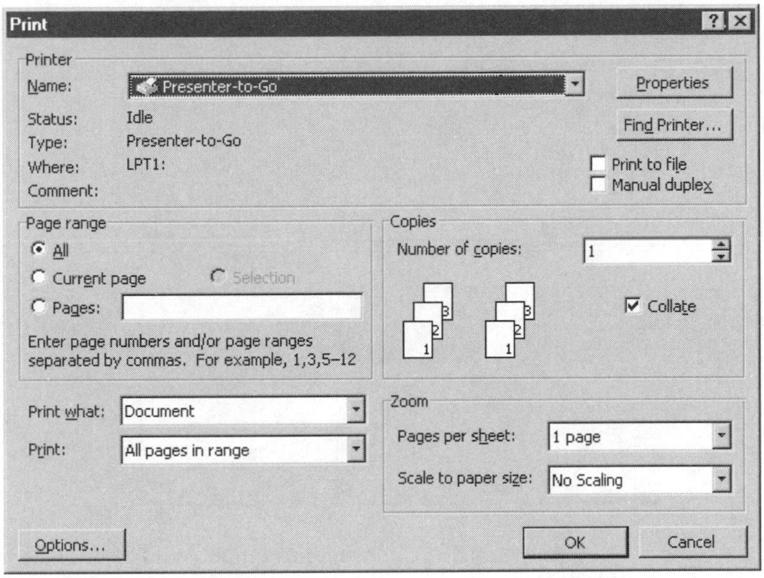

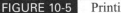

FIGURE 10-5   Printing a Word document to the Presenter-to-Go Printer

10

A PDB file is more compact than the original file and is automatically recognized by the iPAQ as a Presenter-to-Go file. While the files are being converted, Presenter-to-Go displays a status window, shown in Figure 10-6.

Once the document is printed, it is forwarded to the Presenter-to-Go Creator utility (shown in Figure 10-7). Within this utility you can decide whether to generate the presentation or append it to an existing presentation. You can also look at the previous presentations converted by the Presenter-to-Go system, but more on that later in this section.

When the Create button is clicked in the Presenter-to-Go Creator dialog box, the utility generates the presentation and forwards it to the Presenter-to-Go desktop application. This program actually transfers the presentation (the PDB file) to the iPAQ. Simply click the Transfer

Presenter-to-Go Status Window

Pages Processed : 5

FIGURE 10-6   Status window for conversion to the PDB file format

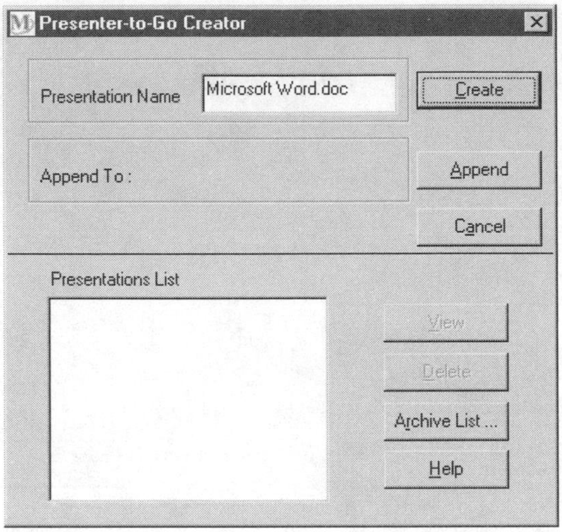

FIGURE 10-7   Create presentations from most documents quickly and easily with Presenter-to-Go Creator.

button in the Presenter-to-Go Desktop dialog box (shown in Figure 10-8), and the file will be transferred. This dialog box also enables you to install the Presenter-to-Go Pocket PC application to the iPAQ (should you prefer to do this from here rather than from ActiveSync).

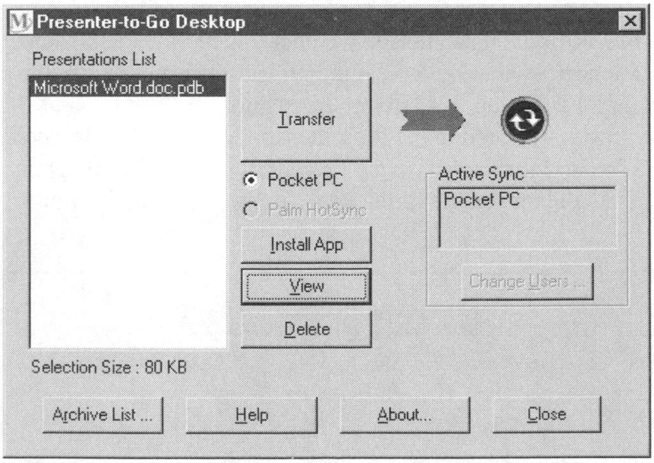

FIGURE 10-8   Transfer your presentations to your iPAQ using the Presenter-to-Go Desktop application.

The presentation can also be viewed (both in a low-resolution preview and in a full-screen presentation) before the transfer is performed. The size of the presentation is displayed on the screen, and you have the option to delete the presentation before transfer. Finally, you can view all the previous presentations that were created and transferred to the iPAQ by clicking the Archive List button—a nice feature if you need access to a large number of presentations, but don't want them to use precious storage space on the iPAQ.

Presenter-to-Go also creates a new icon within PowerPoint. This allows you to quickly convert and transfer your presentation to the iPAQ while maintaining the graphics, color schemes, notes, and animations. After you click the Presenter-to-Go button, you follow the same process as that of the Presenter-to-Go Printer.

You can view your presentations two ways on the iPAQ. You can either run Presenter-to-Go from the Programs menu, or navigate to a PDB file with File Explorer and tap it. Both methods are equally easy, and both launch the Presenter-to-Go application. The only real difference is that when you navigate to a specific presentation, that presentation will be the one opened. When the presentations are transferred to the iPAQ, they are stored in the My Documents\Presenter-to-Go folder.

Once within the Presenter-to-Go application, you have a few choices. If this is a real presentation, you can view not only a list, but also the notes for each frame, and a preview of the presentation. Figure 10-9 shows the three different views: from left to right, List, Notes, and Preview.

You can also hide and display different slides in your presentations by simply clearing or selecting the check box to the left of the slide. From the Presentation menu, you can choose to hide or select all the slides, generate an Auto Slide Show, or delete the presentation. Finally, from the Options menu, you can specify the Preferences for the slide show. These include the delay between slides in the Auto Slide Show, whether to loop the presentation continuously, and an option to preview the presentations in a Left Hand Mode (rotated 180 degrees).

10

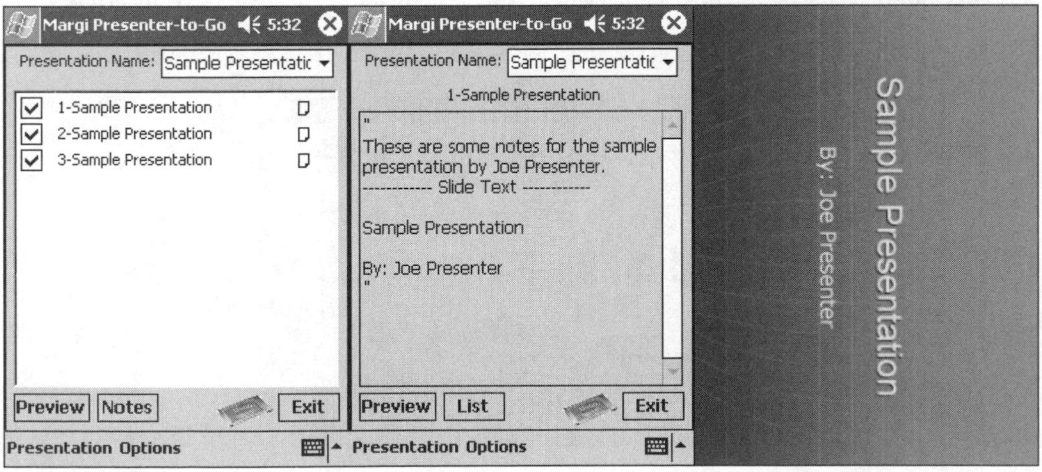

FIGURE 10-9   Presenter-to-Go's List, Notes, and Preview views

One major drawback of Presenter-to-Go is its inability to support shapes or animations. If your presentations contain these features, then you may want to look at some of the other products mentioned in this chapter.

IA Presenter

IA Presenter from IA Style (**www.iastyle.com**) is an advanced application both for viewing your presentations and for making some modifications to them once they are on the iPAQ. A version of IA Presenter ships with both the ColorGraphic Voyager card and the FlyJacket i3800 discussed earlier in this chapter.

Once the application is installed, it installs a desktop component (for setting the ActiveSync conversion options), the iPAQ application, and an ActiveSync converter for converting the file from PowerPoint file format to IA Presenter's IAP format. As you may have noticed, to convert a PowerPoint file to the IAP file format, you simply have to drag it from your desktop to your iPAQ by navigating to it through ActiveSync. When you drag and drop a PowerPoint file, ActiveSync detects the .ppt extension and launches the IA Presenter—ActiveSync Converter application (shown in Figure 10-10). All you need to do now is choose the resolution at which the presentation is to be saved and click the OK button. The presentation will then be converted and copied to the iPAQ.

Like other applications, IA Presenter can be launched in one of two ways. You can either navigate to the presentation file (the IAP file) through File Explorer and tap it, or through the Programs folder in the Start menu of the iPAQ. Again, if you tap a presentation file's icon, IA Presenter will open that file, whereas if you launch the IA Presenter application, you will see a list of presentation files stored on the iPAQ from which you can choose.

IA Presenter enables you to look at your presentation in one of three ways: Normal view (displays the current slide and thumbnails), Slide Sorter view (displays thumbnails only), and Notes Page view (displays the current slide and notes), as shown in Figure 10-11 (from left to

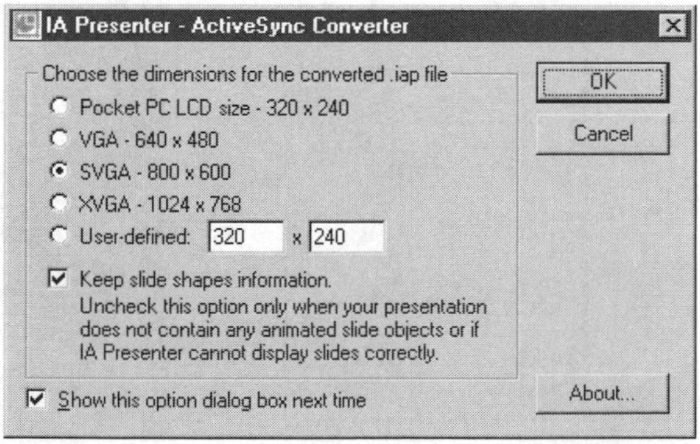

FIGURE 10-10　Transfer your presentations to your iPAQ using the IA Presenter—ActiveSync Converter.

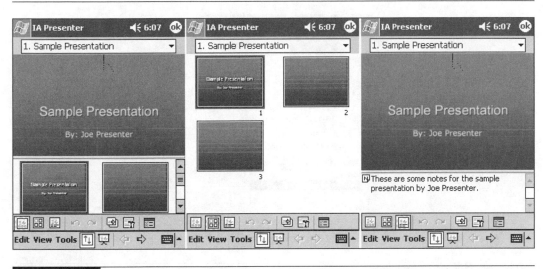

FIGURE 10-11   View your slides in the Normal, Slide Sorter, and Note Page views.

right, respectively). These same views can be selected from the View menu at the bottom of the IA Presenter window.

As we mentioned earlier in this section, IA Presenter enables you not only to view your presentations, but also to make some basic changes to them. You can modify the speaker notes and the slide transitions. To modify the slide transition, you can either click the Slide Transition button on the toolbar (the icon of a slide with an arrow on it) or choose Slide Transition from the Edit menu.

Pocket Slides

Another advanced PowerPoint presentation application is Pocket Slides from Conduits Technologies (**www.conduits.com**). It is similar in many ways to IA Presenter; it can convert presentations on-the-fly through ActiveSync, hide and show slides, view slide thumbnails, and control slide transitions. Where it greatly differs is in its ability to edit not just the speaker notes, but also the text, images, and animations of the slides themselves.

As Figure 10-12 illustrates, Pocket Slides enables you to select text or graphic objects and control how they enter or exit the slide. This includes the order and timing and the effects that are performed on these objects. This application includes many of the features for the creation and modification of slides that are found in Microsoft's PowerPoint.

Much like IA Presenter, Pocket Slides gives the presenter full control over the presentation from the iPAQ before and during the presentation. The speaker notes can be displayed (as shown on the left in Figure 10-13), and the stylus can be used as a pen to highlight information onscreen (refer to the submenu in Figure 10-13).

10

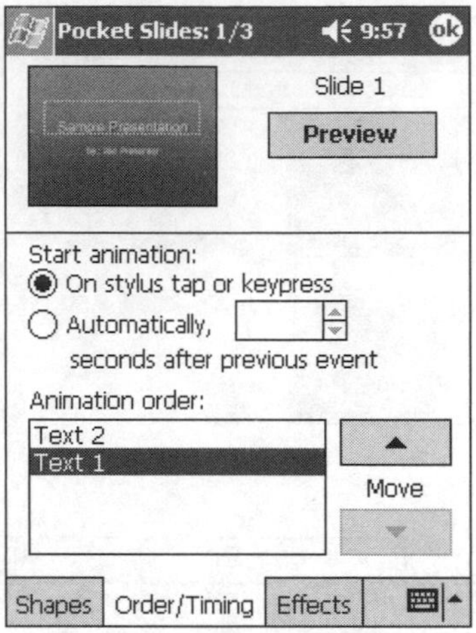

FIGURE 10-12   Modifying the order or timing of a slide

Pocket Slides uses the .cpt extension on its converted PowerPoint files. It can both automatically convert PowerPoint presentations to the CPT file format through ActiveSync and use ActiveSync to automatically convert CPT files to PowerPoint files. To do this, simply drag the CPT file from the iPAQ to the desktop system. At this point, you will be presented with a

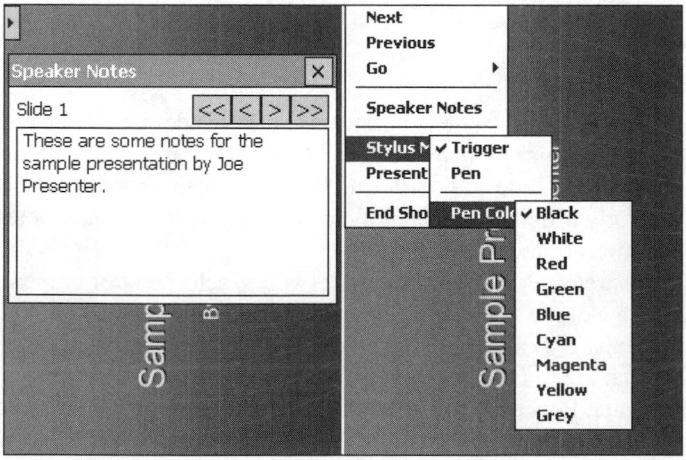

FIGURE 10-13   Controlling the presentation from the Slide Show screen

wizard in which you choose the conversion options for the presentation. This enables you to modify your presentations on either the iPAQ or on your desktop and then move them from one location to the other.

Though we cannot cover all the features of this product, it is by far the most advanced on the market today. It is truly a presentation application. You can create and edit presentations that are almost as complex as PowerPoint presentations.

Pocket SlideShow

Much like the other PowerPoint presentation applications covered in this chapter, Pocket SlideShow from CNetX (**www.cnetx.com**) has several viewing options, can support VGA cards, and enables you to configure slide transitions. Again, it can display the Slide Preview view with either a notes pane or a thumbnail pane (as Figure 10-14 illustrates). A nifty feature is its ability to swap the panes, moving either the notes or thumbnail pane to the top and the preview pane to the bottom.

Pocket SlideShow uses ActiveSync to convert PowerPoint presentations into its own format, using a .pss extension. When a document is copied from the desktop to the iPAQ, a slide conversion wizard will launch, allowing you to choose the resolution at which to convert the presentation. Like some of the other applications covered here, Pocket SlideShow presents a list of all the PSS files on the iPAQ when you first launch the program.

iPresentation Mobile Client LE

iPresentation Mobile Client LE from Presenter (**www.presenter.com**) is a PowerPoint presentation application that requires approximately 2.2MB of memory on the iPAQ. Once you install the

10

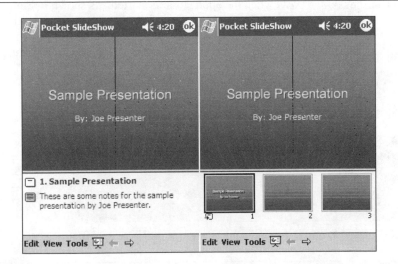

FIGURE 10-14   The different views of the Pocket SlideShow application

product, however, you will quickly realize why it is so large. It supports not only PowerPoint presentations, but also video presentations. This program was designed for the Pocket PC 2000 OS and works very well on it. However, when we tried it, it would only run sporadically on the Pocket PC 2002 operating system, so if you have one of the new 37*xx* or 38*xx* series iPAQs, you may be out of luck for now.

As Figure 10-15 illustrates, the application offers four different views (from left to right): Video/ Slide Title view, Video/Slide Thumbnail view, Thumbnail view, and Preview view. iPresentation Mobile Client LE also enables you to add sound and video to existing presentations, control the timing, and send the presentation directly to the video card.

Converting PowerPoint files to iPresentation Mobile Client format is simple. Again, this application uses an ActiveSync filter to convert from the PowerPoint PPT file format to an IPF file. The first thing you will notice when you copy a PPT file over to the iPAQ is that PowerPoint is launched, the presentation is converted, and PowerPoint is then closed.

AlbatrosSlides

AlbatrosSlides from Albatros (**www.albatros-development.com**) is a simple application for displaying PowerPoint presentations. It is not as powerful as some of the other applications listed here, but is still a good product. Unlike IA Presenter and Pocket Slides, it does not use ActiveSync to convert the presentations. Nor does it use a printer-type conversion process like that of Presenter-to-Go.

It does, however, have a utility, AlbatrosPPConverter, for converting the applications. This utility, shown in Figure 10-16, allows you to choose the existing presentation, the location to store the converted presentation, and the resolution to use during the conversion.

AlbatrosSlides uses the .apv extension for its converted slide presentations and will automatically detect all presentations on the iPAQ when the application is started. As shown in Figure 10-17, AlbatrosSlides has three views (from left to right): Thumbnail view (the number of thumbnails in

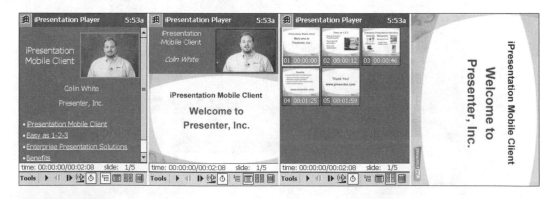

FIGURE 10-15   The iPresentation Mobile Client LE application in action

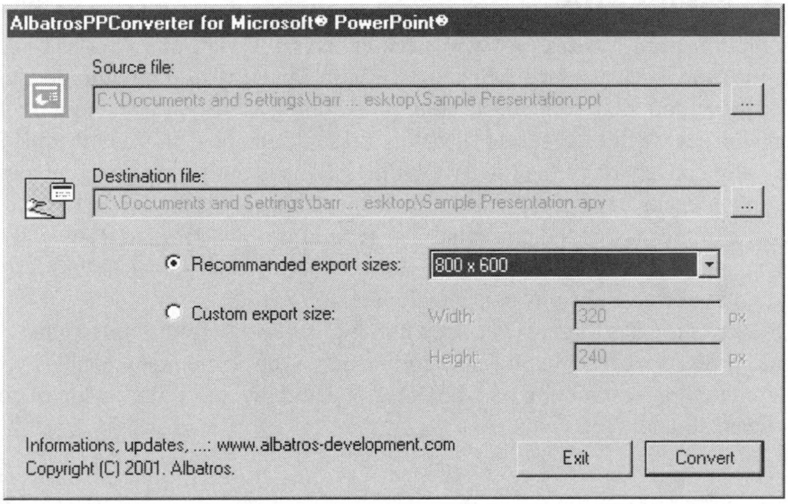

FIGURE 10-16   With the AlbatrosPPConverter you can convert your presentations so that they work with AlbatrosSlides.

this view can be controlled from the Tools | Setting menu), Slide/Speaker Notes view, and Presentation view. Although you can zoom in and out of the presentation, you cannot edit the presentation.

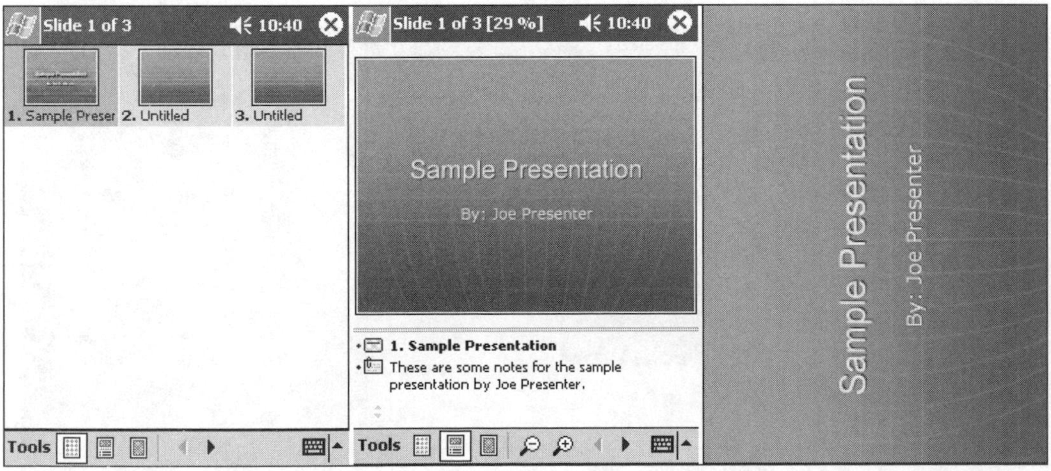

10

FIGURE 10-17   AlbatrosSlides also provides multiple ways to view your presentation— Thumbnail, Slide/Speaker Notes, and Presentation.

ClearVue Presentation

ClearVue Presentation from Westtek (**www.westtek.com**) is a PowerPoint viewer. It requires a secondary application, such as Margi Mirror or Voyager Shadow, to allow it to display a full presentation. It allows you to do some basic editing, including modifying slide order and the timing between slides. One thing that sets ClearVue Presentation apart from the rest is that it does not require any conversion of the PowerPoint files. This is both a blessing and a curse. Not needing a conversion ensures that the presentation is the same as it is on the desktop computer. However, this usually means that the presentations are not optimized for the iPAQ and can be quite large—especially if they contain graphics. Being able to view a PowerPoint presentation that was sent to you via e-mail, however, is a real bonus.

ClearVue Presentation has three views, shown in Figure 10-18 (from left to right): Normal, Slide Sorter, and Slide Show. The Setup Show command on the Setup menu enables you to choose either a manual presentation or an automated one and gives you the option to configure the timings between slides.

Periscope

Periscope from Pocket PC Creations (**www.pocketpccreations.com**) is actually two applications in one. It is the only application covered here that performs both PowerPoint tasks and remote desktop tasks. For this reason, it will be covered in both sections. It is not, however, a PowerPoint presentation application, nor is it a PowerPoint viewer application. It is a PowerPoint presentation remote control application.

Periscope enables you to control a PowerPoint presentation running on either a desktop or a laptop system. You can do this either through the serial/USB port or wirelessly. If it is the wireless

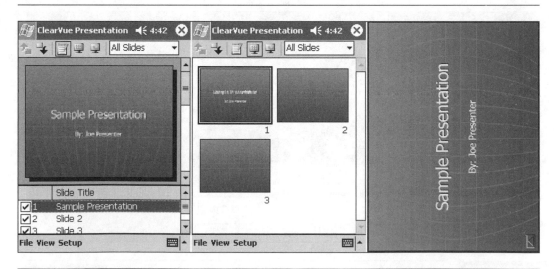

FIGURE 10-18 Viewing your presentations with the three ClearVue Presentation views

solution that you desire, you simply need a wireless network card (covered in Chapter 9) and a network connection (to the same network) on the desktop or laptop system.

As Figure 10-19 shows, once the presentation is launched on the desktop or laptop system, it will be displayed on the iPAQ and can be controlled from there.

Slide Show Commander

Similar to Periscope is Slide Show Commander from Synergy Solutions. Slide Show Commander (downloadable from **www.Synsolutions.com**) allows you to connect, either by wire or wirelessly, to your desktop or laptop system and control the presentation from the iPAQ.

It is a freeware application and therefore does not install as easily or nicely as some of the commercial products covered so far. If, however, you read the Readme file that comes with the application, you should have no problem installing it. Handango has two listings for this software. One is for the freeware application, and one is for a purchased version by Synergy Solutions (**www.synsolutions.com/software/slideshowcommander/PPC.html**).

Remote Desktop Software

Now that we have looked at the presentation applications, it is time to examine some of the remote desktop applications that are out there for the iPAQ. You may wonder why this is in the same chapter as the presentation applications. It's because taking your presentation on the road may also include presenting software on the iPAQ. For example, you may want to view a web

10

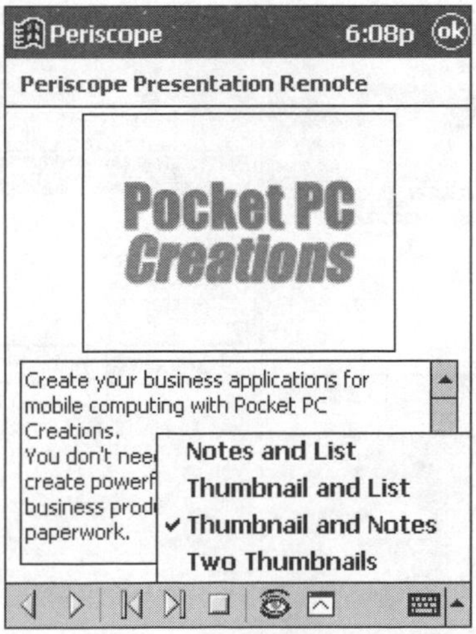

FIGURE 10-19   Using the Periscope application controlling a PowerPoint presentation

page or another application during the presentation. These tools enable you to display the iPAQ screen on your desktop computer.

Remote desktop applications can be divided into two groups. In one group, the applications simply transfer the iPAQ screen at the same resolution as the iPAQ. Anything you do on the iPAQ is echoed on the desktop. In some instances, the reverse is true—anything that is done on the desktop (within the iPAQ screen) is done on the iPAQ. The following applications fall into this category:

- Remote Display Control
- Virtual CE and Virtual CE Pro
- Pocket Controller Enterprise
- Periscope

The second group consists of applications that are used to display the iPAQ screen at just about any desired size. You can then use the desktop's keyboard and mouse to navigate and control the iPAQ. Only one application is in this second group, Handheld Handler.

Remote Display Control

Microsoft's Remote Display Control is part of their PowerToys for the Pocket PC suite of software (**www.microsoft.com/mobile/pocketpc/downloads/powertoys.asp**). It is a free application and consists of two components, a desktop host and an iPAQ client. Remote Display Control can be used over an ActiveSync connection or via a network (wired or wireless). The application is basic and does not have many configuration options. Figure 10-20 illustrates both the host application

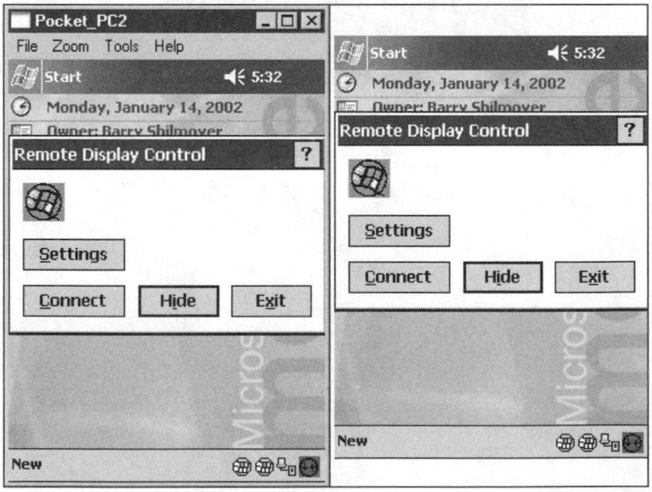

FIGURE 10-20   Controlling your iPAQ from your desktop using Microsoft's Remote Display Control

(left) and the client application (right). You will notice little difference between the two, except for the window and the menu bar at the top.

Virtual CE and Virtual CE Pro

Virtual CE and Virtual CE Pro from BitBank (**www.bitbanksoftware.com/ce**) are remote desktop applications that run over USB, serial, infrared, LAN, WAN/Internet, and ActiveSync connections. Both applications allow you to use your desktop's keyboard and mouse to enter information on the iPAQ, although the Pro version gives you more remote control options and features.

There are two components to the program, a host and a client. The host gives you the ability to not just view the iPAQ's desktop, but also to generate a "skin" so that it looks like your iPAQ, as shown in Figure 10-21. You can also specify the color depth to be used, which speeds up the refresh rate if you are connecting over a slow link. Finally, you can record and play back a session.

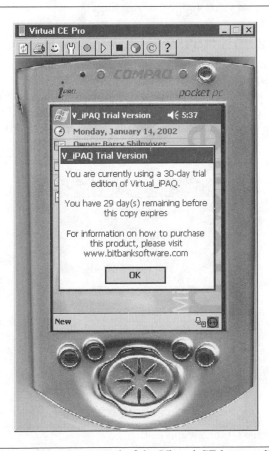

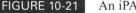 FIGURE 10-21   An iPAQ under the control of the Virtual CE host application

The client application, shown in Figure 10-22, is simple to use. When you first run it, the window is minimized (the application is running in the background). When you switch to it a second time, you can choose one of the connection methods discussed earlier. However, you may run into a problem when you try to connect over a USB or serial port. If ActiveSync is already running and using that port, you will receive an error message informing you that the port is in use. Simply disable ActiveSync, choose a different port, or free the port in the Connection Setting section of ActiveSync.

The following is a list of features found only in the Pro version of Virtual CE:

- Record/play session as key/mouse clicks or AVI video
- Create custom skins to display in the window
- Single-click screen captures to BMP files for convenient and rapid captures of multiple screens
- Toggle toolbar and always-on-top window settings

Pocket Controller Enterprise

Pocket Controller Enterprise from SOTI (**www.soti.net**) differs from the other applications covered here in that it does more than provide remote desktop capability. It also enables you to open an emulated DOS window to the iPAQ (which you can use to copy, delete, and modify files) and a Pocket Manager application (which you can use to view and kill processes and applications running on the iPAQ, as well as to look at system information).

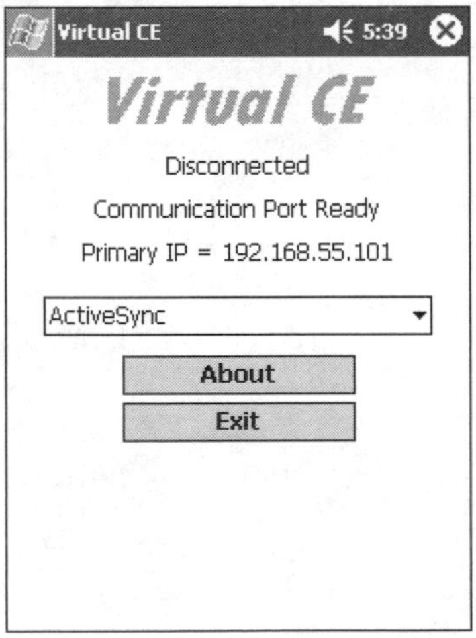

FIGURE 10-22   The Virtual CE client application

Like the other applications, Pocket Controller Enterprise has a host and a client component, although the client component is simply a driver that cannot be configured. The host application, however, has several options, including the ability to automatically start when the iPAQ is connected via ActiveSync, different skins (images of different devices) (all the iPAQ models including the h1910 and the 5450 are available), and the DOS window mentioned previously. Figure 10-23 shows the desktop side of the application.

Pocket Controller Enterprise is also the most flexible of the remote desktop applications. It has the ability to connect the iPAQ to the desktop using a multitude of connections, including Ethernet, Bluetooth, WLAN, ActiveSync, and GPRS.

Periscope

As mentioned in the presentation software section of this chapter, the Periscope application consists of two parts. The first is a remote control application for PowerPoint presentations. The second is the ability to view and control the iPAQ from your desktop.

Periscope has the ability to connect to the desktop wirelessly and does it almost in real time. The protocols used by Periscope make it appear as though the messages are sent instantly between the iPAQ and the desktop.

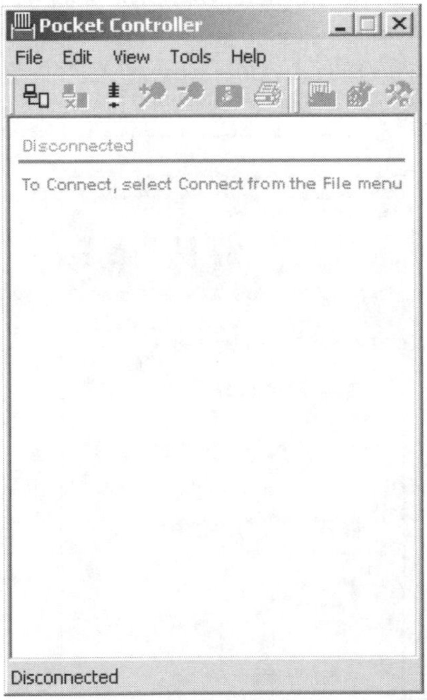

10

FIGURE 10-23   Controlling your iPAQ with Pocket Controller Enterprise

Handheld Handler

The final application covered in this chapter is Handheld Handler from Snowshoe Technologies (**www.snowshoetech.com**). Like the other remote desktop applications, Handheld Handler enables you to view and manage the iPAQ from your desktop, but it also enables you to create a virtual screen that is much larger than that of the iPAQ. In fact, it can simulate screens the size of your desktop screen for applications, such as Internet Explorer and Pocket Word, that benefit from a larger screen.

Handheld Handler creates this virtual screen both on the desktop and on the iPAQ. As you can imagine, viewing a 640×480 screen (or worse, a 800×600 or 1024×769 screen) on the iPAQ's small screen can be painful, but you have the ability to zoom in at any point and navigate the screen with a nifty "compass-like" interface.

Figure 10-24 shows the enlarged iPAQ screen. Notice that the screen is considerably larger than what you would see on the iPAQ and that you have the ability to capture the screen or rotate it as required.

The client application, on the other hand, gives you the ability to select the size of the virtual screen. Be aware that a reset is required whenever you modify the screen resolution, so make sure that you save any data before you make such a change (a warning message will be displayed to alert you).

> NOTE
> *There are two other applications that perform similar tasks to those managed by Handheld Handler: JS Landscape from Jimmy Software (**www.jimmysoftware.com**) and Nyditot Virtual Display from Nyditot (**www.nyditot.com**). The main reason they are not covered in detail here is that they cannot be used to display information on a desktop screen. Instead, they only modify the iPAQ screen so that it can display more information. They do this by "bumping" up the screen resolution to desktop-like resolutions (640×480 and higher).*

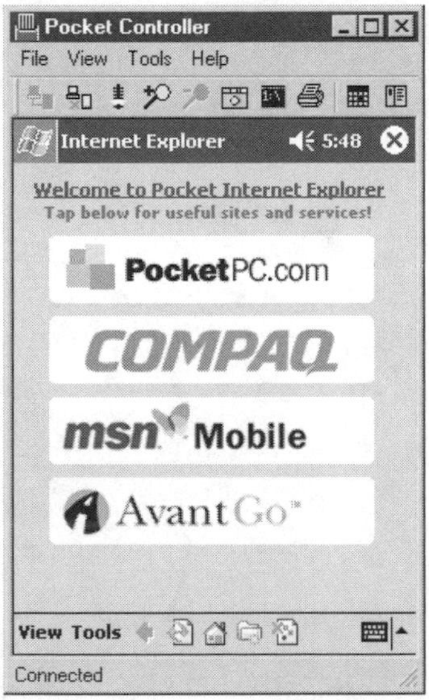

FIGURE 10-24   The Handheld Handler host application runs on your desktop.

Chapter 11

Have Fun, Play Games, Listen to Music, Read Books, and Watch Movies

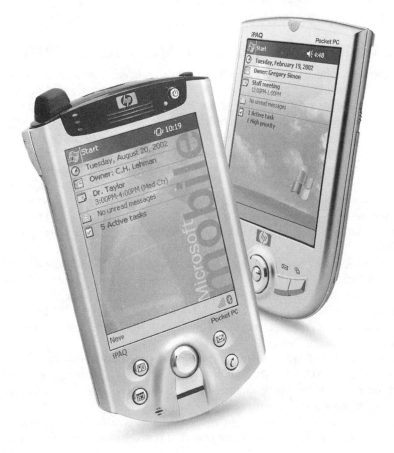

How to...

- Play audio and video
- Read a good eBook
- Find great games
- Take and display digital photos
- Make the most of your hobbies

Lots of Fun Built Into the iPAQ

The iPAQ is a powerful productivity tool, but it's also a lot of fun. A number of applications are built into the iPAQ, and a variety of inexpensive add-ons will help you relax and enjoy yourself after—or during—a hard day of productivity.

Windows Media Player: Video and Music on the iPAQ

Portable electronic entertainment has evolved from car stereos, to transistor radios, to Sony Walkmans, to digital music and portable MP3 players. And with the advent of digital video, we're seeing portable digital video players as well. The iPAQ comes with its own music/video application built in—the Pocket PC version of Microsoft's Windows Media Player.

The newest iPAQs ship with Windows Media Player (WMP) version 8.5 (as shown in Figure 11-1), while others have previous versions (7.0 and 8.0). Pocket PC 2003 devices ship with WMP 9.0. Since the H1910 has the basic version of the Pocket PC operating system installed, it does not ship with Windows Media Player. The Microsoft site **www.microsoft.com/windows/ windowsmedia/download/pocket.aspx** offers WMP for free, but there is no WMP 8.5 installer. Therefore, if you have an H1910 iPAQ, you will be stuck with version 8.0. This site also has links to a control that will allow you to play Windows Media Player videos from within Pocket Internet Explorer.

For audio playback, the Pocket PC version of Windows Media Player supports the traditional MPEG Layer 3 format ("MP3s"). It also accepts music in Microsoft Windows Media Audio (.wma) format and Microsoft Advanced Streaming Format (.asf). If you can connect your Pocket PC to the Internet, Windows Media Player also supports the streaming of WMA and ASF files through the player. Most sites that stream audio or video designed for desktop Windows Media Player will also stream on the Pocket PC.

Windows Pocket Media Player also supports Windows Media Video (.wmv) files in local and streaming format. Like WMA for audio, the WMV format offers better compression than popular MPG and AVI formats for video. However, there's more content available in MPG and AVI formats. Windows Media Player supports downloaded or streaming content.

Microsoft is so sure of the Pocket PC's power as a media player that they have made available a special web site for viewing streaming media on your iPAQ over the Internet. The site can be accessed directly from **windowsmedia.com**.

FIGURE 11-1   Windows Media Player lets you view movies and listen to music on your iPAQ.

How to ... Convert Audio and Video to Windows Media Player Format for Free

Microsoft offers Windows Movie Maker, a free video-editing program for Windows Millennium and XP desktop PCs, on their web site (**www.microsoft.com/windowsxp/moviemaker/**). You can use Windows Movie Maker to capture audio and video to your computer from a video camera, web camera, or other video source. You can also import the following existing files into Movie Maker: video files (.asf, .avi, .m1v, .mp2, .mp2v, .mpe, .mpeg, .mpg, .mpv2, .wm, and .wmv); audio files (.aif, .aifc, .aiff .asf, .au, .mp2, .mp3, .mpa, .snd, .wav, and .wma); and picture files (.bmp, .dib, .emf, .gif, .jfif, .jpe, .jpeg, .jpg, .png, .tif, .tiff, and .wmf). You can piece together any of these resources to create movies with special transition effects, and save the final movie to your computer or to a CD that is recordable (CD-R) or rewritable (CD-RW), depending on your CD recorder. Movie Maker saves the final movie in Windows Media Video format, which can be played using Windows Media Player on the desktop or Pocket PC. Note that a variety of commercial video and audio conversion programs are available from other sources. An Internet search on "video conversion" or "audio conversion" should help you find some of these.

It's worth mentioning here that Windows Media Encoder version 9.0 is a free download from **www.microsoft.com/windowsmedia** and is a focused way of encoding the video. It also has presets for Pocket PCs, although only Pocket PCs running WMP 9.0 will be able to use these presets.

11

Other Audio/Video Players for the iPAQ

A number of third-party players are available for the iPAQ. One of the best is PocketTV, a video program that can play any standard MPEG-1 video file (.mpg or .mpeg extensions), whether content is downloaded to the Pocket PC, or streaming from a web site. PocketTV is free for individual use and can be downloaded on the Mpeg TV web site (**www.pockettv.com**). This is an award-winning program and one of the most downloaded third-party products available, as shown in Figure 11-2. The Mpeg TV web site has FAQs, discussion forums, and tips on how to convert other video formats to MPEG-1.

Another free video/audio player available to iPAQ users is the RealOne Mobile Player from RealNetworks. (**www.realnetworks.com/mobile/player/ppc/index.html**). This lets you view streaming or downloaded audio and video content in the Real (.rm) format. This player is similar to the player you would download to view Real format movies on your desktop computer.

Do you have a favorite TV program you want to take with you? You might want to take a look at offerings from Snapstream Media (**www.snapstream.com/**). Their Snapstream PVS package lets you record video from your TV, VCR, or a video camcorder into a desktop PC equipped with a TV tuner card. You can then use Pocket PVS to synchronize the video recordings to your Pocket PC and watch them using Windows Media Player.

MS Reader: Curl Up with a Good eBook

Sometimes it's relaxing and fun to curl up with a good book. With the iPAQ, you can take one or more electronic books (eBooks) with you and read them anytime you like, with the help of the built-in MS Reader application (see Figure 11-3). MS Reader lets you download and view

FIGURE 11-2   Use PocketTV to view MPEG-1 videos on your iPAQ.

eBooks in Microsoft's LIT file format. MS Reader incorporates ClearType display technology that makes text onscreen easier to read, and you can change the font size from small to large in four steps. MS Reader lets you highlight and bookmark text, insert notes or drawings, move quickly to the last page you read, and more.

The iPAQ has the latest version of MS Reader for the Pocket PC, which lets you view commercial LIT-formatted eBooks protected with Digital Rights Management level 5 (DRM5) security. However, to view DRM5 eBooks, you must first "activate" MS Reader through Microsoft's Passport system. This must also be done with the desktop version MS Reader. The activation process involves connecting your iPAQ to a desktop PC that is connected to the Internet, and then going to Microsoft's MS Reader Activation web page (**www.microsoft.com/reader/info/activation.asp** or **das.microsoft.com/activate**) and registering. It's a simple process, but takes a few minutes. Commercial eBooks are available from a variety of online booksellers, including Amazon, Barnes & Noble, Fictionwise, and others. You'll find a list of online eBook stores, with links, on Microsoft's MS Reader web site (**www.microsoft.com/reader/default.asp**), under "Shop for new ebooks…" You'll also find a link to Microsoft's online eBook Catalog.

MS Reader does not require activation to view eBooks published in DRM1 or DRM3. A wealth of free eBooks is still available to eBook readers in these less restrictive standards. An Internet search on "free eBooks" will help you find these. A variety of eBook links can be found on *Pocket PC* magazine's Best Sites web page, in the Media section (**www.pocketpcmag.com/bestsites.asp**).

Several other eBook readers or viewers are available for your iPAQ. Among the most popular are TomeRaider (**www.tomeraider.com**), Mobipocket (**www.mobipocket.com**), and Palm Reader (**www.palmdigitalmedia.com**).

11

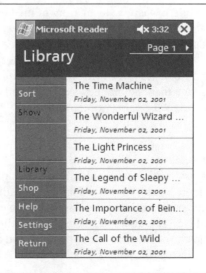

FIGURE 11-3   Viewing a LIT eBook file with MS Reader

Let the Games Begin

Solitaire is probably the most popular game associated with Windows and has shipped with every version of the operating system since 1.0. However, you can download hundreds of games for your iPAQ, and some cost you nothing. The software CD that came with your iPAQ has links to three free games: the classic card game Hearts, Minesweeper, and Reversi. Microsoft also offers a breakout-like game called Cubicle Chaos for free on its downloads web page (**www.microsoft.com/mobile/pocketpc/downloads/cubiclechaos.asp**). In addition, you can check the Downloads section of *Pocket PC* magazine's Best Sites web page (**www.pocketpcmag.com/bestsites.asp**) for freeware sites. Note that Handango, Tucows, and other sites listed on that page also have free Pocket PC software.

The rest of this section is devoted to games you can install on the Pocket PC. Games have been the most downloaded category of third-party software since the Pocket PC was introduced in April 2000. While thousands of games are available for your iPAQ, we mention only a handful of the most popular games.

Most of the games described here are inexpensive commercial programs, but some are free. The vast majority will at least have a free demo version available, so you can try them and see if you like them. Again, this chapter just scratches the surface. Go to some of the web sites mentioned earlier to explore further.

Action Games

Battle Dwarves

www.infiniteventures.com

What happens when you give modern weapons to an army of medieval dwarves? Destruction on a grand level! Arm your team with "bazooookas," frag grenades, railguns, napalm, and more. You battle against a team of computer-generated opponents, using a variety of carefully aimed, specialized weapons. This is a "turn-based" shooting game that takes place in strange landscapes, as shown in Figure 11-4. Each army takes turns firing at the enemy, and the last army with a soldier alive is the victor. It's a "get them before they get you" kind of game, and you need to take advantage of the cover provided in a variety of terrain maps.

Interstellar Flames

www.xengames.com/productsppc.htm

This game pits you against asteroid belts, hostile ships, and waves of enemy fighters. A fleet of alien battleships is approaching our solar system, and only your fighter craft is ready to defend Earth. You'll have to attack huge battle cruisers, and dogfight with enemy fighters while dodging asteroids, as shown in Figure 11-5. You alone must destroy the alien fleet before it enslaves Earth. You can get plenty of power-ups to replenish your fuel and ammunition. The "resume later" feature makes it easy to interrupt the game. This is one of the best interactive action games available.

FIGURE 11-4   Battle Dwarves pits your army of cute dwarves against the computer in no-holds-barred combat.

11

FIGURE 11-5   Interstellar Flames is a great shooter game and a graphical treat.

Metalion

www.ziointeractive.com

This fast-paced 3-D action game lets you pilot the Federation's new fighting weapon (as shown in Figure 11-6), Metalion, in a battle to the death with the evil Red Galaxy Knights from Jupiter. Don't worry too much. You have seven lives and can choose from three types of Metalion, each having different weapons. Still, the bad guys come at you fast and furious. You have to keep your finger on the trigger and your eyes open. In really bad situations you can use the special Super Bomb, but use it sparingly—you only have three per life. And keep an eye out for special symbols that appear on your display (Power-Up, Recover Health, and Super-Bomb). Collect them and increase your chances against the Red Galaxy Knights. Metalion features excellent graphics and fast-paced background music just perfect for an action game.

RocketElite

www.dig-concepts.com

The goal of RocketElite is to fight, fly, and land your rocket on an asteroid. You have to use your thrusters to carefully maneuver your small ship and land and pick up astronauts at strategic locations, as shown in Figure 11-7. RocketElite boasts some impressive features, including fast performance; user-created levels; easy, medium, and hard game play; plenty of power-ups to replenish your ship's fuel and firepower, and more. You can upgrade your ship's fuel system, deflector shield, tractor beam, weapons, and defensive systems. Each level has unique graphics and environmental effects to deal with and adapt to. Finally, RocketElite has single or multiplayer modes. Multiplayer lets you play with other Pocket PC users via IrDA or wireless connections optimized for a high-speed, lag-free gaming experience.

FIGURE 11-6   3-D robotic mayhem

FIGURE 11-7   The goal of RocketElite is to fight, fly, and land your rocket on an asteroid.

Snails

www.snailsgame.com

Your mission is to help an army of snails (the Moogums, the Lupeez, and the Nooginz) defeat each other and conquer the planet Schnoogie by launching strategic attacks with a variety of weapons, as shown in Figure 11-8. Snails is a very polished game with colorful, cartoon-like backgrounds and clever animation. The interface is easy to navigate, and the game has a lot of challenging game play and entertaining scenarios. One hint: you'll have to select your race of snails and choose your weapons carefully if you want to win the war.

FIGURE 11-8   Help an army of Snails conquer the planet Schnoogie.

11

Spawn

www.ziointeractive.com

Spawn is the Pocket PC adaptation of one of the best-selling comic characters of all time. You are a hellspawn (see Figure 11-9) battling against Angels in a world where good and evil are not as clear-cut as they may seem. Spawn for Pocket PC is your chance to join in the battle that has endured for centuries and threatens to tear apart any hope for a peaceful existence on Earth.

Turjah Episode II

www.turjah.com

Turjah II, the sequel to Turjah, is a fast-moving space shootout with great graphics and background sound. An alien force known as the Turjah is once again scheming to destroy Planet Earth, as shown in Figure 11-10. The Galaxy Council has created a powerful warship to stop them, and they need you to fly it. Your enemies drop down on you from above and will circle back to shoot you from behind. Use your game pad or action buttons to move left and right, up and down. When you've got your ship pointed at the enemy, blow them away! Fire your laser cannon or use one of a limited number of super bombs to eliminate all the enemies you see on the screen. (Super bombs are great to use when the screen is clogged with enemies.) Bonuses appear as you shoot the enemies. Grab them to increase your health, power, shield strength, and the number of missiles and bombs you have. This game occupies a lot of memory, but is otherwise excellent!

FIGURE 11-9   Battle good and evil in this First Shooter game

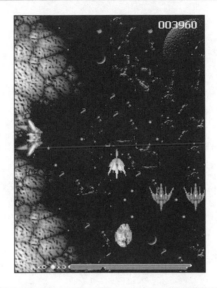

| FIGURE 11-10 | Turjah II is a fast-moving space shootout with great graphics. |

Board Games

Awele

www.hexacto.com

Awele is an award-winning title based on an ancient board game where your goal is to capture as many seeds as possible from your opponent (see Figure 11-11). You are presented with a virtual board with six cups in it. Players take turns distributing or "sowing" their seeds in the different holes. You can play your friends or the computer. The game is relatively simple, but Hexacto has provided polished graphics, professional sound effects, and a detailed help file.

Monopoly

www.handmark.com

Play one of the world's most popular board games on your Pocket PC, captured in Figure 11-12. You can buy, sell, rent, and auction property and practice your Monopoly skills at any time by playing against up to three computer opponents with eight different "identities" and playing styles. Or you can mix any combination of real people and computer players in any game. This is an officially licensed version of the game, and all the artwork is accurate, right down to the silver game tokens. The pop-up menus make it easy to play, save, load a saved game, set preferences, and check the official rules of Monopoly.

FIGURE 11-11   The award-winning game based on an ancient board game

FIGURE 11-12   Monopoly brought to life on your iPAQ

FIGURE 11-13   Sophisticated chess play on your iPAQ

PocketGrandmaster

www.pocketgrandmaster.com
PocketGrandmaster has a sophisticated chess engine, and plays interesting and often aggressive chess (see Figure 11-13). Toolbars and context menus let you access the most-used functions quickly. You can change the look of the game with six different chess-piece sets and eight chessboards. Moves are animated and sound effects realistic. You have an unlimited number of take-backs. PocketGrandmaster supports games with variations, comments, and annotations. The game has a chess clock and an analysis mode for tutoring, problem solving, and hints, and offers different playing modes for both tournament and blitz games.

ChessGenius

www.chessgenius.com
This compact, powerful, and fast program was written by Richard Lang, ten times Computer Chess World Champion (see Figure 11-14). You can play against the computer or another player, or watch the computer play against itself. The game has 30 playing levels: ten easy levels where the game makes deliberate mistakes; ten time-based levels where you have to make a move in a specific number of seconds; and ten Blitz levels, where you have to play the whole game in a specific number of minutes. You can take back moves, step forward, and replay a game. You can save multiple games in one file, which can be imported and exported to desktop PC applications. ChessGenius has a "Tutor" option, which will warn you if you make a mistake or make a weak move.

11

| FIGURE 11-14 | Powerful chess program written by a World Champion |

Emperor's Mahjong

www.hexacto.com

This is a Pocket PC version of the ancient Chinese game of matching tiles. Match a pair of tiles to remove them from the board (see Figure 11-15). When the board is clear, you move on to the next level. The game is simple to play and the graphics are outstanding. The Emperor's Mahjong features 72 different layouts categorized in six themes. Players can also create and save their own layouts by way of the Layout Editor. Three game modes are available. Traditional Shanghai is the most common game mode; just click on tiles by pairs to remove them from the board. The Traditional Shanghai (two players) mode is a turn-based cooperative match until the timer determines a winner after the board is cleared. And finally, there's the Emperor's Challenge, where players try to reach the rank of Emperor by clearing all 72 levels and accumulating Wisdoms. The Emperor's Mahjong features an authentic traditional atmosphere, with rich colors and ambient music that will transport you to ancient China Have fun, but be wise!

Card Games

Championship Hearts, Spades, Euchre, and 500

www.dq.com

These games have existed on the PC since 1994 and have received numerous awards. DreamQuest software recently ported them over to the Pocket PC and markets them individually or bundled into a single package. The games include animated characters who react to how well they are doing in the game (see Figure 11-16). You can ask for hints, undo moves, replay a game, and practice. There are

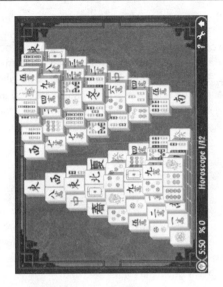

FIGURE 11-15   Ancient Chinese tile-matching game

five difficulty levels, which range from novice to master. There's even wireless capability that lets you play with a friend via infrared communication.

FIGURE 11-16   A popular set of card games brought to the iPAQ

King Sol

www.rapturetech.com
If you like solitaire, you'll love this collection of 70 solitaire games, including Klondiks, Canfield, Cruel, Golf, Elevens, Destiny, and many more. You can pause the game, undo and redo unlimited moves, save and restore games, bookmark your place in a game, auto-play the cards, and more. King Sol maintains a database of your game statistics. You can sort tables by any data field; compare your results against other players; view your results in 3-D charts; set backgrounds, card backs, and sound schemes; and even create backgrounds and card backs from your own image files.

Casino Games

Full Hand Casino

www.hexacto.com
Full Hand Casino includes four games of luck and skill in one package. You can play Blackjack (shown in Figure 11-17), Roulette, Video Poker, or Slot Machine. The games include sophisticated graphics and play by authentic casino rules. Hexacto has a unique online ranking system that lets you compare your "winnings" with other players.

Black Jack Pro

www.g3studios.com
Game play is realistic on this feature-rich adaptation of the popular casino card game, shown in Figure 11-18. You play the game using an intuitive point-and-tap interface. Create up to ten customizable players and play one-, two-, four-, or six-deck games. Play by different casino rule

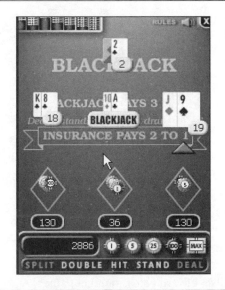

FIGURE 11-17   Four games of luck on your iPAQ

FIGURE 11-18   Feature-rich Black Jack game

sets: Las Vegas Strip, Las Vegas Downtown, Reno, and Atlantic City. You can adjust game speed, customize the interface, and access a tutor that teaches basic Black Jack and two-level card counting strategies to improve your play.

Game Emulators

Video games and other software programs are written for specific hardware and specific operating systems, and a game written for one system (for example, Sony PlayStation) will not run on another system (for example, Microsoft XBox) unless it is reengineered for that system. An *emulator* program allows one computer system to act like and run software for another. Emulators are generally, but not always, freeware programs with little or no technical support, and with idiosyncrasies that can make using them a challenge. Also, emulators generally do not come with the game files themselves. You have to find these on the Web, download them, copy them to your Pocket PC, and use the emulator to run them. The use of these game files (also called *ROM images*) is restricted, so read the copyright notices carefully. Here are a few of the more popular game emulators for the Pocket PC:

MAME CE3 (**www.mameworld.net/mamece3**) is the Pocket PC version of the Multi-Arcade Machine Emulator, a desktop PC program that lets you play hundreds of the older arcade games. The site has a message board where you can post questions and comments. The most comprehensive MAME site is MAMEWorld (**www.mameworld.net**). Again, the emulator does not come with games, but MAMEWorld's "ROMs Links" section lists web sites where you can download the ROM images of well over 2,000 games.

11

FIGURE 11-19   Run most Atari 2600 games on your iPAQ.

PocketNES (http://pocketnes.retrogames.com) is a Nintendo Entertainment System emulator for the Pocket PC. No ROM images come with this one either; do a Web search on "NES ROM" to find them.

PocketVCS (http://pocketvcs.emuunlim.com) is an open-source Atari 2600 emulator that will run most Atari 2600 games. Again, you'll need to download the ROM images of the games yourself. Doing a web search on "Atari 2600 ROM" is a good way to start (see Figure 11-19).

NOTE   *We found a web site that has probably the largest list of emulators for your iPAQ. You can find the site at **www.emulation9.com/wince.html**.*

Puzzle Games

Boxikon

www.shoecake.com/games.html
Boxikon is a Tetris-inspired puzzle game that allows you to drag and drop the pieces anywhere on the board (see Figure 11-20). As with Tetris, when you form a line of pieces, they disappear and you score points. But in this game, lines can be formed either horizontally or vertically. This is still a relatively fast game, but the added dimension makes it more than a test of hand-eye coordination—more planning and strategy are required.

FIGURE 11-20 Boxikon is a Tetris-inspired puzzle game that adds a second dimension to the game play and requires more planning.

Slurp

www.hexacto.com

Your goal here is to "slurp" up the colored drops and clear the board. The smallest round drops cannot be slurped up; the larger ones can. As you tap on the larger drops with your stylus to slurp them up, the remaining drops fall toward the bottom of the screen (see Figure 11-21). The trick with this game is to get as many of the smallest drops to line up with like-colored drops so that they will form larger drops that you can slurp away and thus score points. When no larger drops remain to be slurped up, that level of the game is over, and you start on a new level. However, all of the unslurped small drops remaining at the bottom of the screen turn solid and shrink the size of the next level's screen.

Pop's Pipes

www.hexacto.com

You're Pop the plumber and your goal is to connect pipes that drop from above. You can move the pipe segments left or right as they drop. The more connections you make, the more points you score (see Figure 11-22). A four-piece loop makes a pipe bomb that blows away the surrounding pipes for extra points and more room on the playing board. As with other Hexacto games, you can post your scores on the developer's web site and compare them with others.

FIGURE 11-21   Slurp up the colored drops and clear the board to score points.

FIGURE 11-22   In Pop's Pipes, you are the plumber who must connect pipes to score points.

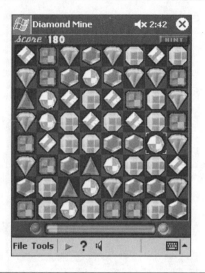

FIGURE 11-23   In Diamond Mine you must match three like-colored gems to score points.

Diamond Mine

www.astraware.co.uk

This game challenges you to swap adjacent gems to make a line of three identical stones (see Figure 11-23). When you do, the gems disappear and the stones above them fall down to fill in the gaps. You can match the gems horizontally or vertically, and the more matches you make, the more points you score. If you ever find yourself at a loss, you can tap on the "hint" button to get a hint about a matching combination. You can play timed or untimed games, disable the background sounds, pause the game, or exit at any time.

Role Playing Games

Gnomes and Gems

www.handango.com

Gnomes and Gems is modeled after classic digging adventure games. You are a greedy gnome digging in dangerous caves looking for treasures (see Figure 11-24). In the depths of the earth you have to watch out for falling boulders and molten lava. You can drown in murky underground rivers if you're not careful. And did I mention the spiders and centipedes that have been known to devour gnomes? If all that isn't enough, you also have to watch out for underground dwellers known as "volcanic imps," who aren't particularly fond of thieving gnomes. This game has more than 100 levels, surprises and puzzles, animations, and sound effects that can be turned off if the situation calls for it.

11

LEAD TIN COPPER IRON SILVER GOLD

SCORE:42   DEPTH :2

EXIT   NEW GAME   PAUSE   SOUNDS ON   HELP

FIGURE 11-24   Gnomes and Gems: Grab your pickaxe and start digging for treasure.

Ultima Underworld

www.ziointeractive.com

This ZIOSoft title is a Pocket PC version of a classic RPG (role-playing game) for the PC. Your goal is to rescue the kidnapped daughter of Baron Almric. You have been implicated as an accomplice and are wanted by the authorities. To find and rescue the maiden, you must explore the Stygian Abyss, a tremendous cavern fraught with peril (see Figure 11-25). You can acquire magic spells, different fighting styles, and new bartering techniques to help you through the abyss. Your goal is to gather eight mystic devices hidden on different levels, which will bring harmony to the abyss and let you rescue the maiden and clear your good name!

Rayman Ultimate

www.gameloft.com

This title is based on the game that was the first PlayStation hit. You are Rayman and your quest is to travel through a variety of worlds and levels to free your friends the "Electoons" from Mr. Dark (see Figure 11-26). You must find the cages where they are held and free them. You have six different worlds to explore with a total of 60 different levels. Watch out for Mr. Dart's creatures while you gather special powers to help you along the way. The graphics are great, the animation smooth, and the sound effects rich and plentiful.

FIGURE 11-25   Based on the classic desktop PC RPG, Ultima Underworld challenges you to explore the Stygian Abyss and rescue the daughter of Baron Almric.

FIGURE 11-26   Rayman Ultimate: Free your friends the Electoons from Mr. Dark.

11

FIGURE 11-27   In Hyperspace Delivery Boy, you are an intergalactic courier who must avoid robots, behemoths, and more to deliver your packages.

Hyperspace Delivery Boy!

www.monkeystone.com

You are Guy Carrington, courier for the Hyperspace Delivery Service. Neither rain, nor snow, nor insane robots, nor dangerous environments, nor even "Sleeping Behemoths" must stop you from delivering your parcels throughout the universe. You have to solve puzzles, dodge aliens, and more, as you make your deliveries (see Figure 11-27). HDB is an enjoyable, overhead scrolling game, with cute cartoon-like characters, great sound effects, and a clear soundtrack. You use the iPAQ's navigation or your stylus to make your way through the various screens in this game. Collect gems and "monkeystones" to receive bonuses, as you play through the 30 levels of this game. Occasionally, you'll find yourself in the "Panic Zone," where you need quick reflexes and thinking to survive.

Shadowgate Classic

www.portable-games.com

Explore the Shadowgate castle, overcome all the hazards, and find the ancient Staff of Ages in this classic role-playing adventure game (see Figure 11-28). You'll meet fantastic beasts, devious puzzles, and heroic challenges. You have to find the ancient Staff of Ages, the one weapon with the power to combat the evil schemes of the hated Warlock Lord. You work your way through a mysterious castle looking for the things you'll need to achieve your quest. Be warned! Death is almost unavoidable. Be sure to use the "save game" feature frequently so that you do not have to start from the beginning after you die. The game has great graphics, interesting sound effects, and more. This is a thinking-person's game, not a fast-reaction-time shooter.

FIGURE 11-28   This RPG challenges you to explore Shadowgate castle in your quest to find the Staff of Ages and defeat the Warlock Lord.

Tower of Souls

www.parystec.demon.co.uk
The goal of this remake of a popular Amiga game is to explore the Fortress of Izlar and defeat Baalhathrok, an evil conqueror (see Figure 11-29). You'll need to pick locks, create potions, and more to make your way through the seven levels and 125 map areas of this game. Your goal is to collect three Nydus Crystals to enter the lair of the enemy and end his evil reign. You should definitely read the manual of this one before you attempt to play it.

Simulations

Ages of Empires

www.ziointeractive.com
Ages of Empires brings the classic Windows game to the iPAQ. Ages of Empires Pocket PC Edition is an epic real-time strategy game spanning 10,000 years, in which players are the guiding spirit in the evolution of small Stone Age tribes. Starting with minimal resources, players are challenged to build their tribes into great civilizations (see Figure 11-30). Gamers can choose from one of several ways to win the game, including world domination by conquering enemy civilizations, exploration of the known world, and economic victory through the accumulation of wealth.

11

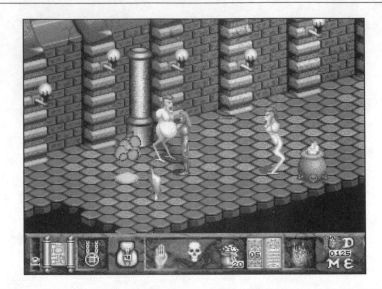

FIGURE 11-29   In the Tower of Souls you must find the magic crystals to enter the lair of Baalhathrok and end his evil reign.

FIGURE 11-30   The classic Windows game on the iPAQ

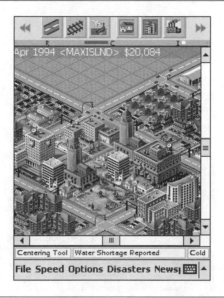

FIGURE 11-31   Design and run your own city complete with citizens and disasters.

SimCity 2000

www.ziointeractive.com

Your goal in this classic simulation game is to design, build, and maintain your own city, as
shown in Figure 11-31. You have to manage resources and cope with disasters, unemployment,
crime, and pollution. You also have to deal with Sims (Simulated Citizens), who build houses,
condos, churches, stores, and factories. They also complain about things like taxes, mayors, and
city planners. If they get too unhappy, they move out, you collect fewer taxes, and the city
deteriorates. This one is based on the classic desktop PC title, considered by many to be one of
the best computer games of all time. Gamers familiar with both say that the Pocket PC version is
very true to the original.

Chopper Alley

www.amazinggames.com

This is a helicopter flight-simulation game with fighting and rescue missions (see Figure 11-32).
You have a variety of helicopters, weapons, landscapes, and missions to choose from. Out of the 25
missions, 14 are immediately available, and you can unlock the other 11 as you play. A detailed
2-D scrolling map can also be optionally displayed on the screen. Play it in either portrait or
landscape mode.

11

FIGURE 11-32 An amazing helicopter flight-simulation game for the iPAQ

Leo's Flight Simulator

http://web.jet.es/leobueno
This flight simulator has excellent graphics (see Figure 11-33) and lets you select from a variety of aircraft to fly over a range of landscapes. It takes a little while to get the hang of the controls. This is a straight simulator—no dogfights.

Motocross Stunt Racer

www.dig-concepts.com
This is a fast-action motocross game with 45 levels and three modes of play: Racing, Stunts, and Free Ride (see Figure 11-34). You can play this game in either portrait or landscape mode. You unlock more levels by scoring a certain number of points in each level. There are plenty of long straightaways, sharp curves, jumps, and shortcuts. This is a fast game that can be controlled via stylus or directional pad.

Sports

iGolf2

www.cecraft.com
Cecraft's iGolf2 has great 3-D graphics, realistic sound effects, and a variety of features that might even satisfy hardcore golfers (on a rainy day). The practice mode lets you select any of 18 holes to practice before you actually play a game. You can select different views of the course: from the tee,

FIGURE 11-33   Fly your very own plane in this high-flying simulator.

from the pin, top view, and target view. You can select your own club, or let the game automatically select it for you, which helps the duffers among us. You can change the different modes of swinging among easy, 2-tap, or 3-tap, as shown in Figure 11-35. For example, in 3-tap mode, the fist tap on the screen starts the swing; the second determines the distance the ball flies; and the third controls

11

FIGURE 11-34   A fast-action motocross game

FIGURE 11-35   Cecraft's iGolf2 has great graphics and realistic sound effects.

the backspin. It will take you a few practice rounds to get the hang of this. Fortunately, you can undo a missed shot.

Tennis Addict

www.hexacto.com

Play a fairly realistic game of tennis on your Pocket PC (see Figure 11-36). Tennis Addict and other Hexacto sports games use PSI (Precise Stylus Input) technology to control all play functions. In this game that means player movement and racquet play. You pick up the feel of this technology pretty quickly. Choose from among 16 different opponents and four court types: indoor carpet, outdoor clay, and real or synthetic grass. You can play a quick game using the Quick Match option or play an entire tournament. You can see your ranking and compare your scores with other players at the Tennis Addict Web Lobby. Hexacto offers two other sports titles that utilize PSI technology: Soccer Addict and Baseball Addict.

Strategy Games

Lemonade Inc.

www.hexacto.com

Test your entrepreneurial skills by trying to sell lemonade. You start with a small lemonade stand and a few dollars in your pocket. Check the latest weather forecast and try to pick the best location for your stand, tweak your lemonade recipe, adjust your price, and manage your inventory. You can reinvest your profits and streamline your production methods if need be, but watch out! If you make

FIGURE 11-36   Play Tennis like a pro.

wrong decisions, you will go bankrupt. There are five maps in the game with different characteristics and attributes (see Figure 11-37). The game can be played in two modes: Open-ended Career mode or 30 days Challenge mode. You can post your high scores on the "Lemonade Stock Exchange," an Internet scoreboard on Hexacto's web site.

11

FIGURE 11-37   In Lemonade Inc., rent is high in the downtown area, but so are the profits.

FIGURE 11-38   Argentum has intense action and great graphics.

Argentum

www.ionside.com

An engaging action/strategy game where you have to deploy your vehicles to seek the precious resource Argentum, which is necessary to build your army and defeat your enemy (see Figure 11-38). The more Argentum you harvest, the more resources you will have to build radars, power plants, tanks, troops, and so on. The game features well-designed missions, great graphics, and excellent sound effects and music. Graphics-intensive games like this are a little hard on battery life and require all the CPU power you can spare. If it seems to be running slow, close all other open applications.

Hobbies, Travel, and More!

This chapter is one of the biggest in the book because there's a lot of fun to be had with your iPAQ. For one thing, you can use it to help you with your hobby.

Digital Photography

Dedicated and occasional shutterbugs can add digital camera capability to the iPAQ Pocket PC via the built-in CompactFlash slot. *Digital camera cards* are available for the Pocket PC. These devices look like a small camera lens sitting on top of a CompactFlash card. Slip them into the CF card slot, and install the software that comes with them. View your images on the iPAQ's screen, tell everyone to say "cheese," and capture a photo or short video. The resolution of pictures from these camera cards is reasonably good, but not the quality of an average, stand-alone digital camera.

FIGURE 11-39   The Veo Photo Traveler

Veo Photo Traveler for Pocket PC

www.veoproducts.com/Traveler_PocketPc/default.asp

This CompactFlash digital camera (see Figure 11-39) lets you capture 24-bit full-color JPEG still images at up to 640×480 resolution. Exposure, white balance, and color control are automatic. The camera lens swivels and has an adjustable focus.

The Pretec CompactCamera

www.pretec.com

The Pretec CompactCamera, shown in Figure 11-40, is capable of taking 24-bit color photos up to 640×480 resolution, and videos at 320×240 or 160×120 resolution. Shutter speed and white balance are automatic. You can add audio notes to the still-image photos and record a voice track with the videos. The camera has an optical as well as digital viewfinder, and a 2X digital zoom. The camera head can be swiveled 180 degrees.

FIGURE 11-40   The Pretec CF camera

11

FIGURE 11-41   The LifeView FlyCAM-CF

LifeView FlyCAM-CF

http://store.yahoo.com/lifeview-usa/

The FlyCAM-CF also lets you capture still images and videos (see Figure 11-41).

In all three cases, software must be installed on the iPAQ to support the cameras. These cameras capture images of reasonably good quality. The software depends on the type of camera you are using and ships with the camera itself.

Chapter 12 Navigate with GPS

How to…

- Use GPS to determine your location
- Navigate to anyone in your Contact list
- Find a restaurant, gas station, bank, or other site in any city
- Play team sports with GPS

Have you ever wished someone were beside you in the passenger seat, guiding you to an unfamiliar address? Or perhaps you've been in a strange city and were trying to find the nearest restaurant or gas station?

Figuring out where we are and where we are going has always been cumbersome and often inaccurate. You can buy a map for a city, but as time passes and things about the city change, it gets less and less accurate. Navigational tools have now been greatly improved courtesy of *Global Positioning System* (GPS) technology.

What Is GPS?

GPS is a network of 24 satellites around the globe that broadcast radio navigation information you can use to determine your exact position anywhere. These satellites act as reference points to determine any position within meters. Actually, these satellites can be used to determine location down to centimeters, but that level of accuracy is only accessible to the U.S. military, who designed and created the system (at a cost of over $12 billion).

Initially GPS devices were still expensive and only practical for large businesses and government. However, continued advancements have reduced a complete GPS system to a few miniaturized integrated circuits, dramatically shrinking the cost and size. GPS has become available to just about everyone and has found its way into cars, boats, planes, construction equipment, and farm machinery, and can even be attached to your iPAQ Pocket PC (maybe future iPAQ versions will feature integrated GPS?).

How Does GPS Work?

GPS works by comparing the signals from multiple GPS satellites (at least four are required for this process to work). A GPS receiver accurately measures the distance from four or more satellites whose positions are known, then uses this information to compute its precise location.

NOTE   *The explanation of GPS used here is simplified. For a more technical understanding of how GPS works, refer to some of the references at the end of this chapter.*

What Do We Use GPS For?

GPS can be used in a wide variety of ways. The possible uses fall into one of five general categories:

- ■ **Location**   To determine where you are. If you are a hiker, you could use GPS with your iPAQ to find your current position. It could also be used with a wireless service to deliver "location-based services." For example, suppose you were looking for a particular type of shoe. When you walked past a shoe store, your iPAQ's location-based services software could determine if that store has your shoes on sale, in stock, and in your size.

- ■ **Navigation**   To get from one location to another. This is generally why you find GPS systems (such as the Hertz Neverlost system) in more and more rental cars and available as options on many new vehicles. Now you can have this functionality in your pocket everywhere you go. If you like to fish, you can use your GPS to locate and easily return to your best fishing holes!

- ■ **Tracking**   To monitor the movement of people or things. Many trucking companies have adopted GPS to help their central dispatching keep track of where all their vehicles are.

- ■ **Mapping**   For cartography. Almost all modern maps are created using GPS technology for precision.

- ■ **Timing**   For accurately determining the time GPS satellites can be used as a form of atomic clock, allowing you to get very precise time on your GPS receiver. Every GPS satellite has its own atomic clock on board.

GPS on Your iPAQ

Your iPAQ will not come installed with a GPS solution. If you want to perform GPS functions with your device, you will need to acquire both a GPS receiver and software. Some sources for this equipment are listed at the end of this chapter. For the purposes of this chapter, we are using a GPS receiver from Emtac. This device uses Bluetooth wireless technology to stay connected to our Bluetooth-equipped iPAQ. It is extremely compact (approximately 3.5"×1.75"×0.5"), easy to use, and has a long-lasting rechargeable battery. Other vendors produce hardware that will plug directly into the bottom of your iPAQ through the serial port. For software we chose Destinator from PowerLOC Technologies (**www.powerloc.com**). You can use any vendor's hardware (check to make sure it conforms to the NMEA standard) or software you like; the techniques discussed in this chapter can be applied to most GPS software packages.

We will not be teaching you every function of Destinator, but rather focusing on the most common GPS navigation activities that an iPAQ user might want to accomplish.

CAUTION   *If you are driving a car, never attempt to interact with a GPS navigation system while the car is in motion. If you need to change an address, you should pull over, or allow a passenger to update the information for you. Most GPS software packages will give you audible instructions through your iPAQ's speaker when you need to turn or perform some other action.*

The main interface of your GPS software will likely contain a large map-viewing area along with a menu or control buttons on one edge, as in Figure 12-1.

12

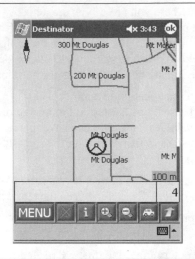

FIGURE 12-1   The Destinator interface contains a large map-viewing window with additional controls at the bottom for changing the view and other options.

In Destinator you have some other common interface elements:

- **Compass**   The top-left corner contains a compass that will always show you which direction is north. North isn't always up, as the map will rotate to face the direction you are going.

- **Status bar**   Below the map area is a bar that will tell you the status information for your system.

- **Scale indicator**   The right side of the map area contains a red-and-white line that indicates the scale. The length of each of the bars is indicated by a number on the bottom right (in Figure 12-1 it is 100 meters).

- **Menu buttons**   The menu buttons are used to launch the Destinator menu, switch to the view of the destination location, show information on location, zoom out, zoom in, switch between driving and walking modes, and switch in and out of 3-D viewing mode.

Note that touching the Menu button will open the main Destinator menu, shown in Figure 12-2, which will get you into the other parts of the software that we will be discussing.

Checking GPS Status

Before you can use your GPS, you need to make sure it has locked into the necessary number of GPS satellites. In the Destinator interface, just above the menu bar, is the status bar. The right side of this status bar shows a number. This is the number of GPS satellites that your receiver is currently communicating with. If this number is less than 4, your receiver will not be able to perform location functions. Incidentally, the GPS transmissions are line-of-sight, so there cannot

FIGURE 12-2   The main Destinator menu is where you will go to enter destinations and manage all your navigation.

be obstacles between you and the satellites. Because of this, your GPS generally doesn't function indoors, in parking garages, or in other such locations.

Selecting GPS Status from the Destinator menu will open the Status screen, shown in Figure 12-3. This screen will tell you important information about your connection with your GPS receiver and its connection with the GPS satellites.

12

FIGURE 12-3   The GPS Status screen will tell you the details of your connection with the GPS satellites.

In this example we are currently connected to four satellites (the minimum). The lines connecting to each satellite indicate the strength of the satellite signal. You can also see your current latitude, longitude, altitude, and velocity (if you are moving!). You can also see the date and time. This is an extremely accurate date and time, as it is based on the atomic clocks aboard each of the GPS satellites you are communicating with. The number that appears beside each satellite graphic is the unique identification number of that particular *satellite vehicle* (SV).

If you are running your GPS with software and hardware from different vendors, you will need to tell them how to talk to each other. To do this, press the Settings button on the top right of the GPS Status screen. This will open the configuration information, as shown in Figure 12-4.

On this screen you can specify the COM port, communication speed, and protocol that your GPS receiver will be communicating with. The easiest way to do this is with the Auto Search button, which will look for a GPS receiver by scanning all the COM ports on your device. Tapping on the Check button will test to make sure that the software is correctly communicating with the receiver. After connecting to a new GPS unit, you may need to do a hot or cold restart using the buttons at the top of the window. Once you have a configuration working, be sure to save it with the Save button.

Now that you have the hardware and software talking, you are ready to start using your GPS!

Finding Your Current Location

Finding out exactly where you are can be useful if you get lost, if you are hiking in the backcountry, or if you work in a situation where your physical location is important to coordinating your work activity, such as bicycle couriers in Los Angeles. Finding your current location is as simple as

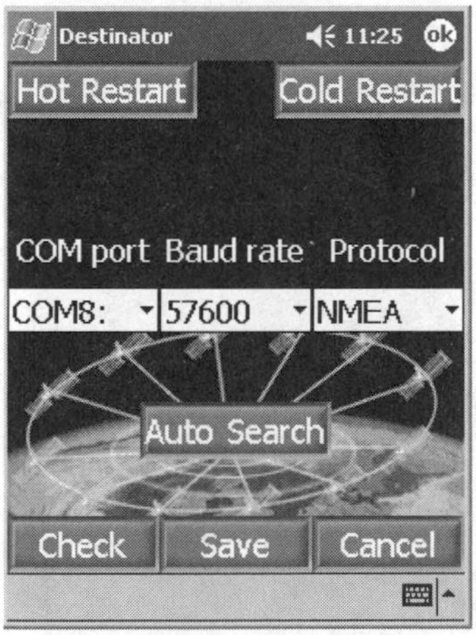

FIGURE 12-4   The Configuration screen allows you to set up how your software communicates with your GPS receiver.

How to ... Use Your GPS When You Are Away from Civilization

The ability to find your current location is also very valuable for hikers, surveyors, marine enthusiasts, and many others. Software like Destinator is useful for navigating cities and streets, but not so useful if you are on the water or hiking in the backcountry. For these uses you will need different software like that offered by MapTech (**www.maptech.com**). Their Pocket Navigator product will allow you to load U.S. Geological Survey maps onto your Pocket PC and navigate with them as shown here.

Of course, if you do plan to use your iPAQ in these rugged conditions, you will need to give special consideration to battery life and rugged conditions. The battery life of your iPAQ won't last you through a multiday hike unless you use the GPS very sparingly. Consider carrying spare batteries, an "electric fuel" battery recharger (a chemical battery that can be used to recharge your iPAQ on the fly), or a solar-powered recharger like the iSUN unit from ICP (**www.icpglobal.com**).

If you are traveling in conditions where your iPAQ is going to be exposed to a lot of moisture or dust, you should consider the iPAQ "ruggedized" case or an alternative case to help protect your device when you need it most. More information on these cases can be found at **www.pocketpctools.com**.

choosing Locate under the Menu button. This will tell you exactly where you are, as shown in Figure 12-5.

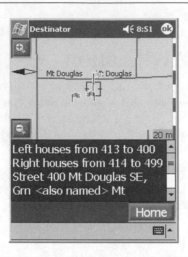

FIGURE 12-5   The Locate option will tell you your current position in a window at the bottom of the map area and indicate it with a yellow flag on the map.

You will get the details of your current information in a window at the bottom of the map-viewing area. In addition, you will see three flags on the map. The red flag is your starting location, the blue your destination, and the yellow is your current position.

Navigating to a Destination

The most common use for GPS on a Pocket PC is to help you find your way from one place to another. We find this particularly useful when we are traveling and have appointments all over town in a city we are unfamiliar with. To navigate to a destination, you must tell your GPS software where you wish to go. You can do this by providing an address, specifying an intersection, or selecting a specific point on a map. In addition, you may have a set of favorite addresses that are places that you go to often, or you can look up a particular contact in your address book to go to their address. Destinator also features a powerful Points of Interest feature that allows you to get a list of the closest restaurants, banks, gas stations, or many other useful destinations. If you find yourself in an unfamiliar location and want to see all the restaurants within three miles, you can find that with this feature.

Specific Address

One of the most common ways to navigate is to enter the address of the location you are going to. Destinator offers a variety of ways to do this, all of which give the same result. Each method simply starts with a different piece of information—City, Street, or ZIP/Postal code. For example, if we wanted to enter a new address, we might start with City. Selecting Menu | Destination | City Street (Menu button, Destination submenu, City Street option) would open the window in Figure 12-6.

FIGURE 12-6 You can enter a specific address to navigate to with your GPS.

You can select your city destination from the drop-down list, or you can start typing the name of the city in the text box at the bottom. After you select your city, you will tap the Street button on the top. This will allow you to select your street destination from the drop-down list. As with city, you can start typing the street name into the text box. When you have input the street, enter the specific street address, as shown here. The valid range of addresses will be offered to you in the box.

Once you have the address fully entered, press the Go! button to calculate the best route from where you are to where you want to go. Your next turn or instruction will appear in the box at the top of the map area, and your path will be outlined on the map with a bold blue-and-white line. As you begin to drive, the maneuvers you will need to complete will be displayed one by one at the top of the map-viewing area until you arrive at your destination. If you have your iPAQ sound turned on, you will also receive verbal instructions on when to turn and what maneuvers to make.

12

Intersection

As an alternative to entering a specific address, you could just specify an intersection. Entering an intersection is usually faster and easier than entering a full address and is useful if you only want to get into a specific area and then plan to navigate manually. I have often used this when traveling. Once, while on business in San Francisco, I decided to meet a friend for dinner in Los Gatos. I knew how to get around Los Gatos, but not the best way to get there from San Francisco. I entered a main intersection in Los Gatos and allowed the GPS to guide me through San Francisco and onto the best freeway to get me to my destination.

To navigate by intersection, you can choose Destination | Intersection. This will open the window shown in Figure 12-7.

First select the city the intersection is in. This doesn't have to be the same city you are currently in, but it must be on the same map that you currently have loaded. (The Pocket PC cannot contain the entire map for most countries in memory at one time, so you must load certain regions.) If your route spans two cities, the software will put you onto the correct highways and calculate the total distance of your trip. After selecting your city, you will select the two intersecting streets using the Street1 and Street2 buttons. Some software is smart enough that after selecting your first street, only valid intersecting streets are shown in the list for Street 2. Unfortunately, Destinator doesn't do this. It is possible to select two streets that do not intersect. If this happens, Destinator will warn you that your two streets don't meet and will show you a map suggesting you "point" at the spot you want to get to using the map cursor (pointing finger, as described in the next section).

Once you have successfully entered your destination, you can use the Go! button to calculate the route and begin navigation, or use the Show button to show the destination on the map-viewing window.

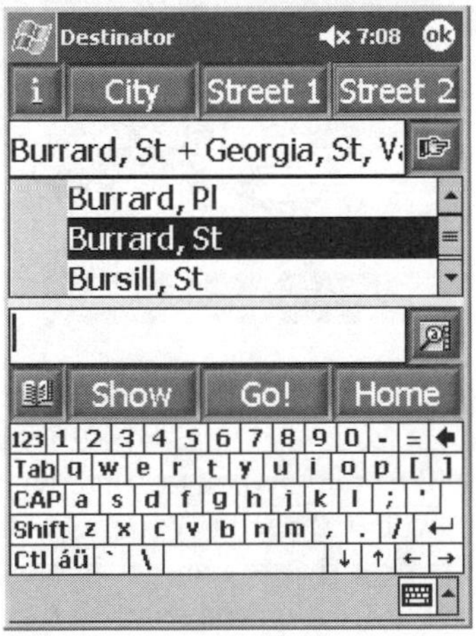

FIGURE 12-7   Navigating to a particular intersection is a quick way to get yourself into a particular part of town.

Get There By Pointing

You don't always have to enter specific street information to get to where you want to go. If you can visually locate where you would like to end up on the map, you can simply point to your destination, and the software will determine where that is. You access this functionality by choosing Destination | Map Cursor (the Map Cursor option of the Destination submenu). This will open the map-viewing window shown in Figure 12-8.

You can use the arrow and zoom controls (magnifying glasses with plus and minus signs) to move around the map. Your current location is shown with a red flag. Once you identify where you would like to go, you can use the Go! button to begin navigation.

Favorites

You might find that there are particular destinations you need to get to often, such as your home, office, day care, or other location. You can set the software to remember a group of "favorite" destinations. I find this useful when traveling in an unfamiliar city, and I often will drive between a variety of meeting locations and my hotel. After picking up my rental car, I will instruct the GPS to navigate me to my hotel. I then make the hotel a "favorite" destination so that I do not have to reenter the information every time I want to return to the hotel.

With previously mentioned techniques for entering a destination location, you can save that location to the Favorites simply by pressing the small Favorites icon with the image of a book shown here.

To navigate to a previously saved favorite location, choose Destination | Favorites. This will open the window shown in Figure 12-9.

FIGURE 12-8   Using the map cursor to point at a destination on the map is another way to tell Destinator where you want to go.

12

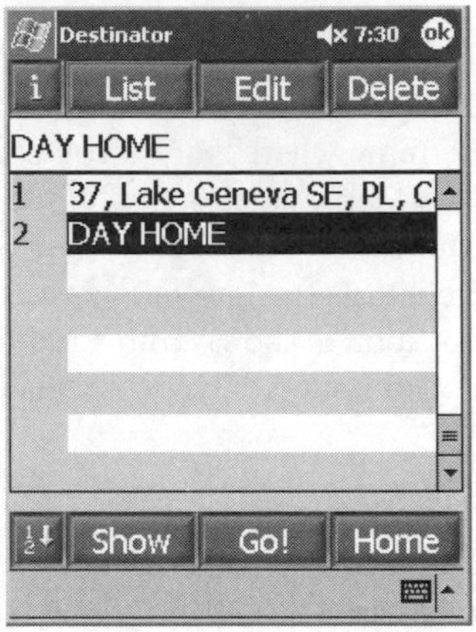

FIGURE 12-9   You can select any of your frequently used destinations from the Favorites window.

You can select any of your favorite destinations from the scrollable list, or type a character or two of the favorite name in the text entry box at the top to quickly scroll through a large list. The list can be sorted either numerically by favorite number or alphabetically by toggling the sort mode; use the icon on the bottom left shown here.

When you first add an address to your favorites list, it will appear as the raw address. You can give this favorite a more meaningful name by tapping the Edit button on the top. This will open a window where you can define a more meaningful name as well as add a comment to the location, as shown next.

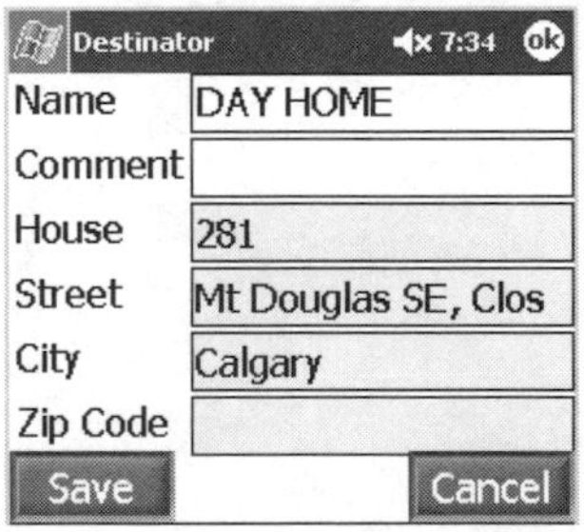

After you select the favorite location, the Go! button will calculate the route to that destination. The Show button will show you where that location is in the map-viewing window.

History

You will find History a very useful option on the Destination submenu. It allows you to see a list of your most recent destinations and simply select from the list to return to that destination.

FIGURE 12-10 You can navigate to the address of any of the contacts stored in your iPAQ Contacts application.

Contacts

Many of the destinations you might want to navigate to are contained within your current contacts on your iPAQ's Contacts application, which was discussed in Part I of this book. You can select from your list of contacts by choosing Destination | Contacts. This may take a moment to load, as Destinator actually loads all of your contacts and addresses into its memory. You will then see a list of your contacts, as shown in Figure 12-10.

A limitation of this particular software is that the address must exactly match the way that the software expects the address to be formatted. For instance, in my hometown, addresses are divided into quadrants. For example, I might want to navigate to "400 Mount Douglas Close SE." Destinator has this address in its map as "400 Mount Douglas SE Close," and thus it cannot plot the address as I have it entered in my contacts. It will bring up an error message saying that the contact I selected does not have an address that matches the current map. If this happens to you, press the Address button on the top, and Destinator will try to map the address you have entered to its closest matching addresses. When the desired address shows up on the list, you can select it and navigate to it.

Points of Interest

The Points of Interest (POI) feature of Destinator is a wonderful, extremely useful feature. It allows you to find the nearest destination from a given category. Imagine you are in an unfamiliar city, and you need to find a gas station or a bank machine. All you need to do is choose Destination | POI. This will open the window shown in Figure 12-11.

12

FIGURE 12-11   It is easy to find the nearest gas station, bank, restaurant, or other key location with the Points of Interest feature.

Select the type of location you are looking for, and tap on the POI List button to see a list of that type of location sorted by proximity, as shown here. Select the destination you would like to navigate to, and press the Go! button to calculate the route.

Maneuvers

Once a route has been calculated, you might want to see a list of all the maneuvers that you will be required to follow to get there. You can pull up this list by tapping on the Maneuvers submenu. This will show you the maneuvers list shown in Figure 12-12.

The current step in the maneuver list is shown in the lighter-colored box at the top of the window. If you would like to see more detail on any particular step, you can select that step and tap the Show button to be taken to the map view for that step. Tapping the Home button will return you to the main map-viewing navigation window.

FIGURE 12-12 The Maneuvers window will let you see all the sequential actions that you will have to execute to get to your destination.

3-D View

An interesting feature in Destinator is the ability to switch from the standard map view to a 3-D view. The 3-D view will show you a view as it might appear to the driver moving along the road. Your mapped path will show up in red. The 3-D view is shown here.

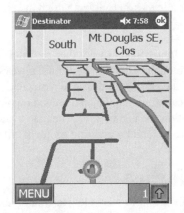

You can toggle in and out of 3-D view at any time by tapping on the arrow button at the bottom right of both the map-view and 3-D view windows.

Loading and Switching Maps

Your iPAQ has a limited amount of memory, and GPS maps are very detailed and need a lot of storage space. If you are planning to do a lot of traveling and need to have a number of

12

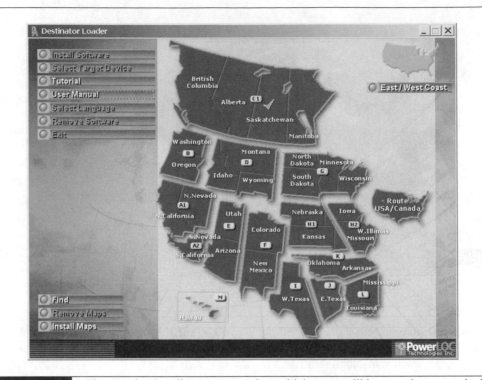

FIGURE 12-13   The map loader allows you to select which maps will be stored on your device.

maps with you, buying a 64MB or larger SD card or other external storage device is highly recommended. If you only travel to one destination at a time, always returning to home in between, you can load and unload the maps you desire as you need them.

Destinator has a complete application for loading and unloading maps. You simply have to insert the CD into your desktop PC and follow the instructions. The map loader shown in Figure 12-13 will let you select the regions you desire to load by clicking on them with your mouse.

GPS Hardware and Software

In addition to the Emtac GPS receiver and PowerLOC Destinator software used in the preceding examples, you should consider many other vendors and configurations of hardware and software for your iPAQ GPS needs. The GPS units come in one of six formats:

- **CompactFlash**   CompactFlash (CF) card GPS units simply connect into the iPAQ via a CF card expansion sleeve. The CF versions tend to be a bit bulkier than their serial port counterparts because the actual receiving antenna must be attached to the CF card itself. Power is usually drawn directly from the iPAQ to power the unit; however, external power sources such as car adapters are available for many models.

■ **PC card**   PC card GPS receivers are similar in size to the CF units, except that they require a PC card expansion sleeve to connect to the iPAQ. These units also usually draw their power directly from the iPAQ or through an external adapter. The advantage of the PC card format is that it can also be used in a laptop computer.

■ **Expansion sleeve**   This type of GPS receiver does not require the addition of an extra expansion sleeve. Instead, the receiver is the expansion sleeve. Although these make the unit very compact, you cannot use any other expansion sleeves at the same time.

■ **Serial port**   This is one of the most common GPS types. It simply clips into the serial interface on the bottom of your iPAQ. You will need to ensure that the unit you purchase matches up with your iPAQ, as different iPAQ versions have different serial port configurations.

■ **Bluetooth**   This is one of the newest types of GPS. It is essentially the same as a serial port unit; however, it makes its serial connection with the iPAQ via a Bluetooth connection and thus is wirelessly connected instead of needing cables.

■ **Stand-alone**   Stand-alone GPS receivers are units that can function with or without the iPAQ (although the iPAQ usually extends the receiver's functionality and usability). These receivers tend to connect to the iPAQ through the bottom serial port. One nice feature about this type of receiver is that you can use it alone or with an iPAQ or with a laptop.

Many GPS hardware vendors offer equipment that will work with your iPAQ. Some of the most common are

■ Navman GPS (**www.navman.com**) comes in the format of an expansion sleeve. You cannot have two expansion sleeves on your iPAQ at the same time, so if you are using an expansion sleeve for storing your maps on an external storage device, this can be a problem. To help get around this, the Navman comes with an integrated CF slot for external storage. The Navman kit includes the expansion sleeve with integrated GPS receiver, SmartPath software, a suction-cup car mount, and power cable.

■ Pharos iGPS (**www.pharosgps.com**) allows you to buy their GPS receiver and software separately if you desire. The Pharos GPS receiver hardware uses a cable to connect to the serial port on the bottom of your iPAQ. This same cable also includes a vehicle power adapter to keep your iPAQ and the receiver powered/charged.

■ TeleType WorldNavigator (**www.teletype.com**) has a variety of formats of GPS units including CompactFlash, PCMCIA, and serial connection. The iPAQ-compatible units can be used with their own integrated antenna, or you can add an external antenna.

■ PowerLOC Destinator (**www.powerloc.com**) sells both GPS hardware and software. Their hardware unit is a serial-connected GPS receiver with vehicle charging/power adapter. You can also use their software with any other standard GPS receiver, as we did in the examples earlier in the chapter.

■ TravRoute CoPilot (**www.travroute.com**) sells their GPS gear in a variety of formats also including an expansion sleeve, serial-connected, or CF format.

12

■ Pretec Compact GPS (**www.pretec.com**) offers a fully integrated CF GPS receiver unit.

■ Socket Communications Bluetooth GPS (**http://www.socketcom.com/product/gps.asp**) offers an OEM version of the Emtac GPS that is well packaged and supported, and actually costs less! I love my Bluetooth GPS and can highly recommend this unit.

Other Software

In addition to the GPS vendors listed earlier, you can consider a few other pieces of software for personal navigation.

Microsoft Pocket Streets

Microsoft's Pocket Streets (**www.microsoft.com/pocketstreets/**) is an extension of their desktop Streets & Trips software. It is not a product that is purchased separately, but is included with the base product (**www.microsoft.com/streets/**). This product includes the ability to export user-generated maps from Microsoft MapPoint, AutoRoute, or Streets & Trips software. This software has very broad coverage for North America, Canada, and several European cities.

Tom Tom CityMaps

One of the biggest issues about GPS systems is the lack of maps available if you are traveling outside North America. A few software companies support maps for non–North American cities. Tom Tom (**www.tomtom.com**) has a database of more than 100,000 cities across Europe that ships on a CD-ROM (some of the larger cities are available in electronic downloads from their web site). This software is well designed and very user friendly.

Where to Go Now

In this chapter we wanted to introduce you to the world of personal navigation with GPS on your iPAQ. It isn't possible to give you a detailed analysis of all the features, software, and hardware products in this space. The vendors listed in this chapter can provide a great deal more detail on their products and features, or you can check **www.PocketPCTools.com** for more detail as well.

In addition to basic personal or business navigation, GPS is rapidly catching on for location-based services (that is, vendors being able to provide you with information when you are near their facilities, or airports being able to tell when you arrive in a parking lot late for a flight that they can automatically rebook you on the next flight or might hold the airplane), and even new sports! A popular new recreational sport has popped up around personal GPS navigation. It is called "geo caching." It involves groups of people hiding or "caching" something in a location and then identifying where these caches are with their GPS coordinates. For more details on this sport, check out **www.geocaching.com**.

If you would like to dive a little deeper into the technology underlying GPS, we recommend an online tutorial put together by one of the major GPS vendors, Trimble. You can find it at **www.trimble.com/gps**.

Chapter 13

Use Your iPAQ in Your Enterprise

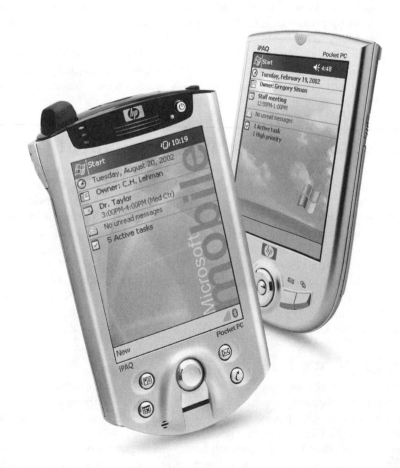

How to…

- Deploy and support iPAQs in your enterprise
- Utilize Exchange 2003 and MS Mobile Information Server
- Support your networks with your iPAQ
- Use your iPAQ in the medical field
- Use your iPAQ for customer service and sales force automation
- Use your iPAQ if you are a pilot, firefighter, or health care worker, and more

As the iPAQ gains popularity, it is increasingly being deployed as a business productivity tool. It is an incredibly flexible platform that can be used for a tremendous range of business purposes. However, deploying these devices as part of the corporate tool set also means that a company must be able to support these platforms.

In this chapter we will focus on the features of the iPAQ, Pocket PC 2003, and third-party applications that make it easier to support and manage iPAQs in your company. In addition, we will look at some third-party tools that will interest you if you are in professions such as information technology, health care, customer service, sales, and others.

Deploying iPAQs in a Corporate Environment

As mentioned at the beginning of the chapter and as you undoubtedly figured out by now, iPAQs are not just personal digital assistants (PDAs). For all intents and purposes, iPAQs are small, yet powerful, computers. As your organization begins to purchase, implement, and support iPAQs, you will notice that supporting them is much like supporting desktop and laptop computers.

Depending on your organization, management may dictate which applications can be installed and deployed on company iPAQs, how corporate e-mail is accessed, how to connect to corporate networks, and what peripherals can be used on the iPAQs. Organizations with central support services may also find themselves having to support these remote, portable iPAQ devices.

This section will look at accessing corporate e-mail using Microsoft's ServerSync technology as well as third-party solutions. We will also discuss some third-party tools for tracking, managing, and supporting these iPAQs.

Accessing Corporate E-mail

E-mail has become a critical component of not just organizations, but also their customers and employees. Many people become so used to e-mail that they find it difficult to live without it. As wireless devices become popular, people start using them as an extension to their contact databases, calendars, and e-mails. The iPAQ is no exception.

All you have to do is drop your iPAQ into the synch cradle, with your system attached to your organization's e-mail system, and it will synchronize those items automatically (once you configure the synchronization settings). The problem with this solution is that these settings change, especially with regard to e-mail and calendar information. Having a calendar on the server is great, but you want to be able to have the calendar synchronize your iPAQ with the server when you are out of the office. This section looks at a few solutions.

Microsoft Exchange 2003 and Mobile Information Server

Microsoft was well aware of the need to synchronize your iPAQ with your Exchange Server infrastructure. Currently Microsoft offers only one way to perform this task, although a second way is coming soon (more on that shortly).

Microsoft released a product called Mobile Information Server 2002 (MIS). MIS is designed to allow organizations to access their Exchange information from hand-held devices. It does this with one of two components: Server ActiveSync and Outlook Mobile Access.

Server ActiveSync performs real-time synchronization between your iPAQ and your organization's Exchange Server over a wired or wireless connection. You configure the iPAQ either through ActiveSync on the desktop or through the ActiveSync application on the iPAQ itself. Appendix A discusses the steps involved in installing and configuring MIS.

About the time this book will be on shelves, Microsoft will release the next version of their Exchange Server product, Exchange 2003 (codenamed "Titanium"). Exchange 2003 incorporates and enhances some of the MIS features.

Outlook Mobile Access has been enhanced in Exchange 2003 to include more protocols, including Wireless Application Protocol (WAP) 2.*x,* XHTML browser-based devices, i-Mode devices, full HTML browsers, and Compact HTML (cHTML). Because Outlook Mobile Access is now part of Exchange 2003, it offers both a lower cost of ownership, since a single server is required for both, and easier management, since the management tools are now simply an extension of Exchange.

Server ActiveSync, now called Exchange Server ActiveSync in Exchange 2003, allows you to work both online and offline by specifying how your iPAQ will synchronize. You can configure it to be either on demand or scheduled, based on the settings on the iPAQ. If you couple it with Outlook Mobile Access, you will be able to access your tasks and your organization's Global Address List (GAL). Figure 13-1 illustrates the configuration tab in Exchange 2003 used to configure a user's mailbox for Exchange Server ActiveSync.

Another feature is one that your iPAQ cannot use…yet. While HP has not announced any plans for this, we hope that they will release an iPAQ that has built-in WAN wireless, such as GPRS or 1*x*RTT. (We think they will do this because the 5450 iPAQ has a GPRS SIM slot, although it is not connected.) Once these devices exist, you will be able to have Exchange send a specially formatted Short Message Service (SMS) message to your iPAQ that will "wake" it up and prompt the device to initiate a synch.

Synchrologic Email Accelerator

Another product that you may want to check out for wireless synchronization with your iPAQ is Synchrologic's Email Accelerator (**www.synchrologic.com**). Email Accelerator, as shown in

13

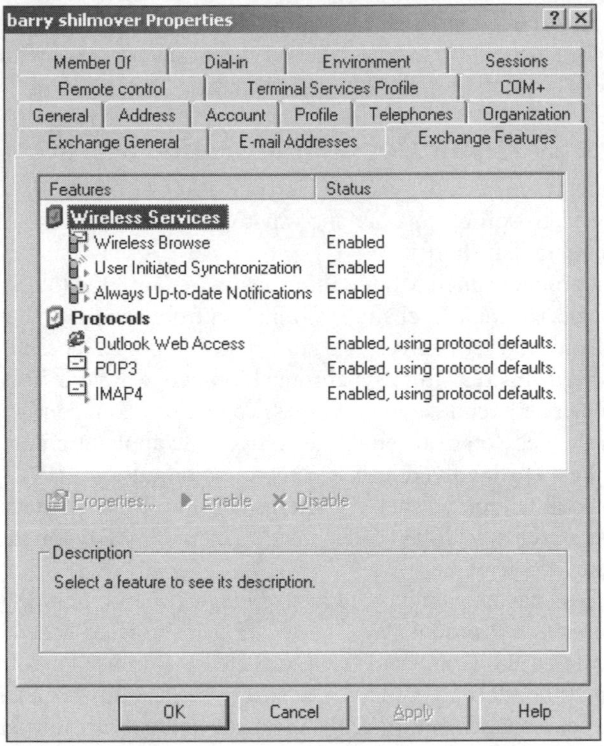

FIGURE 13-1   Configuring a user's mailbox for Exchange Server ActiveSync

Figure 13-2, is similar to the Exchange 2003 and MIS versions in that it allows you to synchronize your e-mail information with your iPAQ. One of the differences is that they allow you to synchronize not only with Exchange Server, but also with Lotus Domino and POP servers.

XTNDConnect Server

The third Product in this section is XTNDConnect Server from Extended Systems (www.XTNDconnect.com). As with the other products mentioned here, it allows you to synchronize your iPAQ with your organization's Exchange system. It also allows you to synchronize your device with Lotus Notes systems. In essence, it replaces your desktop ActiveSync application.

Tracking, Managing, and Supporting iPAQs in the Enterprise

As iPAQs become more prevalent in your organization, the IT department will find that it needs to support them in much the same way as it does desktops and laptops. Software licensing and

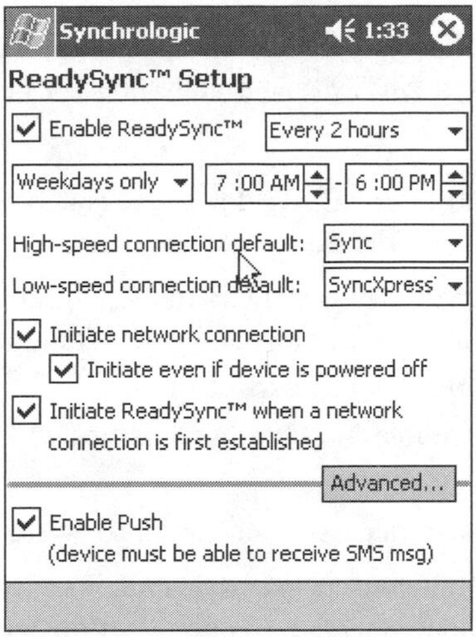

FIGURE 13-2   Synchronizing your iPAQ with Synchrologic's Email Accelerator

usage become an issue, as do hardware peripherals. For example, your organization may purchase a sales automation product for use on the iPAQs for the sales department. If a salesperson then installs a software or hardware product that affects how that application functions, it is up to the IT department to fix it. Problem is, the iPAQs tend to be very mobile and may not be in the same location as the IT department or IT tech.

This section looks at a couple of products that allow the IT department to track and manage their iPAQ devices.

Afaria from XcelleNet

Afaria from XcelleNet (**www.XcelleNet.com**) is a powerful tool that solves mobile management challenges and streamlines systems management. From a central location IT administrators can perform the following tasks:

- Deploy applications for use in the field
- Manage, exchange, and deliver content
- Capture and store hardware and software information, automatically keeping track of mobile devices and their condition
- Provide automated system and data backup and restore capability in the event that data is destroyed or lost
- Synchronize application data on mobile devices

Epiphan CEAnywhere

The final product in the section is CEAnywhere from Epiphan (**www.epiphan.com**). CEAnywhere allows IT departments to connect to your iPAQs and troubleshoot the devices from a central location. Some of the features include

- **Real-time remote control of your iPAQ devices** This provides a "hands-on" experience and virtually places the device in your hand.

- **"Connect Anywhere" portability** The CEAnywhere server can run from almost any location, allowing both your IT department and your Windows CE–empowered workforce to be anywhere in the world.

- **Troubleshooting** It can troubleshoot hardware issues with real-time hardware diagnostics information.

- **Windows CE device registry access** You can make system modifications in real time.

- **CEAnywhere secure session control scenarios** CEAnywhere can be as secure as your requirements dictate. Whether you want to open your device to the world for all to see a sales demonstration, or run a 24-bit secure support session, it is all easily managed through the supplied CEAnywhere user interface, which resides on the server.

- **Client devices connections** Connect client devices via any physical means: dial-up modem, wireless LAN, remote LAN, the Internet, CDMA (Code-Division Multiple Access), CDPD, GSM (Global System for Mobile Communications), and companion PC—as long as they can get a TCP/IP connection back to the CEAnywhere server.

- **File transfer** Quickly transfer files between the iPAQ and desktop.

- **Customizable interfaces** Install multiple skins to get the look-and-feel you require.

- **Quick deployment** Deploy rapidly and install easily with any of our deployment options.

Enterprise Solutions

In addition to the core added value of the iPAQ in the enterprise, the iPAQ can contribute considerably to a significant number of specialized applications. These solutions can be categorized using three broad descriptions:

- **Horizontal** A horizontal solution is one that applies to most organizations regardless of the specific industry of the organization. Some examples of horizontal enterprise solutions include document management, remote desktop access, and systems management. Some would include sales force automation (SFA) and customer relationship management (CRM) in this category, although these are often customized for a specific industry.

- **Vertical** A vertical solution is specific to a particular industry. A good vertical solution can be used by many different companies or organizations within the targeted industry.

For example, a medical solution can be used in a variety of healthcare situations. Solutions for researching court cases could be used by lawyers, judges, and many others.

- ■ **Custom**   A custom solution is developed for a specific company or organization and usually cannot be easily transferred to other companies, even within the same industry.

In each of these categories we will look at some specific examples of solutions, and where possible, show how these solutions are used by real enterprises.

Horizontal Solutions

You can further subdivide the area of horizontal solutions into those solutions that can be installed without any customization, and those that provide a framework, but still need to be customized for your specific use. The standard category is usually less expensive to implement and can provide a faster return on investment. It includes tactical solutions such as mobile systems administration.

The group that needs to be customized is often more expensive because of the manual labor involved in implementing the solution. However, custom solutions are often regarded as more strategic in their ability to fundamentally affect the efficiency of an operation. A solid example of this type of solution is sales force automation, which usually needs to be tweaked for every company that uses it, due to the differences in how each company actually approaches the sales process.

The following are some examples of horizontal solutions that you may be able to implement in your business to add value. This is by no means an exhaustive list, but instead is an introduction to the topic.

> **TIP**   *When looking at any enterprise solution, you will want to carefully examine the security method used to protect the data. One of the drawbacks of the mobility provided by iPAQs is the ease with which the device can be lost or stolen. You should ensure that any solutions that you may implement for your mobile workers never put any of the corporate information or operations at risk. Features you should look for include military-grade encryption of all transmissions. Also, any data stored locally should be encrypted. Simply having a local password is insufficient to protect vital data from techniques for cracking or bypassing these passwords.*

Systems and Network Management

Keeping servers and networks up and running is a critical function for almost every business in the world. Information technology (IT) personnel need to be able to respond to and repair server and network problems from anywhere. Using a wirelessly equipped iPAQ to accomplish this is a natural fit given its portability and wireless capabilities (addressed in Chapter 9).

One product we will look at is the Microsoft Windows Server 2003 Mobile Admin Pack (which uses the sonicadmin product from Sonic Mobility—**www.sonicmobility.com**). With this software, IT support staff have the ability to fully manage the network and server environment from their iPAQ, including managing users, event logs, DNS, printers, files, services, processes, and more. It also includes the ability to talk to any server or network device at the command-line level—not only Windows servers, but also Linux, UNIX, and others.

With the File Explorer interface you can perform many file functions on remote computers right from your iPAQ.

Figure 13-3 shows one of the screens from the Mobile Admin Pack where you can, with your iPAQ, connect to any remote computer and browse the files on its physical and logical drives, just like you would if you were sitting in front of a computer. You can cut, copy, and paste files. If you want to edit a text file, you can pull it down to your iPAQ and make changes, then put it back on the computer you are working on. This is very useful for editing configuration files and other types of system files. If you are on the road and you need a MS Word document that is stored on a server in the office, you can connect to that server, browse to the file, and then e-mail the file to yourself on your iPAQ.

Another common task that IT people need to perform is the starting and stopping of *services*. Services are the programs that run in the background on all Windows-based computers that provide the critical operating functions on the computer. On corporate servers this also includes things such as your mail server and web server. IT personnel often need to be able to stop and restart these services to correct problems. This can be done with remote administration software, as shown in Figure 13-4.

Many other functions can be performed from the iPAQ; in fact, almost all critical functions can be managed remotely using this tool. You can even get right down to a command shell interface. For Windows users, this is the familiar *C:>* prompt, and for users of other operating systems such as Linux and UNIX, this prompt will take a slightly different format. An example of how the command shell interface looks is shown in Figure 13-5.

Another useful tool that is built into the Pocket PC operating system on your iPAQ is a Microsoft Terminal Services client. The Terminal Services client allows you to form a connection

FIGURE 13-4   With the Services window you can start and stop any service on any managed Windows computer on the network.

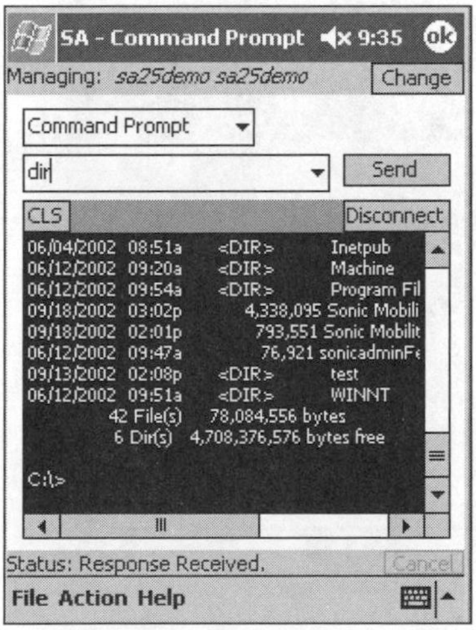

FIGURE 13-5   The command prompt interface allows for low-level access to any managed computer on the network including non-Windows systems and devices.

to a computer running MS Terminal Server. With this you will have the remote computer's screen transmitted to your iPAQ. Any keystrokes you enter on the iPAQ keyboard will be passed along to the controlled computer as its own keystrokes, and any taps you make on your iPAQ screen will be interpreted as mouse clicks on the remote system. Figure 13-6 shows an active Terminal Server session on an iPAQ.

This concept is very valuable for ad-hoc interaction with a remote system for doing things like interacting with a custom order-entry application or other activity. Although useful for those critical situations when you absolutely have to interact with the screen and keyboard of a remote system, this does have a number of limitations when deployed to an iPAQ. The Terminal Server client was never designed to run on a hand-held Pocket PC. As a result, the screen doesn't fit.

Most computers run screen resolutions in excess of 1024×768 pixels. Your iPAQ screen is 240×320 pixels. This means that you can see only a portion of the screen at one time, and you must "pan" around the remote computer's screen to see the portion that you want. You do have the option to "shrink" the remote computer screen to fit into your iPAQ's display; however, this generally makes the interface impossible to read.

Other limitations include the lack of ability to right-click or to double-click, which some PC-based programs require as an interface technique. If you are running on a public carrier wireless network such as GPRS or CDMA, you will also find Terminal Server to run very slowly. If you are running on a higher-bandwidth network such as a WiFi (802.11x)-based network (covered in Chapter 9), you will be less constrained by the speed, but will still face the other challenges.

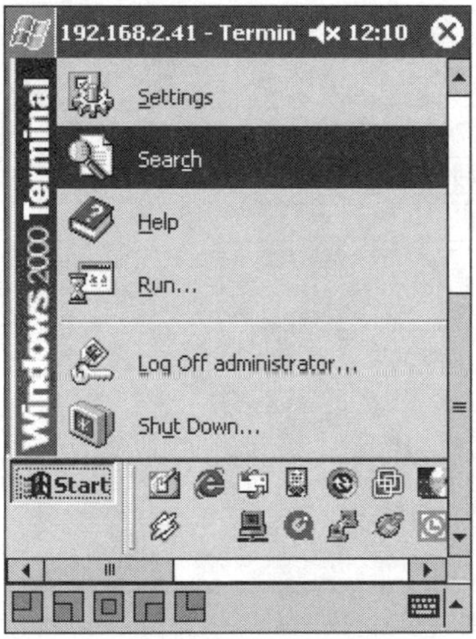

FIGURE 13-6 Terminal Server allows you to see the screen of a remote computer and to "remote control" that system by transmitting your keystrokes and taps from your iPAQ to the managed computer.

Despite its limitations, the Terminal Services client on your iPAQ can be very useful for those important ad-hoc interactions with a computer in your network.

If you would like to read about some companies using mobile administration software or Terminal Services to add value in their enterprises, the following are links to some corporate case studies:

www.sonicmobility.com/sonicadmin_success_stories.htm

www.microsoft.com/mobile/enterprise/casestudies/cs_default.asp

Field Order Entry

Many businesses need to take payments from customers while on the go. This includes pizza deliverers, plumbers, taxi drivers, couriers, and many others. The ability to accept credit cards can be very important for these businesses, but credit card fraud has made accepting credit cards in the field a risky business. Now you can use your iPAQ to accept credit cards and verify them in real time with a wireless connection (as discussed in Chapter 9).

One product that allows you to do this is Pocket Verifier from Merchant Anywhere (**www.merchantanywhere.com**). This product comes in both "lite" and professional versions. With it you can accept credit cards from anywhere you can get a wireless connection, as shown in Figure 13-7.

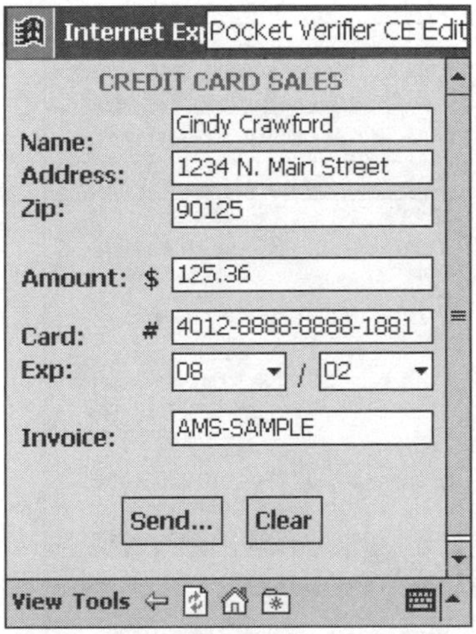

13

FIGURE 13-7   With Pocket Verifier you can accept credit card payments on your iPAQ.

Sales Force Automation

Another common requirement for salespeople is to have access to their sales contacts and deals while on the move. Many businesses use the popular program ACT! to keep track of their critical sales information. If you are an ACT! user, you can use a third-party program called Trans/ACT from Pin Point Tools (**www.pinpointtools.com**) to have all this information at your fingertips, as shown in Figure 13-8.

Trans/ACT will synchronize your contacts, groups, notes, histories, sales opportunities, and calendar with your iPAQ. This includes any custom fields you have created in ACT! and will allow you to even create your own screens on the Pocket PC. This product has a great GUI designer to allow you to build what the screens should look like on your desktop PC and then move them over to your iPAQ.

Vertical Solutions

A very large number of Pocket PC solutions are available for specific industries from aviation to zoology. We will look at a few examples of solutions from the healthcare, aviation, and emergency-response industries.

Aviation

For pilots, the iPAQ is a fantastic lightweight tool. Wherever they happen to be, they can stay in touch by using all the built-in functions of the iPAQ as featured in other parts of this book. However,

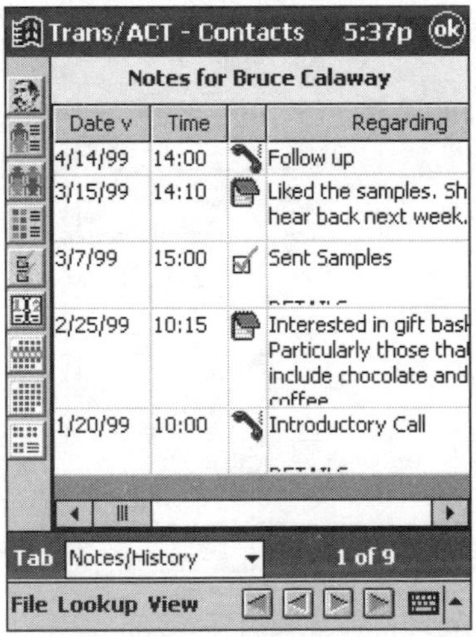

FIGURE 13-8   Take your ACT! information with you on your iPAQ with Trans/ACT from Pin Point Tools.

specific vertical solutions for the iPAQ can add even more value to individuals in the aviation industry. One such product is EFISce, from a UK company called NavTech (**www.palmplan.flyer.co.uk**), as shown in Figure 13-9.

This feature-packed product has many valuable tools for pilots including

- Ability to save, recall, and reverse flight plans
- Fuel planning
- Weight and balance when loading your airplane
- Timer
- Unit conversions
- Connection to GPS for real-time navigation (as discussed in Chapter 12), shown in Figure 13-10
- EFIS or HSI moving map displays
- Wind triangle

EFISce has full European databases available as well as U.S. and New Zealand/Australia databases.

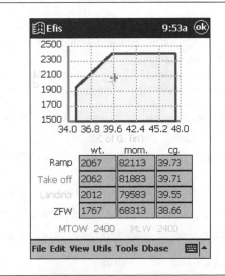

13

 FIGURE 13-9   Tools like EFISce allow pilots to perform many functions from the palm of their hands.

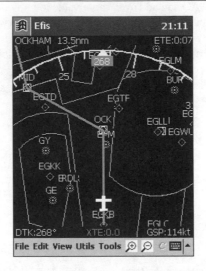

FIGURE 13-10   With an attached GPS you can navigate in real time.

Health Care

The applications for the iPAQ in the healthcare field are extremely broad. The iPAQ is used for patient data tracking, drug guides, prescription transmission, blood tracking, home care, symptom assessment, mobile ECG/EKG, and much more.

Skyscape software (**www.skyscape.com**) produces a wide range of Pocket PC reference products for doctors, nurses, and pharmacists, including products such as

- **Griffith's 5 Minute Medical Consult**   A unique clinical reference for students and practitioners.

- **5 Minute Pediatric Consult**   Physician's and nurse's reference for ailments of infants, children, and adolescents.

- **ABCLabData**   Covers hundreds of common and uncommon laboratory tests.

- **IdentADrug**   Quickly and accurately identifies different medications.

- **OncoMD**   An up-to-date reference on all aspects of cancer chemotherapy.

You can check out many others at **www.skyscape.com**.

One company seeing considerable success with PDA applications in health care is Neoteric Technologies Limited (**www.dataloguk.com**). Their technology is used extensively throughout the UK and is beginning to spread to other parts of the world. Two of their products are PathRequest and SafeTrack.

PathRequest allows hospital staff to order tests at the patient's bedside using a simple profile checklist on their PDA, as shown in Figure 13-11. With a PDA equipped with barcode scanners, hospital staff can positively identify the patient using bar-coded patient identification wristbands. Blood samples are drawn into tubes that have labels printed at the patient's bedside using a portable printer connected to the PDA. The PDA sends the test request to the laboratory via the wireless LAN.

Once the samples arrive at the lab, the bar-coded sample label is scanned and the receipt of the sample confirmed. As all the information about the requested tests is already on the lab system, no further data entry is needed, and analysis can begin immediately. This reduces the turnaround time from sample collection to results arrival. PathRequest can also provide test results and information about other recent tests ordered for each patient.

The PathRequest system has been in use at Queen Elizabeth Hospital in Gateshead, England, since 2001. As a result of the PathRequest installation and other measures taken, the hospital has reduced its clinical negligence insurance costs and has greatly sped up the lab testing process.

"Before PathRequest the fastest we could process a test result was between three and four hours," says Wendy James, project manager at the QE Hospital. "Now the turnaround time can be as little as 30 minutes."

A second Neoteric product is SafeTrack, which handles blood transfusion management. During blood transfusion, patients are potentially vulnerable to mistakes in matching donated blood to their own. Many hospitals use systems that are based upon comparing handwritten patient notes

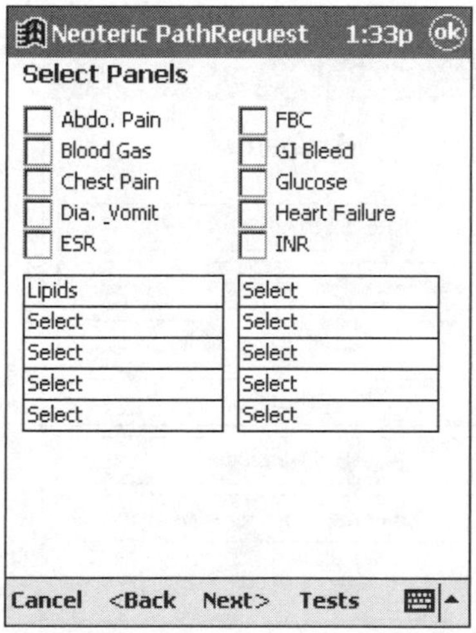

FIGURE 13-11   Hospital staff can use an iPAQ when ordering laboratory tests right from the patient's bedside.

with information printed on a blood bag, and as a result, mistakes are easily made. At Morriston Hospital in Swansea, Wales, the SafeTrack blood transfusion system uses PDAs to simplify and automate the critical checks during the transfusion process.

As soon as a patient arrives on the ward, he or she is given a wristband with all his or her patient information printed clearly and encoded into a barcode. At the blood bank the patient information is matched to the blood to be transfused. When the blood bag arrives on the ward, it is taken to the patient's bedside. There the nurse uses a PDA equipped with a barcode scanner to scan both the wristband and blood-bag label. A match is needed between the barcodes before the transfusion can proceed, virtually eliminating errors. The PDA also leads the nurse through the correct procedure for starting, monitoring, and ending a transfusion, as shown in Figure 13-12, ensuring that all the correct information is collected and that the procedures are completed properly.

"In today's pressured nursing environment, mistakes can easily be made while checking patient details against the blood intended for them," explains Dr. Dafydd Thomas, consultant anesthetist at Morriston Hospital. "We are determined to rule out as many avoidable errors as we can and SafeTrack system is certainly proving successful so far."

Finance

The financial sector is also making extensive use of iPAQs. You see them in the hands of real estate agents, mortgage consultants, stockbrokers, and more. One example of how they can be deployed is with TD Waterhouse, the second-largest discount broker in the world. To facilitate the ability to trade while mobile, TD Waterhouse (in partnership with Microsoft and Compaq)

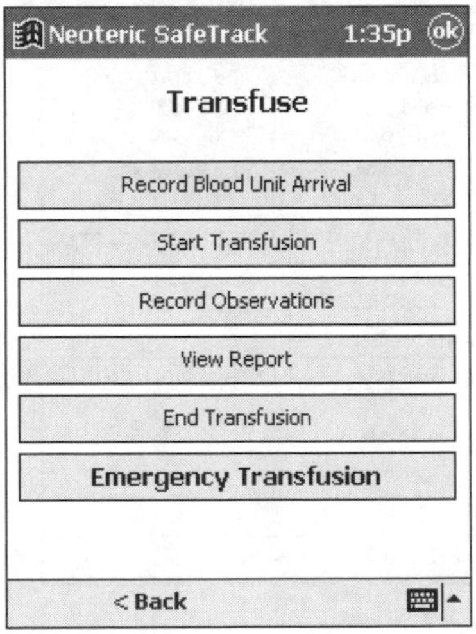

FIGURE 13-12 SafeTrack helps to eliminate blood transfusion errors that occur daily in hospitals around the world.

gave free iPAQs to 5,000 of their top customers. These customers can now connect wirelessly to the TD Waterhouse trading system. This has significantly increased the number of trades from the company's top investors.

Emergency Response

Another important area where iPAQs are making a difference is in emergency response. A company called Pocket Mobility (**www.pocketmobility.com**) has made a name for itself with a suite of products for firefighters, medical/EMS, and law enforcement. Their extensive product set includes software to calculate hydraulic pressure, flow rate, friction loss, pump pressure for firefighters, hazardous materials response information, incident command, and many others.

For medical and EMS personnel, Pocket Mobility has software for emergency foreign-language translations, shift calendar tools, scenario trainers, and so on. Similar packages are available for law enforcement professionals, along with software for quickly identifying suspected criminals.

13

Part III

Select Hardware and Accessories for Your iPAQ

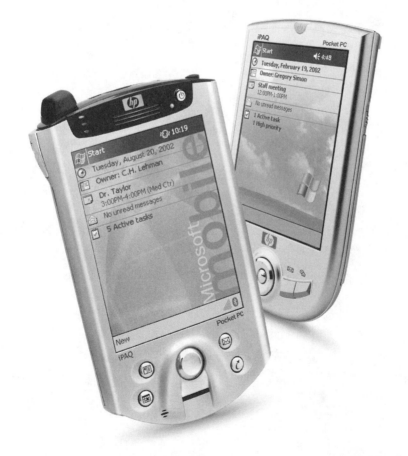

Chapter 14

Go Further with Expansion Sleeves

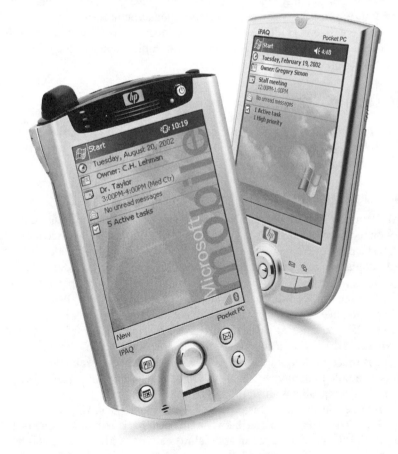

How to...

- Support PCMCIA cards
- Support CompactFlash expansion cards
- Use an expansion sleeve to connect to a GPRS/GSM network
- Use an expansion sleeve to connect to a Bluetooth network
- Use expansion sleeves for medical, multimedia, GPS, and digital photography

Another great feature of the iPAQ is the ability to expand the "naked" iPAQ by adding expansion sleeves to it. An iPAQ fits snugly into the front of an expansion sleeve and interfaces with it to provide new and expanded functionality for GPS location, wireless networking, digital photography, external storage, printing, barcode scanning, and much more. The primary manufacturer of expansion sleeves is Hewlett-Packard (HP), but recently other hardware vendors have gotten into the game. For the most up-to-date list of iPAQ expansion sleeves, check out **www.pocketpctools.com**.

In this chapter, we will look at all the HP expansion sleeves (also known as expansion packs) and discuss what they can do for you. In addition, we will look at some of the third-party expansion sleeves that you can get for your iPAQ.

HP Expansion Sleeves

> TIP *Are you an electronics wizard? Would you like to try making your own expansion sleeve? HP provides all the specs for building an expansion sleeve on their web site at* **http://csa.compaq.com/CSA_For_iPAQ_Developers_CD.shtml**.

HP CompactFlash Sleeve

The standard HP CompactFlash (CF) expansion sleeve is an essential tool for iPAQ expansion if you like to store files on removable media, or want to use any of the dozens of CF-based tools that are on the market. A CF slot can be a lot more than just storage; it can be used for modems, wireless and wired LAN cards, digital cameras, printers, and much more. The expansion sleeve slides onto your iPAQ from the bottom, where it will link into the expansion port on the bottom of your iPAQ. Once connected, it will automatically initialize and get ready to work with your iPAQ. Then you can connect any CF card you like by plugging it into the top of the expansion sleeve.

This sleeve enables you to insert any standard Type I or Type II CF card into your iPAQ, but check to make sure that drivers are available for the version of Pocket PC that you run on your iPAQ. This sleeve is much thicker than it needs to be, but does the job well and is reasonably inexpensive. It is available from anyone who sells HP products. The HP part number is 170339-B21, and it is compatible with all models of iPAQ.

HP recently released an update to this popular CF expansion pack, known as the CF Card Expansion Pack Plus. The main difference between this new pack and the old one is that the new Expansion Pack Plus includes a removable (slim) battery. Additional higher-capacity batteries are also available. Check **http://h18000.www1.hp.com/products/quickspecs/ 11379_div/11379_div.HTML** for more information. The HP part number is 249709-B21, and it is compatible with all models of iPAQ.

HP PC Card Expansion Sleeve

The HP PC card expansion sleeve, shown in Figure 14-1, is the add-on accessory that we use more than any other. It enables you to insert any standard Type II PCMCIA PC card that is compatible with Pocket PC. These are the same cards that we insert into our laptop computers, which enables us to use the same cards in both our iPAQs and our laptops. We use these sleeves extensively for our wireless modem cards and our 802.11b networking cards, giving us real-time access to information while fully mobile.

The range of PC cards available is tremendous. Toshiba makes a 5GB (no, that is not a typo) hard drive that fits into this slot that allows you to store an incredible amount of data. You can also use the expansion sleeve to insert wired or wireless modems and network cards. You can output presentations to a monitor or projector with a VGA card, and much more.

This sleeve also contains an extended battery pack, which is very important; otherwise the power drawn by the PC card would quickly run down your iPAQ battery. The HP part number for this sleeve is 170338-B21. The battery roughly doubles the run time of the iPAQ. Users who primarily use CF cards often use the PC card expansion sleeve with a CompactFlash adapter instead of the CF sleeve in order to have access to this extra battery power.

As with the HP CF Expansion Pack Plus, a new version exists, the PC Card Expansion Pack Plus. This allows you to perform the same tasks as with the older expansion pack, but supports removable batteries. The HP part number for this sleeve is 249708-B21.

HP Dual PC Card Expansion Sleeve

The HP dual PC card sleeve is basically the same as the standard single PC card expansion sleeve, except that it holds two cards simultaneously. This is useful for activities that require two cards at the same time, such as maintaining a wireless connection while showing presentation slides on a projector.

This unit is, however, thick as a brick and will probably only be used by people who *must* have two cards running at the same time as an essential business activity. In addition to the

FIGURE 14-1   The PC Card expansion sleeve from HP is the expansion sleeve that we use more than any other.

14

businessperson who needs to connect wirelessly while simultaneously making a presentation, a medical technician might need a wireless card to connect to the hospital WLAN and another card to plug in a medical device. The dual PC card is made thicker to accommodate the two slots as well as a battery that is twice as big as the single-card sleeve to enable it to power two cards for an extended period. The HP part number for this sleeve is 216198-B21.

HP Bluetooth Wireless Sleeve with CompactFlash Slot

This sleeve is new to the market and will become increasingly useful as more Bluetooth-enabled devices come out. Bluetooth is a wireless communications protocol that allows any Bluetooth-enabled devices within range of each other (usually less than 50 feet) to communicate wirelessly without complicated configuration exchanges. The kinds of things that you can do today with this sleeve include

- **Wireless Internet/e-mail/network access**   If you have a Bluetooth-enabled cell phone, your iPAQ can surf the Web, get e-mail, and run TCP/IP applications by using your cell phone as the data modem.

- **Printing**   You can automatically print documents to printers equipped with this technology.

- **File and information sharing**   Transfer information to any other Bluetooth device, such as another iPAQ for transferring files, meeting notes, contact information, and more.

- **ActiveSync**   You can synchronize your iPAQ with a Bluetooth-equipped PC.

This sleeve looks identical to the standard CF sleeve and also offers a standard CF card in addition to its Bluetooth capabilities. Although Bluetooth is new to the technology, it promises a whole new set of mobile wireless functionality that we have never experienced before.

For example, if you have a Bluetooth-equipped GPRS cell phone in your pocket, your iPAQ can connect to it at any time and surf the Internet, or pull down your latest e-mail. If you are in a meeting in someone else's office, but they have a Bluetooth-enabled printer, you can send your documents to the printer from your iPAQ through the Bluetooth connection without having to make any special adjustments for their network. Perhaps at some point in the future you will see a Bluetooth-enabled vending machine and be able to use your iPAQ to make a purchase from the machine without currency.

HP Wireless Pack for GSM/GPRS Networks

The HP Wireless Pack for GSM/GPRS networks, shown in Figure 14-2, is also a brand-new unit available in limited quantities in limited locations. This amazing sleeve turns your iPAQ into a cell phone. It is a tri-band (900, 1800, and 1900 MHz) GSM phone, which means that it will work on any GSM network (and GSM is the most widely used cell phone network protocol in the world). In addition, it supports GPRS data (it is a multi-slot Class 10 GPRS device), which means that you can use it as your wireless modem to surf the Internet, send and receive e-mail, and anything else that you need to do via the Internet.

This sleeve features "always-on" capability, which enables it to receive a cell phone call or to notify you of a new e-mail message, even when it is powered off. You can use the iPAQ speaker

| FIGURE 14-2 | HP turns your iPAQ into both a cell phone and wireless data device with the GSM/GPRS Wireless Pack. |

and microphone, or use an ear-bud style microphone and earpiece plug-in. We can't wait for this device so that we won't have to carry our cell phone and our iPAQ everywhere we go. This sleeve is still significantly bulkier than the current line of cell phones, but if you are already carrying an iPAQ, why not combine them?

Third-Party Expansion Sleeves

One of the strengths of the Expansion capabilities of the iPAQ is the fact that third party developers can purchase components and build their own expansion packs. In fact, some of the most functional expansion packs are not produced by HP, but are from third party vendors.

Silver Slider CompactFlash Expansion Sleeve

The Silver Slider expansion sleeves (the CF version is shown in Figure 14-3) are modified HP PC and CF sleeves. The manufacturer has removed a lot of the excess plastic to streamline it and has painted the card a metallic silver to match the iPAQ for the fashion-conscious user! There are currently several different versions available:

- Silver Slider 2
- Silver Slider 3
- Dual Slider 3
- Silver Slider 5

14

FIGURE 14-3   The Silver Slider is essentially a modified standard CompactFlash sleeve that is lighter and more retro looking.

This unit is available from the Silver Slider web site at **http://www.silverslider.biz/** or through a second provider, PDAmotion, at **www.pdamotion.com**. If you send in your existing CF sleeve, you'll receive a significant discount. Three different varieties of the CF Silver Slider exist, in addition to one now available for both the single and dual PC card sleeve.

Also, a version from DataNation incorporates the Silver Slider with a vinyl or leather cover to protect the screen.

Navman GPS Expansion Sleeve

The Navman GPS unit was discussed in detail in Chapter 12. It is mentioned here because it is an excellent example of a third-party expansion sleeve for the iPAQ.

With the Navman GPS you can find exactly where you are within a distance of 6.8 meters. In conjunction with navigation software, you can use it to locate and get driving directions to services and points of interest in your area, such as restaurants, gas stations, theaters, and more. You can learn more about the Navman GPS sleeve at **www.navman-mobile.com**.

FlyJacket i3800 (CompactFlash and Multimedia Monitor Output)

The FlyJacket i3800 is a complete multimedia expansion sleeve that also features a CF slot. A multimedia expansion sleeve is one that enables you to send your output to a projector, television, or monitor directly from your iPAQ. You can view full-motion video on the iPAQ. It comes with a pen-sized remote control to advance and back up a PowerPoint slide show running on your iPAQ. The FlyJacket is discussed in more detail in Chapter 10.

The FlyJacket features video input as well, allowing for full-frame video capture from an input source (TV, camcorder, or other). It also includes an additional battery to power all this activity without draining the main battery. More information can be found on the LifeView web site at **http://www.lifeview.com.tw**.

Nexian NexiCam Digital Camera Expansion Sleeve

The NexiCam is a camera expansion sleeve from Nexian. It is a digital camera that will record pictures on its CF card slot or in the iPAQ memory. You can take 800×600-resolution photos, or capture up to 45 seconds of full-motion video.

It won't match the most up-to-date digital cameras in quality or functionality, but for mobile workers who use their iPAQs to enter data and also need to take photos (insurance adjusters and real estate appraisers, for example), this product's all-in-one capabilities make it a great choice. Not only that, but with a wireless modem, you could immediately send the photos to the person who needs them, speeding up the claims process in an insurance case, for example. Watch for information directly from Nexian at **www.nexian.com** or at **www.PocketPCTools.com**.

Nexian NexiPak Dual CF Sleeve

The NexiPak sleeve from Nexian allows for the insertion of two CF cards at the same time, allowing you to run, for example, a wireless 802.11b LAN card and a storage card at the same time. This is similar to the Dual PCMCIA sleeve from HP, but it is CF instead of PCMCIA.

iSwipe Card Reader

The Semtek iSwipe magnetic card reader (**www.semtek.com/products/iswipe.html**), shown in Figure 14-4, securely attaches to the HP iPAQ Pocket PC. It reads magnetic cards encoded to ANSI, ISO, 7811 and 7812, AAMVA, and CA DMV cards. This is a very specialized expansion sleeve for what it does. So, if you need to use your iPAQ to scan credit card information, this is the one for you.

Symbol SPS 3000 Bar Code Scanner Expansion Pack

Symbol Technologies (**www.symbol.com**) put out a great expansion sleeve if you need barcode scanner capabilities. Their SPS 3000 expansion pack, shown in Figure 14-5, allows you to use your iPAQ as a barcode reader for inventory and management applications. You can purchase this expansion pack with either the bar code technology only or with built-in 802.11b WiFi, extra internal battery, and the Bar Code Technology.

14

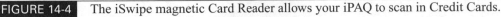

FIGURE 14-4   The iSwipe magnetic Card Reader allows your iPAQ to scan in Credit Cards.

FIGURE 14-5   Convert your iPAQ into a bar code reader with the Symbol expansion sleeve.

SeidioPak Dual CF & Power Pack for iPAQ Pocket PC

Seidio (**www.seidioonline.com**) offers a Dual CF slot that provides not only the dual slots, but also internal removable batteries (see Figure 14-6). The expansion pack uses standard Nokia 8290 detachable and rechargeable Li-ion batteries that can be purchased anywhere Nokia phones are sold.

One drawback of the current SeidioPak is that only one of the CF slots can be used for IO (such as Bluetooth or WiFi). The other must be used for memory storage. We have been informed that this issue is being worked on, and future releases of these expansion packs will support dual IO cards.

These are only some of the expansion packs available for the iPAQ Pocket PC. Check **www.PocketPCTools.com** for announcements and reviews of new expansion packs as they become available.

FIGURE 14-6   The SeidioPack Dual CF and Power Pack gives you the best of expansion cards and extra power.

Chapter 15

Store Important Information Externally or in the iPAQ File Store

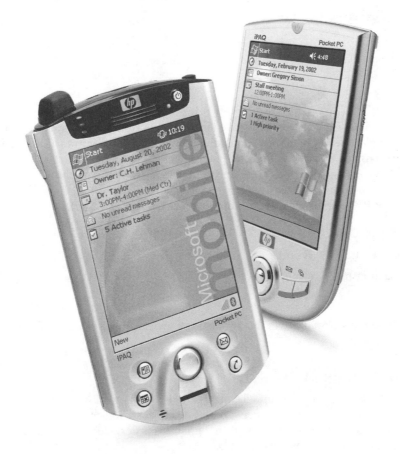

How to...

- Choose a storage medium that makes sense for you
- Understand the differences among the available storage media

In this chapter we will look into some of the products that are available for the iPAQ for external storage. Because we cannot cover all the different products, we have included the ones that we found to be readily available and that we know work with the iPAQ. The number of companies that produce memory continually increases as Pocket PC devices (and other devices using such memory) increase in use.

We've divided these products into three categories and will discuss each in the sections that follow:

- Storage cards
- Hard drives
- Storage peripherals

Storage Cards

A *storage card* is a device that uses solid-state technology to store information. It has no moving parts and is *nonvolatile* (that is, it does not require power to retain its information). Although many of the hard drives that we discuss later in the chapter have the same form factor as the storage cards, they are not the same. They tend to require less power, and they are hardier (they can survive more "punishment") than their hard drive counterparts.

Four types of iPAQ-compatible storage cards are currently on the market:

- MultiMediaCard (MMC)
- Secure Digital (SD) card
- CompactFlash (CF) card
- PC card

In the next sections we will cover the different storage card solutions and some of the vendors who sell them.

MultiMediaCards (MMC Cards)

The MultiMediaCard standard was introduced in November 1997 and was a joint development between SanDisk Corporation and Siemens AG/Infineon Technologies AG. It is very small (24 mm×32 mm×1.4 mm) and weighs less than 2 grams. It is designed to store data for portable devices such as cameras, MP3 players, and PDAs.

NOTE   *For more information on the MMC standard, visit the MultiMediaCard Association web site at **www.mmca.org**.*

HP introduced a Secure Digital/MMC slot with their iPAQ 38*xx* series device. Since then every new iPAQ series (38*xx* series, 39*xx* series, 54*xx* series, and the H1910) includes this slot. The iPAQ will simply recognize the MMC as another storage card and allow you to store information (applications and data) on it. When you first install an unformatted MMC card (or any other storage card, for that matter), you will be presented with a dialog box, shown next, asking whether you would like to format the card. Once formatting is complete (an extremely quick process), you will be able to not only transfer files to it, but also read these cards on a desktop or laptop computer using a special card reader. The card readers are covered later in this chapter.

Be aware that the MMC standard is designed for the connection of storage cards only. As we will see in the next section, Secure Digital (SD) technology allows you to read and write both to MMC cards and to SD cards, which include nonstorage cards such as network cards or modem cards (assuming that the device can handle such cards). Currently the MMC standard only supports memory cards up to 128MB, although 256MB cards are just over the horizon.

In December 2002 Hitachi announced the availability of new MMC cards that are actually half the size of the current MMC memory cards. While as of the writing of this book these cards were not publicly available, you will want to make sure that you purchase the regular-size MMC memory card. The reason for this is a simple one. The iPAQs can only support the older, larger MMC memory card. You would not be able to remove the half-size card once you inserted it.

Following is a partial list of companies that offer MMC memory cards:

- Delkin Devices (**www.delkin.com**)
- Kingston Technology (**www.kingston.com**)
- Lexar Media (**www.digitalfilm.com**)

15

- SanDisk (**www.sandisk.com**)
- Simple Tech (**www.simpletech.com**)
- Viking Components (**www.vikingcomponents.com**)

Secure Digital (SD) Cards

A newer technology that uses the same form factor as MMC cards is Secure Digital. Secure Digital cards have the distinction of not just storing information, but also having the ability to secure the data from unauthorized access (hence the name). Be aware, however, that the iPAQ currently does not support the security features of SD. If you lose an SD card with sensitive information on it, that information will not be secure. SD cards also have a locking read-only switch to protect the data from being erased accidentally.

Another nifty feature of SD cards is their ability to support both storage cards and multifunction cards such as Bluetooth, network cards, GPS receivers, and cameras. This ability is also known as Secure Digital Input Output (SDIO). For your device to handle these types of peripherals, it must support the SDIO standard. Currently, only the 39*xx* and 54*xx* series iPAQs support SDIO.

NOTE *For more information on the SD standard, visit the Secure Digital Association web site at **www.sdcard.org**.*

Like MMC, the SD card is about the size of a postage stamp and has the same dimensions. In fact, you can easily use MMC cards in the SD slot of your 38*xx* series, 39*xx* series, 54*xx* series, or H1910 iPAQ (or in a 36*xx* or 37*xx* series iPAQ with an adapter). Be aware that MMC tends to be considerably slower than SD (although they run at the same speed on the iPAQ).

As with MMC, SD cards are nonvolatile and solid-state. Currently, you can purchase SD cards that are up to 512MB, with 1GB cards on the horizon. Following is a partial list of SD storage card suppliers:

- Compaq Corporation (**www.compaq.com/products/handhelds/pocketpc/options/memory_storage.html**)
- Delkin Devices (**www.delkin.com**)
- Kingston Technology (**www.kingston.com**)
- Kodak (**www.kodak.com**)
- Lexar Media (**www.digitalfilm.com**)
- SanDisk (**www.sandisk.com**)
- Simple Tech (**www.simpletech.com**)
- Viking Components (**www.vikingcomponents.com**)

One of the most common and popular storage cards on the market today is the CompactFlash card. These cards were made popular by digital cameras, since most of the early digital cameras supported their form factor. (Digital cameras are now moving toward SD- and MMC-type cards.)

It is important to note the different form factors of CF cards. Currently there are two CF card types: Type I and Type II. Both CF card types have the same dimensions when you look at the flat side, approximately 1 inch square. Where they differ is in their thickness. A Type I CF card is about 1/8-inch thick, whereas the Type II CF card is slightly thicker. Although they are very similar, that little bit of extra thickness can make all the difference in the world. A Type I CF card will fit into a Type II connector, but the reverse is not true.

As mentioned in Chapter 13, Compaq offers a CF card sleeve for the iPAQ. This expansion sleeve has a CF Type II slot, which allows you to connect any CF device to it. If you are purchasing a non-Compaq expansion sleeve, make sure that it supports Type II. You might be surprised at what types of sleeves have CF slots in them. These can include GPS sleeves, camera sleeves, and sleeves with bar code readers. CompactFlash cards became a hit with iPAQ users because of their small size, low cost, and high capacity.

Several vendors recently announced 1.5, 2, and 3GB CF storage cards. (They use a different method for communicating, however, and currently do not function in the iPAQ. The largest size supported on the iPAQ is currently 1GB.) With these storage capacities, CF cards are quickly catching up to their hard drive brothers for huge storage. As you will see, however, the hard drives that are compatible with iPAQ are getting quite large as well.

PC Cards

The last solid-state, nonvolatile storage card that we will look at is the PC card. These are becoming less popular because of their relatively large size and storage capacity vs. price of the CF cards. The PC card, formerly known as the PCMCIA card, has a large form factor (about the size of a credit card, but much thicker) and is available on just about every laptop around. Although PC storage cards are not that popular, it is interesting to note that one of the reasons the iPAQ was such a big hit when it was first introduced was because it was one of the only devices available with a PC card expansion pack. This allowed people to connect not just storage devices to them, but also full-sized network cards, modems, and other peripherals (such as video cards).

What if you do not have a PC card expansion pack? The solution is not the prettiest or the best solution, but a solution nonetheless. If you positively, absolutely must have a PC card plugged into your iPAQ and you do not want a PC card expansion pack, you can use a *CF-to-PC converter*. The CF-to-PC converter is simply a device that has a CF card on one side connected via a flexible rubber ribbon cable to a PC card connector. The converter is plugged into your iPAQ (with a CF expansion pack), and the PC card is plugged into the other side. While this might seem like a good solution, be aware that it is not guaranteed that all PC cards will work. None of the large, well-known manufacturers currently offers these converters. To find one, simply go to Google (**www.google.com**) and search for "CF to PC converter." A sample one is shown in Figure 15-1.

15

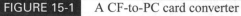

FIGURE 15-1   A CF-to-PC card converter

> **NOTE**   *Although there are a few other storage card technologies, namely Sony's Memory Stick, SmartMedia (SM), and XD cards, they are not covered in this chapter because they are not really popular for the iPAQ. However, several adapters (covered at the end of the chapter) enable you to connect these devices and use them on your iPAQ with a PC card expansion pack.*

You may also notice that PC card memory is known as *ATA memory*. Although the terms can be used interchangeably, "ATA memory" seems to be the more common.

Hard Drives

As technology gets better, smaller, and faster, truly amazing products appear on the market, including the small hard drives that work with the iPAQ. These drives are great for storage since they can store large amounts of information (with 20GB on the way), and they can also be moved into desktops and laptops very easily. In this section we look at two hard drive form factors: the *CF card form factor* and the *PC card form factor.*

IBM Microdrive

IBM's Microdrive is the smallest hard drive available. It measures about 1 inch square and is currently available in three storage capacities: 340MB, 512MB, and 1GB. IBM has also invented a new hard disk technology called "Pixie Dust." This will enable future Microdrives to grow to 6GB with the same form factor as the current drives. The 1GB version is shown in Figure 15-2.

Although several vendors (such as Iomega) resell the IBM Microdrive as their own, only the IBM version is covered here. Table 15-1 lists the specifications of the Microdrive (for models

FIGURE 15-2   An IBM 1GB Microdrive

IBM 1GB Microdrive, IBM 512MB Microdrive, and IBM 340MB Microdrive, and
DSCM-11000, DSCM-10512, and DSCM-10340). For further information, see IBM's
Microdrive web site at **www.storage.ibm.com/hdd/micro/overvw.htm**.

Configuration	
Interface	CF+ (ATA and PCMCIA compatible)
Capacity (MB)	1000 / 512 / 340
Sector size	512
Disk	1
Areal density (max Gb/in.^{2})	15.2
Recording density (max Kbpi)	435
Track density (TPI)	35,000
Performance	
Data buffer (KB)	128
Rotational speed (rpm)	3600
Latency (average ms)	8.33
Media transfer rate (Mbps)	38.8 to 59.9
Interface transfer rate (Mbps)	11.1 (PIO mode 3); 13.3 (DMA mode 1)
Sustained data rate, typical read or write (Mbps)	2.6 (min); 4.2 (max)

TABLE 15-1   IBM Microdrive Specifications

15

Seek Time (Read)		
Average (ms)	12	
Track-to-track (ms)	1	
Full-track (ms)	19	
Reliability		
Error rate (nonrecoverable)	< 1 per 1.0 e 13 bits transferred	
Load/unload cycles	300,000	
Power	**+3.3 V Power Supply**	**+5 V Power Supply**
Voltage requirement (autodetect)	+3.3 VDC, ±5%	+5 VDC, ±5%
Current (write)	250 mA	260 mA
Current (standby)	20 mA	20 mA
Power consumption efficiency (watts/MB)	0.000495/0.000967	0.00085/0.00166
Physical Size		
Height (mm)	5 +0 / −0.10	
Width (mm)	42.80/ ±0.10	
Depth (mm)	36.40/ ±0.15	
Weight (g)	16 (max)	
Environmental Characteristics	**Operating**	**Nonoperating**
Ambient temperature	0 to 65°C (measured at unit)	−40 to 65°C
Relative humidity (noncondensing)	8% to 90%	5% to 95%
Shock (half sine wave)	175 G (2 ms)	1500 G (1 ms)
Vibration (random [RMS])	0.67 G (5 to 500 Hz)	3.01G (5 to 500 Hz)
Vibration (swept sine)	1 G 0-peak (5 to 500 Hz)	5G 0-peak (10 to 500 Hz)

TABLE 15-1   IBM Microdrive Specifications *(continued)*

The IBM Microdrive is available either by itself (with the model numbers listed next) or in the Travel Kit. The Travel Kit includes the Microdrive, a PC card adapter, and a rugged field case for storing the PC card adapter and the drive. The Microdrive also ships in its own little plastic case.

- IBM 1GB Microdrive (Model DSCM-11000)
- IBM 512MB Microdrive (Model DSCM-10512)

- IBM 340MB Microdrive (Model DMDM-10340)
- IBM 170MB Microdrive (Model DMDM-10170)

NOTE *If you are having problems getting your iPAQ to recognize the IBM Microdrive, go to the Compaq Handhelds Software & Drivers page (**h18007.www1.hp.com/support/files/handhelds/us/index.html**), and check to see if your model and operating system require any updates. Some of the older Pocket PC 2000 iPAQs required an update to make the drives function.*

PC Card Hard Drives

The PC card hard drive is becoming more and more popular with PDA and laptop users. The reasons for this are simple. The form factor (a full PC card) allows you to easily transfer the drive from a laptop to your iPAQ to a desktop (assuming that the desktop is equipped with a PC card reader). Before you can use a PC card hard drive in your iPAQ, you will need the Compaq PC Card Expansion Pack (or Dual PC Card Expansion Pack, Expansion Pack Plus, and so on).

Once the PC card hard drive is installed in your iPAQ, you will be able to format the drive, at which point it will be recognized by the iPAQ as just another storage card, as shown in Figure 15-3.

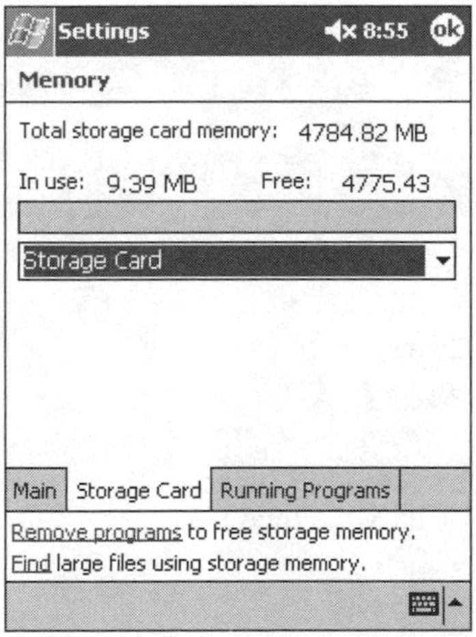

FIGURE 15-3 A 5GB PC card hard drive installed in an iPAQ

15

Currently, two different PC card hard drives are being sold on the market from two different companies. PC card hard drives are available in either a 2GB or a 5GB format and are available from the following companies:

- Kingston Technology (**www.kingston.com/products/pccard.asp**)
- Toshiba (**www.toshiba.com/taissdd/products/features/MK5002mpl-Over.shtml**)

The Kingston DataPak is a PC card-based hard drive. It can be used in either the iPAQ or laptops. Table 15-2 lists its specifications.

Kingston Part Number	5GB	2GB
	DP-PCM5	DP-PCM2
Configuration and Capacity		
Technology	1.8" Winchester hard disk drive	
Storage capacity	5GB or 2GB	
Number of disks	1	
Data heads	2	
Cylinders (logical)	3,900	
Data heads (logical)	16	
Sectors per track (logical)	63	
Rotational Speed	2GB	5GB
	4,200 rpm	3,990 rpm
Seek Times		
Track to track	3 ms	
Average	15 ms	
Maximum	26 ms	
Average latency	7.14 ms	
Data Transfer Rate		
Internal transfer rate	16.25 Mbps (max)	
Start time	3 sec	
Buffer size	256KB	
Power		
Voltage	3 V ±5% or 5 V ±5%	
Spinup current	370 mA (3.3 V) or 380 mA (5.0 V)	
Active read current	360 mA (3.3 V) or 370 mA (5.0 V)	
Active write current	390 mA (3.3 V) or 400 mA (5.0 V)	

TABLE 15-2   Kingston DataPak Specifications

Idle current	150 mA (3.3 V) or 160 mA (5.0 V)
Standby current	70 mA (3.3 V) or 75 mA (5.0 V)
Sleep current	15 mA (3.3 V) or 20 mA (5.0 V)
Physical Size	
Height	0.20" (5 mm)
Length	3.37" (85.6 mm)
Width	2.13" (54 mm)
Weight	1.93 oz (55 g)
Environmental Characteristics	
Operating temperature	5°C to 55°C (41°F to 131°F)
Nonoperating temperature	–20°C to 60°C (–4°F to 140°F)
Relative humidity	5% to 90% noncondensing
Operating shock	200G
Nonoperating shock	1,000G
MTBF	> 300,000 hours
Data reliability	1 nonrecoverable error in 1,013 bits read

TABLE 15-2 Kingston DataPak Specifications *(continued)*

NOTE *Toshiba announced plans for a 10GB and a 20GB PC card hard drive, but we have seen no sign of these drives yet.*

Storage Peripherals

Various peripherals are available to connect the storage cards discussed in this chapter to your iPAQ and your desktop computer, including the following:

- CF adapters
- SD/MMC adapters
- Memory Stick adapters
- Multifunction adapters
- USB adapters

These adapters are fairly self-explanatory. A CF adapter enables you to connect a CF card to a PC card slot. It simply acts as a connector to change the size of the storage card so that it fits into the PC card form factor. The nice thing about this is that you can purchase a PC card expansion pack and use most memory products in that form factor. The SD/MMC and Memory Stick adapters are the same, except that they enable you to connect either SD or MMC storage cards via the PC card slot.

15

The multifunction adapters are fairly new on the market and enable you to use a single adapter to connect a variety of memory cards using the same hardware. An interesting one is the CompactTrio from Pretec. This three-in-one adapter enables you to convert MMC/SD/Memory Stick to CompactFlash. For more information, check out **www.pretec.com/index2/product/ Accessory/CompactTRIO.htm**.

Other adapters include "all-in-one," which will allow up to six different card formats (SD, MultiMediaCard, CompactFlash Type I and II [including the IBM Microdrive], Memory Stick, and SmartMedia). If you do decide to pick up one of these six-in-one devices, be aware that they are available in both USB 1.1 and USB 2.0 formats. Spend a bit extra and pick up the USB 2.0 device, as it transfers data considerably faster than the USB 1.1 version (assuming, of course, that your system supports USB 2.0). For more information on such a device, check out **www.sandisk.com/consumer/sixinone.asp**.

Another device that just has to be mentioned is the SanDisk Cruzer (**www.sandisk.com/ consumer/cruzer.asp**). The Cruzer is pocket-size storage device with upgradeable flash memory. It is tiny (about 3" long, 1.75" wide, and about 0.75" thick) and has two connectors. On one side is a USB connector that slides out and connects into your desktop or laptop computer (a short, compact cable ships with it for those hard-to-reach USB ports). This is what you plug into your desktop, and the Cruzer appears as a removable drive on your system. On the second side is an SD slot. Simply plug in any SD card you desire, and you can easily transfer data between your iPAQ and your desktop/laptop. The Cruzer also ships with software that allows you to encrypt the data stored on the SD card, but this software only works on the desktop/laptop.

The iPAQ File Store

If you have one of the newer iPAQs (37*xx*, 38*xx*, 39*xx*, or 54*xx* series), you will notice a mystery "storage card" on the device. This storage card is called the *iPAQ File Store*. Its size varies between the different units. In the 37*xx* and 38*xx* series it is approximately 6.59MB, 22.22MB for the 39*xx* series, and 21.73 MB for the 54*xx* series. Since the H1910 is a lower-end device, it does not support the iPAQ File Store.

Most of the original iPAQs shipped with 16MB of ROM. It is in ROM that the operating system was stored. A few lucky iPAQ owners got one of the original iPAQs with 32MB of ROM. The reason for the different ROM sizes is that when iPAQs were built, 16MB ROM chips were not available and 32MB ones replaced them. Since the operating system required less than 16MB of storage, this was never an issue.

With the release of Pocket PC 2002, however, the operating system grew to over 24MB (including MSN Messenger, Terminal Services Client, and Microsoft Reader). Since the iPAQ can store information in ROM (for upgrades of the operating system you can flash the ROM), Compaq decided to make the extra ROM available to the user. This extra ROM appears as the iPAQ File Store. One thing, however, differentiates it from RAM. Since it is ROM and can be flashed, it is semipermanent. What this means is that any program that you store in the iPAQ File Store will be retained even if you lose battery power completely and lose all the other data/applications in the iPAQ. It is therefore recommended that you put in File Store the data or applications that you always require on your iPAQ, such as network card drivers.

Part IV

Appendixes

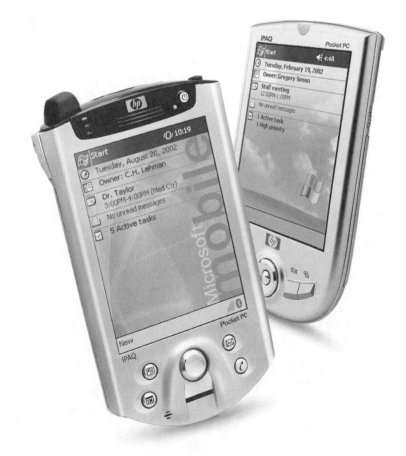

Chapter A

Using Microsoft Mobile Information Server 2002

In this appendix we will look at the Microsoft Mobile Information Server, a new solution for synchronizing your iPAQ directly with your organization's Exchange Server (assuming, of course, that your organization uses Exchange Server for messaging). We will look at the problem with synchronizing your iPAQ as usual, and then discuss the solution in detail.

Some Background

Ask anyone who uses wireless or mobile devices what the "killer application" is, and you will get mostly one answer—e-mail. Before the advent of the Pocket PC, most wireless devices were simply advanced pager solutions for receiving and sending e-mail.

Before we discuss the Microsoft Mobile Information Server, let's take a look at some current methods for sending and receiving e-mail on your iPAQ. You can choose from two e-mail protocols: POP3 and IMAP4.

Pocket Outlook allows you to use either protocol to send and receive e-mail with your iPAQ (see Figure A-1). Be aware that once you choose the protocol to use in a specific connection, you have to re-create the connection if you decide to change it.

We will now briefly describe the differences between the two protocols. Post Office Protocol version 3 (POP3) is the older protocol and therefore not as advanced as its counterpart. POP3 allows you to connect to a POP3-compliant server and retrieve e-mail from a *single* top-level directory. This limitation would be unnoticeable to you unless you use folders to organize your e-mail messages. If you do, then you are out of luck with this protocol.

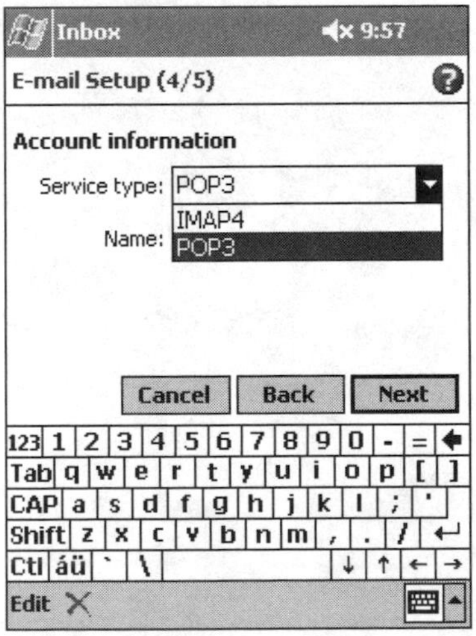

FIGURE A-1   Protocols supported by Pocket Outlook

POP3 also has the limitation that it is an all-or-nothing protocol. When you connect to the server, the client and server exchange information about the e-mails that you have already downloaded. POP3 does this, unfortunately, by comparing all the e-mails every time you connect. As you can imagine, if you have a large number of e-mails in your Inbox, then this process will be time-consuming. The protocol also does not have the ability to control the attachments that might exist in those e-mails. Those attachments will be downloaded whether or not you want them. If you have been using the Internet for more than four years or so, this is most likely the protocol you have used for e-mail thus far.

Internet Message Access Protocol version 4 (IMAP4) is similar to POP3 except that it is more advanced with more features. The IMAP protocol allows you to synchronize information with the server without having to download all the information on the server. Some of IMAP4's improvements over POP3 include the ability to specify what is downloaded, for example, only the message headers, e-mails of a certain size, and attachments of a given size. IMAP4 also allows you to download the list of folders stored on the server.

One of the limitations of both protocols is that they do not allow you to synchronize more than just e-mail. While e-mail is the killer app as we mentioned earlier, Outlook and Exchange also allow you to store tasks, contacts, and calendar information. As you have seen in this book, all these tasks are available with your iPAQ Pocket PC. Wouldn't it be nice if you could synchronize all this information with your organization's Exchange Server? Well, you can...sort of.

Microsoft Mobile Information Server 2002 has a new component that allows you to synchronize three of those options: e-mail, calendar, and contacts.

The Solution

As we mentioned, the solution to this synchronization problem is the Microsoft Mobile Information Server 2002 (MMIS). The following three sections will introduce you to the three components involved with an MMIS installation. MMIS allows you to wirelessly and securely synchronize your calendar, e-mail, and contact information directly with your organization's Exchange Server.

The MMIS Server

In 2002, Microsoft introduced their second version of the Mobile Information Server. MMIS is actually an enterprise server that allows users to browse and access their organization's corporate information on many different devices including Pocket PCs, Palm devices, and Wireless Applications Protocol (WAP)-enabled devices and phones. While these MMIS 2002 features are beyond the scope of this book, a new feature introduced with that version pertains to iPAQ users. That component is known as Server ActiveSync. The rest of this appendix will deal with some of the server, desktop, and Pocket PC components of Server ActiveSync.

Installing a full implementation of MMIS 2002 is not a trivial task. It involves access to Active Directory, extension of the Active Directory Schema, and creation of certificates for the server. Luckily for us, Microsoft thought this out. Instead of having to fully install the MMIS, access Active Directory (AD), and extend the AD Schema, you can simply request that MMIS install the Server ActiveSync component.

A

Installing Server ActiveSync

To install Server ActiveSync on a system, follow these steps:

1. Insert the MMIS 2002 CD into your CD-ROM drive.

2. Choose Start | Run and type *d*:**\setup /vMSAS=1**, where *d* is the drive letter for your CD-ROM.

3. If you have not installed a certificate yet (more on this later), a warning message will appear (as shown in Figure A-2) informing you that you need to install a certificate on the server for authentication.

4. On the Welcome screen click Next.

5. Agree to the Licensing Agreement and click Next.

6. On the per-seat Licensing Agreement page, agree and click Next.

7. Enter the 25-digit CD Key that is on the back of the MMIS 2002 CD case and click Next.

8. Ensure that both the Microsoft Server ActiveSync and Administrative Tools options are selected and click Next.

9. Click Install.

10. On the final installation page, click Finish.

Why Certificates?

Why would you need a certificate installed on your MMIS server? For the same reason you want your bank to install a certificate on their online banking web site when you access your account

---

```
Mobile Information Server - InstallShield Wizard                    _ □ ×

  ⚠    Setup did not detect an SSL certificate on this computer. If this computer is a server that
        processes  synchronization or browse traffic, you should use SSL to encrypt all MIS data. If SSL
        is not used, all data, including user credentials, is unencrypted as it travels over the Internet.


        To exit Setup and install an SSL certificate, click Yes, and then use the IIS Web Server
        Certificate Wizard to install a certificate.


        To continue Setup without installing a certificate, click No. This option is suitable if you are
        installing only the Exchange 2000 Notifications component or Administrative Tools, or if you
        have installed a third-party front-end SSL solution.


                        [      Yes      ]            [      No      ]
```

FIGURE A-2   An SSL certificate must be installed before installing MMIS.

information. Server ActiveSync uses the same technology as your bank to ensure that your e-mail, calendar, and contact information remain secure. That technology is Secure Socket Layer (SSL). Without getting into too much detail on the security features of MMIS, you simply need to know that a certificate needs to be installed on your MMIS Server.

NOTE   *For more information on the way Server ActiveSync deals with security, check out the "How to Install Mobile Information Server 2002 Server ActiveSync White Paper" at **http://www.microsoft.com/exchange/techinfo/deployment/2000/installactivesync.asp**.*

By default, your iPAQ only supports certificates that are issued to you by trusted certification authorities (CAs). For that reason, you will need to install one of these SSL certificates:

- VeriSign/RSA Secure Server
- VeriSign Class 1 Public Primary CA
- VeriSign Class 2 Public Primary CA
- VeriSign Class 3 Public Primary CA
- VeriSign Class 3 Public Primary CA (2028)
- GTE Cybertrust ROOT
- GTE Cybertrust Solutions ROOT
- Thawte Server CA
- Thawte Premium Server CA
- Entrust.net Secure Server
- Entrust.net CA (2048 bit)

NOTE   *If you get an Internet_45 error when you attempt to synchronize with Server ActiveSync, then the certificate you configured is not supported.*

Disabling SSL Certificates in Server ActiveSync

If you need to install and test Server ActiveSync in a test or pilot environment and you do not want to purchase one of the certificates mentioned earlier, you can still use any certificate you want. This does not mean that you can use Server ActiveSync without SSL or security—you still need that. What this does is remove the limitation as to which certificate you use. This allows you to install a certificate on your MMIS server that is generated by any certificate authority, including the certificate services that are available with all Windows 2000 Server systems.

To take advantage of this option, you will need to execute a special CAB file on your iPAQ. This CAB file, called AS_CERT_OFF, can be found on the Mobile Information Server 2002 CD-ROM in the \Support\Tools\Disable SSL directory. Simply copy the CAB file to the iPAQ, and execute it by navigating to it using File Explorer.

A

The Firewall

Before you can access Server ActiveSync from your iPAQ wirelessly, you need to give your iPAQ access to the server through the firewall. While this is again out of the scope of this book (it is covered in detail in the White Paper mentioned earlier in this appendix), we will introduce you to the minimum requirement to make Server ActiveSync work.

You can place your Server ActiveSync system within a perimeter (or DMZ) network, but placing it in your internal network and opening port number 443 to it from the external network will work just fine. Port 443 is simply the port used by HTTPS or SSL.

The iPAQ

The next item you need to configure is the iPAQ itself. Remember that MMIS 2002 arrived long after many of the iPAQs that are on the market today. How can you make your older iPAQ function properly with Server ActiveSync if Server ActiveSync did not exist when you bought it? The good news is that you can upgrade your device if it does not support Server ActiveSync.

To find out if your device supports Server ActiveSync, follow these steps:

1. Tap Start.

2. Tap ActiveSync. (If ActiveSync is not listed on the Start menu, tap Programs and then ActiveSync.)

3. Select the Tools menu, and then tap Options.

4. If you see a Server tab on the bottom of the screen (see Figure A-3), then your iPAQ is capable of connecting to Server ActiveSync with MMIS 2002. If you don't see the Server tab, then your device needs to be upgraded.

If you find that your iPAQ needs to be upgraded with the Server ActiveSync Client Update Software, you will need to install the update on your device. The update consists of a single CAB file (ActiveSyncUpdate.cab). You need to copy this CAB file to your iPAQ and run it. This file has all the required updates necessary for you to be able to synchronize with Server ActiveSync. You can find this file in the \English\Pocket PC directory on the MMIS 2002 CD-ROM.

To install this update, follow these instructions:

1. In the Microsoft ActiveSync window, click the Explore icon to show the files on your iPAQ.

NOTE   *You must turn off the password screen and the owner screen on your iPAQ before you upgrade your device. Failing to do so can terminate the installation prematurely and damage your iPAQ. Also make sure that the iPAQ is* not *running on battery power, but is connected to an external power source.Copy the ActiveSyncUpdate.cab file from the MMIS 2002 CD-ROM to your iPAQ.*

The Server tab

2. On the iPAQ device, tap Start, tap Programs, and then tap the File Explorer icon.

3. Tap the ActiveSyncUpdate.cab file, and follow the instructions to update your iPAQ.

Once your iPAQ is ready to synchronize with Server ActiveSync, you can follow these instructions to configure the synchronization process. Please note that these instructions are done on the iPAQ. In the next section we will discuss the steps involved in configuring Server ActiveSync from your desktop computer with ActiveSync installed:

1. On the iPAQ device, tap Start and then tap ActiveSync to launch ActiveSync. (If ActiveSync does not appear on the Start menu, tap Programs and then ActiveSync.)

2. On the ActiveSync screen, select Tools, tap Options, and then tap the Server tab.

3. Tap the check box next to each data type that you want to synchronize with the Server ActiveSync Server (Calendar, Contacts, and Inbox).

4. In the box under Server Name, enter the name of the Mobile Information Server 2002 server that you set up. If you are going to be using Server ActiveSync with a VPN solution, use the internal name or address of the MMIS system. Otherwise, use the external IP address or name of the server.

5. Tap the Advanced button at the bottom-right corner of the screen.

A

6. Tap the Connection tab.

7. On the Advanced Connection Options screen Connection tab, enter your information in the following boxes:

- User Name
- Password
- Domain

8. If you want to save your password, select the Save Password check box.

9. On the Rules tab select the option that you want to use if there is a conflict between the data on your device and the data on your Exchange 2000 mail server.

10. Tap OK in the top-right corner to save your synchronization settings.

The Desktop

You don't really need to do anything other than install ActiveSync 3.6 on your desktop. ActiveSync comes on the CD you got with your iPAQ, or you can download the newest version from **http://www.microsoft.com/mobile**.

Once ActiveSync is installed on your desktop, you can create a partnership with your iPAQ and your desktop, as well as configure the Server ActiveSync information.

> NOTE   *With Pocket PC 2003, ActiveSync 3.7 is required.*

To configure the Server ActiveSync information:

1. With your device connected to your desktop, right-click on the ActiveSync icon in the notification area of your taskbar, and then select Open Microsoft ActiveSync. You can also double-click on the icon to open ActiveSync.

2. If you are creating a partnership for the first time, when you are prompted to set up a partnership, select "Synchronize with Mobile Information Server and/or this desktop computer," as shown in Figure A-4.

3. On the New Partnership dialog box "Enable synchronization with a server" screen (see Figure A-5), do the following:

- In the Server Name box enter the name of the Mobile Information Server 2002 server your iPAQ will be synchronizing with. If you are going to be using Server ActiveSync with a VPN solution, use the internal name or address of the MMIS system. Otherwise, use the external IP address or name of the server. Also enter the following information:
- In the Domain box enter the name of your domain.
- In the User Name box enter your username.
- In the Password box enter your corporate password.

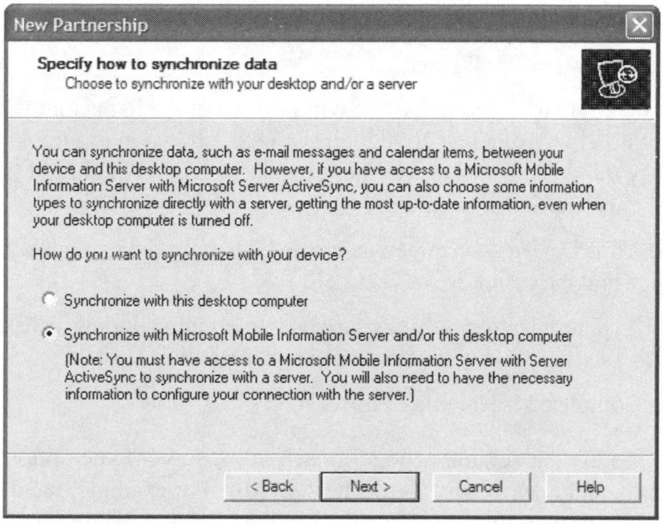

FIGURE A-4   Synchronizing with Mobile Information Server

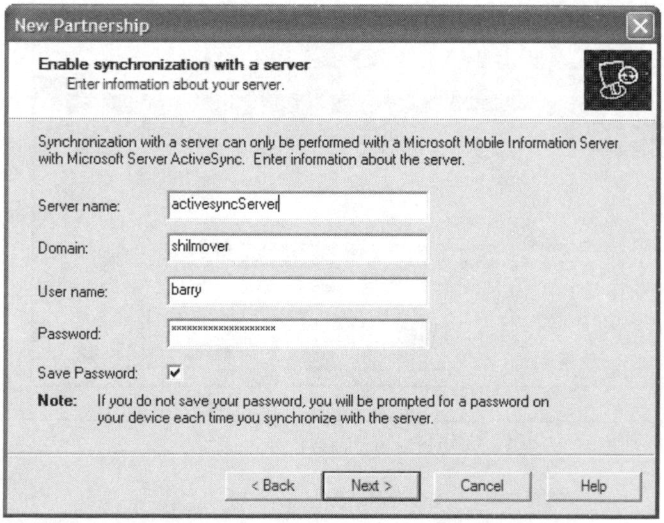

FIGURE A-5   Configuring the Mobile Information Server information

A

4. If you wish to save the password to use whenever you synchronize, select the Save Password check box.

5. To save this information, click Next.

6. On the next screen, in the Mobile Device window, select the items that you want to synchronize with your Exchange 2000 mail server, as shown in Figure A-6. You may want to modify the default settings for these items. To do this, highlight the item to be modified and click the Settings button.

7. On the Name Your Device screen Device Name box, enter the name that you want to use for your device and then click Next.

8. On the Select Synchronization Settings screen, in the main window, select any additional synchronization settings that you want to use and then click Next.

9. On the Setup Complete screen, click Finish.

You may want to modify the default setting for each of the server Sync options, as some of the default settings may not be set to what works best for you. For example, the default setting on e-mail will not synchronize any e-mail over five days old, and you may prefer another amount.

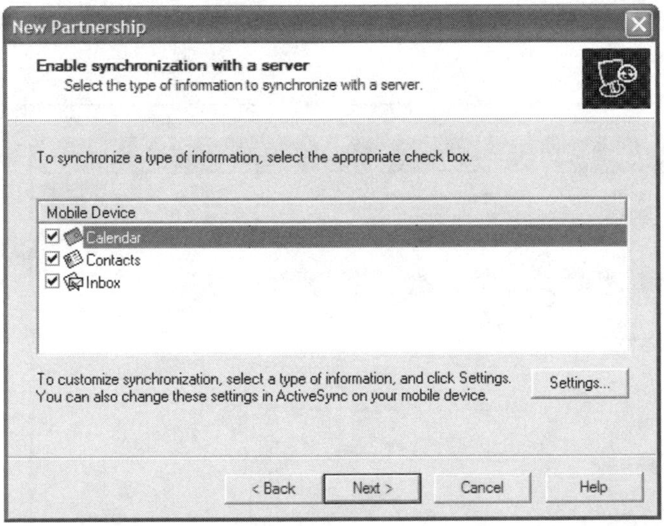

FIGURE A-6   Synchronization categories

The Server

One last step needs to be performed before you can fully synchronize your iPAQ with your organization's Exchange Server. You need to grant your account permission to use Server ActiveSync. Doing that is simple, assuming that you have Administrative rights to your Active Directory Domain Controller. If you do not have this access, you will need to request your Administrator to perform these tasks. In a Server ActiveSync stand-alone installation (that is, you did not extend Active Directory), follow the steps shown next.

To grant your user account access to Server ActiveSync, follow these steps:

1. On the Active Directory Domain Controller, open the Active Directory Users And Computers Administrative snap-in.

2. Expand the Users Organizational Unit.

3. Double-click on the MIS Mobile Users group.

4. Click on the Members tab.

5. Add your account to this group by clicking the Add button and choosing your account.

6. Click OK to save the changes.

If you performed a full installation of MMIS 2002, including the Active Directory Modifications, follow these steps:

1. On the Active Directory Domain Controller, open the Active Directory Users And Computers Administrative snap-in.

2. Expand the Users Organizational Unit.

3. Find your account and double-click it.

4. Click on the Wireless Mobility tab.

5. Select the "Enable wireless access for this user" check box.

6. Choose the "Allow this user to synchronize Exchange data with their device using Mobile Information Server" check box (see Figure A-7).

7. Click the OK button to save the settings.

A

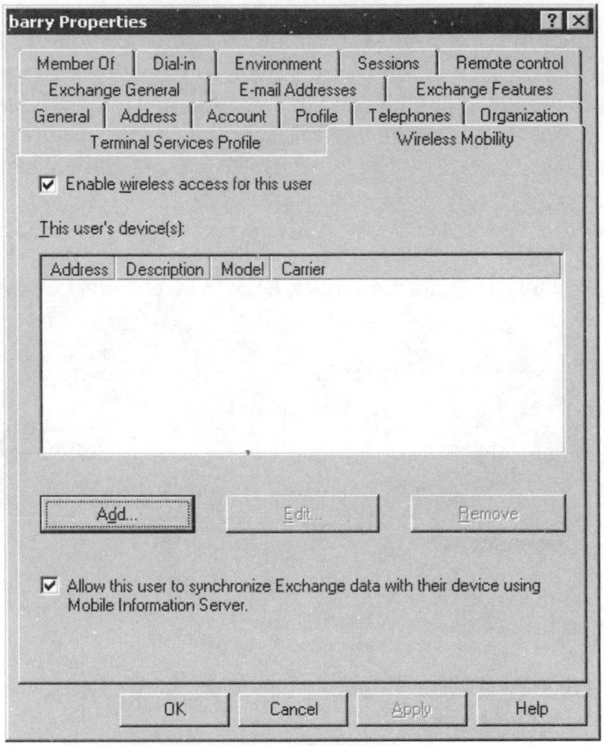

FIGURE A-7   Enabling Server ActiveSync for a user

Appendix B

Where to Go for More Information

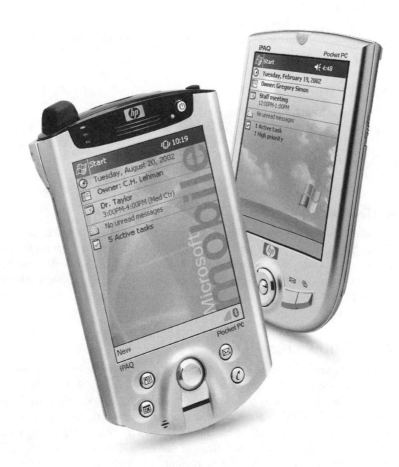

You, the iPAQ owner, can explore many sources of interesting information about your device and the amazing (and not so amazing) things you can do with it. Since the printing of the original edition of this book, the number of sources has exploded! In this list of references you will find information ranging from the practical, such as troubleshooting tips for when your iPAQ won't power on, to the zany, such as determining how well the iPAQ Bluetooth module communicates when immersed underwater in a Ziploc bag.

We have categorized the information sources by type and given a brief description of what you can expect to find at each of these sources. The number of potential information sources is growing so fast that we cannot possibly list them all here. At **www.PocketPCTools.com** we will be hosting an extension to this appendix that will attempt to maintain a comprehensive list of where you can get details on your iPAQ and related products.

Web Sites

Some of the most popular or unique web sites related to Pocket PCs are listed here, followed by a brief list of more sites you might like to check out.

www.pocketpcthoughts.com

Pocket PC Thoughts is a site run by Jason Dunn and a few of his contributors. It is one of the most popular web sites visited by Pocket PC enthusiasts. It is a day-by-day log of new information, reviews, and interesting ideas related to the Pocket PC world, rather like an online newsletter for Pocket PC users. The information you will find on this site is usually brief (with links to more detail) and very informative.

www.pocketpcpassion.com

This site is run by Dale Coffing and is another of the most popular of the Pocket PC sites. It also follows a newsletter format with regular postings by Dale of his experiences with the Pocket PC (which are *very* extensive). Dale attends most of the major trade shows and often can be found working in the Microsoft booth. He is not a Microsoft employee, but works closely with Microsoft to ensure that he is on top of all of the latest information for the Pocket PC. This is a very well-presented and informative site for the Pocket PC user.

www.PocketPCTools.com

This site takes a different approach to giving you information on the Pocket PC. It aims to be complementary to sites such as the first two on this list. It is a database of tools, software, accessories, and everything that you can possibly attach to your Pocket PC. Many of the products are reviewed so that you can see information on their usability, durability, and so on. You can also find out about books and other sources of information and news on your iPAQ or any Pocket PC.

This site is maintained in part by the two authors of this book, Derek Ball and Barry Shilmover. You may also refer to this site for materials supplementary to this book, such as updates to this appendix and other goodies for iPAQ owners.

www.pocketpc.com (www.microsoft.com/mobile/pocketpc)

This site is the official web site from Microsoft about the Pocket PC. It has information about the Pocket PC operating system, hardware, software, and accessories. The most useful attributes of this site for the new Pocket PC owner are probably the online tutorials and support (found under the Club Pocket PC section).

www.cewindows.net

Chris De Herrera is the webmaster of this site. He has been working with Windows CE in its various incarnations for more than five years and has a tremendous depth of experience. On his site you will find essays on the different versions of Windows CE, help for the beginning Pocket PC user, reviews and commentary on popular Pocket PC products, as well as lists of known bugs on these platforms.

www.davesipaq.com

Wow! A site dedicated solely to your new iPAQ. In a newsletter format, this site presents new information on software, hardware, and other news of specific interest to iPAQ owners. You can find out where to buy the cheapest iPAQ, where to obtain the must-have software for your device, and more. This site is run by Dave Ciccone.

www.the-gadgeteer.com

This site is dedicated to reviewing hardware gadgets, mostly but not exclusively for hand-held devices. The site contains a lot of material related to your iPAQ. The reviews are unbiased and usually an interesting read. If you are thinking of acquiring a gizmo for your iPAQ, check the review in *The Gadgeteer*.

www.cebeans.com

This site contains a library of unsupported Pocket PC freeware (software that you can use for free!), which you can download for your Pocket PC.

Other Web Sites

A large number of other sites we wanted to list have relevant information for the iPAQ owner, and more such sites seem to appear daily. One link that will direct you to many of the emerging Pocket PC sites is at *Pocket PC* magazine. They bestow their Pocket PC Magazine Best Sites award, and you can access this list of best sites at **http://www.pocketpcmag.com/bestsites.asp**.

In addition, here are some other sites you may want to visit:

General, News, and Reviews

These web sites focus on general information, news, and product reviews that are relevant to either the Pocket PC world, or the world of mobile computing in general.

www.pocketnow.com

www.pocketpcminds.com

B

www.brighthand.com

www.pocketpccity.com

www.pocketpclife.co.uk

www.pdagold.com

www.winceonline.com

www.pocketpcaddict.com

www.pocketpchow2.com

www.ppcsg.com

www.cewire.com

www.tekguru.co.uk

www.pocketpcpower.net

www.ppcw.net

www.wiredguy.com

www.mobigeeks.com (French-language site)

www.movilpro.com (Spanish-language site)

Software

These sites are focused solely on software. Some are for Pocket PCs only; others have software for a variety of handhelds and mobile devices. Most of the sites have a mixture of freeware, shareware, and trial software. Sites like Handango actually sell the software, and Cnet has free downloads.

www.pocketpcsoft.net

www.pocketpcfreedom.com

www.pocketpcfreewares.com (French-language site)

home.Sidebares.com

http://www.download.com (select Windows CE applications)

www.handango.com

http://pda.tucows.com/pocketpc.html

www.ppc4all.com

www.pocketgamer.org

Other

This section contains sites that didn't fit into any of the previous categories. They have some information that will be relevant to the iPAQ owner.

www.pocketpcthemes.com

www.pocketthemes.com

www.pocketgear.com

Magazines

No magazines focus solely on the iPAQ, but you can find magazines that focus on either the Pocket PC or on the world of mobile computing. A few of the more popular ones are listed here.

Pocket PC Magazine

Published by Thaddeus Computing, *Pocket PC* magazine is focused purely on the Pocket PC world and is chock-full of useful information, news, and reviews of materials that will (usually) run on your iPAQ. They also have a web site, but it does not contain the full version of the magazine (although you can buy an online electronic subscription). You can find them at **www.pocketpcmag.com**.

Pen Computing Magazine

Pen Computing focuses on the world of mobile computing in general. It always contains information relevant to the Pocket PC and iPAQ world, but it also deals with Palm and much more. They have a web site as well, but it does not contain the full version of the magazine. Look for them at **www.pencomputing.com**.

Conferences

Conferences are always an interesting place to get up-to-date information on the Pocket PC world and meet other enthusiasts who use iPAQs and Pocket PCs. Conferences can be a little expensive, but usually the exhibit halls are free.

Pocket PC Summit

The Pocket PC Summit is an annual conference focused solely on the Pocket PC platform. It features a variety of subjects that might be of interest, but is focused largely on the enterprise user of Pocket PC devices. Full information can be found on their web site at **www.pocketpcsummit.com**.

Comdex

The main Comdex conference is held annually in Las Vegas. It is a huge conference related to everything in the high-tech industry. Its coverage is very broad, but Pocket PCs (and iPAQs) are

B

becoming a larger part of the show every year. Smaller regional versions of this show are held in Vancouver, Toronto, Chicago, and Atlanta. The organizers of this conference have now gone global and are holding Comdexes in Greece, Scandinavia, Australia, Saudi Arabia, China, Egypt, Mexico, Japan, Korea, Switzerland, France, and more. More information can be found at **www.comdex.com**.

Mobile & Wireless World

Owned and produced by *Computer World* magazine, this conference focuses specifically on how wireless and mobile technologies are affecting, or may affect in the future, the enterprise workspace. More information is available at **www.mwwusa.com**.

CES

For a more consumer-oriented look at the mobile space, you will find a lot to see at the Consumer Electronics Show (CES) held each year in Las Vegas. This is an extremely large show with over 100,000 attendees annually and over 2,000 exhibitors. It focuses on all aspects of computer electronics, but the Pocket PC is becoming a much more visible fixture at the show. For more information visit **www.cesweb.org**.

Hardware Vendors

Many vendors produce hardware for the iPAQ, and the number is increasing daily. For further news on iPAQ compatible hardware, visit **www.PocketPCTools.com**, where we will endeavor to keep an up-to-date database of all the hardware vendors that carry products compatible with your iPAQ.

www.hp.com

HP will, of course, be an excellent source of information for the iPAQ owner. At the HP web site you can read any advisories or notices that HP feels are important to iPAQ owners specifically. You can also elect to have these notices sent to you by e-mail when they are released. You can download drivers, get technical support, and access a database of useful information about the iPAQ.

www.sierrawireless.com

Sierra Wireless is the manufacturer of PCMCIA card wireless modems for your iPAQ. You can get information on their AirCard line of modems on their web site, as well as download up-to-date drivers for their hardware. Sierra Wireless produces wireless modems for the CDPD, CDMA, and GPRS wireless data networks.

www.novatelwireless.com

Novatel is another manufacturer of PCMCIA card wireless modems for your iPAQ. Their line of modems is known as the Merlin modems. They have modems for CDMA 1xRTT, CDPD, and GSM/GPRS. They have also produced an integrated GSM/GPRS card that can act as a cell phone, allowing a standard iPAQ with a PCMCIA card expansion sleeve to be both your data device and your cellular mobile phone.

www.vajacases.com

If you're looking for a case for your iPAQ, Vaja is one of the premier manufacturers of leather cases for every iPAQ on the market (new and old). Vaja cases are extremely well-crafted, durable, and available in a variety of sizes and colors. You can even get a case customized with a corporate logo!

Index

Numbers and Symbols

= (equal sign), using with formulas in Pocket Excel, 88

? button in Block Recognizer, purpose of, 32

? icon in toolbar, purpose of, 36

3-D view feature in Destinator, using, 313

500 web site, address for, 278

802.11b wireless standard versus wired connections, 232–237. *See also* Socket 802.11b Wireless LANs

54*xx* series, securing, 206–208

5450 built-in wireless LAN, setting up, 233–234

5450 iPAQ, accessing Bluetooth Manager with, 238–239

A

ABC tabs, toggling with Contact Manager, 136

AC adapter for charging batteries, using, 43

Access databases, creating and synchronizing, 52–53

account balances
  displaying with Account Manager, 162–163
  displaying with Account Register, 164

Account Manager window
  in Pocket Money, 162–164
  in Spb Quick, 174–176

Account Register in Pocket Manager, accessing, 162, 164–165

action games
  Battle Dwarves, 270–271
  Interstellar Flames, 270–271
  Metalion, 272
  RocketElite, 272–273
  Snails, 273
  Spawn, 273
  Turjah Episode II, 273–274

ActiveSync program, 44–57
  advisory about Notes feature used with, 51
  advisory about using sync cables with, 44
  Calendar Synchronization Settings dialog options in, 47–48
  Contacts application in, 48–49
  customizing tasks with, 156–157
  downloading current version of, 366
  Favorites options in, 49
  file synchronization options in, 49, 51
  Inbox synchronization performed by, 53
  partnerships in, 44–45
  resolving conflicts in, 55–56
  Rules tab of Options dialog box in, 55–56
  sending and receiving e-mail with, 136–138
  setting up, 44–57
  setting up channels for, 46–47
  Sync Mode of, 55

O

P

INTERNATIONAL CONTACT INFORMATION

AUSTRALIA
McGraw-Hill Book Company Australia Pty. Ltd.
TEL +61-2-9900-1800
FAX +61-2-9878-8881
http://www.mcgraw-hill.com.au
books-it_sydney@mcgraw-hill.com

CANADA
McGraw-Hill Ryerson Ltd.
TEL +905-430-5000
FAX +905-430-5020
http://www.mcgraw-hill.ca

GREECE, MIDDLE EAST, & AFRICA
(Excluding South Africa)
McGraw-Hill Hellas
TEL +30-210-6560-990
TEL +30-210-6560-993
TEL +30-210-6560-994
FAX +30-210-6545-525

MEXICO (Also serving Latin America)
McGraw-Hill Interamericana Editores S.A. de C.V.
TEL +525-117-1583
FAX +525-117-1589
http://www.mcgraw-hill.com.mx
fernando_castellanos@mcgraw-hill.com

SINGAPORE (Serving Asia)
McGraw-Hill Book Company
TEL +65-6863-1580
FAX +65-6862-3354
http://www.mcgraw-hill.com.sg
mghasia@mcgraw-hill.com

SOUTH AFRICA
McGraw-Hill South Africa
TEL +27-11-622-7512
FAX +27-11-622-9045
robyn_swanepoel@mcgraw-hill.com

SPAIN
McGraw-Hill/Interamericana de España, S.A.U.
TEL +34-91-180-3000
FAX +34-91-372-8513
http://www.mcgraw-hill.es
professional@mcgraw-hill.es

UNITED KINGDOM, NORTHERN,
EASTERN, & CENTRAL EUROPE
McGraw-Hill Education Europe
TEL +44-1-628-502500
FAX +44-1-628-770224
http://www.mcgraw-hill.co.uk
computing_europe@mcgraw-hill.com

ALL OTHER INQUIRIES Contact:
McGraw-Hill/Osborne
TEL +1-510-420-7700
FAX +1-510-420-7703
http://www.osborne.com
omg_international@mcgraw-hill.com